DEFEAT INTO VICTORY

'Of all the world's great records of war
and military adventure, this story must
surely take its place among the greatest.
It is told with a wealth of understanding,
a gift of vivid description, and a
revelation of the indomitable spirit of
the fighting man that can seldom have
been equalled—let alone surpassed—
in military history.'

THE FIELD

'Sir William Slim has written something
of more value than a mere military
history. It is the story of how men of
many races endured and triumphed,
how an army found itself, and, perhaps
most valuable of all, it is essentially the
story of himself— a great commander.'

TIMES LITERARY SUPPLEMENT

Also by Sir William Slim

UNOFFICIAL HISTORY

and published by Corgi Books

Field Marshal The Viscount Slim

K.G., G.C.B., G.C.M.G., G.C.V.O.,
G.B.E., D.S.O., M.C.

Defeat into Victory

An abridged edition

CORGI BOOKS

TRANSWORLD PUBLISHERS LTD

A National General Company

DEFEAT INTO VICTORY

A CORGI BOOK 0 552 08757 2

Originally published in Great Britain by
CASSELL & CO. LTD.

PRINTING HISTORY

Cassell edition published 1956
Cassell abridged edition published 1962
Corgi edition published 1971

Copyright 1956 and copyright © 1961 by
Field Marshal the Viscount Slim

This book is set in Baskerville 9/10 pt.

Corgi Books are published by Transworld Publishers, Ltd.,
Cavendish House, 57–59 Uxbridge Road, Ealing,
London, W.5.

Made and printed in Great Britain by
Richard Clay (The Chaucer Press), Ltd., Bungay, Suffolk.

To
AILEEN
a soldier's wife who followed the drum
and
from mud-walled hut or Government House
made a home

PREFACE

A general who has taken part in a campaign is by no means best fitted to write its history. That, if it is to be complete and unbiased, should be the work of someone less personally involved. Yet such a general might write something of value. He might, as honestly as he could, tell of the problems he faced, why he took the decisions he did, what helped, what hindered, the luck he had, and the mistakes he made. He might, by showing how one man attempted the art of command, be of use to those who later may themselves have to exercise it. He might even give, to those who have not experienced it, some impression of what it feels like to shoulder a commander's responsibilities in war. These things I have tried to do in this book.

It is a personal narrative, written from the standpoint of a corps or army commander in the field, whose outlook was often limited by his own surroundings. It is based on a short account I wrote at the time, a skeleton diary, some contemporary papers, and my recollection. For any inaccuracies and, of course, for its opinions and judgments I only am responsible.

If in places I have noticed by name individuals, units, and formations, that is usually because I happened to be near them at a particular time and they caught my eye. I am very conscious that for every one I mention there were a hundred others whose doings were just as worthy of record. Named or unnamed, I shall always be proud to have served with them. Victory in Burma came, not from the work of any one man, or even of a few men, but from the sum of many men's efforts. We all, even those among us who may have seemed to fail, did our best. Luckily, that combined best proved good enough.

W. J. SLIM
Field Marshal

Canberra, Australia

PREFACE TO THE NEW EDITION

This somewhat shortened edition is intended for those who, finding not so great an attraction in accounts of military moves and counter-moves, are more interested in men and their reactions to stress, hardship, and danger. The purely military parts of this narrative have, therefore, been condensed to what is needed for the understanding of the situations encountered and the resulting human problems.

This book is not an attempt to give the history of a campaign but to show how, on the anvil of defeat and difficulty, some men hammered out for themselves and applied those principles of leadership and morale that are basic to success in any great enterprise.

—SLIM
Field Marshal

London

CONTENTS

BOOK I
Defeat

BOOK II
Forging the Weapon

BOOK III
The Weapon Is Tested

BOOK IV
The Tide Turns

BOOK V
The Decisive Battle

BOOK VI
Victory

MAPS

BOOK I: DEFEAT

CHAPTER I

INTO BURMA

It was good fun commanding a division in the Iraq desert. It is good fun commanding a division anywhere. It is one of the four best commands in the service—a platoon, a battalion, a division, and an army. A platoon, because it is your first command, because you are young, and because, if you are any good, you know the men in it better than their mothers do and love them as much. A battalion, because it is a unit with a life of its own; whether it is good or bad depends on you alone; you have at last a real command. A division, because it is the smallest formation that is a complete orchestra of war and the largest in which every man can know you. An army, because the creation of its spirit and its leadership in battle give you the greatest unity of emotional and intellectual experience that can befall a man.

It was especially good to be commanding the 10th Indian Division. We had, as a division, found ourselves. We had scrambled through the skirmishes of the Iraq rebellion, been blooded, but not too deeply, against the French in Syria, and enjoyed unrestrainedly the *opéra bouffe* of the invasion of Persia. We had bought our beer in Haifa and drunk it on the shores of the Caspian. We could move, we could fight, and we had begun to build up that most valuable of all assets, a tradition of success. We had a good soldierly conceit of ourselves. Now, in March 1942, in spite of dust storms, equipment shortages, obsolete armament, and an overdose of digging strong points, it was stimulating to be at what we all felt was a critical spot, waiting for the threatened German invasion of Turkey. If it came, and the Panzer divisions rumbled over the pearl-tinted horizon, we should be the soft-skinned orange flung in front of the steam roller, but meanwhile it was exhilarating to go bucketing about the desert, a hundred miles a day, sweeping our field glasses around a great circle of bare sand. The desert suits the British, and so does fighting in it. You can see your man.

So, when I was called to the telephone at my headquarters in the wrecked flying-boat station at Lake Habbaniyeh, to speak to the army commander in Baghdad, and was told to fly to India within the next three days, my heart slumped.

'Am I sacked?' I asked.

'No, you've got another job.'

'But I don't want another job. I want to stay with my division.'

'A good soldier goes where he's sent and does what he's told!'

And the telephone rang off in my ear.

Constant sandstorms held up my departure for a few days and prolonged the unhappiness of saying good-bye, but at last I was chuffing out into Habbaniyeh Lake to the flying boat. Through the sand, still blowing and stinging my face, I watched the half-dozen figures on my divisional staff who had come to see me off fade quickly into the haze, and I felt as forlorn as they looked, hunched against the driving sand. The flying boat loomed up; I scrambled on board, bumped my head in the low entrance, as I nearly always do, and heard the crew discussing whether the dust storm was too thick to take off. However, the pilot decided it was not, and up we roared. I cheered myself with the thought of the cable I had sent telling my wife to meet me at Delhi, but I was feeling glum enough at leaving my division.

We came down next day on the shrinking lake outside Gwalior, and after a tedious train journey I met my wife at Delhi station. Next morning at General Headquarters, India, no one seemed able, or at any rate willing, to tell me what my job was to be. The only thing that was definite was that I was to fly to Burma almost at once with Lieutenant-General Morris, the chief of the General Staff in India, who was visiting the front to get a first-hand view of a not-too-bright situation. Why I should go in addition I did not know, but this time I was a good soldier, went where I was sent, did what I was told, and asked no questions.

We left early, spent the night in Calcutta, and then flew on to Akyab, a little port on the Arakan coast of Burma. It seemed a very pleasant, peaceful seaside town, much cleaner and better kept than similar places in India—as indeed were all Burmese towns and villages. We sat up late discussing the situation with Air Vice-Marshal Stevenson, the air officer commanding Burma. Rangoon had fallen a few days before, and the British Force had extricated itself with difficulty but was now clear and reorganizing. The position, both on the ground and in the air, was an anxious one.

In the air, in spite of the great numerical odds against us, we had, from the first, gained considerable success, but in our plans for the defence of Burma we had relied too much on the ability of our air forces to stop or at least greatly to delay the enemy advance. Both we and the Japanese were to discover that air attack alone would never succeed in stopping the movement of either side. In any case, the Allied air strength in Burma in 1942 was never on a scale even to attempt it.

When the Japanese invasion began there were only two fighter, one bomber, and two army cooperation squadrons available to meet it. Later three more fighter squadrons and one bomber squadron came as reinforcements, but even then the odds against them were about four to one in fighters. One of the fighter squadrons was from the American Volunteer Group, which, under the dynamic leadership of Colonel Chennault, had been operating with the Chinese long before the United States came into the war. It's crew were as good a collection of fighter pilots as could have been found anywhere.

The Allied airmen were handicapped, in addition to weakness in numbers, by the short range of the British fighters, designed for the close defence of Great Britain, the location of airfields, the meagre complement of anti-aircraft artillery, and the fact that we possessed only *one* radio direction-finding unit.

Rangoon, the main Japanese bombing target, suffered heavily, but in more than thirty raids in the first two months the defenders destroyed a hundred and thirty enemy aircraft with sixty probables. The majority of these fell to the A.V.G. who not only had in the P40 the better figher but were more experienced than the British pilots. These successes had enabled the last convoys to enter Rangoon and its final evacuation to be completed without great loss from the air, but by mid-March the Japanese could put out a daily operational effort of two hundred and sixty aircraft against the Allied average of forty-five. The odds had grown too heavy for even British and American airmen.

Sitting over our drinks that evening in Akyab, we learned that with the fall of Rangoon the remains of the Allied Air Force had been withdrawn to Central Burma. One fighter and one bomber squadron of the R.A.F. and the A.V.G. squadron had gone to Magwe; one R.A.F. squadron to Akyab. No supplies or spares could now reach Central Burma overland or by sea and only the merest trickle by air. The Air Force, like the Army, must live henceforth on its hump. Losses could not be replaced.

Next day we went on from Akyab to Magwe, now our main air base in Burma. We flew over the Arakan Yomas, and I had my first sight of the jungle-clad hills of Burma. Flying over them you can realize what an obstacle they are to vision, but you cannot really appreciate what an obstacle they are to movement. To do that you must hack and push your way through the clinging, tight-packed greenery, scramble up the precipitous slopes and slide down the other side, endlessly, as if you were walking along the teeth of a saw. I often wished afterwards that some of my visitors, who measured distances on small-scale maps, and were politely astonished at the slowness with which I proposed to advance, had walked to my headquarters instead of flown. But all that was to come later. Now, as we roared over these endless, razor-edged ridges, covered to their very summits with the densest jungle, they gave the impression of a thick-pile, dull-green carpet rucked up into fold after fold. It was a relief to me, my eyes for the past year attuned to the bare desert, to come out suddenly on to the Irrawaddy with its narrow strip of comparatively open country on each side of the river.

At Magwe, after a talk with a very confident local air force commander, Morris and I flew, in a smaller plane, to Mandalay, landing, after some hesitation, on a very rough strip cleared among rice fields, a few miles from the town. Here we sat, rather forlorn, until eventually a station wagon appeared, and we drove up the winding road to Maymyo, the summer capital of Burma. It was a delightful spot, with the English houses in the best Surrey stockbroker style, each in its own spacious garden.

Army Headquarters, Burma, was moving in, after its hazardous escape from Rangoon, and it was quite evident that some of it had been considerably shaken by that experience. To begin with, Army Headquarters, Burma, was neither organized, manned, nor trained as a mobile headquarters to command fighting formations in the field. It was, in fact, a miniature peacetime War Office on the Delhi–Whitehall model. Hurried additions and expansions had been made to meet the sudden onset of invasion, but it was very far from being a suitable instrument for the direct control of a campaign. The unfor-

BURMA
& Neighbouring Countries

tunate Lieutenant-General Hutton, who took over command in Burma just as the Japanese attack started, was, as commander in the field, terribly hampered by having to work through a cumbersome headquarters designed for quite different purposes. Given a little time, I have no doubt that Hutton, with his great organizational powers, would have evolved a more suitable instrument, but he was plunged at once into a critical tactical situation when such reforms became well-nigh

18

impossible. However, an unsuitable headquarters was only one of several crippling handicaps under which Hutton and his forces started their war.

In Burma our unpreparedness when the blow fell was extreme, and we paid for it. The basic error was that not only did few people in Burma, and no one outside it, expect that it *would* be attacked, but there was no clear or continuous decision as to who would be responsible for defence preparations or for its actual defence if it *were* attacked. Burma, while politically separated from India, was in every way physically linked to it for defence. It would depend on India for the bulk of its troops and India would be its base. It was essential that the closest ties should be kept without interruption between the two countries. Up to 1937 Burma had been part of India, and its defence, as all its other activities, had been a matter for the Indian government. Then with political separation from India, Burma was made fully responsible for its own military forces.

In September 1939, with the outbreak of war with Germany, a series of bewildering changes began in the higher operational control of the forces in Burma. From India it went to the British Chiefs of Staff in London; then to Far Eastern Command in Singapore. Next back again momentarily to India, only to be snatched away by the crumbling A.B.D.A., the Allied South West Pacific Command in Java, and with the dissolution of that front again to India just as the Japanese were invading Burma. Thus in the space of about sixteen vital months five separate and distant headquarters were in turn responsible for the defence of Burma. To make matters worse for almost the whole of this time operational was separated from administrative responsibility, thus breaking a rule I have never seen violated without someone paying a heavy penalty. These changes alone would inevitably have ensured delay, neglect, confusion, and a lack of understanding of local difficulties. They also resulted in so little progress being made in linking India to Burma by road that when war came there was no overland communication between them, and the Japanese Navy quickly closed all sea routes.

Of our two divisions, the 17th Indian had, like all Indian divisions, been equipped and trained for desert warfare in the Middle East. Its transport was wheeled trucks and except in open country it was incapable of operating off a road. There are few roads in Burma. The other formation, the 1st Burma Division, contained a high proportion of Burmese units raised in a last-minute scramble, untried and without tradition. The allotment of artillery was far below normal and often of obsolete type. An anti-tank battery, for example, was equipped with Austrian 77-mm guns, captured by the Italians in 1918, and, in turn, taken by us twenty-two years later in the Western Desert. These museum pieces were without dial sights and with only one hundred and twenty rounds per gun. When this ammunition had been expended nothing remained but to throw the guns into the river.

January 1942 thus found our two ill-prepared divisions, supported by a tiny air force, pitted against superior numbers of jungle-trained and -equipped troops and vastly preponderant air power.

Our main line of communications, the railway from Rangoon to Mandalay, ran parallel and close to the Siamese frontier, now in Japanese hands. Most of the Burma Division had, therefore, been deployed to meet the most probable enemy advance—an attack from the east on this vulnerable route. Yet when it came, the main Japanese thrust was on Moulmein, well to the south. The 17th Division, its outposts driven in, fought a gallant action against superior numbers at Bilin, but under threat of encirclement was compelled to fall back to gain the cover of the Sittang River. Here disaster overtook it. Part of the division had crossed by the only bridge over the six-hundred-yard-wide stream when in the night it was reported to the divisional commander that the Japanese were about to take the bridge. He had to decide there and then whether to risk the enemy sweeping on across the bridge to Rangoon or to destroy it and leave a large part of his force cut off on the far side. He gave the order to blow. It is easy to say such a decision was wrong, but only those who have faced grim alternatives can understand the weight that presses on a commander at such a time.

The bulk of the division on the east bank fought its way to the bridge only to find it gone. Having destroyed their guns and vehicles, a few rafted themselves across; the rest attempted to swim. Many were shot or drowned; less than two thousand, with five hundred and fifty rifles, ten Bren guns, and twelve tommy guns reached the west bank, without boots and reduced to their underclothing. After this there was little hope of holding Rangoon; it fell on March 9.

No wonder when at Maymyo I first met General Alexander, newly and by sheer luck arrived from Rangoon, I found him, while as calm as ever, obviously worried. The plain fact was that first Hutton and then he had, in turn, found themselves in the normal positions of British generals at the start of a war—called upon to carry out tasks impossible with the means provided.

A moment ago I wrote that General Alexander had escaped from Rangoon by sheer luck. In their attack on Rangoon a Japanese divisional commander had been ordered to sweep around the north of the city and enter it from an unexpected direction, the west. To cover his flank as he crossed the Prome road he put out a strong flank guard which completely bottled up the British as they tried to get away. Several attacks on this road block failed and, had it remained, nothing could have saved the forty-mile-long column strung out along the road south of it. Luckily, as soon as the Japanese main body had crossed the road, its commander withdrew his flank guard. The Japanese division thus entered Rangoon from the west according to plan; the British, finding the cork removed, flowed on, bag and baggage, to the north, also according to plan.

The civil picture was no brighter than the military. The people of the country were quite unprepared for invasion and, as the British suffered defeat after defeat and the Japanese swept forward, they were stunned at the collapse of a power they had always thought, if they thought about it at all, invincible and part of nature. The vast majority had no feeling that the war was their business; they wished only to avoid it. A small minority, mostly soldiers and officials, were actively loyal; about the same number, nationalist politicians, the relics of the old rebels of 1924, students, and some political *pongyis* (Buddhist priests) were actively hostile. These elements were rendered more formidable by the leadership of Japanese-trained Burmans, imported with the invading army, and by the flocking to their standards of numbers of dacoits and bad characters attracted by the prospect of loot. As the Japanese advanced, desertion among the police, the subordinates of all services, and clerical staffs began to spread. The air raids on towns, with their heavy casualties and great destruction by fire, and the swarms of Indian refugees fleeing, not so much from the Japanese, as from the Burmans among whom they lived, all helped in the breakdown of control and communications. The civil administration was crumbling ahead of the Japanese.

There was, however, one bright gleam on the otherwise murky scene—the Chinese. At Christmas 1941 Generalissimo Chiang Kai-shek had generously offered the Chinse Fifth and Sixth Armies to cooperate in the defence of Burma. General Wavell had accepted at once the most readily available division of the Sixth Army and moved it into Upper Burma, the two remaining divisions of the Army were to follow. Later, during February, the three divisions of the Fifth Army, considered the best-equipped and -trained force in China, began to move towards Toungoo. Much hampered by lack of transport, it was not until mid-March 1942 that the first division, the 200th, reached Toungoo, with the rest of the Fifth Army slowly following.

On the arrival of the Chinese, General Alexander intended to transfer the 1st Burma Division from Toungoo in the Sittang Valley across to the Irrawaddy Valley to join the 17th Indian Division. He would then have two groups, a Chinese and a British, separated by the tangled, jungle-covered hills of the Pegu Yomas.

To add to General Alexander's difficulties, command in the Chinese group was somewhat uncertain. In mid-March the American commander, Lieutenant-General Stilwell, arrived, in the double capacity of commander of all Chinese forces in Burma and chief of staff to the Generalissimo. In the first, he was subordinate to General Alexander, but not, of course, in the second. Stilwell was much hampered by inadequate staff and signals. Moreover, there was a commander in chief of the Chinese Expeditionary Force, General Lo Cho Ying, through whom all his orders had to go to the army commanders. These officers evinced considerable independence in selecting which of the orders they would accept, and even divisional commanders at times showed a tendency to pick and choose. They were able to back up their refusals with some show of legality as Chiang Kai-shek had not actually given Stilwell his official seal as commander in chief. And, if this were not enough, there was, seated at Lashio with a Chinese mission, a General Lin Wei, who, as the Generalissimo's direct representative, blandly disclaimed all operational responsibility, but, as he modestly put it, 'exerted influence.' Such was this 'influence' that no Chinese army commander would carry out an Alexander–Stilwell–Lo order unless it had been passed by him.

A Chinese 'army' corresponded to a European corps and usually consisted of two or three divisions. The division itself was not only much smaller than its British or American equivalent, having a strength of from seven to nine thousand, but only two-thirds of the men were armed; the other third replaced the absent animal or motor transport and acted as carriers. As a result the rifle power of a Chinese division at full strength rarely exceeded three thousand, with a couple of hundred light machine guns, thirty or forty medium machine guns, and a few three-inch mortars. There were no artillery units except a very occasional anti-tank gun of small calibre, no medical services, meagre signals, a staff car or two, half-a-dozen trucks, and a couple of hundred shaggy, ill-kept ponies. Nevertheless, the Chinese soldier was tough, brave, and experienced —after all, he had already been fighting on his own without help for years. He was the veteran among the Allies, and could claim up to this time that he had held back the Japanese more successfully than any of the others. Indeed, he registered his arrival in the forward areas by several minor but marked successes against enemy detachments.

In Maymyo I had talks with many staff officers, often old friends with whom I had served in years gone by, and attended several conferences, including one with a Chinese general who had played a great part in the only real victory the Chinese had won against the Japanese up to that time—Changsha. I drew him to one side and listened very carefully, through an interpreter, to his account of the tactics of that battle. His experience was that the Japanese, confident in their own prowess, frequently attacked on a very small administrative margin of safety. He estimated that a Japanese force would usually not have more than nine days' supplies available. If you could hold the Japanese for that time, prevent them capturing your supplies, and then counterattack them, you would destroy them. I listened to him with interest—after all, he was the only Allied commander I had heard of who had defeated the Japanese in even one battle. There were, of course, certain snags in the application of this theory, but I thought its main principles sound. I remembered it and, later, acted on it.

I was still quite ignorant as to why I had been brought to Burma, and again no one seemed willing to enlighten me. My secret fear was that I was going to be told to take over Chief of Staff to General Alexander in place of Hutton, who was going back to India. General Alexander would have been a charming and unselfish master to work for, but, apart from the fact that I could never be in the same class as Hutton as a staff officer—he was outstanding in that capacity—I had never fancied myself in that line at all. I had been a second-grade general staff officer in India ten years before, and for a short time in early 1941 I had been a brigadier, General Staff. I had had enough experience, anyway, to convince me, and I think others, that whatever I was like as a commander I was certainly worse as a staff officer.

A day at Mandalay while we waited for an aircraft gave us an opportunity to look around. We saw a number of units and details that had been withdrawn for various reasons from the fighting to reform or be used as reinforcements. Gunners who had lost their guns—the most pathetic people in the world— staffs of broken-up formations and evacuated camps, a hotch-potch of bits and pieces, odd groups, and individuals. The British looked worried, the Indians puzzled, and the Burmese sulky. I had a suspicion that, unless someone very quickly took hold pretty tightly, a rot might set in behind the front.

We started on our return journey to India still without my future being revealed, and I began to fear an even worse fate—I might be destined for some staff job in India. However, it was no good worrying. I should have to be told soon. I got no farther than Calcutta. There, immediately after breakfast on the day of my arrival, in the gloomy and, I suspect, insanitary Government House, I was sent for by General Wavell. He was standing in one of the visitors' sitting rooms, in his usual firmly planted attitude. He had seen swept away, in overwhelming disaster, Malaya, the Dutch East Indies, the Philippines, and Allied sea and air power in the Far East. He held at that moment the most difficult command in the world—India and Burma. Yet it gave one confidence to look at him. I had seen him at the height of dazzling success, and he had stood and looked calmly and thoughtfully at me in the same way as he looked at me now. He asked some questions on what I had seen in Burma. When I had answered, he said, 'I see,' and we lapsed into silence. He broke it by saying without any preliminaries, 'I want you to go back to Burma to take command of the corps that is to be formed there.'

My heart gave a thump. This was better than a staff job! But I knew enough now to realize that a command in Burma was more likely to be a test, and a tough one, than a triumph.

As if he knew my thoughts, he went on, 'Alexander has a most difficult task. You won't find yours easy.' Another pause, and then, 'The sooner you get there the better.'

'I'll start tomorrow morning,' I assured him.

'I see.'

A pause.

Emboldened, I asked him why Singapore had fallen as it did. He looked steadily at me for a moment and then told me. He wished me luck. We shook hands, and I left.

Back in my room I sat under a slow-moving electric fan, and thought. There was a good deal to think about—what I had heard and seen in Burma and what General Wavell had told me about Singapore. With a map on my knees I reflected how little I knew about Burma. I did what I always do in such circumstances—reduced the map to a rough diagram with the distances between the main places marked. When you have got such a diagram into your head you have a skeleton of the terrain and can cover it with the flesh and features of further knowledge without distortion. I reflected also how very ignorant I was of the Japanese, their methods and their commanders. In 1938, when I was commanding the 2/7th Gurkhas, I had taken the Japanese as enemy in my annual battalion training in the hills round Shillong. I had also used some officers and men of the Asaam Rifles, a military police force who controlled the tribes of the eastern frontier, to give us instruction in jungle fighting. Sitting in Government House, I thought with a little spasm of conceit that my unit had been one of the very few in the British Empire that had done *some* jungle training, and I smiled, wryly, when I thought of it now in the desert with my old 10th Indian Division. It *is* a bit hard always to train British forces for the *next* war as so many voluble advisers urge us! I tried to recall the Japanese organization as I had learned it for that battalion training, but my knowledge had only been sketchy and my recollection was hazy. I really did know very little.

Then more immediate personal details forced themselves to my attention. I had been travelling light, with not more than twenty or thirty pounds of kit. My baggage with all my camp equipment and the rest was somewhere between Baghdad and

Bombay. I got hold of an A.D.C. and asked him to produce me an Indian tailor. Within half an hour the *darzi* had run the tape over me, noted my measurements on the edge of a newspaper, and departed with an order to produce three khaki drill bush shirts, three pairs of slacks and shirts by five o'clock the next morning. He swore he would—and he did, by dint of sitting up stitching all night.

That evening, after dinner in the great dining room of Government House, we went in a party to an air-conditioned cinema. Watching the usual inane picture seemed rather a stupid way of spending one's last evening in civilization, but the resources of the city for intelligent recreation were limited, and I did not feel that more thinking in my room would get me anywhere.

I rose early, packed the fruits of the tailor's labour in my valise, and prepared to set out. However, as so often happened, an inquiry by telephone made it clear that my aircraft would not be ready at the time originally given. I spent a couple of hours, therefore, in shopping for a few extras, accompanied by the helpful A.D.C. This young man worked hard on me, using all his charm—and he had a lot—to persuade me to take him to Burma. Apart from a reluctance to rob my kind host, the governor, of an A.D.C., I discovered that the boy had by no means recovered from a serious wound got in North Africa. But his heart was all right.

At the revised time I went to Dum Dum aerodrome, on the outskirts of Calcutta. It was an infuriating place for a passenger, and remained so until Air Marshal Coryton put it in order in 1945. After the usual difficulty in finding anyone who knew anything about one's projected journey, or indeed about anything at all, I eventually located the pilot and the Lysander that were to take me to Burma. The pilot was a cheerful young Sikh of the Indian Air Force, who, strangely enough, had flown me once or twice in Iraq. We strapped on our parachutes and climbed into our seats. The aircraft then refused to start. It went on refusing for half an hour. At the end of that time my Sikh, cheerful as ever, started off to find another Lysander. Eventually he did, and we transferred to it and took off.

Petrol capacity compelled us to proceed by a series of hops. At Chittagong swarms of coolies had to be cleared before we could land, and I thought my lighthearted Sikh would write a few of them off and possibly us, too. But I need have had no fears, he was a most skilful pilot. Time was getting on when, after a cup of tea, we took off again, and flew on over what seemed interminable jungle. The sun had set and petrol was getting a bit low when suddenly we saw the glistening Irrawaddy, and crossed it by a white pagoda that showed up in the dusk. My pilot's navigation had been excellent; he had struck the river just opposite our destination, the airfield at Magwe. We circled, waiting for a signal from the ground, but no lamp flickered, so we landed and taxied up the runway. No one emerged to guide us, and we halted at the end of the strip. Still no one appeared. Darkness was falling rapidly, and all around us parked closely together were aircraft. I got out and walked towards some huts, which were evidently the control station. The door of the first was open. It was an office, but empty; so were the others. My pilot joined me, but, as far as we could discover, the airfield and the bulk of the British aircraft in Burma were completely deserted. The Sikh found a telephone but failed to get any response from the other end, wherever that was. While he still hopefully went on ringing, I wandered to the road that skirted the airfield, and at last a truck with some Burma rifles in it came along. I hailed it, got the pilot, and we drove into R.A.F. Wing Headquarters in Magwe, some two or three miles away. There I found everyone in good heart and cheer. When I suggested that it was a bit rash to leave so many aeroplanes on a deserted airfield in the midst of a not-too-reliable population, I was told that it was the army's business to look after their safety. Although I knew warning had been sent from India, I never discovered whether I had really been expected or not. It was a strange arrival, and not too reassuring as to either the standard of staff work in Burma or the safety of our precious aircraft.

CHAPTER II

FIRST IMPRESSIONS

Next morning, March 13, 1942, I flew south to Prome, and there met General Alexander and the two divisional commanders, who had been called in for a conference. The 1st Burma Division was under Major-General Bruce Scott; the 17th Indian Division under Major-General 'Punch' Cowan. By a trick of fate for which I shall always be very thankful, Scott, Cowan, and I all came from the 1st Battalion, 6th Gurkhas. We had served and lived together for twenty-odd years; we—and our wives—were the closest friends; our children had been brought up together in the happiest of regiments. I could not have found two men in whom I had more confidence or with whom I would rather have worked. I have never heard of any other occasion on which the corps commander and both his divisional commanders came, not only from the same regiment, but from the same battalion. So unique a coincidence demanded that the corps should be brilliantly successful. Alas, we were thoroughly defeated, but whatever the reasons for that, they were certainly not in the divisional commanders. I was fortunate in finding at the heads of my divisions such examples of the able, highly trained, and truly professional younger leaders that the British and Indian Armies had quietly produced in surprising numbers, while their countrymen were laughing at cartoons of 'Colonel Blimp.'

General Alexander, finding it unnecessary to introduce my divisional commander, issued his directive to my corps. The situation briefly was that the 17th Division, not yet by any means fully re-equipped or reorganized after the Sittang disaster, was re-forming some thirty miles south of Prome, and was at the moment out of touch with the enemy. The 1st Burma Division was about Toungoo, some eighty miles to the east and the other side of the jungle hills of the Yomas, holding the Sittang Valley. The Chinese Fifth Army was moving in to relieve it, so that it could be transferred to the Irrawaddy front. As the Chinese would not go south of Toungoo, 1st Burma Corps would cover Prome. Thus the Allied Army would hold a roughly level front right across Burma, while the Chinese assembled and my corps collected together.

After this short conference I turned to have a first look at my corps headquarters. It consisted of a handful of officers collected mainly from Burma Army Headquarters, a few clerks, and a small, very small detachment of Burma Signals with four wireless sets. Altogether not more than about sixty officers and men, sitting on their valises and kitbags. I asked about office equipment, messing arrangements, tentage, and transport. There was ludicrously little of any of these for the normal set-up of any unit let alone a corps headquarters. The only thing that really reassured me was the Chief of Staff, Brigadier 'Taffy' Davies, who had been with Hutton in the same capacity. I had known him for a long time, and he had commanded a battalion in my brigade at the beginning of the war. Taffy Davies was something more than a brilliant staff officer; he was a character in his own right. His tall, bony figure grew more and more emaciated as the retreat dragged on while he gave himself no rest, either physical or mental. But he got—and kept—that scratch headquarters working. From nothing and almost with nothing, he formed, organized, and infused it with his own spirit. It never reached one fifth the size of any other corps headquarters I have seen, or had one tenth of its equipment, but we were never out of touch with our formations; we quickly knew their dispositions and movements, we never failed to feed and ammunition them to the extent possible, and we never failed to get our orders to them in time. We were, of course, a tactical battle headquarters only, and orders were more often than not verbal. We issued, I think, only four written directives. All things considered, that headquarters was a surprisingly good effort, but it could not have continued for more than a few months at the pressure under which it worked; officers and men could not have stood the strain indefinitely. I had got with Davies a small group of key officers who rivalled even him in energy, unselfishness, ability, and devotion. Simpson, who as 'A.Q.', was responsible for a nightmare of improvised administration; Pattison-Knight his right-hand man, whom nothing ever flurried or dismayed; Montgomery the G.2, who never seemed to need sleep; Wilson the engineer, who achieved miracles and died of sheer exhaustion as we reached India. One of the greatest attributes a commander can have is the ability to choose his staff and commanders wisely, but I can claim no credit for the staff I got at Burcorps; that I suspect should belong to Hutton. Whoever was responsible, I am grateful to him.

As I left with Punch Cowan to visit his division, Taffy Davies was shepherding my headquarters into the Prome Law Courts, while the redoubtable Pattison-Knight proceeded to rustle up an officers' mess by the simple expedient of collecting cooking pots, crockery, and cutlery from abandoned European bungalows, and a mess staff from the roadside. A ceaseless stream of Indian refugees of all types and classes was pouring into the town. When a man passed who looked as if he might have been a servant, he was grabbed, interrogated, and, if suitable, installed as cook, waiter, washer-up, or sweeper. It was thus that Anthony, our mess butler, was procured. I doubt if the British forces would have got out of Burma at all without Anthony. Corps Headquarters certainly could not have kept going. He ran a reasonably decent senior officers' mess in circumstances of incredible difficulty, and we owed him a great deal. I think he made sure we paid him, but who would grudge him that?

The 17th Division was moving into an area just south of Okpo, and Cowan drove with me there in his armoured wheeled carrier. The fact that he had anything left that could be recognized as a division at all was a great tribute to his troops and above all to him. When we arrived at Divisional Headquarters, in the stilt-raised houses of a Burmese village, almost the first man I met was Brigadier Welchman. I had said good-bye to him in the hospital at Khartoum where we had both been taken from Eritrea, after being shot up in the same truck. Here he was, cheerful as ever, and still carrying the spear that had always accompanied him in Africa. 'Welcher' was, next to Punch Cowan himself, the greatest morale raiser I had ever met. I thought it wrong that one divisional headquarters should have both of them, and as I lacked a commander for the corps artillery, of which incidentally there was extremely little, and Welcher was a superb gunner, I deprived Cowan of him.

The troops of the 17th Division looked fine-drawn, as well

they might, and I was shocked at their terrible shortages of equipment and clothing, but their spirit was surprisingly good. With the strengths of units disturbingly low, it was an unhappy thought that, with Rangoon gone, we had no further hope of replacements.

Cowan had with his division 7 Armoured Brigade, under Brigadier Anstice, a tough, battle-tried formation from the Middle East. Its two regiments, 7th Hussars and 2d Royal Tanks, made up for the weakness of armament and armour of their old light tanks by the quality of their crews.

This was not the first, nor was it to be the last, time that I had taken over a situation that was not going too well. I knew the feeling of unease that comes first at such times, a sinking of the heart as the gloomy facts crowd in; then the glow of exhilaration as the brain grapples with problem after problem; lastly the tingling of the nerves and the lightening of the spirit, as the urge to get out and tackle the job takes hold. Experience had taught me, however, that before rushing into action it is advisable to get quite clearly fixed in mind what the object of it all is. So now I sat down to think out what our object should be.

What the overriding intention of the campaign was—whether a last-ditch stand to hold part of Burma, a desperate attempt to retake it, or to withdraw the army intact to India—we did not know. Indeed it was never, until the last stages, made clear to us, and we were hampered increasingly in all our plans until it was.

Still, whatever our eventual purpose, from all points of view it was necessary, somehow or other, to wrest the initiative from the Japanese. That meant we must hit him, and hit him hard enough to throw him off balance. Could we do it? I thought so. As far as we could make out our 17th was opposed by the Japanese 33rd Division with possibly some attached units, and an unknown number of hostile Burmese. When the 1st Burma Division joined us we should, therefore, for the first time be in at least equal, perhaps superior, strength on our front. The Japanese, judging by their form up to date, were bound to attack, and almost certainly at the same time to make a turning movement round our left through the Yomas. If we could collect a mobile reserve, let them commit themselves to the attack, and then strike back in real strength, either at the turning movement as it issued from the jungle or straight down the road at their vitals, we might give them a considerable jar. I made up my mind, therefore, that our object in Burma Corps should be to concentrate our two divisions with a view to counterattacking at the earliest possible opportunity.

Within the next day or two, as I moved about among the troops or sat in the judge's gloomy room, lined with heavy law books, which was my office, several factors—none of them reassuring for the success of our plans—made themselves obvious:

(i) *Our intelligence was extremely bad.*

There was no Burmese intelligence organization, either behind the enemy's lines or in our own territory, while our air reconnaissance was meagre and, owing to the nature of the terrain, negative and unreliable. We had no prisoners, for the Japanese did not surrender, and our only source of information was the identification of enemy dead and the study of their documents. Even this was limited as we had in the whole corps only *one* Japanese interpreter. The truth was, we were like a blind boxer trying to strike an unseen opponent and to parry blows we did not know were coming until they hit us.

(ii) *We were ill-trained and ill-equipped for jungle warfare.*

Our troops were a match for the Japanese in the open but not in the jungle. Our transport was mechanical and we were thus tied to the single road through the jungle, while the Japanese, equipped and trained to do so, could move wide round our flanks to block the road, our life line, behind us—a manoeuvre to which, as yet, we had no real answer.

(iii) *Combat units were much below strength.*

Casualties had been heavy, desertion in the Burmese units was increasing, and we had no prospect of replacing losses. If a battalion went into action two hundred men short and lost another hundred, it would inevitably fight next time three hundred short. We suffered from an incurable wasting disease.

(iv) *The local inhabitants were not helpful.*

While the hill tribes were generally actively loyal to us, the Burmans of the plains and the townsfolk were in the main apathetic and terrified, wanting only to avoid becoming involved with either side; a small minority were actually hostile.

(v) *There was a wide gap between the Allied forces in the Sittang and Irrawaddy Valleys.*

The Chinese and ourselves were separated by eighty miles of

the roadless, jungle-covered hills of the Pegu Yomas. Unless covered somehow, the Japanese would certainly penetrate this gap and encircle us.

(vi) *Morale was threatened.*

The troops up to now had fought well, but losses, hardship, and lack of success were having their effect, especially in rear areas where there were a lot of shaken people about. The Chinese, ill-trained and badly equipped, were at this time an unknown factor.

It is one thing to know what is wrong; it is another to put it right. I was to find that to retrieve the past in the midst of a fierce and relentless present is no easy matter.

The first necessity was to improve our information and we founded the 'Yomas Intelligence Service.' Scattered through the forests of the area were numbers of Burmans who, in happier times, had cut and brought out timber for various British firms. These men we made the framework of our organization; their officers we recruited from the British employees and from the government forestry services. We had no time to follow the usual channels, via Gazettes and the rest, in their appointment, so my divisional commanders and I simply told these young men they were officers and gave them suitable temporary rank. Such was the poverty of our resources that we could not provide them with rank badges, until one of them solved the problem by cutting small squares from his black evening socks—which he was not likely to require for some time—and stitching them on his shoulder straps, thus adequately indicating his new status. This method we followed for the rest.

Actually, I should say, as a class our best intelligence officers were not the government civilians, but the outside up-country members of the business firms who had a closer knowledge of the country and its people. It was noticeable that parliamentary government, which had progressed far in the central government and in local administration, seemed to have forced officials to become more and more office-bound. Business, too, seemed among all grades in Burma to have been a better training than government service for initiative.

Our improvised intelligence screen had considerable weaknesses. First it required time to establish itself, secondly it had no means except runners, or at the best ponies, of getting its news back to a roadhead, and thirdly it had to stay put. Whether we advanced or retreated, we should lose almost all the Burmans in it because they worked from their homes.

We, of course, asked urgently for more Japanese-speaking officers or men. We were told that numbers were just starting to learn the language in universities and classes in England and India; as soon as they were proficient we should get them. I am afraid the Japanese got us out of Burma quicker than the brightest students got out of their universities!

Jungle skill was as hard to improve as intelligence; the major difficulty was opportunity. If troops are to be trained they must be pulled out of the fight even if only for a month, and we could not do this—every man we had was needed at the front. Experience taught us a good deal but, with the Japanese as instructors, it was an expensive way of learning. The problem of lightening our equipment to some extent solved itself, as realizing that mobility and survival were synonymous, units jettisoned more and more of their baggage. We could not, however, shake loose the tin can of mechanized wheeled transport tied to our tail and we remained largely road-bound, while air supply was an obvious solution but still in the dim future awaiting aircraft. The standard of jungle craft rose only a little, but I do not know what more we could have done in the time and the circumstances.

Few problems are insoluble, but our wasting strength was one. The most we could hope was to slow up the decline. We combed out combatants or potential combatants behind the line, but, in a theatre where almost all administrative personnel were Burman or lower-grade Indian, little could be scraped up from this source. Army Headquarters cooperated and we speeded up the return of men from hospital and of convalescents, but this is a method not without danger. Our medical services were much below what they should have been in establishment, and, even working as devotedly as they did, could not reduce the sickness rates. The tendency was, in fact, for sickness to rise as medical supplies grew scantier and men suffered more from prolonged strain, fatigue, and privation.

In East Africa, where, through the night, we had beaten the Ethiopian emperor's rallying call on his royal drums to summon his subjects from the Italian regiments back to their allegiance, I had thought, 'How terrible to be an Italian officer and wake each morning to find more of your men gone.' Now I was learning what it was like. Reports of desertions from Burmese units increased. The Indian soldier has three loyalties: to his home, to his religion, and to his regiment and his officers. The Burman soldier, too often, had not had time to develop the third, so the fear of leaving their families unprotected in a Japanese-held Burma made men slink off along the jungle paths for home. There was no way of putting that right except by victory and advance.

As we could not hope to find enough troops to hold the dangerous gap between ourselves and the Chinese, we attempted, in addition to our Yomas Intelligence Service, to produce a few mobile units of the mounted infantry type. The mounted portion of the Burma Military Police, whose men were Indians domiciled in Burma, were to form the nucleus, but there was a great shortage of ponies. I remember discussing on one occasion the provision of these ponies with an elderly, tired, and depressed civilian who, in other matters, it seemed to me, had shown no great nerve. On this subject, however, he roused himself and became positively animated, 'Ah!' he volunteered. 'Ponies! The man you should have gone to was X. He could lay his hand on any number of ponies, exactly the sort you want!'

'Grand!' I said, thrilled that we were at last getting somewhere. 'Where is he? Fetch him along.'

'Alas!' answered my civilian, dropping back to his usual lugubrious tones. 'Poor X! He died three years ago!'

Hard things have been said and sometimes written about the civil services and of the collapse of the administration in Burma. My general impression was that many of the British senior government officials were too old, too inflexible in mind, and too lacking in energy and leadership really to cope with the immense difficulties and stark realities of invasion. But before soldiers criticize too much, I think they would be well advised to remember that in the defence of Burma, right from the start of the war with Germany, the vital decisions were made by the fighting services. The civil services could at the best only conform to these decisions and cooperate in them. My experience was that, with very few exceptions, British civilians, both governmental and commercial, and many Burmans stood to their posts with courage and devotion. Nor did we always realize the extent to which, in the districts, the civil officials were hamstrung by the defection of their sub-ordinate Burmese staffs. An inspector of police whose constables have mostly disappeared, the president of a municipality whose clerical and public utility staffs have taken to the jungle, a deputy commissioner whose subordinates have gone on indefinite leave on urgent private affairs, is liable to appear ineffective to a soldier, who, however difficult the situation, still has somebody who will take his orders. When all is said, the real reason the Burman civilian, like his soldier brother, left his post was that he doubted that we, the soldiers and airmen, could hold back the Japanese. The only thing we could do to help the civil administration was to keep the closest touch with them so that we could pool our information, give warning of our demands, and provide such help as we could in the maintenance of order, the control and evacuation of refugees, and a thousand other things. I asked for a senior but active civil officer to be attached to Corps Headquarters to assist this cooperation. I received Mr. Tom Phelips, who was invaluable, not only in the work for which he was appointed, but in the effect his courage, energy, resource, and devotion to duty had on all of us. He was invariably cheerful, but with the cheerfulness that, far from irritating when things are black, raises the spirit. His laugh was like a battle cry to us, and, I am sure, to the Japanese too, for they must often have heard it. Phelips was the embodiment of the highest tradition of the Indian civil service; he was an example to us soldiers.

Our last and most fundamental danger would be a collapse of morale in our own troops. Success is, of course, the easy foundation on which to build and maintain morale—if you have it. Even without success, confidence in their leaders will give soldiers morale. Difficult as it is to attain without the glamour of victory, we were better off here. The Army Commander was a great name after Dunkirk, to the British element at least. He showed himself forward freely and lived up to his reputation for personal bravery. The greatest assets for morale that we had, however, were the two divisional commanders, who had and held the confidence and indeed affection of their troops, British, Indian, and Gurkha, in a remarkable degree. The hard test of battle had brought forward some excellent brigadiers, like Jones and Cameron, who were real leaders, and they too played a noble part in keeping up tails that had every reason to droop.

The most important thing about a commander is his effect on morale. I was known to a number of the more senior officers, especially those of the Indian Army from the rank of battalion commanders upward, but little to the troops. As far as morale was concerned, I therefore started pretty well from scratch, which is not a bad thing to do. It has often happened in war that a fresh commander has taken over after a period of ill-success just as the reinforcements, improved armament, and increased supplies arranged by his predecessor are beginning to arrive in the theatre. The troops naturally identify him with the improved conditions, and he finds a ready-made foundation on which to start building until he can give them a victory, and thus, in the only permanent way, consolidate their morale. This advantage neither General Alexander nor I would have. We had to expect the exact opposite. The loss of Rangoon meant not only that our resources and amenities would be progressively and drastically reduced, but, combined with the fall of Malaya, that a tide of Japanese reinforcements would sweep in through the port. Clearly I must get about among the troops and see and be seen. Luckily there was no public relations department at my headquarters to greet my arrival with the clumsy beating of the big drum. A commander, if he is wise, will see that his own troops know him *before* the press and other cymbal clashers get busy with his publicity. All that can be most helpful *afterwards*.

The broad conclusion of my survey of the situation was the not very brilliant or original one that what was required for morale, and for all our other troubles, was a good recognizable victory. We had a chance of getting this, I thought, if we could bring over the 1st Burma Division, reorganize the 17th, and carry out the overdue maintenance of our tanks, so that we could hit back with a united corps. If neither the pressure of the Japanese on our front nor events elsewhere forced us to undertake comparatively large-scale operations before we had managed to do these things, we might reasonably hope that the enemy would offer us an opportunity.

Our most urgent task was to bring the 1st Burma Division across to the Prome area. In the Sittang Valley the Chinese Fifth Army was now moving in, but it would not go beyond Toungoo. This was unfortunate as it meant that the 1st Burma Division which had been conducting offensive operations to the south had to pull back and, in doing so, to abandon one of our best rice-growing areas, with consequent bad effects on supply and among our Burmese soldiers who found themselves withdrawing from their home districts. The Japanese followed up closely; our rear guards fought stoutly, inflicting losses on them, but the division, when it passed through the Chinese at Toungoo, was considerably exhausted. On March 22, I ordered it to concentrate fifty miles north of Prome. I chose this area rather than Prome itself for administrative reasons and so that the division, which of necessity would arrive piecemeal, could collect without interruption. I estimated that from ten days to a fortnight would be required to complete its concentration.

Meanwhile, the 17th Division showed its spirit. On March 17 a young major, Calvert, later to become the best known of Wingate's column commanders, led a daring raid on the Japanese-held river fort of Henzada. At about the same time the 1st Gloucesters surprised a Japanese battalion in billets eighty miles south of Prome and chased it into the jungle—a most sprightly affair. There was obviously a great deal of fight in the 17th Division.

Nevertheless, I decided to pull it and the Armoured Brigade closer to Prome. The country south of the town was suitable for tanks and the move would ease maintenance difficulties. I was anxious to gain time for the corps to concentrate undisturbed and I hoped the withdrawal would delay enemy plans to attack. All the same, I think I would have done better to have left the 17th Division forward and brought the 1st Burma Division to Prome. Apart from all else, it was a mistake to begin my command by a withdrawal if it could have been avoided.

One brigade (63) in Prome itself covered the main road from the south, another (16) in Sinmezwe-Hmawza held the southeastern approaches, and the third (48) was echeloned back in the Wettigon area as reserve and to meet any hostile move round the flank. The 7 Armoured Brigade was in rear with the reserve brigade, hoping to find an opportunity for tank maintenance. The left flank was protected by the Yomas Intelligence screen and detachments of the Burma Frontier Force; the right by the Marines in their river craft and commando parties on the west bank of the Irrawaddy working with them. Corps Headquarters in Prome was now perhaps rather near the actual front, but I had no intention of going back if we could avoid it, so it remained.

Prome was bombed by Japanese aircraft, usually not in much strength, every other day or so, invariably at breakfast time. I had been bombed often enough before, but never in a town, and I found it much more frightening than in the desert or the bush. We had difficulty in controlling the fires that broke out, and, even when there were no air raids, fires still occurred. These mysterious fires in towns we occupied became an annoying feature of the campaign. Sometimes we caught Burmans in the act of starting them, and they got short shrift, but to the end it was one of the favourite activities of the fifth columnists of whom there appeared to be plenty. Prome was, unfortunately, the centre of an area that was notable for its hostility. What with air raids, fires, and refugees, it was, in spite of its attractive situation, its bungalows and gardens, not a comfortable place. The thousands of wretched Indian refugees, many with smallpox and cholera, bivouacked all over its streets and river wharfs, waiting to cross the Irrawaddy and to trudge down the Tangup track to the Arakan coast, were in pitiable case. They were, in addition, quickly reducing the town and its water supply to a state that threatened an epidemic among the troops. The civil authorities with such help as our administrative staffs and units could give—which was not much—worked devotedly and passed thousands over the river to eventual safety in Bengal. The cleaning of the streets was a problem, as the municipal conservancy services had melted away under air attack. We solved it to a considerable extent by taking gangs of convicts from the local jail and giving them liberty in return for a few days' work as street cleaners. We began with the least criminal and gradually worked up the scale of guilt. The residue of really bad men, the violent criminals, we finally shipped upstream for confinement in Mandalay. The barge on which they were being towed was, however, attacked by Japanese aircraft. Convicts and warders took to the water together; some of the criminals were shot, some drowned, but none, I think, reached jail in Mandalay or anywhere else. I hope the survivors were a great trouble to the Japanese during their occupation; I fear they must have been to their fellow countrymen.

CHAPTER III

A CHAPTER OF MISFORTUNES

While we had registered only a couple of minor offensive scores on the ground, the Royal Air Force in Burma had achieved a more notable success. On March 21 nine British bombers and ten Hurricanes fought their way into Rangoon, shot down eleven Japanese fighters in the air, and destroyed sixteen aircraft on the ground for the loss of one Hurricane.

The same afternoon the enemy retaliated and over the next twenty-five hours nearly two hundred and fifty bombers and fighters in waves attacked Magwe airfield. By the evening of the 22d almost all Allied aircraft there had been destroyed and the few still capable of flying had left, the British for Akyab, the American for Loiwing. Burwing Headquarters and the personnel of the Allied squadrons also left rather hurriedly by road for Lashio and Loiwing. The Japanese then repeated their attacks on Akyab with the same result. Akyab was abandoned; the last of the R.A.F. left Burma.

From then onwards my corps was totally without air reconnaissance, defence, or support. Any aircraft we saw in the sky was hostile—and we were to see many. We were even blinder than before, forced more and more to move at night, and by day to greater dispersion. Buildings became death traps to be avoided; we took increasingly to the jungle. The actual casualties to fighting troops inflicted by the Japanese air force, even after it had absolute freedom of the skies, were surprisingly small. The effect on morale, while not so great as might have been expected, at first was serious, but later the troops seemed in some way to become accustomed to constant air attack and to adjust themselves to it.

Now great wedges of silver bombers droned across the sky, and one after another the cities of Burma spurted with flame and vanished in roaring holocausts. Prome, Meiktila, Mandalay, Thazi, Pyinmana, Maymyo, Lashio, Taunggyi, largely wooden towns, all of them crumbled and burned. The Japanese used pattern bombing, coming over in faultless formation, giving themselves a leisurely dummy run or two, and then letting all their bombs go in one shattering crump. They were very accurate. We always said they had in each formation only one leader capable of aiming, and all took the time from him. It was certainly effective with the civil population. The police, hospitals staffs, air-raid precaution units, public services, and railways collapsed. Labour vanished into the jungle; towns were evacuated. Only a few devoted British, Anglo-Burmans, and Burmese carried on nobly.

General Wavell, the commander in chief in India, had decided that to commit his pathetically meagre air resources on the Burma front without a warning organization against overwhelming numbers would be inevitably to destroy them. There is no doubt this was a right decision, but it was cold comfort to us and made our chances of counterattack much more slender.

With the disappearance of our air force came further disturbing events which were to affect the whole campaign. The leading Chinese division, the 200th in Toungoo, had suddenly, on March 24, been cut off by the Japanese 55th Division. The nearest Chinese troops were a single regiment of their 22d Division sixty miles north with the rest of that division 300 miles away, while its third division, the 96th, had not yet reached the Burmese frontier. The situation was critical. On March 28 General Alexander, urged by the Generalissimo, ordered me to take the offensive at once in order to relieve pressure on the Chinese. Two of Stilwell's staff came to see me, also, with a message stressing his need.

It was quite contrary to my intention thus to attack before my corps was concentrated and I doubted if anything we could do in our present state would really help the Chinese. However, it was an order, and it was up to us to make an attempt, even if not a very hopeful one, to help our ally.

Although our information of the enemy was poor and the 17th Division was still trying to re-equip, I ordered Cowan with the strongest force he could make mobile to advance astride the main road and railway towards Okpo, sixty miles southeast of Prome, and to destroy any enemy encountered. In addition, to prevent enemy forces reported on the west of the Irrawaddy from crossing the river behind Cowan, I organized a small detachment to move down that bank. I was far from happy about these operations, but they were the best we could do to carry out General Alexander's orders.

Cowan formed a striking force of a tank regiment, a battery, and three infantry battalions, all at half strength, under Brigadier Anstice, and ordered him to occupy Paungde, a big village thirty miles south of Prome. Although a few days earlier we had raided Paungde and driven out a Japanese detachment, we now found it strongly held. While severe fighting was going on for possession of this village, Anstice received reports of Japanese approaching the road behind him and a liaison officer returning to Divisional Headquarters had a shock when he found Shwedaung, a town on the main road only ten miles south of Prome, full of Japanese. Cowan then ordered Anstice to withdraw, and sent two weak Indian battalions to clear Shwedaung from the north.

Meanwhile, our small force on the west bank had been ambushed by enemy concealed by villagers in their houses. After desperate resistance most of our men were killed, but twelve, all wounded, were kept till next day when, tied to trees, they were used by the Japanese to demonstrate bayonet fighting to the villagers. This was only one of many instances in the campaign of bestial outrage. The Japanese conduct towards their prisoners will always remain a foul blot on their record.

With the loss of this detachment the enemy began to cross to the east in large numbers, bringing with them several hundred of the Japanese-officered Burman National Army. These at first, believing themselves invulnerable to bullets, fought fanatically, but their ardour cooled as they realized their error. Nevertheless, they were an aggravation to the troubles of our withdrawal. Casualties on both sides in this action at Shwedaung were heavy. We lost ten tanks, two guns, numerous vehicles, and more than three hundred and fifty killed and wounded in the infantry alone. These were losses which at our reduced strengths and without hope of replacement we could not afford.

Unpleasant as they were, the effects of the Shwedaung fight were nothing like as serious as the loss of Toungoo on the Sittang front which occurred at about the same time. The Chinese 200th Division, cut off in the town, resisted stoutly, but when the other troops of the Chinese Fifth Army disregarded Stilwell's order to attack to relieve the garrison there was no alternative to starvation or surrender for it but to cut its way out. Only remnants of the 200th Division, without guns or vehicles, escaped, and a general Chinese withdrawal towards Pyinmana followed. The loss of Toungoo was, in fact, a major disaster, second only to our defeat at the Sittang bridge.

It was now a question whether we should continue to hold Prome. The eastern half of the line across Burma had gone; the state of the town itself was desperate. It had been almost completely burned, cholera among refugees was increasing, and there had even been a few cases among the troops. There was a considerable quantity of stores, mainly rice, on the river-side quays, and we began to back load. As there was no railway and our spare road transport was negligible, this had to be done by boat, a difficult and risky proceeding under a completely dominant hostile air force. I moved my headquarters to Allanmyo, thirty-five miles north of Prome, where, on April 1, I had a visit from Generals Wavell and Alexander. After a review of the somewhat gloomy situation, General Wavell decided that a further withdrawal was necessary, and I was ordered to concentrate my corps in the area Allanmyo–Kyauk padaung–Thayetmyo to defend the oil fields and Upper Burma. I was glad this decision had been taken as it helped me to achieve what was my main immediate object—the concentration of my corps. The 1st Burma Division was coming in as fast as Scott could urge it, but it was unavoidably arriving in bits and pieces which had to be put together. I was horrified at its low scale of equipment. It had never been up to even the standard of the 17th Division in this respect—the whole division, for instance, could muster only one improvised carrier platoon, instead of one per battalion. It was shockingly short of artillery. A considerable proportion of its infantry and administrative units was Burmese. Although the division had acquitted itself well, there had already been numerous desertions, and, in spite of many good British and Burmese officers, things were not getting better. As the enemy threat on the west bank was increasing, it was necessary to split the division, a thing I dislike doing very much, by sending 2 Burma Brigade over the river to hold south of Thayetmyo, the town opposite Allanmyo.

On the evening of General Wavell's conference at Allanmyo the Japanese made their contribution to the question of

43

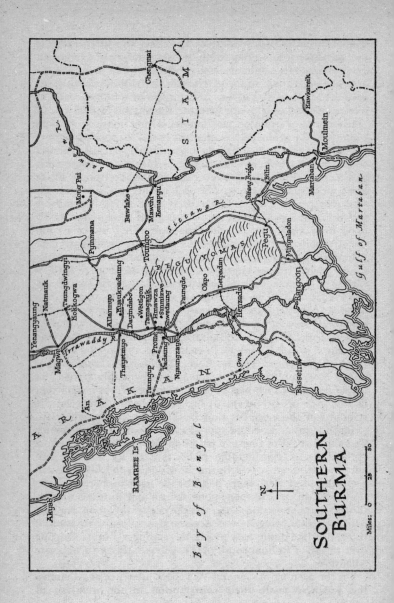

SOUTHERN BURMA

Miles: 0   25   50

whether we should hold Prome. They attacked the brigade of the 17th Division holding south of the town and at the second attempt infiltrated between our positions in the dark into the houses. Several other attacks were repulsed but through this gap the enemy poured into the town and attacked the defenders in the rear. Gradually our troops were pushed out to the north. Our brigade four miles east of Prome bloodily repulsed all attack and intercepted and roughly handled a Japanese force coming in from that flank but, as the enemy were pushing north through the town, had to be pulled across to the main road to stop them. Cowan's reserve brigade had gone forward, the situation in the dark was confused, and I now received circumstantial reports—which later proved false —that a new Japanese force was coming in from the east to get between my two divisions. I therefore ordered Cowan to bring back the whole of his division to Allanmyo, behind the 1st Burma Division.

His men had a trying march. They had been fighting all night and much of the day. It was very hot, very dusty, and there was no water on the route. In addition, the Japanese air force gave them no respite, strafing and bombing them constantly. In spite of this, they passed under the wing of the 1st Burma Division on April 3, complete and in not too bad shape.

My corps was now concentrated, not *where* I had hoped originally, or, for that matter, *how* I had hoped. Still, concentrated it was, and it now remained to decide how I should carry out my task of denying the oil fields to the enemy and defending Upper Burma. The first thing was to choose where we should stand and fight. A reasonable defensive line could have been found running from Allanmyo up into the higher ground to the west, but this would have left a gap of many miles between us and the Chinese. To avoid this, General Alexander had ordered me to hold Taungdwingyi in strength as the junction point where the Chinese front would meet mine. To hold both banks of the Irrawaddy at Allanmyo and a line to Taungdwingyi fifty miles to the north-northeast would mean stretching my two very weak divisions—now not equal in strength to one full one—over some sixty or more miles. It seemed to me that I must shorten my front, in the only way I could, by moving farther up the Irrawaddy until I was nearer to Taungdwingyi. I decided, therefore, to fall back to just south of Magwe and to hold to the south of the west-east Magwe–Taungdwingyi lateral road. I did not like the idea of another withdrawal; we were fast approaching the dangerous state when our solutions to all problems threatened to be retreat, but I hoped this would be the last.

We held south of Allanmyo long enough to demolish the small oil field on the opposite bank of the river, evacuated the town on April 8, and withdrew through a lay-back position to the final line. The Japanese did not follow up in strength and only minor skirmishes occurred when we got on to the new line. It was clearly no use sitting down, strung out in this way, waiting for the enemy to attack; we had somehow to collect a striking force for counterattack. This was by no means easy. One brigade had to be west of the river and two weak divisions, less this detachment, on a forth-mile front held out little hope that we could scrape together for the counterattack anything really effective. I, therefore, strongly pressed the army commander to make the Chinese, who were now in the north of Pyinmana, take over the eastern end of my line. He agreed, and Stilwell ordered General Tu, commander of the Fifth Army, to relieve me with a regiment, and later a division, in the Taungdwingyi area.

These were my first active contacts with Stilwell, who had arrived in Burma a few days after me. He already had something of a reputation for shortness of temper and for distrust of most of the rest of the world. I must admit he surprised me a little when, at our first meeting, he said, 'Well, General, I must tell you that my motto in all dealings is "buyer beware," ' but he never, as far as I was concerned, lived up to that old horse trader's motto. He was over sixty, but he was tough, mentally and physically; he could be as obstinate as a whole team of mules; he could be, and frequently was, downright rude to people whom, often for no very good reason, he did not like. But when he said he would do a thing, he did it. True, you had to get him to *say* that he would, quite clearly and definitely—and that was not always easy—but once he had, you knew he would keep to his word. He had a habit, which I found very disarming, of arguing most tenaciously against some proposal and then suddenly looking at you over the top of his glasses with the shadow of a grin, and saying, 'Now tell me what you want me to do and I'll do it.' He was two people, one when he had an audience, and a quite different person when talking to you alone. I think it amused him to keep up in public the 'Vinegar Joe, Tough Guy' attitude, especially in front of his staff. Americans, whether they liked him or not—and he had more enemies among Americans than among British—were all scared of him. He had courage to an extent few people have, and determination, which, as he usually concentrated it along narrow lines, had a dynamic force. He was not a great soldier in the highest sense, but he was a real leader in the field; no one else I know could have made his Chinese do what they did. He was, undoubtedly, the most colourful character in Southeast Asia—and I liked him.

The Burma Corps had now entered the 'Dry Belt.' The country, instead of being green and thickly covered, was brown and bare, with occasional patches of parched jungle. The water courses, worn through the low, undulating hills, were dry, and the general effect was of heat and dust. Yet the terrain was too cut up by nullahs and stony hills for the free movement of motor transport off roads. We had, as far as we were able, reorganized our fighting troops' transport. Infantry brigades were now partly on a pack basis, and vehicles with divisions had been reduced to meet only their more essential needs. The vehicles thus saved had been formed into a corps pool of mechanical transport, which was held back and allotted as required. Apart from tactical reasons, if we were to continue to supply the troops this reorganization would have been forced on us by our losses in vehicles by air attack, destruction in battle, and above all through lack of proper repair facilities and spares. The greater flexibility in rear thus obtained, combined with the increased pack element forward, would, we hoped, enable our striking force, when we had collected it, to attack in flank any Japanese columns that might penetrate the front.

Relying on the Chinese to take over Taungdwingyi, we planned to form under Scott's 1st Burma Division this striking force of one brigade from each division and the armoured brigade. The line astride the Irrawaddy we should have to hold, inevitably very thinly, with the rest of the corps. This was all very well, but neither could the striking force be collected nor the defensive dispositions be taken up until the promised Chinese arrived at Taungdwingyi. We waited expectantly for them.

We waited in vain. I kept my headquarters in Taungdwingyi in the attempt to make direct contact with the Chinese. Messages via Burma Army Headquarters and Stilwell brought vague answers. The regiment was on its way. It would arrive next day, two days hence. It was held up by supply difficulties; if we would send rice, it would come. Officers were sent out to look for it. It was reported here, there; the reports were then cancelled. At last *some* Chinese were actually contacted and disappeared again. This was repeated. It was rather like enticing a shy sparrow to perch on your window sill. We dumped supplies of rice. Chinamen appeared, collected them, and melted away again. We dumped the rice a little nearer Taungdwingyi each time, and at last a Chinese unit did appear there. But, alas, it was not the promised regiment, only what was called a 'guerrilla battalion' and a very small one at that, quite insufficient and quite inadequately equipped to take over by itself any part of the line. So the 17th Division had to remain in and about the town, which was made into a real stronghold. Large parts of it were levelled by controlled burning, not only to improve fields of fire and increase freedom of movement, but to avoid the complete destruction such as had befallen Prome. It was as well this clearing was done, as air attacks became frequent and heavy.

One raid occurred as divisional commanders and others were assembling at Corps Headquarters for a conference. Some of us were just finishing breakfast when the alarm went and in a group we walked towards the slit trenches, I still carrying a cup of tea. Looking up, we could see the usual tight wedge of twenty or thirty bombers coming straight over. The mess servants and others saw them, too, and began to run for shelter. I had been insistent on stopping people running at these times, as it had led to panic, so continuing our move at a slow and dignified pace, I called out to them to stop running and walk. I remember shouting in Hindustani, 'There's plenty of time. Don't hurry!' a remark that almost qualified for the famous last words series. At that instant we heard the unmistakable scream of bombs actually falling. With one accord two or three generals and half-a-dozen other senior officers, abandoning dignity, plunged for the nearest trench. Scott, being no mean athlete, arrived first and landed with shattering impact on a couple of Indian sweepers already crouching out of sight. I followed, cup of tea and all; the rest piled in on top, and the whole salvo of bombs went off in one devastating bang.

Poor Scott, crushed under our combined weight, feeling warm liquid dripping over him, was convinced that I had been blown into the trench and was now bleeding to death all over him. His struggles to come to my assistance were heroic but almost fatal to the wretched bottom layer of sweepers. We hauled ourselves and them out, and slightly shamefacedly returned to our conference.

On April 8 I moved Corps Headquarters to Magwe, on the other flank, a much better communication centre and not quite so much in the front line, though equally annoyed by air attack. It was also on the main road and much nearer to Yenangyaung, where the oil fields were now being prepared for demolition. I spent a good deal of my time on the lateral road from Magwe to Taungdwingyi which ran just behind our front, and I do not think I have ever disliked a road more. It was, for most of its course, unshielded from the air, and throughout the hours of daylight the Japanese kept a constant patrol of two or three fighters over it. A jeep was the safest vehicle; from it you had a clear view of the sky, and it was easy to spring in one bound from your seat to the ditch. One often did! Once, when I was visiting his area, Curtis who commanded 13 Brigade, went ahead in a closed car with the colonel of the Inniskillings beside him. A Japanese fighter swooped and riddled the back of the car. The colonel was killed instantly, and when we came up we found Curtis bleeding from three wounds, all luckily superficial. Bandaged but completely unshaken, he took me around his positions without any further reference to the incident. I have rarely seen a better instance of steady nerves.

It soon became evident that the Japanese were preparing a strong push for the oil fields. From such indications as we were able to get, it looked as if their main thrust would come directly up the east bank of the river. Japanese reinforcements, we knew, had been pouring in through Rangoon. Their old formations would have been made up in strength again and there would almost certainly be new ones added. The blow, when it came, would be heavy. All this made me more anxious to pull the 17th Division out of Taungdwingyi, even if only to free 48 Brigade for the striking force. The promised Chinese regiment, however, showed no sign of turning up, and Army Headquarters were very insistent that the corps should keep a strong force in the town. True, it would have been the point of junction between the Allied Armies, but I ought, I think, when I could not persuade Army Headquarters to agree to weakening the garrison, to have done it myself.

The expected enemy advance began on April 10, covered by numerous small parties of hostile Burmans and Japanese, disguised as peaceful villagers. These tactics were difficult to counter as the countryside was covered by numbers of genuine refugees trying to escape from the battle area. It was always a toss-up for our men whether the group of Burmese men, women, and children, wandering past their positions with their creaking bullock carts, were what they seemed or Japanese with concealed machine guns.

Early on the 11th the advanced posts of 1 Burma Brigade were in touch with large, formed bodies of the enemy. A little later 13 Brigade south of the main road was engaged with a Japanese regiment, while 48 Brigade was dealing with parties, sometimes trying to pass as Chinese, attempting to infiltrate north. There was heavy fighting that night when the Japanese real attack was fiercely pushed home against both 1 Burma Brigade on our right and 48 Brigade at Kokkogwa. Both attacks were repulsed. That against 48 Brigade was one of the bitterest-fought actions of the whole campaign. The enemy attacked fanatically and in strength. It was a pitch-dark night, lightened fitfully by violent thunderstorms. By dawn on the 12th, after fierce hand-to-hand fighting that had swayed back and forth in attack and counterattack, the Japanese were flung back and the tanks moved out to a good killing. Unfortunately, while these attacks, both on 1 Burma Brigade and on 48 Brigade, were being repulsed, other considerable Japanese forces infiltrated between our groups and established themselves in positions from which they could fire on the road. Throughout the day pressure up the east bank increased and hostile aircraft constantly struck at any movement.

I took General Alexander with me when I visited both divisional headquarters, and we saw something of the start of the battle. We were machine-gunned from the air at Scott's headquarters, which although well hidden in a big clump of forest were betrayed, I think, by tracks leading into the trees, or perhaps by Burmese agents. General Alexander, as usual, was quite unperturbed and refused to take shelter in a trench, as I did very briskly, preferring to stand upright behind a tree. I was very annoyed with him for this, not only because it was a foolhardy thing to do, but because we had been trying to stop the men doing it. We had lost a number in this way. It was all right as long as the hostile aircraft did not come from more than one direction and if they did not drop the small anti-personnel bombs some of their fighters carried. If, as often happened, they did either of these things, results were apt to be unpleasant for everyone not in a trench or flat on the ground. This was not the only time I found the army commander's courage above my standard.

Returning from Taungdwingyi late that afternoon, we found 48 Brigade had just cleared the main road of a big Japanese infiltration party that had tried to put a block across it. Our car was held up as the fight was still going on about eight hundred yards south of the road, and the enemy, with what appeared to be a single infantry gun, were shelling a bridge over which we had to pass. Their shooting was not very effective, but they might score a bull in time, so I whistled up a couple of light tanks that were standing by and suggested to General Alexander that he get into one and I into the other to cross the bridge.

'What about my car and the driver?' he asked at once.

'Oh, he'll have to stand on the gas and chance it,' I replied.

'But it'll be just as dangerous for him as it would be for me!'

'Yes, but he's not the army commander.'

'All right,' said Alexander. 'You go in a tank. I'm staying in the car!'

So, of course, we both went in the car.

During the night of April 12–13, the Japanese resumed their attacks, and 48 Brigade again heavily repulsed the one on their front, but we were not so fortunate on our 1 Burma Brigade flank. During the 12th Scott, expecting this attack, had ordered the reinforcement of the forward troops on the river-bank while he prepared to strike the enemy assault in flank next morning with his main mobile reserve. Unfortunately, his division was lamentably short of signal equipment, especially wireless, while telephone cable was constantly cut by saboteurs and agents. As a result, orders went astray and moves were delayed. Meanwhile, in the dark, Japanese dressed as Burma Rifles and as civilians surprised the Burma Rifles and Burma Frontier Force dug in on the riverbank. Strong Japanese forces followed up and when our delayed reinforcements, not knowing this had happened, approached next morning they were ambushed. Although they rallied, counterattacked, and rescued some of the prisoners taken in the night, they were compelled to fall back, leaving the way to the north open. Japanese pressure against 1 Burma Brigade increased, there was considerable infiltration by strong enemy parties, and certain of our units gave way. The striking force, moving down to counterattack, became involved in a series of fights with enemy groups, and exhausted itself by marching and countermarching to deal with them. Finally 1 Burma Brigade, in much confusion, fell back to the main road, exposing the whole of our right flank and giving the enemy a clear run for Magwe.

The first news we had at Corps Headquarters was a warning from Scott that the situation on the riverbank was obscure, but that he feared something unpleasant had happened. This was quickly followed by the arrival of certain fugitives, who, as is the way of fugitives, described the heroic fight they had put up and assured us they were the sole survivors. I had enough experience to know that things are never quite so bad—or as good—as first reports make them, but this was obviously serious. Something had to be done at once to reconstitute our right flank. There was very little available; nothing, in fact, except a handful of exhausted units we had pulled out for a short rest. These, hurriedly organized into some sort of force, were sent off. First, in mechanical transport, the 2d King's Own Yorkshire Light Infantry, now very weak in numbers indeed, to hold Myingun and block the enemy advance along the riverbank; following them the 1st Cameronians, also only a skeleton battalion, and one of our Indian Mounted Infantry detachments. I also brought a battalion from 2 Burma Brigade back across the river to form a fresh reserve.

Corps Headquarters, somewhat hampered by a couple of air raids, packed rather hurriedly and stood by for a move. It was on these occasions, far too frequent, that we congratulated ourselves on the smallness of our staff and lightness of our equipment.

By the morning of April 14, it was clear that there was a wide gap beween our two divisions, the road from Magwe to Taungdwingyi was completely cut, and very strong Japanese forces were astride it between 13 Brigade and 48 Brigade. Neither of these brigades was now on the offensive; both were fighting hard, defensive battles against superior numbers. I agreed with Scott that there was no prospect now of getting his striking force going again. For this reason and because the failure of communication made it practically impossible for the Burma Division to control it, I reverted 48 Brigade to the 17th Division. Immediately south of us the improvised force sent to reconstitute the flank was heavily engaged. The Yorkshiremen were, indeed, surrounded—they eventually most gallantly cut their way out—and the remaining units had not the strength to hold the Japanese. There was nothing for it but to pull back this flank to the deep, dry watercourse of the Yin Chaung, which, starting just north of Taungdwingyi, meandered from east to west to enter the Irrawaddy some eight miles south of Magwe, and to try, with the 1st Burma Division, to hold that obstacle. If we could not, then our next halt would for reasons of water supply have to be on the Pin Chaung, north of Yenangyaung. In other words, we should lose the oil fields.

It was, in fact, now evident that unless we quickly reunited our two divisions we could hardly hope to hold the enemy. I was sure the time had now come when it was imperative to draw in the 17th Division, but General Alexander was loath to do anything that might adversely affect the Chinese. He still insisted on keeping the 17th Division in Taungdwingyi. Luckily, while Corps Headquarters had still been there, we had, by removing the lines and planking the bridges of the railway that ran north out of the town to Kyaukpadaung, turned its earth formation into a rough road. Had this not been done, it would have been impossible, when the Magwe road was cut, even to maintain the 17th Division. The conversion of a railway to a road had been a fine bit of work by the sappers who carried it out under frequent air attack.

For the next two days the 1st Burma Division pulled back, devotedly covered by tanks of 7 Armoured Brigade, to the Yin Chaung. On the night of April 16–17 the Japanese attacked 1 Burma Brigade along this obstacle. At first the brigade resisted stoutly and inflicted considerable losses by ambushing the leading enemy units, but a battalion of Burma Rifles gave way, thus allowing an Indian battalion to be surrounded. The Indians fought their way out, but the whole front was broken. It must be remembered that at this time units were very weak, few battalions having as many as three hundred men, and those tired, ill-fed, and lacking equipment. The 1st Burma

Division had no option but to save what it could by ordering a retirement of both 1 and 13 Brigades across the country to the Magwe–Yenangyaung road.

We had already sent the bulk of our administrative units and a portion of Corps Headquarters back to Yenangyaung. When a mountain battery started firing from just behind my headquarters I went out and asked what range they were firing at. An officer told me, 'Two thousand yards,' but when he added, 'We're just reducing to fifteen hundred,' I thought it time for the rest of Corps Headquarters to go.

The retreat through the oil fields had begun.

CHAPTER IV

DISASTER

It was a great disappointment that our efforts to stage a counter-blow on the Magwe–Taungdwingyi line had failed so badly, and I drove into Yenangyaung to check the final arrangements for the inevitable demolition in no happy frame of mind. Every gallon of gasoline was precious now and the gallant oil-company staff were keeping up some production until the last moment.

Meanwhile, by the forced retirement of the 1st Burma Division on its right and the withdrawal north of the Chinese on its left, the 17th Division had become isolated and exposed at Taungdwingyi. I now wished to abandon that town but Army Headquarters still insisted that, as the Chinese were in difficulties, Taungdwingyi must be held.

My headquarters passed through Yenangyaung and halted in the scanty cover of some low scrub-covered hillocks on the banks of the Pin Chaung, just north of the town, where I heard that General Alexander was sending me the newly-arrived 38th Chinese Division and I asked that it should be concentrated at Kyankpadaung as soon as possible. It was generous of Stilwell to make no protest at this, as he cannot have been happy about the situation on his own front. I also tried to reconstitute the reduced and shaken 1 Burma Bigade by giving it yet another battalion I drew from the west of the Irrawaddy as the 1st Burma Division made its way up the waterless road towards Yenangyaung. It was a melancholy march. The troops suffered greatly from heat and thirst and were frequently attacked by hostile aircraft. 7 Armoured Brigade again covered the withdrawal; what we should have done without that brigade I do not know. By evening we had managed to pass the rear echelons of the divisional mechanical transport safely back to Gwegyo, twenty-five miles north of Yenangyaung.

Our information of enemy moves from ground sources was

far from full, but it was ominous; from the air it was non-existent. As I could not risk the oil field and the refinery falling intact into Japanese hands, at 1300 hours on April 15 I gave orders for their demolition. At once a million gallons of crude oil burned with flames rising five hundred feet; the flash and crash of explosions came as machinery, communications, and buildings disintegrated; over all hung a vast, sinister canopy of dense black smoke. It was a fantastic and horrible sight.

On the 16th we moved Corps Headquarters from the Pin Chaung back to Gwegyo and it was as well we did so, for soon after dark the Japanese, disguised in Burma Rifles uniforms, pounced on the road at the exact spot we had left. We put in a brisk counterattack with such troops as we could raise and, after some very rough fighting in the dark, cleared the road. Transport again began to come through, but some anti-aircraft guns were ambushed and almost captured. Another counterattack rescued them, and I met them coming out, one gun with its tyres burning, its British gunners smoke-blackened but cheerful. Nor was their shooting affected, for they brought down seven aircraft later in the day. There was no lack of targets.

The 1st Burma Division, wearily making its way up the road, still south of Yenangyaung, heard in the early hours of the 17th that the enemy were in the town ahead of it. Scott began to concentrate his men, tired and thirsty, on the southern outskirts while his leading troops pushed on. Another Japanese attempt to block the road at the old Corps Headquarters site was again flung back, but returning in much larger numbers they succeeded, after considerable loss, in establishing a block near the ford just north of Yenangyaung, and all movement out of the town ceased.

I had now practically nothing further with which to counter-attack, and it was with relief that I heard that the first regiment of the Chinese 38th Division was just arriving in Kyaukpadaung. I dashed off in my jeep to get them moving.

Apart from the guerrilla battalion that had so reluctantly come to us at Taungdwingyi, this was the first time I had had Chinese troops under me. I found the regimental commander in the upstairs room of one of the few houses still standing in Kyaukpadaung village. He was a slight but tough-looking little Chinaman, with a real poker face, a pair of field glasses, and a huge Mauser pistol. We were introduced by the British liaison officer with the regiment, who spoke perfect Chinese. We shook hands, and got down to business with a map. As I described the situation, the Chinese colonel struck me as intelligent and quick to grasp what I wanted. This was to bring his regiment, in lorries which I had ready, down to the Pin Chaung at once, and then sent back the transport to fetch the next regiment as quickly as possible. I explained that it was my intention to attack with those two regiments, or, if possible, with the whole division, across the Pin Chaung early on the 18th in cooperation with a breakout by the 1st Burma Division. Having explained all this fully, I asked him, through the interpreter, if he understood. He replied that he did.

'Then let's get moving,' I said cheerfully. The translation of this remark brought a flow of Chinese. He could not, he said, budge from Kyaukpadaung until he had the orders of General Sun, his divisional commander.

'But,' I explained, 'General Sun has been placed under my orders. If he were here I should tell him to do what I have told you to do, and he would do it. Isn't that right?'

'Yes,' agreed my regimental commander readily.

'All right, then let's get going.'

'But I cannot move until I get the orders of General Sun.'

And so it went on for an hour and a half, at the end of which I could cheerfully have shot the colonel with his own pistol. At last, just when I was feeling desperate, he suddenly smiled and said, 'All right, I will do it!'

Why he changed his mind I do not know. I suspect some of the Chinese of various ranks who had flowed in and out of the room throughout our interview must have brought a message from Sun, telling him to do whatever I wanted. Once he got moving, I had no complaints about my Chinaman. Indeed, within the next few days I got to like him very much.

In fact, I got to like all, or almost all, my Chinese very much. They are a likeable people, and as soldiers, they have in a high degree the fighting man's basic qualities—courage, endurance, cheerfulness, and an eye for country. In dealing with them I soon discovered that we got on very well if I remembered three things about our allies:

(i) Time meant nothing to them. No plan based on accurate timing had a hope of success. Whether it was attacking the enemy or coming to dinner, eight o'clock might mean four or just as likely twelve.

(ii) They would steal anything that came near them: stores, rations, lorries, railway trains, even the notice boards from our headquarters. It was no good getting fussed about this or even finding it extraordinary. After all, if I had belonged to an army that had been campaigning for four or five years without any supply, transport, or medical organization worth the name and had kept myself alive only by collecting things from the other people, I should either have had much the same ideas on property or have been dead.

(iii) The most important thing to a Chinaman was 'face.' I suppose 'face' might be defined as the respect in which one Chinaman is held by others. In practice, if a proposal can be put to a Chinaman so that carrying it out will enhance his prestige among his associates he will almost invariably accept it. Whatever 'face' is, and however annoying its repercussions may be to an Occidental, it is well to remember it is a very human thing. The Chinese are not the only people who bother about what the neighbours think.

Later in the day Lieutenant-General Sun Li Jen, commanding the 38th Division, arrived. He was a slight but well-proportioned, good-looking man, who might in age have been anything from twenty-five to forty-five. He was alert, energetic, and direct. Later I found him a good tactician, cool in action, very aggressively minded, and, in my dealings with him, completely straightforward. In addition, he had the great advantage that he spoke good English with a slight American accent, having, as he was rightly proud to tell, been educated at the Virginia Military Institute. The Institute could be proud of Sun; he would have been a good commander in any army.

I discussed with him the details of the attack next morning. He was suspicious, having, I think, been warned somewhere to look out for the slick British trying to put one over him. All our Allies at first suspect us of being terribly clever; it is flattering, but a bit disconcerting. I was impressed by Sun, and it was essential to gain his confidence. His division had no artillery or tanks of its own, and I was therefore arranging that all the artillery we had this side of the Pin Chaung and all available tanks should support his attack. I decided there and then that these arms should not be 'in support of' but 'under command of' his division. Long-suffering Brigadier Anstice, commanding 7 Armoured Brigade, threw me the look of a wounded sambhur when he heard me give this out, but, as always, he rose to the occasion and he and Sun got on famously together. I had in fact, arranged privately with Sun, as I would have done with a British divisional commander inexperienced with tanks, always to consult with Anstice before employing them. Sun, being an extremely sensible man, did so. He was, as far as I know, the first Chinese general to have the artillery and armoured units of an ally placed actually under his command, and his 'face' with his own people was accordingly vastly enhanced.

The rear guard of the 1st Burma Division closed up on Yenangyaung during the night of the 17–18th. They were still almost without water as the Japanese were now between them and the Pin Chaung, and, having arrived by boat, held the riverbank as well. My only link with Scott was by radio from Tank Brigade Headquarters to the small tank signals detachment he had with his one squadron. We used, as far as we could, code for our talks, and here again I found it a tremendous advantage to have a close friend as divisional commander. Our speech was so interlarded with references to things such as our various children's ages, the numbers of the bungalows we had lived in in India, and other personal matters, to say nothing of being carried on largely in Gurkhali, that he would have been a very clever Japanese who could have made much of it. In this way we coordinated the attack for next morning.

The plan was roughly for the 1st Burma Division to break out north while the Chinese came down to the Pin Chaung, cleared up the road block at the ford, and took in rear the Japanese trying to hold the Burma Division. I was still a little doubtful whether my friend the Chinese regimental commander, who was to lead the attack, would be quite as pushing as he should or whether some scruple might not delay him as it had yesterday. I mentioned this to Sun, who at once said, 'Let's go and see.' Off we went to Regimental Headquarters, where the colonel, as far as I could see, had his battalions all ready for the attack. The colonel knew what I had come for, and so, with something of a twinkle in his narrow eyes, he said :

'We will now go to a battalion.'

We went.

At the Battalion Headquarters, which was well forward, the

commanding officer, through Sun, told me his company dispositions. Feeling quite sure that our Allies meant business, I announced my satisfaction, and prepared to go back; but I was not to get away so easily. The colonel, twinkling even more pronouncedly, said :

'We will now go to a company.'

I was not sure that a company, just as the attack was starting, was where I wanted to be, but it was a question of 'face' for me now. So, not liking it very much, I went on, dodging along shallow nullahs to a company command post. We had not been there long when the attack went off. There was no hesitation about these Chinese soldiers. I think a lot of them must have had experience under fire, as they used ground skilfully. The Japanese made a lot of noise as the Chinese broke cover, but, as usual, their shooting was high and bad. The colonel turned to me. For one awful moment I thought he was going to say, 'We will now go to a platoon!' but he did not. Instead, he looked at me and grinned. Only a good and seasoned soldier can grin at you like that when bullets are about.

The Chinese attack we had watched reached the Pin Chaung and cleared the north bank, but failed to take the strongly held road block at the ford. Even the tanks, prevented from closing by the soft sand of the river bed, could not drive out the defenders. Sun got busy preparing another attack, but with communications as bad as his were and with the units by now rather mixed up, I did not think he could renew the assault as quickly as he hoped.

Meanwhile, the Burma Division had begun in real earnest the Battle of the Oilfields. And a brutal battle it was. The temperature that day was 114 degrees; the battlefield was the arid, hideous, blackened shale of the oil field littered with wrecked derricks, flames roaring from the tanks, and shattered machinery and burning buildings everywhere. Over it all hung that huge pall of smoke. And there was no water.

At six thirty in the morning the Burma Division attacked. Progress was made, under cover of artillery, but the guns were running short of shells. Then some Burman troops faltered. In spite of this a by-pass road was cleared and a good deal of transport got down almost to the Pin Chaung itself, only to be held up by Japanese on the south bank. The British and Indian troops of the division fought doggedly over low ridge after ridge, the Japanese defending each one to the last man. A detachment of the Inniskillings struggled through to the Pin Chaung and enthusiastically greeted the troops it found there, believing them to be Chinese. They were Japanese who lured the Irishmen into an ambush. The tanks made a last attack on the road block, but it was defended by several anti-tank guns, and the tanks, bogged in the soft sand, became sitting targets. The attack, like that of the Chinese from the other side, petered to a standstill.

More Japanese were coming in from the east and were reported on the river. The situation was grave. At half past four in the afternoon Scott reported on the radio that his men were exhausted from want of water and continuous marching and fighting. He could hold that night, he thought, but if he waited until morning his men, still without water, would be so weakened they would have little or no offensive power to renew the attack. He asked permission to destroy his guns and transport and fight his way out that night. Scott was the last man to paint an unduly dark picture. I knew his men were almost at the end of their strength and in a desperate position. I could not help wishing that he had not been so close a friend. I thought of his wife and of his boys. There were lots of other wives, too, in England, India, and Burma whose hearts would be under that black cloud a couple of miles away. Stupid to remember that now! Better get it out of my head.

I thought for a moment, sitting there with the headphones on, in the van with the operator crouching beside me, his eyes anxiously on my face. Then I told Scott he must hang on. I had ordered a Chinese attack again with all available tanks and artillery for the next morning. If the Burma Division attacked then we ought to break through, and save our precious guns and transport. I was afraid, too, that if our men came out in driblets, as they would in the dark, mixed up with Japanese, the Chinese and indeed our own soldiers would fail to recognize them and their losses would be heavy. Scott took it as I knew he would. He said, 'All right, we'll hang on and we'll do our best in the morning, but, for God's sake, Bill, make those Chinese attack.'

I stepped out of the van feeling about as depressed as a man could. There, standing in a little half-circle waiting for me, were a couple of my own staff, an officer or two from the Tank Brigade, Sun, and the Chinese liaison officers. They stood there silent and looked at me. All commanders know that look. They see it in the eyes of their staffs and their men when things are really bad, when even the most confident staff officer and the toughest soldier want holding up, and they turn where they *should* turn for support—to their commander. And sometimes he does not know what to say. He feels very much alone.

'Well, gentlemen,' I said, putting on what I hoped was a confident, cheerful expression, 'it might be worse!'

One of the group, in a sepulchral voice, replied with a single word:

'How?'

I could cheerfully have murdered him, but instead I had to keep my temper.

'Oh,' I said, grinning, 'it might be raining!'

Two hours later it was—hard. As I crept under a truck for shelter I thought of that fellow and wished I *had* murdered him.

Throughout the night, as we sat inside a circle of laagered tanks just above the Pin Chaung, we could hear and see the crump and flash of Japanese shells and mortar bombs flailing Scott's wretched men. His guns did not reply. They were down to about twenty rounds per gun now, and he was keeping those for the morning. Time and again the Japanese put in infantry attacks, attempting to infiltrate under cover of darkness and shelling. These attacks, one after the other, were beaten off, but certain of the Burma troops panicked and abandoned their positions, throwing extra strain on the British and Indians.

The day began for me before dawn with a severe blow. The Chinese attack across the Pin Chaung to take Twingon, a village about a mile south of the ford, which I had hoped would start soon after daylight, could not be got ready in time. After a good deal of talk it was promised for twelve thirty as the earliest possible hour. I was then faced with the problem of either telling Scott to hold his attack, which was due to go in at seven o'clock, or to let it go as arranged. I decided to let it go, rather than keep his men and transport sitting cramped and waterless under artillery, mortar, and air attack.

At seven o'clock the Burma Division resumed the attack, but a reinforced Japanese defence held it after it had made some progress. Meanwhile, on the north bank, while still urging the Chinese to hurry their preparations, we had managed to scrape up a small British force which attacked and, during the morning, actually got a squadron of tanks and some of the West Yorkshire Regiment across the Chaung. This small success might have been expanded had not one of those infuriating mishaps so common in battle occurred. An officer some distance in the rear received a report that strong enemy forces were advancing to cut off the transport assembled about Gwegyo. Without realizing the situation forward, and still less that the threatening forces advancing on him were not Japanese but Chinese, he ordered back the tanks and accompanying infantry to deal with this new but imaginary danger.

The Burma Division was once more halted in a tight perimeter and was being heavily shelled. The heat was intense, there was still no water, the troops were exhausted, and they had suffered heavy casualties, their wounded, of course, being still with them. At this stage the Burma battalions, in spite of the efforts of their officers really disintegrated. 1 Burma Brigade reported that the bulk of their troops were no longer reliable; even 13 Brigade said that some of theirs were shaky. It was hardly to be wondered at; their ordeal had been terribly severe.

The Chinese attack, promised for 1230 hours, had now been postponed to 1400 hours. Just before that time it was again put back to 1600 hours. We managed, however, to get it off at 1500 hours instead. These delays were of course maddening, but I had not then learned that time means little to the average Chinaman. Actually, with their lack of signal equipment, of means of evacuating wounded, and of replenishing ammunition, and their paucity of trained junior leaders, it was not surprising that to sort themselves out, reform, and start a fresh attack took time. The trouble was not with Sun, who was all energy and desire to attack, but with so many of his subordinates, who promised but did not perform, and in the delays and errors that occurred in getting his orders to them. One of their troubles, and a real one, was water. They could not attack until water had been replenished, and they had no means of fetching it up except in a few petrol tins slung in pairs on a bamboo and carried, willow-pattern plate fashion, across a man's shoulder. We got one of our few remaining water lorries and ran it up nearly to their front line, with orders to make continuous trips backward and forward. It went the first time and did not return. Eventually the British driver appeared on foot. He said, with soldierly embellishments, that having emptied the tank of water, the Chinese, in spite of his protests, emptied the radiator also, and, when he left to get help, were trying to empty the petrol tank as well! Sun dealt with that incident; we got the water lorry back and it ran regularly. Even so, when I was at one of the forward Chinese headquarters a large and very fat Chinese officer protested volubly that it was impossible to attack as none of his men had water. He was deeply moved about it. I noticed that all the time he was so passionately describing the sufferings of his men he had a very large water bottle hanging from his belt, and that even at his most gesticulatory moments it lay snug against his ample posterior. I walked quietly up to him, lifted it, and shook it. It was full to the cork. There was a pause in his flow of language, and a moment's hush among the specta-tors. Then all shouted with laughter—in which the fat officer joined. Without more ado he agreed they could attack by 1500 hours, and they did.

Unhappily, before that time communication with Scott had ceased and his last desperate effort to break out could not be coordinated with the Chinese attack. His squadron of tanks had found and cleared a rough track, leading east, down to the Pin Chaung, over which it was hoped vehicles could move. Scott himself formed up the column, guns in front, wounded in ambulances and trucks next, followed by such vehicles as had survived the bombardment. With a spearhead of tanks and infantry the column lurched down the narrow, uneven path, through the low hillocks. But the trail turned to sand; the leading ambulances were bogged and the column stopped. As many wounded as possible were piled on the tanks, and Scott gave the order to abandon vehicles and fight a way out on foot across the Pin Chaung. This his men did, some in formed bodies, some in small groups, and on the other side they met the Chinese. At the sight of the water in the Chaung the mules which had come out with them went mad, and the men flung themselves face downward into it. The haggard, red-eyed British, Indian, and Burmese soldiers who staggered up the bank were a terrible sight, but every man I saw was still carrying his rifle. The two brigades of the division had reached Yenangyaung at a strength of not more than one; there they had lost in killed and wounded 20 per cent of that small number, with a considerable portion of their guns, mortars, and vehicles. None of these losses, in either men or equipment, could be replaced. After its ordeal the division would be of no fighting value until it had rested, and, as best it could, re-organized. We collected it that night about Gwegyo.

When the Chinese did attack they went in splendidly. They were thrilled at the tank and artillery support they were getting and showed real dash. They took Twingon, rescuing some two hundred of our prisoners and wounded. Next day, April 20, the 38th Division attacked again and with tanks penetrated into Yenangyaung itself, repulsing a Japanese counterattack. The fighting was severe and the Chinese acquitted themselves well, inflicting heavy losses, vouched for by our own officers. Sun now expected a really heavy Japanese attack at dawn on the 21st. I discussed this with him and agreed that he should come out of the town, back to the Pin Chaung. His division had done well and I did not want it frittered away in a house-to-house dogfight for the shell of Yenangyaung. In spite of the stories I had heard from American sources, of Chinese unwillingness to fight, I had remembered how enthusiastic officers, who had served with our own Chinese Hong Kong regiment, had been about their men, and I had expected the Chinese soldier to be tough and brave. I was, I confess, surprised at how he had responded to the stimulus of proper tank and artillery support, and at the aggressive spirit he had shown. I had never expected, either, to get a Chinese general of the calibre of Sun.

A number of our badly wounded had of necessity been left in the ambulances when the Burma Division had finally broken out. A young gunner officer volunteered to go back to discover their fate. Under cover of darkness he did so. The ambulances were still standing on the track, but every man in them had had his throat cut or been bayoneted to death.

We were not alone in our misfortunes. When the Chinese Fifth Army had been driven out of Toungoo towards Pyinmana, their Sixth Army was spread out to the west along the Mawchi–Loilem–Takaw road. Its leading division, the 55th, was attacked at Mawchi by part of the Japanese 56th Division and on April 17 the enemy cut the road behind it near Bawlake. The Chinese fought hard to escape, but suddenly all telephone and wireless communication with the 55th Division ceased; it had been overrun and scattered. Moving fast by side tracks, small Japanese mobile columns then cut the main

Thazi–Loilem–Kentung road behind the Sixth Army, which broke and fell back pellmell, leaving all bridges intact. On April 20 its remnants halted twelve miles west of Loilem, one hundred and thirty miles north of Mawchi.

When, on April 19, General Alexander, Stilwell, and I met to decide what should be done next, not knowing the full extent of the collapse of the Chinese Sixth Army, we planned on the basis that, while pressed, it could still, in such extremely good defensive country, hold the small forces that were all the Japanese could bring against it. General Tu, commanding the Fifth Army about Pyinmana, had still three intact divisions, and hoped to stage another 'Changsha' battle there—it was for this reason that he had ignored Stilwell's order to take over Taungdwingyi—but the Japanese discovered the trap and refused to walk into it. The last Chinese Army to arrive, the Fifty-sixth, had now one division in Mandalay and a second moving into Burma, so that Stilwell was, or rather thought he was, able to dispose of eight divisions, his 9th, the 38th being under my command.

As a precautionary measure Burma Army Headquarters had prepared an outline plan by which the Chinese armies would, if compelled, withdraw to China via Lashio, accompanied by our 7 Armoured Brigade and by a brigade group of the 17th Division. The remainder of the British forces were to make for India via the Hukwang Valley and Kalewa. The objects of this scheme were to cover the entrances into China and India and, by sending a British force with them, to ensure that the Chinese remained active Allies. I did not like this plan at all, especially the sending of any British formations into China. Their administration would be almost impossible, they would arrive in a shocking state, and be no advertisement for us. Besides, I thought there was a chance that even now we might turn the tables on the Japanese.

I had come to the conference armed with a suggestion, worked out by Davies, my chief of staff and my mainstay in these difficult times, and myself, to take advantage of the exposed position of the Japanese 33d Division in Yenangyaung, to attack and destroy it. To do this I hoped to get on loan for a short time another, or, if possible, two more Chinese divisions to join my 38th. With these I proposed to attack Yenangyaung from the north and east, while the 17th Division, at last released from Taungdwingyi, swept up through Magwe and fell on the enemy rear from the south. With the reconstituted 1st Burma Division, now about the strength of a brigade, to hold various 'stops,' I felt we had a good chance, if we acted quickly, of smashing the 33d Division. When we had done that, and I calculated it would take a week from the time the attacking divisions reached Yenangyaung, we should be in a position to move over to the Sittang and take the Japanese opposite the Fifth and Sixth Chinese Armies in flank and rear. A little ambitious, I know, but still a chance, and, as both Stilwell and I recognized, about our last chance. I found him, as he always was, ready to support an offensive move and prepared to go a long way to help me. He was naturally anxious also to do anything that would prevent any further withdrawal of my corps to the north, as that would expose the Fifth Army to flank attack from the Japanese Irrawaddy forces. He promised me the 200th Chinese Division from the Fifth Army, and I asked for it at Kyaukpadaung as soon as possible. General Alexander gave this transfer of a Chinese division his blessing, but he still refused to sanction the withdrawal of the 17th Division from Taungdwingyi, as he felt that to do so would expose the Chinese flank. This, of course, took a good deal of the sting out of our plan, but I felt the main thing was to get the Chinese to Kyaukpadaung. Then we would see what would happen to the 17th Division. I returned to my headquarters at Gwegyo more cheerful than I had been for some time, and Davies got down to preparing our masterpiece— Burma Corps Directive No. 5, which was to put paid to our account with the redoubtable Japanese 33d Division. Alas, it was never issued!

Events on the Chinese front were moving to a climax. By April 21, their Sixth Army had practically disintegrated. The Japanese, moving swiftly in relatively small columns with motorized infantry, tanks, and armoured cars, had constantly hooked round and cut off the Chinese forces trying to hold main roads on narrow fronts. On that day, the Japanese reached Hopong; the next, the 22d, they drove the Chinese out of positions to the east of it and towards Loilem on the road to China. Loilem itself was bombed from the air and burned, while the Chinese again tried to hold astride the road, some eight miles west of it. Another hook, and the Japanese had Loilem, and General Kan, the Chinese Army commander, with three hundred men, all that was left to him, was a fugitive on the Lashio road. The Chinese 93d Division had advanced from Kengtung to within twenty miles of Loilem, when it heard the Japanese were in the town. It turned and withdrew. General Kan with his remnant came across country to Kengtung, where he joined what was left of the 49th and 93d Divisions and the stragglers of the 55th Division. Having collected these, he, and with him the last traces of the Sixth Army, moved into China. Kengtung was then occupied by Siamese forces under Japanese control. The road north to Lashio was open to the enemy.

All unconscious of these disasters, we at Burma Corps were very pleased at the speed with which Stilwell carried out his promise to send us the 200th Chinese Division from the Fifth Army. In spite of difficulties in finding transport, it reached Meiktila, and the leading regiment began to roll in by lorry to Kyaukpadaung. From the look of it I thought the 200th would be nearly as good as the 38th Division. I had come back to our headquarters in the evening of the 20th after spending some time seeing Chinese soldiers debussing, and Davies and I were sitting after dinner putting the finishing touches to our famous Directive No. 5 when a staff officer came in and said 'Do you know that all the Chinese at Kyaukpadaung are packing up and going back again?' And they were!

Stilwell, at last having received something approaching accurate information of the Sixth Army debacle, had recalled the 200th Division for a desperate attempt to retrieve the situation. When they drove the Chinese out of Loilem, the Japanese had also occupied Taunggyi, only sixty miles from Thazi, which, if they seized that, too, would cut off the whole of the Chinese Fifth Army. Stilwell himself leading the 200th Division and a regiment of the 22d retook Taunggyi on April 24. Pushing eastward, he drove the enemy out of Hopong, killing some five hundred, and occupied Loilem. It was a magnificent achievement, made possible only by Stilwell's personal leadership with the very front units, but it could only be a last effort—the disintegration of the Chinese forces had gone too far. Stilwell had to return to his headquarters, the counter-stroke petered out, and, left to themselves, the Chinese made north up the Lashio road.

Meanwhile, even as we were holding our conference on April 19, the Japanese had turned on the Chinese Fifth Army and by a series of frontal attacks and hooks round its flanks had driven it out of Pyinmana and Pyawbwe. By April 25, its motor transport in a *sauve-qui-peut* dash had reached Lashio and its two divisions, having ceased to be fighting formations, were streaming back in disorganized groups through Thazi towards Mandalay.

Between April 26 and 29 parts of two divisions of the newly-arrived Chinese Sixty-sixth Army reached Lashio, where there was great confusion. On the 29th the enemy attacked Lashio with thirty light tanks, a few armoured cars, twelve guns, and two battalions of lorry-borne infantry, and took it. The remnants of this Chinese Army, about three thousand men, made their way out into China while the Japanese pressed on to take Bhamo on May 4; other enemy columns pursuing the Fifth Army were in Meiktila on the 8th. The Chinese 200th Division and the regiment of the 22d Division that Stilwell had led to Taunggyi, finding Lashio occupied by Japanese, after some wanderings made their way to China. The only Chinese troops now left in Burma out of the original nine divisions were my 38th Division, still intact, and the fleeing remnants of the Fifth Army.

On April 25, General Alexander and I met Stilwell, just returned from the taking of Taunggyi, at Kyaukse, twenty-five miles south of Mandalay. The complete disappearance of the Sixth Army and the rapidly spreading disintegration of the other two Chinese armies were the dominating facts of a grim situation. There was no longer any chance of staging a counter-offensive; the Japanese were about to seize Lashio and with it would go our hopes of holding northern Burma. With the Chinese rapidly passing out of the picture, realism demanded that we should now decide to get out of Burma as intact as we could, with as much as we could. Recognizing this, the army commander ordered a general withdrawal north of Mandalay, and, as the Chinese were no longer able to protect themselves during such a move, he ordered my corps to extend to its left and act as rear guard to the fugitive Chinese Fifth Army as it made north along the Meiktila–Mandalay road and railway. The retirement was to begin at once; indeed, as far as the Chinese were concerned, it was already in full, disorderly swing.

There was no time to be lost if we were to stop the Japanese pouring over the Irrawaddy at Mandalay on the heels of the fleeing Chinese, and 7 Armoured Brigade was ordered at once

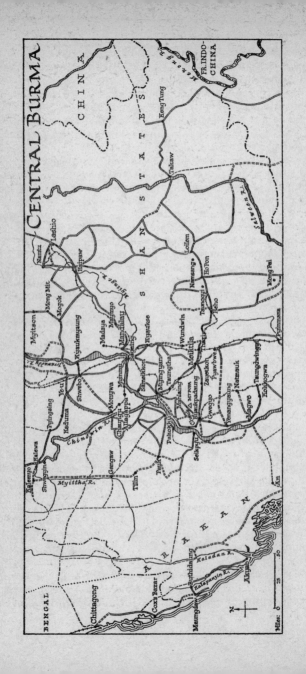

with all speed to Meiktila. Back once more at Corps Headquarters, Davies and I, instead of our precious, stillborn Directive No. 5, issued orders for:

(i) The 38th Chinese Division to cover Kyaukpadaung.

(ii) The 1st Burma Division (less its 2 Brigade on the west of the Irrawaddy) to complete its reorganization and be ready to move on Taungtha.

(iii) The 17th Division to evacuate Taungdwingyi, move rapidly to the area Mahlaing–Meiktila–Zayetkon, and with 7 Armoured Brigade, cover the withdrawal of the Chinese Fifth Army.

On the evening of the 25th tanks of 7 Armoured Brigade interposed east of Mektila between the Chinese and the pursuing Japanese. They surprised an enemy armoured and mechanized column, shot it up, and dispersed it with considerable loss. The 17th Division, having evacuated Taungdwingyi and Natmauk, was firmly established in the Meiktila–Zayetkon area, supporting 7 Armoured Brigade in its thrusts against Japanese columns advancing astride the main road and railway. There were many small parties of fugitive Chinese scattered over the country, and these were passed back and directed on Kyaukse.

My corps, now very weak, was terribly stretched on a seventy-five mile line from Seikpyu, on the west of the Irrawaddy, to Meiktila, and as all Chinese were now north of this line I ordered Cowan to establish a brigade in Kyaukse and then fall back to cover the road and railway bridges over the Myitnge River south of Mandalay. This he did during the night of April 26–27. I was extremely pleased with the way in which the 17th Division and 7 Armoured Brigade were carrying out these trying rear-guard tasks so hurriedly thrust upon them.

Throughout this time, it was very difficult to get any reliable information of the locations of Chinese troops of the Fifth Army. Obviously both the 96th and 22d Divisions had disintegrated and were making their way back in leaderless parties as best they could. All higher control seemed to have disappeared, and neither the Chinese nor American headquarters could give any reliable estimate of the position or when the fugitives would be over the Myitnge River. An occasional

Chinese officer appeared fleetingly at corps or 17th Division Headquarters with appeals, usually for transport, or with requests for information about his own troops. On one occasion a Chinese colonel, whose men were to entrain at one of the stations north of Wundwin to which a few trains had been sent by night, asked for our troops to be posted on and close to the railway station. If this were not done, he feared that the first Chinese troops to arrive would panic, rush the trains, and drive off, leaving the others behind. In answer to his request, a small detachment from the 17th Division was sent back and duly occupied obvious positions on and around the station. Some of General Stilwell's staff, vainly trying to get order into the retreat, arrived at the station, saw our troops there, and jumped to the conclusion, no doubt confirmed by the Chinese, that this was the rearmost portion of the British rear guard. Knowing many Chinese were still well to the south, the harassed Americans reported that the British were beating the Chinese in the race north. Stilwell, infuriated, sent a message accusing me in emotional terms of having failed to carry out my duty as rear guard. I dare say my nerves were nearly as stretched as his—we were neither of us having a very good time—and I was furious at this injustice to my troops who were at that moment fighting briskly far to the south of his Chinese. I replied with a very astringent refutation of the charge. This was the only time Stilwell and I fell out, but a few days later he sent me a message withdrawing the accusation and coming as near to an apology as I should think he ever got.

On April 28, with Lashio about to fall and little or nothing to stop a Japanese dash for Bhamo and even Myitkyina, I received from General Alexander directives for the final withdrawal to India. Recognizing that our hold on the Mandalay–Irrawaddy line could only be temporary, the plan, given in some detail, was:

(i) Two brigades to fall back astride the Chindwin, delaying the enemy as far south as possible.

(ii) A strong detachment to be left in the Myittha Valley which runs north, roughly parallel to, and some thirty miles west of, the Chindwin.

(iii) The remainder of the corps to move via Ye-u on Kalewa, leaving a detachment to cover this route, and to see out of Burma by the Shwegyin track all administrative, civil, and other refugees not escaping by other routes.

(iv) The 38th Chinese Division and possibly other Chinese troops to accompany Burma Corps.

I had pressed hard that the 38th Chinese Division should come with my corps into India. Sun had welcomed the idea, and I was glad to see that General Alexander now intended the division to march out with me. The remainder of the Chinese were, as far as I could judge, already making their way as best they could to China.

It was not easy to arrange this withdrawal while we were closely engaged in a rear-guard action, with the Irrawaddy, one of the great rivers of the world, crossed by only one bridge, behind us. The Burma Army had directed the corps to cross by the ferries at Sameikkon and west of Mandalay. I was a bit doubtful about these ferries, as we had already experienced the difficulty there was in keeping the civilian crews who manned them at work under air attack and the threat of the Japanese advance. I made a hurried reconnaissance with Swift, my chief engineer. It was as well we did so. One ferry consisted of nothing at all, another of one dumb barge aground some yards from the bank, and the third of a small craft capable of taking one or two vehicles at a time. I do not doubt Army Headquarters had made preparations, but it was becoming increasingly difficult to hold administrative detachments in place and our prospects of getting three divisions, with the Japanese on their heels and no air cover, over by these ferries did not look too promising. However, Swift and the chief engineer of the 1st Burma Division were not easily defeated. The river fleet of the Irrawaddy flotilla was being sunk in Mandalay. Swift rushed there, seized some of the vessels, and brought them downstream to the ferries, barges were pulled off sand banks, approaches improved, and ferries of a sort provided. We christened the provision of ferries by the Burma Army that 'blanket' system of administration, from the old story, 'And we says to 'im, "Jump, and we'll 'old the blanket." And 'e jumped. And there worn't no blanket!' Luckily we looked before we leapt.

On April 28 corps orders were issued directing:

(i) 1st Burma Division to cross the Sameikkon ferry and

move to Monywa. There 13 Brigade was to cross to the west
bank of the Chindwin to secure the town from the south
and southwest.

(ii) 1 Burma Brigade to move from Monywa to Kalewa by
boat.

(iii) 2 Burma Brigade (now on the Irrawaddy west bank)
to withdraw via Pauk and Tilin into the Myittha Valley, to
deny that route to the enemy and eventually make touch
with the rest of the 1st Burma Division west of Kalewa.

(iv) 17th Division (less 63 Brigade) to cross and hold the
north bank of the Irrawaddy from Myinmu to Allagappa.

(v) 63 Brigade of the 17th Division to cover the road
thence to Monywa.

(vi) 38th Chinese Division and 7 Armoured Brigade to
hold the river from Sagaing to Ondaw.

The Ava bridge had been allotted to the Chinese Fifth Army,
for the crossing of the Irrawaddy, but I obtained permission
from Burma Army Headquarters to use it also for 7 Armoured
Brigade. It appeared to me, however, that if the 17th Division
was to cover the last of the Chinese over the bridge they might
as well follow themselves before destroying it. The 17th Division was therefore ordered to hold Kyaukse until all the
Fifth Army were north of the Myitnge River, then follow with
7 Armoured Brigade, cross, and destroy the Ava bridge.

Having seen 1st Burma and 38th Chinese Divisions well
started, with the Japanese showing little inclination to follow
too closely but being very annoying from the air, I set off to
visit the more dangerous 17th Division flank. On the road to
Kyaukse we ran into plenty of evidence of Burmese atrocities
against Indian refugees and Chinese stragglers. Luckily we fell
in with a mobile column from the 17th Division just in time to
rescue two Indian sepoys—one badly mutilated—who had
been repairing a telephone line and to bring down just retri-
bution on the gang responsible for the outrage.

In Kyaukse, bombed and burned out with many of its inhabitants and their cattle lying dead in the streets, we found
four weak battalions of Gurkhas, some guns, and a few Sappers, in all about eighteen hundred men. They had small
lorried detachments pushed out well to the flanks and to the
south and were expecting the rest of the 17th Division to pass
through that night. I left feeling this brigade would give a

74

good account of itself. It did.

April 29 began with some brisk clashes between enemy infantry and tanks and our detachments, which, during the day, in face of much superior force, fell back slowly on Kyaukse. At 2200 hours in bright moonlight the Japanese launched a fierce attack on our positions astride the road. The Gurkhas held their fire until their yelling assailants were a hundred and fifty yards away and then let them have it. The attack withered away. At midnight a Japanese transport column blundered almost into the defences and was heavily shelled and mortared. Half an hour later, another attack was met by close-range fire and destroyed; at 0515 hours, still in darkness, a third attack was flung back in confusion. At dawn on April 30, tanks and Gurkhas sallied out and cleared a burned-out village, killing many Japanese and capturing mortars and light automatics. The enemy belonged to the 18th Division and in the opinion of the Gurkhas were much inferior in both courage and skill to their old opponents the 33d Division.

During the 30th it was clear that the whole 18th Division was deploying to outflank our positions and, after repulsing another attack in the afternoon, the brigade was ordered to pull out as soon as it was dark. This it did under cover of one of its battalions, embussed a few miles up the road, and drove across the Ava bridge to Myinma. A most satisfactory piece of rear-guard work.

On the night of the 27th I returned to Corps Headquarters, now at Sagaing. Mandalay was full of dumps, stores, and camps of every kind—almost all of them deserted. A few officers and men of the administrative services and departments remained, but there had been a general and not very creditable exodus. We were to find more and more that demoralization behind the line was spreading. From now on, while the fighting troops, knowing that their object—to get out intact to India—was at last clear, actually improved in morale and fighting power, the amorphous mass of non-fighting units on the line of communication deteriorated rapidly. In its withdrawal the corps was from now on preceded by an undisciplined mob of fugitives intent only on escape. No longer in organized units, without any supply arrangements, having deserted their officers, they banded together in gangs, looting, robbing, and not infrequently murdering the unfortunate villagers on their route. They were almost entirely Indians and very few belonged to combatant units of the army. Most of them were soldiers in name only, but their cowardice and their conduct brought disrepute on the real Indian soldiers who followed. It was not to be wondered that as we retreated we found villages burned and abandoned and such inhabitants as were not in hiding frightened and unfriendly.

It was impossible to guard all the stores lying unattended in Mandalay. On one dump—of special octane petrol for our tanks—we did, however, put a small guard. We were growing greatly anxious about fuel supply for tanks, and the find was a godsend, but when the tanks arrived next day to refill they found nothing but twisted and blackened drums. A senior staff officer, alleged to be from the Burma Army, had appeared and ordered it to be destroyed, and so, with the help of the guard, it was. In the growing confusion, mistakes of this kind were almost inevitable but none the less damaging.

Numbers of Fifth Army Chinese were collected in Mandalay, and attempts were being made to get them away to the north by train. At the same time I was anxious to rescue some of the more important items such as rifles, bren guns, ammunition, medical stores, and boots, without which we could not continue to fight. With this object, two or three small trains were being loaded under the direction of a few stout-hearted British and Anglo-Burmese railway officials who set a magnificent example of devotion to duty. My Chinese of the 38th Division came one afternoon and told me that a certain Chinese general had discovered these trains and was coming that night with his troops to seize them and to escape north. I was in a quandary. I had not enough troops to guard them against the numbers who would appear, nor did I want a fight with our Allies. I sent warning to our railway friends and asked them to steam the engines ten miles up the line. In due course the Chinese arrived, piled themselves in, on, and all over the wagons. The general ordered the trains to start. He was then told there were no engines, as on my orders they had all been taken away. There was nothing for my Chinese friend to do but to call off his men and think of some other way of stealing a train. Eventually he succeeded in doing so and got away, but it was not one of my trains. I met him frequently afterwards in India. We never mentioned trains, but I noticed that he regarded me with an increased respect.

The corps, with the exception of 63 Brigade, that still held the approaches to the Ava bridge on the south bank, was now all safely over the Irrawaddy. There had been an anxious moment with the tanks. I found a line of them halted on the south side of the bridge with officers in consultation. A Stuart tank weighs some thirteen tons, and a notice warned us that the roadway running across the bridge on brackets each side of the railway had a maximum capacity of six tons. I asked who had built the bridge and was shown a tablet with the name of a well-known British engineering firm. My experience has been that any permanent bridge built by British engineers will almost certainly have a safety factor of 100 per cent, and I ordered the tanks to cross one by one. I confess I watched nervously to see if the roadway sagged under the first as it made a gingerly passage, but all was well. Good old British engineers! At last even the Chinese commander in chief agreed that all his men were over, and so 63 Brigade was withdrawn across the bridge. With a resounding thump it was blown at 2359 hours on April 30, and its centre spans fell neatly into the river—a sad sight, and a signal that we had lost Burma.

CHAPTER V

EVACUATION

The whole of the Burma Corps had crossed the Irrawaddy by the Ava bridge and the ramshackle ferries with much less trouble than I expected. The vigorous Japanese follow-up at Kyaukse was not repeated against the 1st Burma Division farther west, and there, what might have been a very hazardous operation, was interfered with only by air attack. By the evening of April 28, the 38th Chinese Division, 7 Armoured Brigade, and the bulk of the 17th Division were in position along the north bank of the river from Sagaing to Allagappa. The 1st Burma Division was also over the river and about to move to Monywa. I made a quick tour of the river line and returned to my headquarters, now in a monastery near Sagaing. I was relieved that the crossing had gone so smoothly and reassured by the condition of the 17th and 38th Divisions.

There was still, however, plenty to cause anxiety. It was clear that, with the Chinese armies in the state they were and with the Japanese pushing so rapidly north on the east of the Irrawaddy, our positions along the river west of Mandalay could not be held for long. Apart from this tactical consideration, the next stage of our long retreat must start soon to avoid the monsoon rains. Our road would run through Ye-u to Kaduma, twenty miles to the northwest, and there it would plunge into the jungle for a hundred and twenty miles until it reached the Chindwin at Shwegyin. For that distance the route was no more, and often less, than an unbridged, earth cart track, with frequent sharp bends, steep gradients, and narrow cuttings. Long stretches, sometimes as much as thirty miles, were completely without water. It crossed several wide stream beds of soft sand, difficult enough now for vehicles, and, when rain came, likely to be unfordable rivers. When Shwegyin was reached, the track ended and there was a six-mile river journey upstream to Kalewa. Then came a long trek up the malaria-infested Kabaw Valley, through dense jungle to Tamu to reach the unmetalled road that we hoped was being built from Imphal in Assam. Whatever happened it would be an arduous march; if the monsoon rains came before we had completed it, it could be an impossible one. The informed consensus was that the monsoon could be expected to start in earnest about May 20, but, of course, there might well be heavy rain before that.

I was, from what I heard of the route, doubtful if, even without rain, our heavier and bulkier vehicles could be got through. To test this and to discover where the track must be improved, I ordered a reconnaissance party with engineers to take a column consisting of one of each type of large vehicle, tank, anti-aircraft gun, lorry, etc., and go over the route to check its feasability. Burma Army Headquarters were now working as hard as they could to improve the track and to stock it with supplies and, where needed, with water, while General Headquarters, India, were, we were told, working similarly from the other end. But time was short and the way would be long and hard.

I was sitting outside my headquarters at Sagaing, musing on these things, when I was surprised to see a civilian motorcar drive up and disgorge half-a-dozen Burmese gentlemen dressed in morning coats, pin-stripe trousers, and grey *topis*. There was a definitely viceregal air about the whole party. They asked to see me. They were a deputation of influential Burmese officials from the large colony who had taken refuge in the Sagaing hills in the bend of the Irrawaddy opposite Mandalay. They submitted a neatly typed resolution duly proposed, seconded, and passed unanimously at a largely attended public meeting. This document stated that the Burmese official community had received an assurance from His Excellency the Governor that no military operations would take place in the Sagaing hills, a locality held in particular veneration by the Burmese people. Trusting in this, they and their families had removed themselves there. Now, to their dismay, Chinese troops had entered the hills and were preparing defences, even siting cannon. They therefore demanded that I, as the responsible British commander, should order out the Chinese and give a guarantee that, in accordance with His Excellency's promise, no military operations should take place in the Sagaing hills.

79

I was terribly sorry for these people. They were all high officials of the Burma government, commissioners, secretaries, judges, and the like; their world had tumbled about their ears, but they still clung to the democratic procedure of resolutions, votes, and the rest that we had taught them. They brought me their pathetic little bit of paper as if it were a talisman. When I told them that, as far as I was concerned, I had no wish for military operations in their hills—I might have added truthfully nor anywhere else at that moment—but that the Japanese general was equally concerned and not likely to be so obliging as to agree, they departed, polite but puzzled. The impressiveness of the proceedings was somewhat marred by one gentleman, who came back and asked could he not be issued with a six months' advance of pay? I do not blame him—it would be a long time before he would draw his British pay again.

The only Chinese now left as organized formations were our 38th Division, in good shape, and the 22d Division, badly mauled but still holding together. We had developed a real affection for Sun and the brave, cheerful, uncomplaining rascals he commanded, so that when Stilwell asked for them to be returned to him and General Alexander agreed, we were sorry to let them go. The 7 Armoured Brigade was also left temporarily as rear guard to the Chinese.

On April 30 the 17th Division was holding the riverbank from Sagaing to Allagappa, and my headquarters was a few miles north of Monywa in a grove of trees around a small Buddhist monastery. The town itself was garrisoned by a weak detachment, while the headquarters of the 1st Burma Division were bivouacked four miles to the south and two of its brigades, still twenty miles away, were plodding wearily north towards Monywa. Very foolishly I had allowed the division's third brigade, on the west bank, to move off to secure the Myittha Valley, which was reported to be threatened and, if occupied by the Japanese, would cut our escape route to India. As a result the approaches to Monywa on the west bank were left unprotected for two days. Forgetting the speed with which the Japanese might come up the river by boat, I had chosen to meet the wrong threat, and we paid heavily for my mistake.

We were sitting, after our rather meagre dinner, in the twilight under the trees—Davies, one or two others, and myself. We had just received a visiting staff officer from Army Headquarters, and I was behaving rather badly to him. I was, in fact, telling him what I thought about the 'blanket' system of administration. I was being quite unjust, because Goddard, General Alexander's chief administration officer, had done an astounding job in circumstances of fantastic difficulty, and in any case the victim before me was not responsible. But tempers were frayed, and one or two things had that day annoyed me—more were going to! So, really enjoying myself, I was relating the administrative enormities that had been perpetrated against my long-suffering corps. At the end of each catalogue of crimes of commission and omission I said, 'And you can tell Army Headquarters *that*!' My litany was still in full swing, when, looking up, I saw, standing in the gloom, two or three white-faced officers whom I did not know.

'And what do you want?' I asked, still in a bad temper.

One of them stepped forward.

'The Japs have taken Monywa,' he said, 'and if you listen you will hear them mortaring!'

A deathly pause fell on the gathering. Then, sure enough, softened by distance but unmistakable, came the *wump, wump, wump*! of Japanese mortars. The silence was broken by Taffy Davies.

'And you can tell Army Headquarters *that*!' he said.

The situation was a nasty one. Scott's divisional headquarters just south of Monywa, with only a platoon of Burma Rifles, was in no state to defend itself and we were little better. I sent an officers' patrol off at once to investigate and collected all available troops, about three hundred mixed British and Burmans, sending them to hold any Japanese met as far south as possible. Burma Division was called up and told to concentrate its two brigades at Chaungu, fifteen miles south of Monywa. At the same time, I ordered the 17th Division to send by rail, under cover of darkness, its 63 Brigade also to Chaungu and another brigade back to hold Ye-u. In answer to my urgent request General Alexander returned to me two squadrons of tanks, one to Ye-u, the other to Chaungu. Our only local protection was sentry posts from our Burmese Defence Platoon, in which I had no great faith—it deserted in a body a few nights later—and we now stiffened it with a handful of British clerks. I then ordered Corps Headquarters to pack ready to move.

After that there was little we could do but wait. If the

Japanese had really taken Monywa, it was a tossup whether they would turn south or north from the town. If south, it would be unpleasant for headquarters, 1st Burma Division; if north, for us. I lay on the hard wooden platform that had been the abbot's bed in an upper room of the small monastery, round which our headquarters were grouped, listening to occasional distant explosions and the faint chatter of machine guns. A Japanese force of any size in Monywa would cut me off from almost the whole of my corps, and I reproached myself for having let the brigade on the west bank continue its march before it had been replaced.

Actually the Japanese had not at this time taken Monywa, although we believed they had. Mortars and machine guns had suddenly opened on Monywa from the west bank at seven o'clock in the evening, and throughout the night enemy parties had crossed the river south of the town. At five o'clock, on May 1, a considerable force of Japanese, with some Burmans, had attempted to rush headquarters, 1st Burma Division. Under Scott, the divisional commander, British and Indian clerks and staff officers had put up a stout fight, falling back towards Chaungu. Several officers and men were killed or wounded, all kit and much equipment were lost, but ciphers and secret papers were saved. It says much for the spirit and toughness of Scott and his men that within a few hours they were functioning again as a divisional headquarters.

Early on the same day several large Japanese naval launches came upriver and embarked six or seven hundred troops from the west bank. Our small garrison in Monywa opened fire with every weapon it had and inflicted numerous casualties as the ships were crossing, but the heavy Japanese artillery and mortar retaliation overwhelmed our few posts on the river front. The enemy landed, were reinforced, and cleared the town.

During the morning of May 1, 63 Brigade arrived by rail, detrained eight miles from Monywa, and at once advanced. They were held up about the old Burma Division headquarters, where, in a village, the enemy had considerable strength. During the late afternoon one squadron of tanks and 13 Burma Brigade joined them outside Monywa, and 1 Burma Brigade reached Chaungu. The division laid on an attack by all three brigades for next morning.

Meanwhile, communication with the 1st Burma Division

having been lost, Corps Headquarters was without news of all this, but during the day General Alexander came to Ye-u, met Stilwell for the last time, and ordered the withdrawal from the Mandalay–Irrawaddy line. He sent the remainder of 7 Armoured Brigade back to me from the Chinese and agreed to Stilwell's taking the 38th Chinese Division and remnants of the Fifth Army to Katha and thence probably to India. As soon as dusk gave cover from the air, Corps Headquarters, except for a small tactical group that remained with me, moved to Ye-u, where headquarters, 17th Division, had arrived.

The attack to recover Monywa by three brigades under the 1st Burma Division went in on May 2. One talks of brigades, but they were by now sadly depleted and the whole force did not amount to a normal brigade group. By 1500 hours, after severe fighting—the railway station changed hands three times before it was ours—we were well into the town. Another attempt by the Japanese to push naval launches up the river was frustrated by our mortar fire. All was going well when Scott received a signal ordering his division to withdraw to Alon, north of Monywa. At this time equipment was so short that communication was largely by relaying via tanks, and somewhere in the precarious chain, a garbled message had crept in. After some doubt it was accepted as genuine, and obeyed. However, the effect, though disappointing, was not really great. All transport had already by-passed Monywa and reached Alon; the division collected there during May 3 and its rear guard having given the enemy a sharp rap, joined the two brigades of the 17th Division at Ye-u, thus concentrating the whole corps in this area.

The Japanese moving by the Chindwin were clearly making a great effort to cut us off from India, either at Shwegyin, where our escape track reached the river, or at Kalewa or Kalemyo. It was essential for us to reach these places first and, on May 3-4 we pushed 16 Brigade of the 17th Division as hard as we could down the Shwegyin track. It arrived in time and occupied all three towns.

My headquarters and those of the 17th Division outside Ye-u were within a couple of miles of one another. During the night of May 3-4 some Japanese parties infiltrated through the covering troops and attacked the 17th Division Headquarters with grenades and light machine-gun fire. An enemy jitter party also made noises and threw grenades round Corps Headquarters, while we, bereft of our defence platoon, stood to half the night. The proceedings were further enlivened by an agitated British sergeant suddenly dashing into our midst, staggering up to Welchman, my chief gunner, and gasping out, 'The battery's overrun. They're all dead and the guns lost.' He then fainted gracefully but heavily into the brigadier's arms. Of course the battery was all right. The sergeant had been awakened from an exhausted sleep by a bang as someone threw a grenade or firework, and, still alseep, had panicked. Men's nerves were wearing thin. I do not altogether wonder that I said myself at this time, 'If somebody brings me a bit of good news I shall burst into tears!' I was never put to the test.

Sun from his Chinese 38th Division visited me at Ye-u and asked me not to leave there until he was well to the north. I was very ready to do this to help him and, in any case, there were in the neighbourhood many refugees, including European women and children, and more than two thousand wounded, whom it would take time to evacuate. We gave up what transport we could for these unfortunates, but we had few ambulances left and the wounded, in lorries and some civilian buses we had picked up, had a nightmare journey, which many, I fear, did not survive.

Meanwhile, the 1st Burma Division, with one regiment of tanks, held a rear-guard position in an arc south of Ye-u while the 17th Division moved off to form laybacks at Kaduma, at the entrance to the jungle track, and at Pyingaing, known always as 'Pink Gin.' We pushed ahead also some sapper units to improve the route, and put in water ponts and ration dumps. It was as well this was done; otherwise, the march would have been well-nigh impossible. To relieve the already-critical congestion at Shwegyin River crossing, I sent 1 Burma Brigade, without vehicles, northwest through the jungle to cross the Chindwin at Pantha and make for Tamu, which, after an arduous march, it reached on May 16. Two companies of Gurkhas were, at the same time, sent from Shwegyin southwest to the river, where a tributary entered it, to guard against any Japanese attempt to strike inland up this stream and cut us off. As a precaution rations were further reduced.

We now had three major anxieties. First that the Japanese might cut us off from India; second, that our supplies might fail; and third, that the monsoon would catch us. This last was the worst, for if the rain came while we were still on this track,

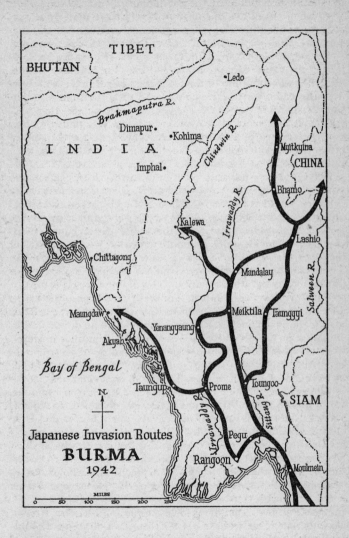

Japanese Invasion Routes
BURMA
1942

we should be immobilized and undoubtedly starve. The odds were we might escape one or even two of these perils, but our chances of avoiding all three were slender. Actually, it was the Japanese who got us first.

To begin with the withdrawal went reasonably well. I moved my Corps Headquarters to 'Pink Gin,' and the whole, or rather what was left, of the 1st Burma Division passed safely over the Chindwin; 63 Brigade of the 17th Division, ferrying in its remaining lorries, reached Shwegyin, and its other brigade (48) and most of 7 Armoured Brigade halted at 'Pink Gin' as rear guard. Still, to avoid our three enemies, Japanese, hunger, and monsoon, speed in crossing the Chindwin was essential.

But speed was not easy to attain. Shwegyin was one huge bottle-neck. There had originally been six river steamers, each of which would take five or six hundred men packed tight, but not more than one lorry, two or three guns, and a couple of jeeps. Loading was slow from the single rickety improvised pier, which, incidentally, was submerged by a sudden rise in the river in the midst of our exodus, and had to be rebuilt. There was no direct crossing. Steamers leaving Shwegyin had to proceed six miles upstream to Kalewa, unload, and return—a round trip of several hours. Nor was there even a cart track on either bank; from Shwegyin to Kalewa everything, except a man walking or a mule, had to go by river. The difficulties of embarkation were greatly increased by the hundreds of derelict civilian cars dumped by refugees, regardless of obstruction, in all the scanty open spaces and approaches to the ferry, and by numbers of Indian refugees hoping to cross the river.

The road to the pier ran for about the last fifteen hundred yards in the 'Basin.' This was a horseshoe-shaped, flat space about a thousand yards wide, mostly open but with small clumps of jungle, surrounded on three sides by a steep two-hundred-foot escarpment, almost precipitous on the inside, but not so steep on the outside slopes which were covered with jungle. From the edge of this escarpment the whole of the 'Basin' was displayed at one's feet. Looking down, one felt it could be a death trap, and now it was literally full of soldiers, refugees, animals, motor vehicles, guns, and tanks. It was obvious that if we were to get all these to Kalewa we should require the uninterrupted use of all six steamers for several days. Pattison-Knight of the Corps 'Q' staff and several officers from Burma Army Headquarters, left behind for the purpose by Goddard, were working heroically to load steamers throughout the twenty-four hours, but, try as they might, it was a terribly slow business. Every gun had to be manhandled on to a deck where stanchions, railings, and fittings seemed specially designed and sited to make stowage difficult. Lorries and trucks had to be manoeuvred most delicately; one slight misjudgment and a vehicle jammed on the gangway or hanging into the river might mean hours of delay. I had already ordered only four-wheel-drive vehicles to be shipped; if we were, as seemed likely, only to get out a portion of our transport we had better have what would be most useful. The embarkation of men was, of course, easy, as they had no kit to worry about except their arms. Before embarking all men had to cut wood for fuel, and as they filed on board each man, as if in payment for his trip, threw a log on to the pile for the engine.

Burma Army Headquarters, when organizing the withdrawal of themselves, the administrative units, and refugees that preceded us, had installed Brigadier Ekin with a small staff as area commandant at Shwegyin. This was most helpful, as it saved us from having to detach a brigade headquarters from one of the divisions, and gave a much-needed continuity of control. The defence of the 'Basin' was not easy, as it was surrounded by dense jungle, running, on the outside, right to the top of the escarpment. We had already pushed forward the Gurkha commando detachment to watch the most likely approach from the river. In addition, to prevent the passage of Japanese naval craft, a floating boom had been built from bank to bank about two miles south of Shwegyin, where a battalion and the small Marine flotilla were disposed to cover both sides of the river. The close-in defence of the 'Basin' along the escarpment was entrusted to another Indian battalion and some detachments. Units were so weak that the defence was thin, but there were almost always troops waiting in the 'Basin' to embark who formed a reserve. We relied on our outlying defence screen for enough warning to give time to get these into position. To guard against air attack, which was a terrible danger in a place like this, we concentrated all our available anti-aircraft artillery—an amount that in any other theatre would have been regarded as pathetic.

Everyone—staff, sappers, Marines, Irrawaddy flotilla officials

—was working all out and considerable progress was being made when on May 7 and 9 the Japanese put in several heavy air attacks on what must have been an ideal target. Casualties were not so heavy as one would have expected, for the troops by now, without waiting for orders, automatically dug slit trenches, though a good many vehicles were destroyed or damaged. The boom was broken twice, but replaced at night. It was great good fortune that none of the steamers was hit, but the bombing, not unreasonably, proved too much for many of the civilian Indian crews. They deserted in large numbers, and those that stayed refused to bring their ships downstream of Kalewa. We put guards of soldiers on board to force them to work, but it was impossible to prevent the lascars from slipping overboard. It was only owing to the courage of the British ships' officers and of a few stout-hearted Indian subordinates that any of the steamers at all could be got to the Shwegyin jetty. The number of ships and the rate of turnaround both decreased alarmingly.

On the evening of May 8, Cowan with his rear guard of 48 Brigade and a regiment of tanks, to avoid the congestion that would have resulted from coming into the 'Basin,' halted two miles down the track northeast from Shwegyin. Very wisely on the 9th he sent forward the 7th Gurkhas to reinforce the troops holding the escarpment. The battalion arrived after dark and bivouacked in the 'Basin.'

At my headquarters in the jungle just outside Kalewa I was very worried at the delays caused by air bombing and the fear that either the Japanese or the monsoon would be on us before we could complete the crossing. Having collected the officer responsible for river transportation, and assured myself that he had done all a man could at the Kalewa end, I started off in the dark by launch early in the morning of May 10 to visit Shwegyin and see what could be done there. My A.D.C. and I reached the jetty at about 0530 just as it was getting light. A steamer was alongside but loading for the moment was interrupted while the sappers repaired the pier damaged by a lorry. Followed by my A.D.C., I walked across the steamer's deck on to the jetty. Just as I set my foot on it a stream of red tracer bullets cracked viciously overhead and at once, from the south side of the escarpment to my right, a terrific din of rifle, machine gun, mortar, and some artillery fire broke out. It was the most unpleasant welcome I have ever had. Obviously

88

something quite big in attacks was starting and it was already close. What had happened to our outer defences I had no idea; they must have been either by-passed or overrun.

I was now by myself, my A.D.C. having decided rather sensibly that, whatever was happening, I should want breakfast and that he had better fetch the box containing it. Rather put off by my reception, I walked up the track from the jetty, past a number of parked tanks, and turned off right towards Ekin's brigade headquarters. A lot of stuff was coming over, all too high to be dangerous, but, judging by the noise, just ahead, a proper fight seemed to be developing. I found myself crossing one of the larger open spaces, where, crouching behind every little mound and bush that dotted it, were men of the 7th Gurkhas, the battalion that had arrived the previous night. My inclination to run for cover, not lessened by a salvo of mortar bombs that came down behind me, was only restrained by the thought of what a figure the corps commander would cut, sprinting for safety, in front of all these little men. So, not liking it a bit, I continued to walk forward. Then, from behind a bush that offered scant cover to his bulky figure, rose my old friend, the subadar major of the 7th Gurkhas, his face creased in a huge grin which almost hid his twinkling almond eyes. He stood there and shook with laughter at me. I asked him coldly what he was laughing at, and he replied that it was very funny to see the General Sahib wandering along there by himself *not knowing what to do*! And, by jove, he was right; I did not!

It is a funny thing how differently the various races react to such a situation. A British soldier would have called out to me to take shelter and would have made room for me beside him. The average Indian sepoy would have watched anxiously, but said nothing unless I was hit, when he would have leapt forward and risked his life to get me under cover. A Sikh would have sprung up, and with the utmost gallantry dramatically covered me with his own body, thrilled at the chance of an audience. Only a Gurkha would stand up and laugh.

But it was no use standing there being laughed at by a braver man than I was. So I went on a little farther to Brigade Headquarters. There I found Ekin and alarm, but no panic. It was clear—only too clear—that somehow a considerable force of Japanese with mortars and infantry guns had got through our outer guard and was now attacking the Indian battalion holding the escarpment in its southern sector nearest the jetty. This attack seemed to be being held—but only just.

What had actually happened, although we did not, of course, know it at the time, was that the previous afternoon some seven hundred Japanese, with guns and mules, had landed from naval craft about eight miles south of Shwegyin. The landing craft had immediately turned around and brought in more during the evening and night. At the same time a larger force had come ashore on the west bank about six miles south. The party on the east bank moved inland to avoid the battalion defending the boom and ran into the Gurkha commando party, who only wireless set failed to get in touch with the Brigade Headquarters at Shwegyin. For some reason the commander of the party did not attack the Japanese column, but attempted to withdraw, keeping his men between the enemy and the 'Basin'. In the dark the Gurkhas lost touch with one another and broke up into small groups, which made their way back as best they could. The officer himself was drowned trying to swim the Chindwin to escape capture. Some of his men arrived mingled with the Japanese, others made their way back individually, a large number were lost—and no warning was given.

While I was at Brigade Headquarters a second and heavier attack came in, rather more to the east, and after making some progress was beaten back, but the Japanese were now heavily mortaring the 'Basin.' Their mortar, the equivalent of our three-inch, was their most effective weapon, and they handled it boldly and skilfully; a high proportion of our casualties in most of our engagements came from it. Fortunately its shell was not so powerful or lethal as our own or the effects would have been more serious, but it was unpleasant and trying enough for troops penned in a narrow space. Some time after the second attack, or more probably during it, numbers of Japanese infiltrated between our rather widely spaced posts and got on to the forward edge of the escarpment, dominating the eastern side of the 'Basin.' The Gurkhas, with my old friend the subadar major well to the fore, then put in a very spirited counterattack, right up the cliffs. There followed very confused fighting in which the Gurkhas and the Indians, who were still clinging in places to their positions, savagely clashed with large numbers of enemy in the precipitous jungle around the 'Basin's' edge. The situation was restored, but enemy snipers continually crept forward and made themselves a nuisance. At one moment the Japanese brought up to the rim of the escarpment an infantry gun—the small fieldpiece that their battalions had—and proceeded to fire at point blank range. A Bofors gun of an Indian light anti-aircraft battery engaged it and a duel ensued. It was quickly over; the Bofors scored several direct hits on the gun, turned it over, and wiped out its crew. Japanese aircraft flew over frequently but did not attempt any actual attack, probably because from the air it was impossible in that close fighting to distinguish British from Japanese.

After the Gurkha counterattack I returned to the neighbourhood of the jetty to try to get in touch through the tank signals with Cowan and 48 Brigade. I could not get Cowan himself, but learned he was already on the move towards the 'Basin.' A steamer was alongside the jetty, its skipper, an official of the Irrawaddy flotilla, holding it there by sheer will power and courage, in spite of its crew. The twenty-five-pounders of 7 Armoured Brigade were being embarked, and as the guns were brought down to the water's edge they were kept firing until the last moment. Wounded were coming down the track in a trickle and being carried on board, while certain administrative troops filed across the gangways. The loading went on steadily, but at the highest pressure, and there was no sign of panic. Even a crowd of about a hundred Indian refugees, cowering in the shelter of a bank, did as they were told and huddled there in mute misery. One poor woman, near the tank from which I was speaking, lay propped against the side of the track dying in the last stages of smallpox. Her little son, a tiny boy of four, was trying pathetically to feed her with milk from a tin a British soldier had given him. One of our doctors, attending wounded at the jetty, found time to vaccinate the little chap, but nothing could be done for his mother. She died, and we bribed an Indian family with a blanket and a passage on the steamer to take the boy with them. I hope he got through all right and did not give smallpox to his new family. At the last minute, when the steamer was fully loaded and casting off, I let the rest of the refugees scurry on board, to cling precariously to rails and fill every crevice in the ship. It was no longer possible, as enemy pressure increased, to get ships alongside the jetty. Another and fiercer attack broke into the 'Basin' itself and penetrated towards the track. Everyone who could be scraped up was pushed out to hold back this vital thrust. Pattison-Knight, my 'Q' staff officer, who had been at Shwegyin for some days supervising embarkation and was a conspicuous figure in his exquisitely cut, but by now somewhat soiled, jodhpurs, took a tommy gun and went into the fray. About an hour later he came back and exchanged the tommy-gun for a rifle, explaining that 'The little yellow baskets are a bit farther off now!'

Ekin had handed over to Cowan, who had fought his way into the 'Basin,' losing his A.D.C. wounded at his side in the process. Thinking with his arrival that this was no place for a corps commander and that I should be of more use if I could get some of the ships lying upstream to come down again, I took to my launch and visited them. Three extremely gallant skippers, two civilians of the Irrawaddy flotilla (their names, I think, Murie and Hutchinson), and Lieutenant-Commander Penman of the Burma Naval Volunteer Reserve, in turn brought their ships inshore a few hundred yards above the jetty, under a cliff which gave shelter from mortar fire. Here they embarked wounded and administrative units for the last trips. After that no crews, whatever their skippers did to induce them, would come downstream again. That was an end to the last chance of getting anything out of Shwegyin except mules and men and what they could carry over the roughest and steepest of paths.

At about 1400 hours a desperate attempt by the 7th Gurkhas to dislodge a strong Japanese party that still held a hill commanding the 'Basin' failed. All embarkation had stopped, and Cowan, who had my authority to do so, made the only possible decision—to get out before more Japanese arriving finally cut him off. Rear guards were laid out covering the track along the east bank, guns were ordered to waste down their ammunition, and all nonessentials started off up the track. At about eight o'clock that evening all guns put down a concentration on the escarpment as the Gurkhas and Indians holding it withdrew. It was by far the heaviest artillery concentration we had put down in Burma; for the first time the gunners were not stinting their ammunition, and they fired all they had in twenty minutes. Under cover of this barrage the last troops passed through the rear guard, leaving the 'Basin' lit by flames and explosions as guns, tanks, and vehicles were destroyed. It was a sad ending to all the effort that had brought them so far.

but at this stage it was better to lose matériel than risk the destruction of the whole force. We had saved about one-third of the guns, and a fair portion of the best mechanical transport, the four-wheel-drive lorries, but the loss of the tanks was a terrible blow. True, they were worn out and in any case obsolete, but even they would be hard to replace in India, and they held such a sentimental place in our esteem for what we owed to them and their crew that it was like abandoning old and trusted friends to leave them behind.

The march along the track to Kaing, opposite Kalewa, was arduous for weary, burdened men. The path was narrow, in places precipitous, and everywhere rough, but the Japanese did not follow up. Their losses had been heavy and they were busy trying to salvage what they could in the smoking 'Basin.' Although we did not then know it, we had fought the last action of the campaign. The 48 Brigade and some other units were taken upstream from Kalewa to Sittang, whence they marched through the hills to Tamu, while the steamers that carried them were sunk to avoid capture. The rest of Burma Corps marched from Kalewa, ninety miles through the Kabaw Valley, well termed Death Valley because of its virulent malaria, to Tamu—a grisly march!

While the main body of Burma Corps was suffering these vicissitudes, 2 Burma Brigade, which had withdrawn up the west bank of the Irrawaddy and turned northwest to follow the Myittha Valley, had plodded steadily on. It had several skirmishes with large bands of armed Burmans, but had not been followed by Japanese. The brigade had supplemented its scanty pack transport by locally impounded bullock carts which carried its wounded and sick. Its feelings may be imagined, therefore, when an officer of the line of communication services, retiring ahead of the corps, demolished the only bridge over the wide Manipur River while 2 Brigade was still south of it. The carts had to be abandoned and the brigade with difficulty ferried itself across. It rejoined us at Kalemyo, west of Kalewa, tired, hungry, and angry.

Even then we were not without further alarms. Our greatest danger was that the Japanese coming upriver in their naval craft might land south of Kalewa and, moving across country, cut the track between Kalewa and Kalemyo. Sure enough, one day we received apparently reliable and circumstantial news that the worst had happened. The Japanese, in strength, had established a road block between Corps Headquarters, then just north of Kalemyo, and our rear guard, a few miles east of Kalemyo. The rear guard was cut off. In one of our few remaining jeeps I at once returned to Kalemyo, where a couple of battalions of the 1st Burma Division were bivouacked. As I looked around the gaunt, ragged men, lying exhausted where they had dropped at the end of the day's march, my heart sank. I thought, 'Nothing can rouse them. They have reached the end of endurance!' Yet, when their no less weary officers called on them, they struggled into their equipment, once more grasped their weapons, formed their pitifully thin ranks, and, turning their backs on safety, tramped doggedly off to another fight.

There was, thank God, no fight. We had not gone far when the officers I had sent ahead to reconnoitre returned and told us that the alarm was false. There were no Japanese and no road block. A staff officer, seeing from a distance our own troops making a traffic-control barrier across the road, and hearing at the same time the noise of a Japanese fighter strafe in the neighbourhood, had in his tired imagination combined the two into an enemy road block. The troops were turned about, and, muttering curses on generals who disturbed them without cause, went back to their broken rest. I sent for the officer responsible for the alarm and told him what I thought about him in a way which, I fear, showed that my nerves were little better than his.

Next day we resumed the march. The track through the jungle seemed unending. We had only fifty lorries and these were used to ferry troops forward, but, of course, the bulk did the distance, as they had done so many weary miles, on their feet. In too many cases literally *on* their feet, for their boots had given out. Clothing was in rags, officers and men had only what they stood up in. Beards were common as shaving kit had grown scarcer and scarcer. I had tried growing a beard myself at one time in the retreat when it was becoming rather fashionable, but mine appeared completely *white*, and the probable effect on the troops of having a corps commander who looked like Father Christmas was such that I resumed shaving with the relic of a blade.

While Burma Corps had been thus laboriously and perilously making its way back to India, the remnants of Fifth Chinese Army, covered by Sun's 38th Division, fell back from

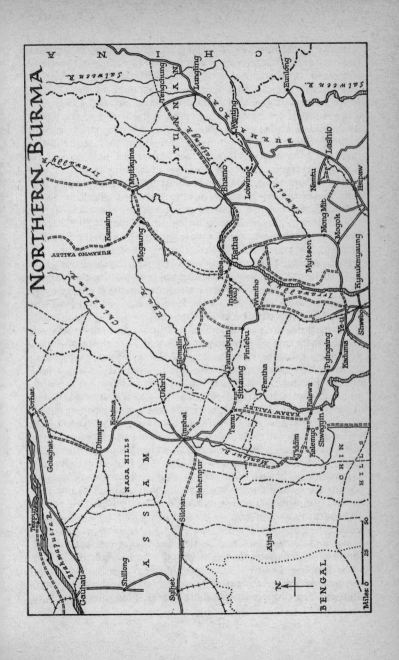

Shwebo to the north. Fifth Army Headquarters with parts of the 22d and 96th Divisions, after great hardships, eventually staggered out through the Hukawng Valley. Their conduct on this terrible retreat was, perhaps understandably, not such as to endear them to either local inhabitants or fellow fugitives. They seized trains, ejecting our wounded and refugees, women, and children, took all supplies on evacuation routes, and looted villages. Their necessities knew no law and little mercy. General Stilwell with the American portion of his headquarters remained at Shwebo until May 1 when, any further effort to control the Fifth Army being obviously useless, he moved to Wuntho on the railway a hundred miles farther north, with a view to reaching Myitkyina and flying out. There he learned that he could not reach the airport before the Japanese, and he was compelled to strike west, by car, as long as the road lasted, then on foot with some pack transport to the Chindwin about Homalin, and through the hills to Imphal. It was a gruelling march and the party owed its survival to the astringent encouragement of the elderly general himself, who proved the stoutest-hearted and toughest of the lot. His party reached Assam on May 15.

Meanwhile, the 38th Division, still intact and now operating without any superior command, followed Fifth Army to Naba, fifty miles north of Wuntho, on the Myitkyina railway. There, learning that it would be impossible to reach Myitkyina ahead of the Japanese, Sun turned south again back to Wuntho, where he met the Japanese now in occupation and had a skirmish. With his 113 Regiment as rear guard he then struck across the hills to the Chindwin at Paungbyin where on May 14 he collided with a Japanese force coming up the river in the attempt to cut off Burma Corps. He held them off, crossed the river, and reached Imphal on May 24. Unfortunately, 113 Regiment of his division was cut off and almost destroyed. Nevertheless, Sun's withdrawal was a bold and skilful one and he was the only Chinese commander who brought his troops out, starving and in rags, it is true, but still a fighting formation.

We had already had one or two heavy showers to give us a foretaste of what the monsoon would do to us, when, on May 12, it burst in full fury. On that day our rear guard was leaving Kalewa and our main body toiling up into the hills. From then onward the retreat was sheer misery. Ploughing their way up slopes, over a track inches deep in slippery mud, soaked to the skin, rotten with fever, ill-fed and shivering as the air grew cooler, the troops went on, hour after hour, day after day. Their only rest at night was to lie on the sodden ground under the dripping trees, without even a blanket to cover them. Yet the monsoon which so nearly destroyed us and whose rain beat so mercilessly on our bodies did us one good turn—it stopped dead the Japanese pursuit. As the clouds closed down over the hills, even their air attacks became rare.

A couple of marches south of Tamu we received our first helping hand from India. An Indian mechanical transport company met us, but its recruit drivers had been so scared by the stories fugitives from Burma had told them and by the perils of the half-made road that many of them would not drive any farther south. When ordered to do so they took their lorries into the jungle and hid. This difficulty was overcome by putting beside each driver a man from 7 Armoured Brigade who saw to it that they went where they were told—a last service of this magnificent formation. Then the company was of inestimable value in ferrying wounded and sick and sometimes whole units forward.

On the last day of that nine-hundred-mile retreat I stood on a bank beside the road and watched the rear guard march into India. All of them, British, Indian, and Gurkha, were gaunt and ragged as scarecrows. Yet, as they trudged behind their surviving officers in groups pitifully small, they still carried their arms and kept their ranks, they were still recognizable as fighting units. They might look like scarecrows, but they looked like soldiers, too.

CHAPTER VI

AFTERMATH

The men of Burma Corps, when they reached Imphal, were physically and mentally very near the end of their strength. They had endured casualties, hardships, hunger, sickness, and, above all the heartbreaking frustration of retreat to a degree that few armies have suffered and yet held together as armies. They were, even at the last, as I had proved, ready if called upon to turn and fight again, but they had been buoyed up by the thought that once over the border into India, not only would other troops interpose between them and the enemy to give them relief from the strain they had supported so long, but that welcome and rest would await them.

Instead, they found that the only forces India had been able to provide on this threatened frontier were a single infantry brigade of raw troops, with a promise of the gradual arrival of the remainder of a division. Instead of rest behind covering troops, they were harshly told to do the covering themselves. They did not expect to be treated as heroes, but they did expect to be met as soldiers, who, even if defeated, were by no means disgraced. Yet the attitude adopted towards them by certain commanders and their staffs was that they were only to be dragooned into some show of soldierly spirit by hectoring and sarcasm. Apart from its lack of comradely feeling, this was profoundly bad psychology. How much wiser was the treatment of the troops who escaped from Dunkirk. Their hardihood in the face of great material odds was generously recognized, their courage in retreat and defeat acclaimed; at once they were received as if they had won a great victory, not suffered a disaster. My men had endured a longer ordeal with at least equal courage; they deserved an equal welcome. The one they got, intensely resented by commanders and troops, would have had more serious consequences had it not been for the efforts of Scott and Cowan, the divisional commanders, on one side, and of Major-General Savory commanding the 23d Indian Division, which provided the troops from India, on the other. Savory was a tough, war-experienced, and successful leader, proved in the Middle East, who understood the handling of men. Although he had troubles enough of his own with his raw division, he was always ready to help the less fortunate troops of Burma Corps, and to his soldierly understanding they owed a great deal.

Savory recognized at once that the fighting troops of Burma Corps, who came out in their disciplined ranks, every man with his weapons but little else, were very different from the hotchpotch of improvised units, rear organizations, noncombatants, civil and military deserters, officerless men, refugees, and riffraff that had swarmed out ahead of them. Others did not, and my soldiers suffered for the sins of those who had preceded them; nothing could have been more galling to tired, exasperated fighting men, who knew they had done their duty.

If our welcome into India was not what we expected, the comfort provided was even less. As the wasted units marched wearily into Imphal, through the sheets of monsoon rain, they were directed into areas of jungle on the steep hillsides and told to bivouac there. It seemed to them that no preparations at all had been made for their reception. They had arrived with nothing but the soaked, worn, and filthy clothing they stood up in; they had no blankets, no waterproof sheets, no tentage. Nor did they find any awaiting them. On those dripping, gloomy hillsides there was no shelter but the trees, little if any clothing or blankets, no adequate water or medical arrangements. As Taffy Davies, indefatigable in labouring to ease the sufferings of our troops, wryly said, 'The slogan in India seems to be, "Isn't that Burma Army annihilated yet?"'

The men were bitter, and who could wonder at it, but it was not fair to criticize too fiercely the material failure of India to be ready to receive us. Imphal was a thousand miles from Calcutta at the extreme end of a most rickety line of communication, stretched to breaking point. India itself was deficient of everything, and it was impossible to get forward over that distance at short notice what a destitute corps required. The fault was a lack of foresight, months before, when preparation should have begun. Yet here, as everywhere, the frequent changes and divisions in the higher responsibility for the Burma campaign had prevented any smooth, long-term development of Assam as a base for an army. The administrative and medical staffs on the spot made superhuman efforts to cope with the tragedy, but they had not a tenth of the resources required. If we had come out of Burma a fully equipped corps, with our proper complement of transport, tentage, and medical supplies, we might have managed, but we had not. We had practically nothing—even if that, as was pointed out to us, *was* our own fault. Still, the effect of such a reception on tired men, keyed up by the expectation of something very different, can be imagined. Many lost the will to fight longer against the malaria, dysentery, and exhaustion that attacked them. I should estimate that 80 per cent of the fighting men who came out of Burma fell sick, and many died.

Obviously the whole Burma Army should have been sent on leave or to hospital in India as fast as the transportation system would allow. Unfortunately, the slow arrival of reinforcements from India and the possibility of a Japanese advance against Imphal compelled the retention of the whole of the 17th and of some units of the 1st Burma Division. Actually, although one would not have gambled on it at the time, the monsoon effectively put a stop to any further Japanese follow-up, and the two armies settled down for some months out of touch with one another.

The 17th Division, while very reduced in numbers, was still capable of functioning as a division. The 1st Burma Division had at various stages towards the end of the retreat sent to their homes most of its Burmese. Each man was given his rifle, fifty rounds, and three months' pay, told to go to his village, wait for our return, and be ready to join any organization we should start to fight the Japanese in Burma. These men, mainly Kachins, Chins, Karens, and other hillmen, almost without exception did so, and in due course formed the backbone of the resistance movements that grew in strength as the Japanese occupation continued. Their loss and the casualties its British and Indian units had suffered made it no longer possible for the 1st Burma Division to continue as a division. Its headquarters and the bulk of its remaining units were gradually returned to India and absorbed into the 39th Indian Division, which became a training formation.

Of the one-hundred and fifty guns of all kinds that Burma Corps had possessed at one time, seventy-four had reached the Chindwin, but of these only twenty-eight had crossed into India. The total mechanical transport of the corps on arrival at Imphal was fifty lorries and thirty jeeps. Our casualties had been some thirteen thousand men killed, wounded, and missing, besides, of course, those evacuated sick. The Japanese losses had been only a third of this—four thousand six hundred killed and wounded. I kept a record of all we had lost in men, guns, tanks, and vehicles. Someday I hoped to balance the account with perhaps a little interest added.

On May 20, I handed over all my troops to IV Corps, and Burma Corps ceased to exist. There was then nothing more for me to do in Imphal. I said good-bye to Scott and Cowan and to as many units as I could reach. I had a horrible feeling I was deserting them, and the friendship and loyalty that officers and men showed me when I bade them farewell only made it worse. To be cheered by troops whom you have led to victory is grand and exhilarating. To be cheered by the gaunt remnants of those whom you have led only in defeat, withdrawal, and disaster, is infinitely moving—and humbling.

Burma Corps Headquarters left for India a few days ahead of me. We had handed in all transport, including my own jeep, so I tried to make the journey to railhead at Manipur Road in a civilian refugee car found derelict on the roadside and tinkered into some sort of mobility by my faithful Cameronian bodyguard. Bl luck and with nursing we got it to Kohima, but there its tired engine gave out. We coasted down the hill to within a few miles of the railway where a rise finally stopped us, and we finished the journey ignominiously in a passing lorry. Even then we had a day to wait for a train, as the railway had been bombed and most of the staff had vanished. At last some military railway operating officials arrived with a train which had to stop at the points outside the small junction. A colonel and a major of Engineers, with a couple of senior railway officials, assembled in the signal cabin and an earnest debate took place as to which lever should be pulled to allow the train to enter the station. At last the fateful decision was made. We watched the colonel seize the lever and fling it over with a professional crash. No signal moved, no point shifted. The wires had been cut, and so we never discovered if it was the right lever, after all.

I slept sitting up nearly all the long, crowded journey to Calcutta, and on to Ranchi in Bihar where Burma Corps

Headquarters had preceded me. I found it pathetically reduced. Malaria had taken a heavy toll, starting with Taffy Davies, and running right through the party. It was a particulary virulent type of cerebral malaria which struck a man down, sent his temperature rocketing into delirium, and often killed him in three or four days. It was noticeable that the older men, the forty-fives and upward, seemed to suffer less from disease and exhaustion than the younger ones. In fact, almost the only members of my staff to escape hospital were these presumably well-salted veterans. We tried to pretend it was because we were a tougher generation, but it was actually due, I think, to the greater care we took of ourselves, and the greater docility with which we obeyed medical instructions.

I had now an opportunity for a few days to sit down and think out what had happened during the last crowded months and why it had happened. The outstanding and incontrovertible fact was that we had taken a thorough beating. We, the Allies, had been out-manoeuvred, outfought, and outgeneralled. It was easy, of course, as it always is, to find excuses for our failure, but the excuses are no use for next time; what is wanted are causes and remedies.

There were certain basic causes for our defeat. The first and overriding one was lack of preparation. Until a few weeks before it happened, no higher authority, civil or military, had expected an invasion of Burma. They were all grievously pressed in other quarters, and what was held to be the comparatively minor responsibility of the defence of Burma was tossed from one to another, so that no one held it long enough to plan and provide over an adequate period. The two great errors that grew from this were the military separation of Burma from India and the division of operational from administrative control. An army whose plan of campaign is founded on fundamental errors in organization cannot hope for success unless it has vast superiority over the enemy in numbers and material. Another fatal omission, springing from the same cause, was that until too late no serious attempt was made to connect India and Burma by road, so that when Rangoon fell the army in Burma was for all practical purposes isolated.

A most obvious instance of the lack of preparation was the smallness and unsuitability of the forces provided to defend Burma. Two ill-found, hurriedly collected, and inexperienced divisions, of which one had been trained and equipped for desert warfare and the other contained a large proportion of raw and unreliable Burmese troops, were tragically insufficient to meet superior Japanese forces in a country of the size and topography of Burma. The arrival of the Chinese adjusted the numerical balance in favour of the Allies and, if they could have been got up to the front in strength before Rangoon fell, they might, in spite of their lack of almost all the necessities of a modern army, have changed the result. It is perhaps doubtful if, with the transport and supply resources available, their forward concentration could have been achieved; the pity is it was not tried. Even if it had been, the refusal of the Chinese to obey Stilwell's orders would probably have ensured defeat.

The completely inadequate air forces and their total elimination in the campaign were most grievous disadvantages to the army. Had we, however, had enough well-trained and suitably-equipped divisions I do not think this handicap, serious as it was, would have been fatal; we could still have beaten the Japanese. Nor would a superior air force have enabled us to defeat the Japanese with the troops we had. It would have helped greatly and relieved the army of a terrible strain, but we had to outfight the enemy, soldier for soldier, on the ground.

In Burma we ought, whatever our strength, to have had one great advantage over the Japanese—we should have been fighting in a friendly country. The inhabitants should have been not only on our side, but organized and trained to help us. They were not. It is easy to say the Burmans disliked British rule and were therefore hostile to us, but I do not think that was actually so. A very small minority was actively and violently hostile. I should estimate it as certainly not more than 5 per cent—a figure that compares favourably with the number of collaborators in many European countries. These were drawn mainly from the intensely nationalist youth of the towns and the remnants of the old rebels of the twenties. Naturally, in a country such as Burma, notorious always for its dacoits, they were joined by considerable numbers of bad characters as soon as our defeats and withdrawals gave opportunities for looting. A larger section of the Burmese population was actively loyal as long as it seemed we should hold their native districts, while many of the hill tribes remained faithful to the British at great cost to themselves even during the Japanese occupation. The fact was that to the main mass of the peasant population the invasion was an inexplicable and sudden calamity; their only interest was, if possible, not to become involved in it and to avoid the soldiers of both sides.

Up to December 1941 even the military regarded the likelihood of invasion as remote, so it was not surprising that the civil government did not take comprehensive measures to educate and prepare the population for it. When it became evident that war was imminent, the civil authorities were reluctant to organize evacuation schemes, refugee control, intelligence machinery, the militarization of railways, or anything in the nature of a Home Guard. There was a fear, which seems often to afflict other administrations than the Burman, that if the people were told unpleasant things about an unpleasant situation they might become depressed and panic. As a result, no one was prepared for war and the series of British reverses was a stunning surprise.

The Burmese fighting forces themselves were affected in much the same way as their civilian brethren. They were hurriedly expanded with raw recruits who had no military tradition, and had incorporated in them civil armed corps such as the Burma Frontier Force and the Burma Military police who were neither equipped nor trained for full-scale war. The position of their families was what really undermined the reliability of the Burmese soldiers, the police, and the lower grades of all the civil services. As we retreated their homes were left in the dangerous no-man's land between the lines or in the crudely and brutally administered Japanese-occupied territory. Small wonder that many Burmans deserted to protect their families. Indians in the Burmese services, and there were many, were in an even worse plight, for their families not only suffered all the dangers that the Burmese did, but in addition were liable, without British protection, to the savage hostility of Burmans, only too ready to seize an opportunity to vent their hatred. If the families of Indians, Anglo-Indians, and Anglo-Burmese in government employ could have been evacuated to India at the start of the campaign it might have caused some despondency among the local population, but it would have increased the reliability of the Burmese military and civil services very considerably.

In spite of all these disadvantages we could have, if not defeated the Japanese, at least made a much better fight of it with even the small force of reliable troops we possessed, had they been properly trained. To our men, British or Indian, the jungle was a strange, fearsome place; moving and fighting in it were a nightmare. We were too ready to classify jungle as 'impenetrable,' as indeed it was to us with our motor transport, bulky supplies, and inexperience. To us it appeared only as an obstacle to movement and to vision; to the Japanese it was a welcome means of concealed manoeuvre and surprise. The Japanese used formations specially trained and equipped for a country of jungle and rivers, while we used troops whose training and equipment, as far as they had been completed, were for the open desert. The Japanese reaped the deserved reward for their foresight and thorough preparation; we paid the penalty for our lack of both.

To me, thinking it all over, the most distressing aspect of the whole disastrous campaign had been the contrast between our generalship and the enemy's. The Japanese leadership was confident, bold to the point of foolhardiness, and so aggressive that never for one day did they lose the initiative. True, they had a perfect instrument for the type of operation they intended, but their use of it was unhesitating and accurate. Their object, clear and definite, was the destruction of our forces; ours a rather nebulous idea of retaining territory. This led to the initial dispersion of our forces over wide areas, an error which we continued to commit, and worse still it led to a defensive attitude of mind.

General Alexander had been confronted with a task beyond his means. He had been sent to Burma with orders to hold Rangoon, presumably because it was obvious that, if Rangoon fell, it was almost inevitable that all Burma would be lost. On his arrival he found the decisive battle of the campaign, the Sittang bridge, had already been lost, and with it the fate of Rangoon sealed. The advent of the Chinese may have roused a flicker of hope that its recovery was possible, but the loss of Toungoo and the state of the Chinese armies soon quenched even that glimmer. It was then that we needed from the highest national authority a clear directive of what was to be our purpose in Burma. Were we to risk all in a desperate attempt to destroy the Japanese Army and recover all that had been lost? Ought we to fight to the end on some line to retain at least part of Burma? Or was our task to withdraw slowly, keeping our forces intact, while the defence of India was prepared? Had we been given any one of these as our great over-all object it would have had an effect, not only on the major tactics of the campaign, but on the morale of the troops. No such directive was ever received. In the comparatively subordinate position of a corps commander, immersed in the hour-to-hour business of a fluctuating battle, I could not know what pressures were being exerted on the local higher command, but it was painfully obvious that the lack of a definite, realistic directive from above made it impossible for our immediate commanders to define our object with the clarity essential. Whoever was responsible, there was no doubt that we had been weakened basically by this lack of a clear object.

Tactically we had been completely outclassed. The Japanese could—and did—do many things that we could not. The chief of these and the tactical method on which all their successes were based was the 'hook.' Their standard action was, while holding us in front, to send a mobile force, mainly infantry, on a wide turning movement around our flank through the jungle to come in on our line of communications. Here, on the single road, up which all our supplies, ammunition, and reinforcements must come, they would establish a road block, sometimes with a battalion, sometimes with a regiment. We had few if any reserves in depth—all our troops were in the front line—and we had, therefore, when this happened, to turn about forces from the forward positions to clear the road block. At this moment the enemy increased his pressure on our weakened front until it crumbled. Time and again the Japanese used these tactics, more often than not successfully, until our troops and commanders began to acquire a road-block mentality which often developed into an inferiority complex.

There was, of course, nothing new in this idea of moving around a flank; it is one of the oldest of stratagems, and there were many answers to it. The best answer would have been to do the same to the Japanese before they did it to us, but we, by reason of our complete dependence on motor transport and the unhandiness of our troops in the jungle, could not carry out these hooks successfully in any strength. They were only possible for forces trained and equipped for them. Another counter would have been to have put in the strongest possible frontal assault on the enemy while the flanking force was still distant in the jungle and he was divided. Japanese tenacity in defence and our lack of artillery, however, were such that before our assault had made much progress the flank blow was likely to be delivered. If we could have arranged our forces in more depth we might have held off the hook when it approached the road, but we never had enough troops to allow this. In any case, if we had, we could have employed them more profitably offensively. Lastly, there was at least a partial answer in supply by air, which would, temporarily at any rate, have removed our dependence on the road, but that needed aircraft and we had literally none. Equipped and trained as we were in 1942, we had no satisfactory answer to the Japanese road block.

The most infuriating thing was that, while we guessed these movements around our flanks were almost certainly going on, we could never get warning of them. Contrary to general belief, their columns did not move fast through the jungle; their progress was steady but slow, almost leisurely. They did not start very early, halted during the midday heat, and allowed themselves ample time to cook before a full night's rest. They took few precautions, often moving in dense columns without protective detachments. For warning of our proximity they relied largely on Burman informers, and for their routes on local guides. Apart from the absence of air reconnaissance and the lack of cooperation of the inhabitants, we felt terribly the want of light, mobile reconnaissance troops, who could get out into the jungle, live there, and send back information. Our attempts to form such units did not have much success. The extreme inefficiency of our whole intelligence system in Burma was probably our greatest single handicap.

As to the two corps commanders, neither Stilwell nor I had much to boast about. His difficulties were greater than mine, and he met them with a dogged courage beyond praise, but his Chinese armies were, as yet, not equal to the Japanese. He was constantly on the lookout for an aggressive counterstroke, but his means could not match his spirit. He could not enforce his orders nor could his inadequate staff and communications keep touch with his troops. When he saw his formations disintegrate under his eyes, no man could have done more than, and very few as much as, Stilwell, by personal leadership and example to hold the Chinese together, but once the rot had set in the task was impossible.

For myself, I had little to be proud of; I could not rate my generalship high. The only test of generalship is success, and I had succeeded in nothing I had attempted. Time and again I had tried to pass to the offensive and to regain the initiative, and every time I had seen my house of cards fall down as I tried to add its crowning storey. I had not realized how the Japanese, formidable as long as they are allowed to follow undisturbed their daring projects, are thrown into confusion by the unexpected. I should have subordinated all else to the vital need to strike at them and thus to disrupt their plans, but I ought, in spite of everything and at all risks, to have collected the whole strength of my corps before I attempted any counteroffensive. Thus I might have risked disaster, but I was more likely to have achieved success. When in doubt as to two courses of action, a general should choose the bolder. I reproached myself now that I had not.

In preparation, in execution, in strategy, and in tactics we had been worsted, and we had paid the penalty—defeat. Defeat is bitter. Bitter to the common soldier, but trebly bitter to his general. The soldier may comfort himself with the thought that, whatever the result, he has done his duty faithfully and steadfastly, but the commander has failed in *his* duty if he has not won victory—for that *is* his duty. He has no other comparable to it. He will go over in his mind the events of the campaign. 'Here,' he will think, 'I went wrong; here I took counsel of my fears when I should have been bold; there I should have waited to gather strength, not struck piecemeal; at such a moment I failed to grasp opportunity when it was presented to me.' He will remember the soldiers whom he sent into the attack that failed and who did not come back. He will recall the look in the eyes of men who trusted him. 'I have failed them,' he will say to himself, 'and failed my country!' He will see himself for what he is—a defeated general. In a dark hour he will turn in upon himself and question the very foundations of his leadership and his manhood.

And then he must stop! For if he is ever to command in battle again, he must shake off these regrets, and stamp on them, as they claw at his will and his self-confidence. He must beat off these attacks he delivers against himself, and cast out the doubts born of failure. Forget them, and remember only the lessons to be learned from defeat—they are more than from victory.

BOOK II: FORGING THE WEAPON

CHAPTER VII

THE THREE V's

Apart from my not too cheerful musings on the past campaign I had little to occupy me for the few days I was in Ranchi, except visits to hospitals. These visits were as depressing as my thoughts. No one had expected the proportion of sick among the returning troops to be so appallingly high. The hospital provision was inadequate. Inadequate in amount, in accommodation, staff, equipment, and in the barest amenities. To supplement the few existing hospitals new ones were being improvised and hurriedly raised medical units swept up from all parts of India to man them. Schools and other large buildings were requisitioned, the medical staffs arriving barely ahead, sometimes indeed after, a swarm of patients. It was no unusual thing to find a desperate hospital staff frantically organizing the unloading of their equipment and the clearing and cleaning of rooms left by previous occupants in no very sanitary state, while the sick lay on verandas and under trees awaiting admission. I saw many of my staff and hundreds of my officers and men lying grievously sick or wounded, some dying, in the squalid discomfort of these places. It was months before the hospitals of eastern India reached even a reasonable standard of comfort. That they were able to function at all in the summer of 1942 was owing to the superhuman exertions of commanding officers and their matrons and to the devoted, unceasing labour of their staffs, British and Indian.

The British population, small and often scattered, rallied to our help and did more in direct service to the troops than I had thought possible. They had another distinction, too: they were the only community I have ever heard of who *asked* for conscription to be imposed on them. There were no other conscripts in India.

At the moment there was little for me to do, so although

quite fit, even if a stone or two lighter, I asked for, and got, a couple of weeks' leave. Just as I was off to join my family in Simla I was ordered to Calcutta to take over the newly formed 15 Indian Corps whose sign, the three V's for fifteen and victory, gives its name to this chapter. I travelled down to Calcutta (with General Broad, who commanded Eastern Army, of which the corps was part) and after a hurried take over entered on a series of fresh tasks and problems.

The situation in June 1942 was an anxious one, likely at short notice to become critical. Eastern Army, with its headquarters at Ranchi in Bihar, was responsible to General Headquarters, India, at Delhi, for the internal security and external defence of all eastern India, which included, of course, the conduct of the war in Burma. The forces at its disposal were meagre and of necessity spread over a vast area. In Army Reserve, about Ranchi, were the 70th British Division and 50 Armoured Brigade. To safeguard strategic railways and to support the various provincial civil administrations, a number of small garrisons were scattered at great distances from one another. Forward, the army had two corps deployed to hold the Burma frontier (against the Japanese) and to safeguard the Bengal–Orissa coast line. The IV Corps, with its headquarters at Imphal in Assam, faced the enemy roughly along the northern portion of this frontier. It contained the newly arrived 23d Indian Division and what was left of the troops who had come out of Burma in the 17th Indian Division, not yet re-equipped, fever-ridden, and much below strength, but still, wonderful to relate, with fight in them.

South of IV Corps, in the jumbled mass of forest-covered hills on each side of the Indo-Burmese border, was a gap of nearly a hundred miles before the left of XV Corps in Arakan was reached. This gap, although quite unguarded, was not at the moment so dangerous as it might appear because the monsoon was in full blast, and even the Japanese at this season could hardly bring any appreciable force through such country. Still, it was a disquieting factor, and would become a real danger when the rains stopped.

To hold the southern Burma front, my XV Corps had only the 14th Indian Division under Major-General Lloyd, who had outstandingly distinguished himself as a fighting brigadier in the Middle East. The division was complete and mobile on a mixed animal and mechanical transport basis, but it was not yet battle tried and its jungle training left much to be desired. It was concentrated mainly about Comilla, east of the Meghna River, with detachments at Chittagong and a rather nebulous forward line of outposts watching the Japanese. My other division, the 26th Indian, located mostly around Calcutta, had as its tasks the internal security and coastal defence of Bengal and Orissa. It was not then a mobile or battle-worthy division at all, being woefully short of all forms of transport; nor could it, by any stretch of the imagination, be regarded as a trained formation. Besides its two divisions, the corps had a few other combat units, such as the Calcutta garrison, tied to the soul-destroying duties of internal security in a great city. My only armour was one Indian States Forces armoured car regiment.

Two infantry divisions, only one of which was operable, were not much with which to face an increasing Japanese army, to control an uneasy area as large as a major European country, with a population of millions, and to defend against probable invasion seven hundred miles of coast, uncovered by any naval force. The supporting air force, recovering as it was from the disasters of the Burma retreat, was far too small and ill-equipped to meet the demands that might be made on it. Help, if it came at all, would not be great, and it might take some time to come—gloomy thoughts that could be dispelled only by action.

In the steamy heat I assessed my tasks. They were three: the campaign on my part of the Burma front, the internal security of my area, and defence against invasion from the sea.

On the Burma front the Japanese seemed as little prepared as we were to advance during the monsoon and we might look for a breathing space during which to build up a limited offensive after the rains. The internal situation in eastern India was, however, not reassuring. The Congress party, by far the most powerful political organization in India, was rapidly working up anti-Allied feeling. It not only urged Indians to refrain from the war effort but conducted a campaign against recruiting and attempted to suborn sepoys from their allegiance. The Moslem League, the next most important political body, while not so actively hostile, rather shamefacedly refused cooperation.

Recruiting and the loyalty of Indian troops were not affected by all this, but fanned by unscrupulous propaganda and fantastic rumours the vast civil population developed a restlessness that might at any time break out in violence. The fact that all our communications to the Burma front ran for hundreds of miles through Bengal and Bihar did not lessen anxiety, which remained and mounted but was not immediate.

It seemed to me, thinking these things over, that the most imminent threat and the one we were least prepared to meet was invasion from the sea. The Japanese could send a fleet into the Bay of Bengal secure in the knowledge that we had no naval forces nearer than East Africa and that even these were incapable of challenging it. Our air forces would be hardly able to face a combination of land planes, based on Burmese airfields, with those from carriers. Landings in the monsoon would be hazardous, but the Japanese had shown a disconcerting skill in getting ashore in places and at times our experts had declared unlikely. In any case, as soon as the monsoon subsided, conditions for a large-scale attempt would be favourable.

The most likely hostile approaches were up the Hoogly with a direct thrust at Calcutta, or by infiltration through the Sunderbans to cut off our forces to the east and threaten Calcutta from the rear. The Sunderbans, a complicated delta of waterways through which the combined Ganges and Brahmaputra, on a front of two hundred miles, reached the sea, was an invitation to amphibious penetration. We had neither the troops to deny even the main channels nor the road or water transport to make mobile a useful striking force. For warning we had to depend on local civilian coast watchers most inadequately trained.

Most of the area was without telephones, wireless was unprocurable, and reports, hurriedly written in imperfect English, went by bicycle, runner, or boat to an often-distant telegraph office. What was surprising was not that messages were inaccurate, garbled, and delayed, but that we had any watching organization at all. As the R.A.F. slowly grew, the chance of surprise landings lessened, but the risk of the Japanese coming, observed or unobserved, remained, and we passed anxious nights when invasion scares called us from our beds.

We know now that the enemy never seriously contemplated a landing but at the time it loomed constantly over us. Yet the effort and determination that we put into our preparations to meet it raised our morale. It is a simple rule that the worse the situation the more should the troops be kept fully and actively occupied, and ours were tirelessly working to improve their training, equipment, and mobility.

There were two answers to the problem of the Sunderbans —an overwhelming air force or a flotilla of river craft. The first was, at this stage, out of the question, so we fell back on the second. We turned to the Navy. Our requests followed a descending scale. We asked first for a force of light naval craft. It was regretted they were not available. A few coastal motor-boats? The same answer. All right, we would provide the ships; but could we have some naval officers and ratings to man them? Alas, not one. Finally, with memories of the gallant detachment I had in the Retreat, we asked for a few Royal Marines. None could be spared. So we settled down to raise our own navy.

We based its organization on three functions:

(i) Reconnaissance—fast, light motorboats.

(ii) Fighting—small steamers as heavily armed and protected as we could make them.

(iii) Support—several larger steamers, enough to carry up to a brigade group to land and form road and river blocks.

Few, if any, of the river craft we obtained were really fitted for their roles. Most were old, worn out, and generally ill-found. It often seemed a toss-up which would happen first— their card-board-thick boilers blow up or rock loose on their seatings and go through the fragile sides of the ships. Nevertheless, based on the existing Army Inland Water Transport Service, which carried supplies on the rivers, we formed our fleet of more than a hundred vessels.

We manned it by enrolling the civilian crews of the ships in the I.W.T.; a process that only partially turned them into disciplined servicemen. Our officers were volunteers, merchant seamen, amateur yachtsmen, marine engineers of sorts. These, with the stalwarts already in the I.W.T., formed the navigational crews. For manning the armament and for signalling we fell back on the medieval expedient of drafting soldiers on board. We found an ideal commander for our flotilla, Lieutenant-Colonel Featherstonhaugh, a regular soldier, who had sailed before the mast, got a coastal mate's certificate, and had his wings as an airman. He had led commandos in Norway and was just the man to handle such a military-nautical set-up and, it must be confessed, the sometimes queer types that gravitated towards it. The main armament of our fighting ships was the two-pounder anti-tank gun; for anti-aircraft defence we relied on Bren guns. Dockyard maintenance, a big item in so decrepit a fleet, was undertaken by workshop companies of the I.W.T. which we established at various river ports. They did noble work but lacked much essential machinery. For major repairs we had, therefore, to rely on civil firms in Calcutta.

In spite of all difficulties we were able, in July 1942, to stage a grand combined exercise with the flotilla and the R.A.F. Our fleet, steaming down the winding channels to the sea, was an impressive sight—especially its smoke. At the conclusion of the exercise we felt that, combined with the fighters of the R.A.F., our flotilla gave us a reasonable hope, not only of discovering Japanese infiltration, but of seriously delaying and even checking it. The spirit of its men was that of the young soldier ship commander who sent the signal, *'Large Japanese submarine reported off mouth of Meghna River. Am proceeding to sea to engage.'* His heaviest armament was a two-pounder, his speed, with the safety valve screwed down, eight knots, and his rickety river steamer was never meant to venture to sea, least of all in the monsoon. The submarine would do eighteen knots on the surface and have a four-inch gun. But he went to look for it! Later the officers and men of the flotilla gave many examples of high courage and initiative in Arakan. When the time came for serious landings on that coast, however, more orthodox forces were available. All the same, we were proud of our flotilla; anyway, it was *ours*—no one had helped us much in the making of it.

I moved XV Corps Headquarters out of Calcutta to Barrackpore, a few miles farther up the Hoogly. Here we installed ourselves in a spacious Georgian house, once Lord Wellesley's country residence. My headquarters was the lineal successor to the old Presidency and Assam District Headquarters, which in various forms had functioned in Calcutta Fort since the days of Clive. As I watched the loads of files, books, and papers being moved, I could well believe it. When I looked at some of the staff, too, I realized that it had indeed been a static headquarters. It is hard to ask men whose lives had for years been a matter of routine to change not only the tempo of their work

but their whole scale of values in it. Some can and do. Then
their experience and their sense of duty are invaluable. Some
cannot. The only thing then is to find some niche where they
can still be useful; a mobile, live, fighting headquarters is no
place for them. Once again, through no merit of my own, I
was fortunate in the chief of staff I inherited. Brigadier Tony
Scott, with his judgment, energy, and dash of the dramatic, was

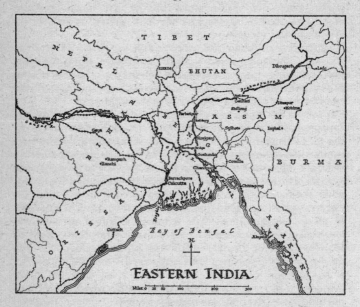

EASTERN INDIA

just the man to act as yeast in a rather lumpy headquarters
and get it moving physically and mentally.

We divided the Barrackpore house with Air Headquarters
Bengal and Burma, under Air Vice-Marshal Bill Williams, an
inspiring commander for his own service and an unselfish colleague to us. I never shared his belief that, owing to air action,
every Japanese soldier was already starving, but Williams laid
the foundation of that cooperation with the army on which
the air supremacy we later gained, and so much else, depended.

Calcutta, that swarming city, next to London the largest in
the British Empire, was itself a problem. We had to ensure its

tranquillity, defend it by land, sea, and air, organize it as the main base of Southeast Asia, and make it the leave centre for British, Indian, and American troops. At the moment the city was quiet, but for how long no one knew. An incursion of Japanese surface forces into the Bay of Bengal had recently cost us heavily in merchant ships, and every air raid sent the vital dock and factory labour streaming back to its villages. If invasion came, Calcutta would be the enemy's primary objective, and all XV Corps could hope to do was to delay the Japanese until Eastern Army's meagre reserves and anything else that could be scraped together came to our help. Our movements would be terribly hampered by the estimated three million refugees on the roads, and our defence was so thin that all installations in the city, not essential to the civil population, were prepared for destruction.

Meanwhile, in hope of better times, the docks had to be kept working at increasing capacity and the whole industry of Bengal expanded and turned to war production. Gradually, from Tatas, then the largest and most modern steel works in the British Empire, to the smallest Bengal workshop the hum of industry was rising to a crescendo, and it was the European 'Box Wallahs,' the commercial community, who in those hot, anxious months by their energy, efficiency, and above all by their calmness turned eastern India into a main workshop and supply source of every war theatre in Southeast Asia and the Middle East. They deserved well of their country; if they made a profit, they earned it.

The British or American serviceman is a townsman, and after a spell in the jungle he yearns for the distractions of the city. Calcutta alone could offer those—and did, from excellent cinemas, restaurants, and clubs to doubtful dance halls and, running down the whole scale of vice, to disease ridden-dens of perversity. With no help beyond local resources, we set out to provide wholesome amusement in such abundance that the soldier would not be lured into these darker byways. This we slowly achieved. Statistics of venereal disease and absence without leave, both high in Calcutta, fell rapidly as we tightened our discipline and cleaned up the worst plague spots. Before very long the close alliance of the army with all decent elements in the city improved it out of all recognition as a leave centre.

Parallel with these activities we conducted an energetic

campaign to clear up the worst of the plague spots. British and American Military Police—there was a rapidly increasing influx of American Air Force and administrative units—cooperated closely with the Calcutta police. The work of the joint Anglo-American police patrols was effective and not without a humorous aspect. During a fracas, involving both British and American soldiers, one such patrol sailed into the mêlée and sorted out each its own nationals. One American G.I., however, proved particularly truculent. A burly American policeman drew his nightstick, removed the soldier's cap, and slugged him hard on his bare head. As the man subsided unconscious to the floor, the policeman carefully replaced the cap. 'Why,' asked an admiring British colleague, 'did you take off his cap? The way you hit him it wouldn't have mattered if you'd left it on!' 'Say,' was the reply, 'that hat is the property of Uncle Sam. Don't you respect government property in the Royal British Army?'

The training of the formations in Bengal and of their staffs was pushed on at high pressure, under conditions more suitable to ducks than to men. Mobile columns were formed and exercised, some of them in boats, and tactical schemes carried out. Many of the Indian units were newly raised, several from races that had no tradition of military service and could not, therefore, provide their own N.C.O.s or Indian officers. For the bulk of the British troops this was their first experience of India, and there are better introductions to the glamorous East than being marooned in mildewed Bengali towns and dumped in sodden paddy fields. They took it all very well, and I wish I could have been easier with them, but they had to be trained. I am afraid, also, that a number of commanders and staff officers for various reasons failed to make the grade, and were removed. They took that very well, too.

I was, of course, much occupied simultaneously with current operations in Arakan and with preparations for an advance, but what befell there I leave to the next chapter. In July, however, Lieutenant-General Irwin, Eastern Army commander, told me that he wished himself to exercise direct control of the forthcoming Arakan offensive, and for this and other reasons his headquarters and mine would shortly change places. He would take direct command of the 14th and 26th Divisions, and I should form and train a new XV Corps at Ranchi. Whether it was wise to eliminate a corps headquarters in the chain of command to the Arakan I doubt, but Barrack-pore was certainly a better location for Army Headquarters. It put the equivalent land and air commands together, and was an incomparably better communications centre.

Before the date of our move arrived, internal trouble, so grave as to be in effect an organized rebellion, broke out in Bengal and Bihar. The Cripps Mission had ended in failure, and Gandhi had proclaimed civil disobedience throughout India with the avowed object of driving out the British. No government at any time, and certainly not in war, with the enemy at its gates, could ignore such a challenge. Gandhi and the Congress chiefs were arrested and imprisoned, but their subordinate leaders plunged into the struggle, translating Gandhi's order 'to do or die,' in the only way they under-stood—incitement to violence. Widespread disturbances broke out. In Calcutta the students, joined by the large numbers of hooligans always ready to take advantage of any weakening or preoccupation of the forces of order, came into the streets and serious rioting began. Most annoying to us were the attacks on government motor transport, attempts to decapitate motorcycle despach riders by stretching wires across roads, and the cutting of telegraph and telephone cables. At first it looked as if we might have really serious trouble in the city, but when the rioters realized, as they quickly did, that the troops were not prepared to stand as Aunt Sallies under showers of bricks but would hit back, they revised their ideas. With practically no casualties among the troops and very few indeed among the rioters, the disturbances in Calcutta petered out.

Those in the countryside were much more serious. Here, especially in Bihar, they took the form of concerted attacks on strategic rail communications. Large gangs, numbering often several hundreds, armed with primitive but effective weapons and some firearms, assaulted railway stations all over the country. Signalling instruments were destroyed, station build-ings burned and looted, lines torn up over considerable dis-tances, and European passengers dragged from trains to be hacked to pieces. The flow of supplies to the Burma front was cut off for days at a time, the large cities of Patna, capital of Bihar, and Gaya were isolated, and Calcutta itself was left little better off. Requests for troops to restore order and re-open communications flowed in from all sides. The police in many districts were besieged in their own police stations; large areas passed out of control of the civil authorities.

The urgent need was to reopen the main railways so that we could move troops as required to deal with the disturbances and restart supply to the Burma front. Eastern Army wisely relieved XV Corps of responsibility for most of Bihar and the British 70th Division, scattered through the worst areas of that province, quickly began to restore the situation. We, with all Bengal and Orissa left as our responsibility, had to bear in mind the possibility that the rebellion was concerted with the Japanese and that an invasion might be attempted simultaneously, or at least some desperate airborne support given to the rebels. There was no definite indication of such a link-up between Congress and the Japanese, but the public utterances of its leaders and the systematic wrecking of strategic communications lent colour to the idea. Enough, at any rate, to make us hesitate to disperse all the 26th Division in detachments to restore order. So it was with one eye on possible Japanese intervention that we proceeded to clear up our area. Before we had finished we were reduced to any expedient to get more troops. First we emptied reinforcement camps, improvising units from the soldiers in them. Then those in convalescent depots were turned out to replace fit men in more static defence duties. When my last available battalion had been sent north of the Ganges to reopen the railway to Assam—and incidentally itself been cut off with the line both ahead and in rear of it uprooted—I was reduced to the expedient of forming my final and only reserve from the venereal patients in the Calcutta and Barrackpore hospitals. A route march or two, and guard duties, had a very good effect on them.

After an anxious two or three weeks the situation in Bengal was well in hand, although that in Bihar was still far from happy. The Japanese had made no move, for in actual fact they had heard little or nothing of the disturbances until long afterwards. It would have been a great relief to me to have known that, but at the time, I am afraid, we rather overestimated the efficiency of the Japanese intelligence. By the end of August we were able to carry out our exchange of locations with Eastern Army Headquarters, and we moved to Ranchi without incident.

The Ranchi Plateau was almost ideal for the training we needed. Its climate was vastly preferable to the steaming heat of Bengal, malaria was much less, and the tawdry distractions of Calcutta were absent. There were great areas of jungle, wide stretches of more open country, and rivers and streams of all sizes. Here, as the first instalment of the new XV Corps, we took over the 70th British Division, 50 Armoured Brigade, and some corps units. The division was still spread about Bihar dealing with the rebellion, which, though it kept on flaring up in odd places, was coming increasingly under control. The civil administration of the province had been badly shaken. While some of the district officials had tackled a most alarming situation with resolution, others had allowed their areas to slip completely out of their grasp. The police, too, on whom so much depended, gave me the impression of having been grievously neglected. Even their uniforms were in such a state that I gave them some hundreds of pairs of khaki shorts. A policeman with his shirt showing through the seat of his trousers is at a disadvantage in his attempts to uphold the majesty of the law. Apart from this the lot of the Indian policeman was a particularly unhappy one. He was called upon to suppress and jail the very people whom he shrewdly and rightly suspected would tomorrow be the government and have absolute control of his and his family's fate. The astonishing thing is, not that there were some mutinies and troubles in the police, but that so many remained true to their salt.

Gradually the rebellion subsided into sporadic attacks on isolated stations and attempts to derail trains. A practical preventive to these outrages was found by enforcing village responsibility under which the inhabitants living along the railway guarded their own local stretches of line. They were willing to do this provided there were troops in the neighbourhood and that they were rewarded promptly for any success they achieved. British soldiers, as usual, proved the best of peacemakers. In spite of one or two nasty incidents in which a few of them were murdered, they kept their tempers admirably and were soon on good terms with the population. Civil power was slowly re-established, still rather shaky in places, and the 70th Division collected again for training.

Meanwhile, we had really got down to training ourselves— the Corps Headquarters. As a battle fighting headquarters it was neither mobile nor efficient, and we had to make it both. I think we got most fun from making it mobile. First we had to make the individuals who composed it, staff officers, signallers, cooks, clerks, mess waiters, and menials, themselves mobile. Physical training started the day, with route marches increasing in length and toughness as time went on, varied by a little brisk drill under selected instructors from the 70th Division. At first protests, mainly from the Indian clerical establishment, were indignant and vigorous. Our worthy *babus* averred that:

(1) In many years of honourable service they had never been subjected to such an indignity as parades.

(2) The drill instructors were harsh men who used rude words.

(3) The exhaustion consequent on these warlike goings-on rendered them incapable of performing their clerical duties.

(4) If compelled to continue this violent exercise, all the internal organs of their bodies—enumerated with unblushing detail—would cease to function and they would indubitably die.

(5) Their boots would wear out.

On the third morning before a route march the whole of the Indian clerks of one section of the headquarters paraded sick, complaining of divers obscure but incapacitating aches, pains, and distresses. I told the doctor attending them that, whatever was or was not the matter with them now, I relied on him to see that they really did feel ill within the next couple of hours. What dismal drench he administered I do not know, but, pale and shaken, they were on parade next morning. When I asked how they felt and inquired whether they would not like to see the doctor again, they assured me most earnestly that they were in no further need of medical attention.

It had been vividly impressed on me during the Retreat from Burma that in the jungle there are no noncombatants, so, with this physical toughening, we introduced weapon training for everybody. The whole headquarters from the corps commander downward went through qualifying courses in rifle, pistol, Bren gun, bayonet, mortar, and grenade. I was not much good with the Bren gun, but kept my end up with the other weapons. My Gurkha orderly, Bajbir, when I ordered him to parade at the rifle range, protested:

'What, *me*!'

'Yes, you.'

'Me! On a *range* to shoot at a paper *target*?'

'Yes, on a range, at a target.'

'But I've killed *five* Japs!'

All the same he paraded with the rest of us. He was a superb shot, and, having scored near possibles in all positions, at all ranges, and with all weapons, he was mollified by being made an instructor.

After the first month there were no attempts to avoid parades, and everyone took a pride in toughness and soldierly skill. The efforts of some, handicapped by nature and years of soft and sedentary living, may have been pathetic, but they were gallant. As one of the British N.C.O.s said of a *babu*, ' 'Is feet's horful, sir, but 'is 'eart's all right!' The physical effect on the men was plainly noticeable; not only did they look cleaner, fitter, and healthier, but they moved with the brisk and confident carriage of men sure of themselves. We began to get a very good feel about headquarters.

Having got the individuals mobile, it remained to achieve the mobility of the headquarters as a unit. The first step towards this was to limit the number of lorries allotted to each section for its baggage, tentage, office equipment, and messes, to an essential minimum. Heartrending appeals to increase these allotments were sternly refused. The next step was to order everything to be packed in 'yakdans,' those leather-covered boxes, fitted with rings and chains, that can be slung one on each side of a pack saddle. This ensured that, not only was no superfluous equipment carried, but that all the impedimenta of Corps Headquarters could, without repacking, be loaded at once on to either trucks, boats, aeroplanes, or even mule transport. We were, I knew, likely to use all these, and change rapidly from one to the other. The accumulation of paper at any headquarters has to be seen to be realized. Every fortnight each section was ordered to sort its papers and destroy everything not essential. My order, rigidly enforced, was, 'When in doubt, burn.' We constantly practised moving until the drill for it was thoroughly mastered; we could pack in a couple of hours and open up a properly camouflaged working headquarters in the bush in less. A large part of headquarters I kept permanently in tents and we frequently moved out into the jungle for several days at a time. At last even Tony Scott was compelled to admit we were mobile. If we were, it was largely thanks to him.

Making ourselves mobile, essential as it was, was only one step towards being operationally efficient. Most of our junior staff officers were only partially trained, our clerks had a lamentably low standard of efficiency, our mess staff left much to be desired, and our signals needed a great deal of attention. Courses were held for staff officers, classes for clerks. Those of us who had wives in India were able to get them to Ranchi, and they at once set to work, in hospitals, canteens, or at any job required, including instruction in shorthand and type-writing.

The operational efficiency of our organization was based on two nerve centres—the War Room and the Information Room. In the War Room, where the second grade operational staff officer reigned supreme, there were thoughout the twenty-four hours always on duty an operational and an intelligence officer. The War Room had also, either present or at immediate call, an administrative staff officer and a Royal Air Force representative. All signals both in and out came straight to the War Room, where one copy was posted on the appropriate board, others went direct to the branches of the staff concerned for action, and, unless really secret or not of general interest, a final copy went to the Information Room. Admission to the War Room was, of course, restricted to the principal staff officers and heads of branches, who could at any time bring themselves completely up to date on the situation and the activities of other departments from the signals and the marked maps. The Information Room, on the other hand, was open to all ranks. It was divided into two sections, one dealing with the operations of the corps and its immediate neighbours, the other with more distant fronts and the war in general. It played a large part in keeping even the most subordinate in touch with events. I had long ago decided that any risk of leakage from such a source was more than out-weighed by the increased keenness and intelligence developed by this feeling of being in the know. There was nothing very original in any of this, although we had to work out most of it for ourselves by experiment. We tested our system pretty thoroughly in exercises and manoeuvres and assured ourselves it worked. I doubt if any headquarters ever had harder or more intensive training, and I am sure no body of men could have responded to it more wholeheartedly and effectively. Within three months we were a mobile and efficient fighting headquarters, very different from the static and rather stodgy crowd who had left Calcutta.

As the 70th Division, under Major-General George Symes, reassembled around Ranchi, I was able to get to know it well. It was one of the best British formations I have met, with a magnificent battle-hardened spirit gained in the Middle East. It was a tragedy that it was never allowed to fight in Burma as a division. 50 Tank Brigade, equipped with Valentines, was the corps armoured formation, and I liked the look of it very much. With these formations, and an increasingly alive Corps Headquarters, we began serious training.

This training was based on a short memorandum I had drawn up, giving what I considered to have been the tactical lessons of the 1942 campaign. The chief of these were:

(i) The individual soldier must learn, by living, moving, and exercising in it, that the jungle is neither impenetrable nor unfriendly. When he has once learned to move and live in it, he can use it for concealment, covered movement, and surprise.

(ii) Patrolling is the master key to jungle fighting. All units, not only infantry battalions, must learn to patrol in the jungle, boldly, widely, cunningly, and offensively.

(iii) All units must get used to having Japanese parties in their rear, and, when this happens, regard not themselves, but the Japanese as 'surrounded.'

(iv) In defence, no attempt should be made to hold long continuous lines. Avenues of approach must be covered and enemy penetration between our posts dealt with at once by mobile local reserves who have completely reconnoitred the country.

(v) There should rarely be frontal attacks and never frontal attacks on narrow fronts. Attacks should follow hooks and come in from flank or rear, while pressure holds the enemy in front.

(vi) Tanks can be used in almost any country except swamp. In close country they must always have infantry *with* them to defend and reconnoitre for them. They should always be used in the maximum numbers available and capable of being deployed. Whenever possible penny packets must be avoided. 'The more you use, the fewer you lose.'

(vii) There are no noncombatants in jungle warfare. Every unit and subunit, including medical ones, is responsible for its own all-round protection, including patrolling, at all times.

(viii) If the Japanese are allowed to hold the initiative they are formidable. When we have it, they are confused and easy to kill. By mobility away from roads, surprise, and offensive action we must regain and keep the initiative.

These were the lessons I had learned from defeat and I do not think I changed them in any essential throughout the rest of the war. There was, however, one big omission, as I gave them to XV Corps. I did not mention air supply. This was intentional. Most of us had long ago recognized that air transport could solve some of our worst problems, but as yet we had no transport aircraft. My experience was—and is—that it only does harm to talk to troops about new and desirable equipment which others may have but which you cannot give them. It depresses them. So I made no mention of air transport until we could get at least some of it.

The troops lived in tents or *bashas*, the bamboo huts, thatched with leaves, that were so familiar to us. Reasonably cool and certainly airy, they were pleasant enough in dry weather, but far from waterproof in wet. The aboriginal tribes of the Ranchi Plateau were a friendly race of excellent physique. Their men made our roads, and their young women provided most of the labour for our camps. On my first visit to a camp under construction I was startled to find, working among the troops, gangs of these cheerful girls, most of whom wore nothing above the waist. I was more than a little apprehensive of the results of such a display of dusky but by no means unattractive femininity. It says much for both parties, the girls and the soldiers, that there was practically no trouble of any kind. Later a Bihar regiment was raised, and when I inspected it in Burma, where it did well, and complimented the men on their appearance, one of them laughingly replied, 'Ah, but, sahib, you should see our women!' I told him I had and admired them. A friendly, cheerful, free people who deserve to remain so.

In our training we had as neighbours our old friends, the Chinese. Sun's sorely tried 38th and the remnants of Liao's 22d Chinese Division had been collected after the Retreat at

Ramgarh, some forty miles from Ranchi. In spite of their reduced state, Stilwell, indomitable as ever, planned to raise on
this nucleus a strong, well-equipped Chinese force of several
divisions that would re-enter northern Burma and open a road
to China. Only Stilwell believed that was both possible and
worth the resources it would demand. The Chinese themselves
were by no means enthusiastically cooperative; the Indian
government, not without justification, felt considerable appre-
hension at the prospect of thousands of Chinese about the
countryside. With a few notable exceptions, the Americans
had little confidence in anybody—in the Chinese, in the British, or in Stilwell.

Stilwell was magnificent. He forced Chiang Kai-shek to
provide the men; he persuaded India to accept a large Chinese
force, and the British to pay for it, accommodate, feed, and
clothe it. The American 'Ferry Command' then flew thirteen
thousand Chinese from Kunming over 'the Hump,' the great
mountain range between Assam and China, to airfields in the
Brahmaputra Valley, whence they came by rail to Ramgarh.
This was the first large-scale troop movement by air in the
theatre and was an outstanding achievement. The young
American pilots of the Hump should be remembered with
admiration and gratitude by their countrymen and their
Allies.

The two Chinese divisions were reconstituted. Good food,
medical care, and regular pay achieved wonders. I have never
seen men recover condition as quickly as those Chinese
soldiers. Intensive training, under picked American instructors, began on mass-production methods, which were most
effective. I was very impressed by the rapid progress of the
infantry who were converted to artillery, and who in an aston-
ishingly short time were turned into serviceable pack batteries.
No doubt they were apt pupils, but the major credit went to
their teachers, under Colonel Sliney, one of the best artillery
instructors any army has produced. Everywhere was Stilwell,
urging, leading, driving.

I saw a good deal of Sun and Liao, as well as a number of
Chinese regimental and battalion commanders whom I had
met in Burma. The mass system of instruction left these senior
Chinese officers little to do but watch their men being trained
by the American experts, and they feared a loss of face. Sun, I
think, especially felt this, but when I advised him to make the

best of it and reap the benefit later, he was too sensible not to agree. If it surprised us to see our Chinese friends coming on at such a rate, it had an even greater effect on the Americans themselves, an effect which spread even to their headquarters in Delhi. At last they began to catch some of Stilwell's faith and to believe that the Chinese could, with training, equipping, and leadership, be made fit to fight the Japanese.

Some weeks later another division, the 7th Indian, joined XV Corps. It had not been tried in war, but there was a freshness and a keenness in all it did, which received an imaginative lead from its new commander, Major-General Frank Messervy. He had been chief staff officer of the 5th Indian Division when I had been a brigade commander in it, and later, with his audacious Gazelle Force in East Africa, he had made a great name for hunting the Italians. He had had his ups and downs as a divisional commander in the Middle East, but I welcomed him as an offensively minded leader, steadied by experience and misfortune in a hard school.

Shortly afterwards, the 5th Indian Division itself arrived from the Middle East. It has been overseas since August 1940 and had seen as much and as varied fighting as any division. It had a spirit and a self-reliance that come only from real fighting. It owed much to its commander, Major-General Briggs, and like all good divisions—and bad ones—reflected its commander's personality. The war had found him in command of a battalion in this division—a battalion that in some extraordinary way was always where it was wanted, that always did what was wanted, and was ready to go on doing it. So Briggs got a brigade. His brigade was just as steadily successful as his battalion had been. It went into the toughest spots, met the most difficult situations, and came out again, like its commander, still unperturbed and as quietly efficient as ever. So, while others fell by the wayside, Briggs got his division. I know of few commanders who made as many immediate and critical decisions on every step of the ladder of promotion, and I know of none who made so few mistakes.

Towards the end of our stay in Ranchi another new Indian division, the 20th, joined the corps. It was commanded by Douglas Gracey, a fellow Gurkha, whom I had known for many years, and who, as a brigade commander, had cooperated with my 10th Division against the French in Syria in 1941. Full of energy and ideas, he had a great hold on his Indian and

Gurkha troops.

I was indeed fortunate in these three divisional commanders. Messervy, Briggs, and Gracey all served with me later in Burma. Messervy became an inspiring corps commander, Briggs a most successful commander in chief in Burma during the trying time after the war, and Gracey, after brilliantly commanding his division, carried out in an outstanding manner a most difficult military-political task in Indo-China.

My stay in Ranchi was interrupted by two visits to Arakan: once by myself, and once with most of my headquarters, as I shall relate. In spite of this, training in Ranchi was continuous and progressive. There were infantry battle schools, artillery training centres, cooperation courses with the R.A.F., experiments with tanks in the jungle, classes in watermanship and river crossing, and a dozen other instructional activities, all in full swing. Our training grew more ambitious until we were staging interdivisional exercises over wide ranges of country under tough conditions. Units lived for weeks on end in the jungle and learned its ways. We hoped we had finally dispelled the fatal idea that the Japanese had something we had not.

As I went from division to division and saw their keenness, their toughness, their jungle craft, and their speed of movement, I began to feel that, when the time came, we should live up to the XV Corps sign of the three V's, for 15 and victory.

CHAPTER VIII

THE FIRST ARAKAN CAMPAIGN

When we withdrew, rather precipitately, from Akyab Island in April 1942, chaos and civil war spread throughout Arakan. First, the local inhabitants fell on the wretched Indian refugees, who were still in thousands trying to escape by the coastal route. This exodus was followed by a bitter internecine struggle for land and power between the Arakanese and the Mughs, two sections of the population. The Mughs got the worse of it and many were driven across the Naf River to take shelter in territory still held by us, there to make yet another refugee problem. Faction fights among the victorious Arakanese then became the order of the day, until the Japanese, pushing up to Buthidaung, restored some sort of uneasy peace.

This was the position when I took over XV Corps and with it responsibility for the Arakan front. The first necessity was to improve our intelligence of Japanese movements and intentions and, to this end, we extended into our area an organization, 'V' Force, already working on the Assam front. British officers, when possible those with local knowledge, were sent into the most forward areas where they built up a network of agents, who, operating behind the enemy, collected and brought back information. The Japanese had much the same spy system—often employing the same men—and a fascinating duel developed between the rival organizations. Our officers and methods were more popular with the inhabitants and, as a result, we gained the better of these exchanges. 'V' Force later extended its activities to include minor raiding operations and became a valuable part of the intelligence framework.

The bulk of Lloyd's 14th Division was still north of Chittagong and, as yet, he was reluctant to stretch farther south but whether we remained on the defensive, or, as I intended, passed to a limited offensive, a proper screen well ahead of the main force was clearly essential. I sympathized with Lloyd's wish to keep his division concentrated for training, but that could be carried out even more realistically farther south. I had, besides, at my first inspection of Chittagong found a disturbing nervousness among its small garrison, and I ordered the forward move to begin.

I had every confidence in Lloyd and in his chief staff officer, Colonel Warren, whom I had taught at the Staff College. Warren concealed, under an at times infuriating deliberation, a determination and an imperturbability that were later to stand him and his commanders in good stead.

In July General Headquarters, India, became firm on the intention to order a modest offensive in Arakan, with the objects of clearing the Mayu Peninsula and seizing Akyab Island. Prospects seemed good. As far as we knew the Japanese then had only four divisions in Burma: one in the far north-east watching the Yunnan Chinese; two on the Assam front; and one, the 55th, in western Burma. Of this only one regiment and some other units were in Arakan, and so, in the opening stages at least, Lloyd would have a handsome margin of superiority.

There were, as always, in war, other factors besides numbers. The ground was one—the most important. The Mayu Peninsula is some ninety miles long and about twenty wide at its northern end, whence it tapers to a point just short of Akyab Island. Down its centre runs the Mayu Range, a razor-sharp ridge, from one to two thousand feet high, almost precipitous but jungle covered. The lower slopes, in a tangle of broken spurs, approach to within a thousand yards or so of the sea on one side and of the Mayu River on the other. The narrow strips of flat ground on each side are split by innumerable streams or *chaungs*, which on the west especially are tidal with treacherous banks of mud at low tide. Such a terrain would afford, at frequent intervals, ideal positions for defence and gravely hamper the deployment of an attacking force.

Before Eastern Army had decided itself to control the offensive, we at XV Corps had prepared plans for it. Knowing something of Japanese tenacity, we had felt that a straightforward advance, even in superior force, would be slow and costly. We had hoped to stage a three fold attempt: the main thrust by the 14th Division down the peninsula; a series of short amphibious hooks down the coast by our flotilla; and

Wingate's brigade, now training, swinging well out to the east to come in on Akyab by the back door. I think that would have worked.

However, Eastern Army when its turn came, had to give up all idea of using Wingate's brigade as General Wavell had decided to use that in the north to cooperate with an expected Chinese advance from Yunnan. Then Eastern Army developed —perhaps understandably—doubts about our cherished flotilla, so in the end, relying on their preponderance of force, they came down in favour of one simple, direct advance down the west side of the peninsula.

This, our first offensive in the theatre, was never intended to accomplish more than the very limited objective of taking Akyab. Its most important effects would not be the minor improvement in the tactical situation that the possession of Akyab would give, but the moral effect that *any* successful offensive would have on world opinion, on our Allies, and, most important of all, on our own troops. Morale in places was not too high and we badly needed a victory of some sort. It was a mistake to blazon the advance as an invasion of Burma. Even if the limited success aimed at were attained, it would not come up to the expectations raised, and, if we failed, the depression would be the greater. It is better to let a victory, if it comes, speak for itself; it has a voice that drowns all other sounds. If it does not come—and victory is never certain—the less preliminary drumbeating there has been the better.

From Ranchi, to which we had moved in August, we watched with growing anxiety the progress of the Arakan offensive, now no longer our responsibility. The weather, difficulties in collecting supplies and equipment, and other reasons, delayed its start, and it was not until mid-December that the 14th Division began in earnest its ninety-mile move on Akyab. The advance was made on both sides of the Mayu Range, along the seacoast and astride the Mayu River, with a flanking detachment still farther east in the Kaladan Valley. The central spine of the range was not occupied; it was judged too precipitous and too thickly jungle covered to be passable. For most of the way, therefore, it effectively separated the two prongs of the advance.

To begin with, all went well. The little port of Maungdaw on the estuary of the Naf River, and the town of Buthidaung were taken against slight opposition. The west-to-east road between them, which pierced the range by two tunnels—relics of a vanished railway—was occupied, giving us the only lateral road in the peninsula. The last days of 1942 found Lloyd's troops on the right of the range in the coastal plain just short of Donbaik, ten miles from the tip of the peninsula; and on his left, approaching Rathedaung in the Mayu River Valley, about fifteen miles from Foul Point. A carrier patrol even reached that point, separated by only a narrow channel from Akyab Island, and returned to report no enemy seen.

An unfortunate pause in the advance until January 6 then occurred, which gave the Japanese time to bring up reinforcements and to dig in at both Donbaik and Rathedaung. Our left attack on Rathedaung, gallantly pressed, was repulsed; two set-piece frontal attacks on the right across the paddy fields on Donbaik also failed disastrously. The Japanese held Donbaik with little more than a battalion, with other troops in reserve, yet, so skilfully were their positions sited and hidden that an attack on the restricted front between the ridge and the sea failed to dislodge them. For the first time we had come up against the Japanese 'bunker'—from now on to be so familiar to us. This was a small strong point made usually of heavy logs covered with four or five feet of earth, and so camouflaged in the jungle that it could not be picked out at even fifty yards without prolonged searching. These bunkers held garrisons varying from five to twenty men, plentifully supplied with medium and light machine guns. They were quite impervious to bombardment by field guns and even the direct hit of a medium bomb rarely penetrated. They were sited in groups to give mutual support, so that it was impossible for assaulting troops to reach a bunker without coming under fire from at least two others.

Some reports and many rumours of these setbacks in Arakan spread through the Eastern Army. The high hopes inspired by the drumbeating that had preceded the offensive died down and heads began to be shaken. Reinforcements were sent from India to give renewed impetus to the attack, until eventually four fresh Indian brigades and one British brigade had been added. The 14th Division now had nine brigades and it was, I think, the largest that ever went into action. To overcome the bunker difficulty, XV Corps was ordered to send one troop of Valentine tanks to Arakan. The tank brigade commander protested against such a small detachment and I supported him, as it was against all my experience in the Middle East and Burma. 'The more you use, the fewer you lose.' I argued that a regiment could be deployed and used in depth even on the narrow front chosen for attack. We were overruled on the grounds that more than a troop could not be deployed and that the delay in getting in a larger number across the *chaungs* was more than could be accepted. Reluctantly we sent the troop, and the secret of its move was admirably kept. This and the gallantry of the crews were the only admirable things about the episode.

The third assault on Donbaik went in, but the handful of tanks was knocked out almost at once, and the attack again failed. After a pause to bring up fresh troops a fourth attack on the same frontal model, but now without tanks, was made on February 18. By sheer gallantry, Punjabi troops penetrated to the bunkers, but were eventually thrown back after suffering very heavily. The Japanese technique was, when our troops reached the enemy positions, to bring down the heaviest possible artillery, mortar, and machine-gun concentrations on them, irrespective of any damage they might inflict on their own men. Actually, as the Japanese defenders were mostly in bunkers they suffered little, while our troops, completely in the open, had no protection from this rain of projectiles.

In the second week of March I was summoned to Calcutta by the army commander, General Irwin, who told me he wished me to visit Lloyd in Arakan. I asked him if, now so many brigades were operating there, he intended to send my headquarters with me to take over control. He replied that he did not want me to take any operational command, nor did he think a corps headquarters necessary at this time, but he might decide to send us there later. All I was to do now was to look around, get into the picture, and report to him.

My impressions in Arakan were, first, that nine brigades and a long and difficult line of communication were far too much for any divisional headquarters to control; second, that morale was definitely on the downgrade. Lloyd had been ordered to make yet another attempt to break through at Donbaik and had been given 6 Brigade of the 2d British Division for the purpose. His plan, a direct frontal attack, seemed to me too like its predecessors. I told him I thought he was making the mistake we had made in 1942 in considering any jungle, even that on the Mayu Range, impenetrable; it would be worth while making a great effort to get troops along its spine. However, Lloyd and his brigadiers were convinced it was impassable and, in any case, he said, he could not afford the delay. He was quite confident of success this time.

Back in Calcutta I reported to the army commander, but having studied the question and having had the opinions of subordinate commanders on the spot, he concluded that any flanking move via the ridge was impracticable. I had the idea that rather against his inclination he was being hurried into this attack by Delhi. On his assurance that I should not be wanted, I asked for and was granted ten days' leave to Simla, where my wife and young daughter were then living.

On March 18 6 Brigade made a desperate attempt to break through the strengthened Japanese defences. Advancing again, straight in the open, over the dead of previous assaults, they got among and even on the tops of the bunkers; but they could not break in. Like the Punjabis, they were caught by the merciless Japanese counterbarrage and bloodily driven back. It was a magnificent effort, and it was the last. Donbaik remained impregnable, and all hope of taking it was abandoned.

Now, having brought us to a standstill, it was the Japanese turn to attack. A strong enemy column, which had marched from Central Burma, suddenly fell upon our flank detachment in the Kaladan and scattered it. Other Japanese detachments led by a Colonel Tanahashi, afterwards to become only too well known to us, broke into the Mayu Valley and struck behind 55 Brigade opposite Rathedaung. After fierce fighting the brigade extricated itself and, badly shaken, fell back up the Mayu River. Lloyd reacted by a counterattack, but the army commander, who had hurried to the front on the news of disaster, relieved him, took command of the division himself, and redisposed the forward troops to hold any further Japanese advance. For a short while it appeared as if the front was stabilized and the army commander, handing over to Major-General Lomax, who arrived to replace Lloyd, returned to Calcutta.

At four o'clock in the morning of April 5 at Gaya, I was awakened by a banging on the door of the railway carriage in which my wife and I were returning from Simla to Ranchi. I was told by a railway official that I was wanted urgently on the telephone and the train would be held up for me. In my pyjamas I staggered over the recumbent figures that invariably litter every Indian platform at night to the station master's office. Here I heard Tony Scott speaking from Ranchi. Dramatically he proclaimed, 'The woodcock are flighting!' 'Woodcock' was the code name for the move of Corps Headquarters to Arakan. I was to go straight on in the train to Calcutta; my wife would be picked up at the junction for Ranchi; Scott would be off that morning for Chittagong with the Corps Headquarters.

At dawn on a dismal station platform I said good-bye to my wife and left her rather forlorn, hoping that someone *would* come and take her to Ranchi. We had had too many partings of this kind in the last twenty years, but this was, I think she would agree, one of our most hurried and most miserable. Late in the morning I arrived in Calcutta and spent some hours with General Irwin, getting his view of the situation as it was known to him and receiving his instructions. Things in Arakan were obviously again going wrong; but how seriously was not clear. I was to set up Corps Headquarters in Chittagong as soon as possible, but I was not to take operational control until told to do so by him. I was not, even when I assumed operational command, to have administrative control; that would remain with Army Headquarters, who on all such matters would deal direct with the division. I was, therefore, to leave almost the whole of my administrative staff behind in Ranchi. I did not like this separation of operational and administrative control, especially as a corps could have relieved the overworked division of much of its administrative burden, but the army commander was insistent. The situation in Arakan was further complicated as at this juncture the 26th Division Headquarters from Calcutta was in process of replacing the 14th Division Headquarters, which, together with certain brigades, it was intended to bring back to India.

Early next morning I flew to Chittagong, where I picked up a fighter escort as Japanese aircraft were busy, and landed on a forward air strip near Divisional Headquarters. I had never met Lomax, the new divisional commander, but I was at once impressed by his calm level-headedness. He would have had plenty of excuse for nervousness had he shown it. The situation as far as it could be discovered was fantastically bad. Lomax, barely arrived, had just begun to study the dispositions he had inherited from General Irwin, was learning the names of his brigadiers, and meeting a completely strange staff, when the Japanese struck again. Using not very large forces with the greatest boldness and rapidity, they had crossed the Mayu River in the night, fallen on the flank of 47 Brigade which had been extended to cover the eastern side of the range, and rolled it up. The brigade disintegrated and, losing practically all its equipment, struggled out over the hills in

small starving parties. As far as we knew at Lomax's headquarters that brigade had ceased to exist—as, indeed, it had—and his left flank was crumbling, if not already gone. The Japanese, without pause, had exploited to the full the opportunity this gave them. Straight over the Mayu Range they came, following or making single-file tracks through the jungle and over the precipitous slopes that we had complacently considered impassable. On the night of the 5th Japanese infantry and pack guns debouched from the foothills on to the coastal strip west of the range. They struck into the rear of 6 Brigade as it pulled back from Donbaik. The Brigade Headquarters was rushed by howling Japanese streaming out of the darkness, most of the staff were killed, and the brigadier, Cavendish, was captured, only to be killed a little later either by his guards or by our own artillery fire. Everywhere the units of 6 Brigade found Japanese in between them, behind them, and around them. It says much for the stubborn courage of the British soldier that, in these conditions, with control temporarily gone, battalions, companies, and batteries rallied, cleared their immediate localities with the bayonet, and began to fall back, holding off a fanatical enemy, delirious with success.

The position as Lomax and I looked at it next day was grim, so grim as to have almost a comic element. With the left flank, east of the range, gone, the right along the coast looked like a Neapolitan ice. First and farthest south, as far as we could discover, were some British artillery, then a wad of Japanese, next half 6 Brigade minus its headquarters, again more Japanese, and lastly the rest of 6 Brigade.

For myself, I was in a strange position, which was new to me, and which I did not like. I have rarely been so unhappy on a battlefield. Things had gone wrong, terribly wrong, and we should be hard put to it to avoid worse. Yet I had no operational control and, even if I had, no troops in hand with whom I could influence events; Lomax already commanded everything. In spite of all this I would have had no hesitation in assuming tactical command at the front, as General Irwin had done with Lloyd and as I had done myself on occasion, but for one thing—Lomax. I did not know him; I had been with him only a matter of hours, but they were testing hours. Never had a divisional commander, immediately on taking over a strange formation, in a new type of war, been confronted with a more desperate situation. I was filled with admiration for the way in which he took hold. Wherever he went he inspired confidence by his steadiness, decision, and obvious competence. Was this his true form? Would it last? I was prepared to bet it was and would. In fact, I did not flatter myself that I could handle the immediate situation any better than he could. On the other hand, I did know there were a hundred ways in which, at Corps Headquarters behind him, I could take some of the strain.

Quietly, without fuss, Lomax regrouped his rear brigades to cover the vital Maungdaw–Buthidaung road, and reorganized the units already shattered. In this latter task I did what I could to help. There was no doubt that the disaster had tragically weakened morale in a number of units, British and Indian. Those of 6 British Brigade, in spite of the hammering they had taken, were an exception. They had not liked it, but they were still staunch.

Not the least of Lomax's difficulties was that the tired but efficient headquarters of the 14th Division had been replaced by the untried staff of the 26th Division, newly arrived, unacquainted with most of the brigades, and finding the contrast between a fast-moving battle and the static life of Calcutta only too painful. The rapid recoil of our front made it necessary to move back Divisional Headquarters, and it was evident from the resulting confusion that, if it found it so difficult to move itself, it was not likely to be very efficient at getting others to move. With my concurrence, Lomax made a clean sweep of several of the divisional staff, whom I replaced for him by the temporary loan of officers from Corps Headquarters. In a few days we managed to produce as chief staff officer for the division Colonel Cotterill-Hill. He and Lomax made a splendid pair, and from the day of his arrival the 26th Division Headquarters began to sort itself out. Lomax was, at the same time, relieved of the strain of reorganizing the headquarters himself and could devote his energies more freely to the proper functions of a commander in battle.

I stayed with Lomax for a few days and I hope he did not find my presence a handicap. My original opinion of his leadership was confirmed, indeed I never changed it throughout the war. When things at the front were rather more under control I rejoined Corps Headquarters.

Chittagong, once an attractive town, was now a melancholy place. Most of its inhabitants had fled from bombing and those who remained, the poorest, were menaced by approaching famine. The railway workshops had been demolished but the docks, thanks to a stout-hearted naval captain named Hallett, were showing reviving activity. Corps Headquarters, installed in a college, functioned one-sidedly without its administrative half. In the town, too, was 224 Group R.A.F., under Air Commodore Gray, whose pilots had achieved marvels of sustained efforts in covering the recent withdrawals.

The front, which I frequently visited, was now, temporarily at least, stabilized on both sides of the Mayu Range and we had at last troops in position along its spine. It was evident that the Japanese would not rest satisfied with their easy successes; they would attack again. When their push came, I was sure it would be on the east of the range in the form of a strong drive to get across the lateral Maungdaw–Buthidaung road. If it succeeded, we should have to abandon Buthidaung —its supply would be impossible—and our hold on Maungdaw would become precarious.

Lomax had no intention of sitting down waiting for this to happen, and, with my full approval, he planned a counter-stroke in the nature of a trap. The Japanese striking force was to be shepherded into a box. When it was well in, the lid was to swing to behind it with a bang. One side of the box was two battalions on the ridge itself; the other was two more along the Mayu River. The bottom of the box, its northern end, was yet again two battalions holding the hills south of the Maungdaw–Buthidaung road. The lid was a mobile striking force of a brigade less a battalion, placed behind the river side of the box, ready to swing in. That all sounds nicely geometrical and simple, but translated into tired troops, many of them badly shaken, holding positions among tangled jungle hills and streams, it was not so tidy, and much less simple. I was more than a little anxious as to the outcome. It would all have been so easy if we could only have washed out the last four months of defeat and frustration. Then the troops would have been mentally and physically fit for this sort of battle, but time is the one thing you cannot regain in war. I had no doubt the Japanese would walk into the trap. They did. Their attack began as we expected and, according to plan—our plan. Feeling stiff opposition on their flanks, they pressed rapidly forward in the centre and flowed into the box. So far, so good. Now was the time to crash down the lid. Lomax was just giving the order for this when the bottom fell out of the box and out of our plan. The two battalions south of the lateral road failed to hold. First one then the other gave way. The Japanese broke through and seized the Point 551 feature which dominated the eastern half of the Maungdaw–Buthidaung road. In the confused fighting that followed we not only failed to retake Point 551, but were pushed back, and the Japanese got astride the road. That meant we could no longer maintain a force in Buthidaung, as the road was its only means of access. Even more serious, it put paid to most of the wheeled transport east of the range. We had now no route by which to get it away, and when the troops pulled out of Buthidaung by jungle tracks over the hills they destroyed their vehicles. It was too much like 1942 over again, with the added bitterness that this time we had been defeated by forces smaller than our own.

It was no use crying over spilt milk. In war you have to pay for your mistakes, and in Arakan the same mistakes had been made again and again until the troops lost heart. I got very angry with one or two units that had not behaved well, and said some hard things to them, but thinking it over I was not sure the blame was all theirs. In any case, what was wanted now was not recriminations, post-mortems, and witch hunts, but some clear—and quick—thinking.

Could we hang on to the tunnels area and the western part of the lateral road? Could we hold Maungdaw? If not, where should we go back to? Bawli Bazaar, Cox's Bazaar, Chittagong? Frankly, the troops that had been in action for the past weeks were fought out and many of them could not be relied on to hold anything. I had asked for the 70th Division from Ranchi to enable me to send back to India the bulk of worn-out formations, and it was coming in bit by bit, but less than a brigade had yet arrived. It would have taken a month or two to stock up Maungdaw, while ships coming in would have to run a Japanese gauntlet. To hang on to Maungdaw as a matter of prestige—and it had now no other value—would have been to invite a siege and a disaster. I urged its abandonment. The army commander was naturally reluctant, but I was quite sure, whatever the effects in Delhi, we must get out, and he finally agreed. Our only hope of stabilizing the front, if the Japanese really pushed us, was to hold the ricefield country. Our men were still untrained for the jungle and they feared it more than they did the enemy. We had to select areas where we could give our troops reasonable fields of fire and open manoeuvre. The first place where this could be done was about Cox's Bazaar, and here we planned a layout for a division of three or four brigades, astride the main line of advance to Chittagong. Bawli we would hold as what amounted to an outpost position. It was very galling to be thrown back on these defensive tactics, but at the moment there was no alternative.

I was constantly flying between Lomax's and my headquarters. On one occasion, when seeking a forward brigade, I got a bad fright through landing on an air strip we had already abandoned, but which luckily the Japanese had not yet taken over. The situation was not improved by the pilot of my Lysander stopping his engine before we realized where we were, and then being unable to restart it! Before he got it going again I was sweating with more than the heat.

With great skill and very little loss Lomax broke contact with the Japanese. On May 11 we evacuated Maungdaw and pulled back to the new positions. The rain came, and the enemy, almost as tired as we were, sat down on his gains at Buthidaung, the Tunnels, and Maungdaw, making no serious attempt to follow us to Bawli.

Here we were back where we had started, a sad ending to our first and much-heralded offensive. Our actual losses in killed, wounded, and missing were not high, about twenty-five hundred, and, while we had not inflicted so many on the enemy, he had suffered, too. Malaria had taken a heavy toll, far above our battle casualties, and we had lost a good deal of equipment. Neither these serious losses nor the abandonment of territory was as damaging as the loss of morale. It was no use disguising the fact that many of the British and Indian units which had fought in Arakan were shaken and depressed. As so often happens, too, the troops in the rear areas, who greatly outnumbered those at the front, suffered an even greater decline in morale. It was plain that our main task during the respite of the monsoon must be to rebuild that morale. At this critical time two men, each almost the antithesis of the other, one indirectly, the other directly, came to our help. The first was Brigadier Orde Wingate; the second, General Sir George Giffard.

I had first met Wingate in East Africa, when we were both fighting the Italians, he with his Abyssinian partisans, whom in those days we impolitely called *shiftas* or brigands, and I with my more orthodox Indian infantry brigade. I had already in 1941 and 1942 had several lively discussions with him on the organization and practice of guerrilla warfare. With many of his ideas I was in agreement, but I had doubted if methods based on his Abyssinian experience would succeed equally well against a tougher enemy and in country not so actively friendly. Wingate was a strange, excitable, moody creature, but he had fire in him. He could ignite other men. When he so fiercely advocated some project of his own, you might catch his enthusiasm or you might see palpable flaws in his arguments; you might be angry at his arrogance or outraged at so obvious a belief in the end, his end, justifying any means; but you could not be indifferent. You could not fail to be stimulated either to thought, protest, or action by his sombre vehemence and his unrelenting persistence.

Just at this time he had returned from his first raid into Burma.

Passing through the IV Corps outposts along the Chindwin, his brigade in a number of columns, all supplied by air, had pushed two hundred miles eastward into Japanese-held Burma. They had blown up bridges and cuttings on the Mandalay–Myitkyina railway that supplied the Japanese northern front, and attempted to reach across the Irrawaddy to cut the Mandalay–Lashio line. Exhaustion, difficulties of air supply, and the reaction of the Japanese prevented this, and the columns breaking up into small parties made for the shelter of IV Corps. About a thousand men, a third of the total force, failed to return. As a military operation the raid had been an expensive failure. It gave little tangible return for the losses it had suffered and the resources it had absorbed. The damage it did to Japanese communications was repaired in a few days, the casualties it inflicted were negligible, and it had no immediate effect on Japanese dispositions or plans. The abandonment of a projected enemy offensive through the Hukawng Valley was not owing to this raid, but to the fact that the Japanese 55th Division, which was to take part in it, had to be diverted at the end of 1942 to meet the British threat in Arakan. If anything was learned of air supply or jungle fighting it was a costly schooling.

These are hard things to say of an effort that required such stark courage and endurance as was demanded of and given by Wingate and his men. The operation was, in effect, the old cavalry raid of military history on the enemy's communications, which, to be effective against a stout-hearted opponent, must be made in tactical coordination with a main attack elsewhere. Originally, Wingate's raid had been thus planned to coincide with an advance by Chinese forces from Yunan. Later, although it was clear that this Chinese move would not materialize, General Wavell sent Wingate's force in alone. It was a bold decision, and, as it turned out, it was justified, not on military, but on psychological grounds. It cannot be judged on material results alone. While, like the Arakan offensive, it was a failure, there was a dramatic quality about this raid, which, with the undoubted fact that it had penetrated far behind the Japanese lines and returned, lent itself to presentation as a triumph of British jungle fighting over the Japanese. Skilfully handled, the press of the Allied world took up the tale, and everywhere the story ran that we had beaten the Japanese at their own game. This not only distracted attention from the failure in Arakan, but was important in itself for our own people at home, for our Allies, and above all for our troops on the Burma front. Whatever the actual facts, to the troops in Burma it seemed the first ripple showing the turning of the tide. For this reason alone Wingate's raid was worth all the hardship and sacrifice his men endured, and by every means in our power we exploited its propaganda value to the full.

On May 21 I heard that General Giffard had replaced General Irwin as commander in chief, Eastern Army. Except for a brief visit to my headquarters ten days earlier, I had not met him. He called me to Calcutta at the end of the month and we had a very full discussion on the Arakan situation. The new army commander had a great effect on me. A tall, good-looking man in the late fifties, who had obviously kept himself physically and mentally in first-class condition, there was nothing dramatic about him in either appearance or speech. He abhorred the theatrical, and was one of the very few generals, indeed men in any position, I have known who *really* disliked publicity. The first impression he gave was of courtesy and consideration, and this was a lasting impression because it was based on thought for others.

But there was much more to General Giffard than good taste, good manners, and unselfishness. He understood the fundamentals of war—that soldiers must be trained before they can fight, fed before they can march, and relieved before they are worn out. He understood that front-line commanders should be spared responsibilities in rear, and that soundness of organization and administration is worth more than specious short cuts to victory. Having chosen his subordinates and given them their tasks, he knew how to leave them without interference, but with the knowledge that, if they needed it, his support was behind them. I returned to Calcutta—with some difficulty, as the weather forced back my aircraft twice—feeling that the new army commander was a man I could work with, and for, wholeheartedly.

Within a few days General Giffard came with me on an Arakan tour. He visited the forward troops, my own headquarters, and the rear areas. He met officers and men and spoke to them. He was at his best talking to individuals. As a speechmaker he was neither eloquent nor picturesque, but he had two things that impressed soldiers—he knew his stuff and he was dead honest. *The* quality that showed through him was integrity, and that was the quality which, as much as any other, we wanted in our army commander. Without any shouting from the housetops or organized publicity stunts, belief in the new army commander spread, and with it spirits began to revive. Those who, like myself, commanded under him, built on the foundations he laid in morale and organization, and later, when we succeeded him, often received credit that should justly have been his.

After a few weeks tidying up Arakan, getting tired formations out, building up supplies, and doing the hundred-and-one things necessary to give the troops in their sodden trenches and leaky *bashas* as much comfort as possible, Corps Headquarters, leaving Lomax and his 26th Division to hold the front, returned to Ranchi. General Giffard's instructions to me were to have the divisions already at Ranchi, and those he would send me later, fit for a real offensive immediately after the monsoon.

With him I discussed the forthcoming Arakan offensive, which he was entrusting to XV Corps. For it I was to have the 5th and 7th Divisions. The 20th Division was to go to IV Corps at Imphal; the 70th Division would remain in Army Reserve. The 26th Division, when relieved by either 5th or 7th, would remain in Arakan, as reserve for that front. The old Sunderbans flotilla had by now largely reverted to transport duties, and though we had hoped for landing craft and naval forces for a minor landing, they were not yet available. We should thus again be reduced to a straightforward advance overland with only amphibious feints. I was anxious to avoid the old move on a narrow front, and I asked for an additional formation to send down the Kaladan River on the left flank, always the dangerous spot in Arakan. This would be independent of the main advance, and would have to be supplied entirely by air. General Giffard accordingly made available for me the 81st West African Division, less one brigade, and provided enough air transport from our growing resources to supply it.

This was the first time a normal formation such as a division was to be committed to complete air maintenance. General Giffard's staff with mine worked out the organization required. We very soon realized that if we were going to make the best use of this great new weapon of air supply we must, with our limited resources in aircraft, provide a simple, flexible organization of control and operation that would suit any normal formation without elaborate preparation. We approached the problem from the starting point that transportation by air was no more extraordinary than movement by road, rail, or boat; it was merely one method of moving things and men. There is indeed only one test of air-mindedness, and that is not whether you can fly an aeroplane, but whether you regard it as a vehicle. If you do, you are air-minded; if you regard it as anything else—a weapon, a sporting adjunct, or a bag of tricks—you can be an air marshal, but you are not air-minded.

The 81st West African Division was training in the jungle near Bombay, and I flew down to spend a few days with them. Their discipline and smartness were impressive, and they were more obviously at home in the jungle than any other troops I had yet seen. They had neither animals nor vehicles with their fighting units, but were organized on a man-pack basis. In order to see what this meant, I did what I have often found very enlightening with a new organization. I had a formal parade. A battalion and a battery at war establishment were drawn up for inspection, with every man in his place. I was at once struck by two things. First, by the horde of unarmed porters who were needed to carry supplies, ammunition, baggage, and the heavier weapons; second, by the large number of white men in a unit, fifty or sixty to a battalion. Accustomed as I was to Indian battalions in the field with usually only seven or eight Europeans, it struck me as an unnecessarily generous supply. I never changed that view and later experience confirmed it. This I know is rank heresy to many very experienced 'coasters.' I was constantly told that, far from being too many, with the rapidly expanded African forces, more British officers and N.C.O.s were needed. But these large British establishments in African units had great drawbacks.

The only way to fill them was to draft officers and N.C.O.s willy-nilly to them, and this did not always give the right kind. The European who serves with native troops should be not only much above average in efficiency and character, as he must accept greater responsibility, but he should serve with them because he wants to, because he likes them. Another effect of so many British was to stifle the initiative of the Africans. All commanders, even down to seconds-in-command of platoons, were British; the African N.C.O. thus had, at least during training, a white man always at his elbow to whom he could turn for orders. Naturally he did so, and when in battle the Britisher became a casualty or for some other reason the African was left on his own, he was lost. The Sudan Defence Force units, the only other African troops I had, up to then, commanded, seemed to me even after their expansion to have got a better answer, with their few but picked British officers and their Sudanese officers and N.C.O.s, temperamental perhaps, but trained to be full of initiative.

As the monsoon drew to a close our divisions slipped quietly away from Ranchi. The 5th and 7th went to Arakan, where they took over the front from the 26th Division, which went into Corps Reserve at Chittagong. The 81st West African Division was already collecting for its move down the Kaladan, when early in October XV Corps Headquarters was established in the jungle a few miles south of Bawli. On October 6 I left Ranchi, and, after a day with the army commander, flew to my new headquarters and took command of the Arakan front. Our plans for the offensive had been made, and all that was required at the moment were the usual final checks.

I had hardly had time to make a tour of the front by air, launch, and jeep, when I was summoned to Calcutta to act for General Giffard as commander in chief, Eastern Command. Lieutenant-General Sir Philip Christison, whom I knew very well, having been a fellow instructor at Camberley Staff College, was to replace me at corps. I left with many regrets, not only at parting from my staff, who had served me so very well, and for all of whom I had, and still have, a real affection, and from the troops, but at not having had the chance of wielding with my own hand the weapon I had seen forged.

I flew to Calcutta on October 15, 1943, without even an A.D.C. Nigel Bruce, who held that thankless post, had broken his leg immediately on arrival in Arakan, and I missed him badly. My aircraft, piloted by Air Commodore Gray, who had insisted on paying me this compliment, made an unexpectedly quick trip, and I arrived considerably ahead of time. No one was at Dum Dum airfield to meet me—I never did have much luck there—and so I wandered off rather forlornly to try to find a car. Eventually I forced a protesting Indian driver, who said he was waiting for a brigadier, to take me. A mile or so outside the airfield I met Brigadier Steve Irwin, the chief of staff of Eastern Command, coming to meet me at the correct time, and changed cars. I hope the other brigadier was not kept waiting too long.

As we drove out to Barrackpore I watched an army commander's black-and-red flag fluttering over the bonnet of the car, and wondered where I was really going.

CHAPTER IX

THE FOUNDATIONS

It was strange to find myself back at Barrackpore as an army commander, in the same room, at the same desk I had left a few months before as a corps commander. The scene was little altered, except that the rooms were more congested with staff officers and clerks, there were now huts all over the grounds, and more despatch riders noisily came and went under the windows. Yet great changes were in progress.

The army of which I took command was still the old Eastern Army of India, and I was thus, at the moment, under General Auchinleck, who had recently succeeded General Wavell as commander in chief, India. However, in August 1943 the British and United States governments had formed a new Southeast Asia Allied Command to control all forces in Burma, Ceylon, Malaya, the Dutch East Indies, Siam, and Indo-China. Admiral Mountbatten was appointed supreme commander, with, under him, three commanders in chief, for sea, land, and air. General Sir George Giffard was to be the land commander in chief at 11th Army Group, and I, as commander of the newly formed Fourteenth Army, should serve under him. This reorganization dividing Southeast Asia Command from India was carried out during the next two months. It entailed splitting my headquarters between the new Fourteenth Army and the revived Indian Eastern Command, and it gave me one immediate advantage—it relieved me of all responsibility for Bihar, Orissa, and most of Bengal, an immense weight off my shoulders.

I do not believe in the system, so popular in the war, of commanders when promoted taking with them from the formations they leave the cream of their staffs. These travelling circuses, grouped around particular generals, cause a great deal of heartburning and confusion. Not only is the subordinate headquarters skimmed of its best officers, but in the higher, a number of efficient and worthy officers are abruptly thrown out to make room for newcomers. I am not at all sure either that the practice is good for the generals concerned themselves. So, as usual, I arrived at Eastern Army without a following, and took over the complete staff as I found it.

Again, through no merit of my own, I was lucky. I soon found that Steve Irwin, who had recently been appointed brigadier-general staff, was an outstanding staff officer, with a first-class brain that grasped, and what was more important held to, the essentials of any plan or organization. Unruffled by crisis, he had a dry, keen wit in the summing up of people and affairs that I found refreshing. The transfers to other headquarters that now had to be made, did, however, give me an opportunity to introduce some officers of my own choosing. Chief among these was 'Alf' Snelling, to whom I had said good-bye in the sandstorm on Lake Habbaniyeh eighteen months before. He came to me now as my major-general in charge of administration. I knew that the campaign in Burma would above all be a supply and transport problem, and I was determined to get the best possible man to take charge of that side of it for me. I think I did.

Immediately on taking over I found myself confronted by three major anxieties—supply, health, and morale.

Supply was, of course, largely a matter of communications. The Fourteenth Army was deployed on a seven-hundred-mile front, from the Chinese frontier beyond Fort Hertz to the Bay of Bengal. Along the Indo-Burmese border, in a shallow curve, sweeps the wide belt of jungle-clad, precipitous hills, rail-less, roadless, and, for six months of the year during the monsoon rains, almost trackless. Sparsely populated by wild tribes, disease infested, and even unmapped in places, much of this great area had been penetrated only by occasional Europeans and then only in the dry season. It could fairly be described as some of the world's worst country, breeding the world's worst diseases, and having for half the year at least the world's worst climate. To move even small pack caravans by the few dry-weather tracks from Burma to India was so difficult that no proper trading route existed. To supply, move, and fight great armies in or through the mass of jumbled hills had for so long been regarded as impossible that no serious defence measures had ever been taken on India's eastern frontier. Nor had any effective communications either for trade or war been built.

Such roads, railways, and navigable rivers as there were stopped abruptly each side of the mountain barrier, a couple of hundred miles apart.

From the Indian side the fighting areas could be reached—but only circuitously—by railway and river; there were no through roads. From Calcutta the broad-gauge railway, for about half of the distance a single track, ran for 235 miles to Parbatipur. Here hordes of coolies unloaded the wagons and noisily transferred the contents to the ramshackle metre-gauge train that, if all had gone well, would be waiting. This then wandered up the Brahmaputra Valley to the ferry at Pandu, four hundred and fifty miles from Calcutta. The coaches and waggons were uncoupled and pushed, with much clanking and banging, on to barges. A slow river crossing and the laborious process was repeated in reverse on the opposite bank. Over at last and reassembled, the train rattled monotonously on to Dimapur, the terminus for the Central Front, over six hundred miles from Calcutta. If bound for the northern front, it continued its journey, even more slowly, to Ledo, more than eight hundred miles from Calcutta.

The line had been built mainly to serve the Assam tea gardens, and in peace its daily capacity had been only 600 tons. By the time the Fourteenth Army was formed, this had risen to 2,800, but even this was quite inadequate to supply British forces at Imphal, the Chinese at Ledo, and the ever-rising tonnage required on the American airfields for the traffic to China. Plans for increasing capacity were in hand, but it was obvious that India could produce little more in the way of railwaymen, and there was no possibility of getting British. The American Army came to the rescue with the offer of six battalions of railway troops, some four thousand seven hundred fully-trained railwaymen. Early in 1944 these troops took over the operation of the line, and by October they had raised capacity to 4,400 tons and by January 1, 1946, to 7,300 tons a day. This was possible owing to the large additional American staffs—on the lengths of line normally in charge of two British or Indian officers, the Americans were able to put twenty-seven officers, all professional railwaymen—because of the arrival of more powerful locomotives from America and Canada, and because of the drive and energy put into the task. Thus to treble the capacity was a great achievement without which the vast and mounting air supply to China could not have been undertaken. But this is anticipating. We had in the summer of 1943 to work on 2,800 tons capacity, and this would not nearly meet demands for stocking the bases at Dimapur and Ledo, the construction of the American airfields and the Ledo road, the lift for China, and the move of reinforcing formations, all added to normal maintenance. This railway, until we took Rangoon, remained our chief transportation link, and for the next year at least was a terribly limiting factor, indeed something of a nightmare. I remember once saying, 'Well, that railway's been washed away by floods, put out by bombing, swept away by landslides, closed by train wrecks; there's not much more that can happen to it.' But there was. We had an earthquake that buckled rails and shifted bridges over a hundred miles of it.

It was also possible to reach almost to the northern front by river. Leaving Calcutta by a winding route through the Sunderbans, the main stream of the Brahmaputra was reached and followed to Dibrugarh, a distance of 1,136 miles by water. For the Central Assam front, the river-head was Gauhati, near Pandu, but the capacity of this route was limited by the bottleneck of the metre-gauge railway, already overloaded, between Gauhati and Dimapur. The southern front in Arakan was reached by a tortuous combination of broad-gauge, river steamer, and metre-gauge, which ended at Dohazari railhead, thirty miles south of Chittagong.

To bridge the gaps between the railheads and the fighting lines, main all-weather roads were under construction in the autumn of 1943—from Ledo to the Chinese front, from Dimapur to the central front, and from Dohazari, south of Chittagong, for Arakan. The most important of these was that serving the main front, which climbed through the hills from Dimapur to Imphal and then wound down again almost to the Burmese frontier. This road, a truly magnificent engineering achievement, was of a quality and permanence beyond any other on the Burma front. There was something splendid in its sweep through jungle, along mountain flanks, and over torrents. Day and night without break thousands of lorries swung around its curves and ground in low gear up its gradients. Then from this main artery, at Imphal, branched off that crazy road to Tiddim, 180 miles away in the Chin Hills, zigzagging up cliffs, meandering through deep valleys, soaring again literally into the clouds. The making of this road was hardly a more wonderful feat than keeping it open against the spates, subsidences, and the great landslides of the monsoon. The Arakan road had its own difficulties to overcome. It did not cross the great mountains of the others, but it encountered innumerable *chaungs*, tidal creeks running up inland from the sea. It went through a country that produced no stone for road metal, and it was impossible to bring in the thousands and thousands of tons that would be required. My engineers proved equal to the need. They built the road with bricks, millions and millions of them. Every twenty miles or so was a great brick kiln, looking in the distance rather like a two-funnelled ship. We imported skilled brickmakers from India, brought the necessary coal by rail, boat, and lorry, and baked our bricks. A brick road is terribly apt in rain to sink into the earth, but constantly having fresh bricks relaid it held, a monument to ingenuity and determination.

These three roads were pick, shovel, and basket roads, made by human labour, with an almost laughable lack of machinery. The men who built them worked under the most arduous conditions of climate and with the most elementary scale of accommodation, often with the enemy within striking distance. The whole of the labour, many thousands, was Indian, and much of it came from the Indian Tea Association, which organized, officered, and controlled some forty thousand of its own workers. Without this contribution we should never have built either the roads or the airfields that were vital for the Burma campaign and for the supply of China.

Pushing forward also at this time, under the vigorous direction of American engineers, was the Ledo road, intended eventually to link up with the old China–Burma road via Myitkyina. This road was, in its standards, even more ambitious than the Imphal one. For its construction the Americans had available a quantity of road-making machinery that made our mouths water—and they knew how to use it. With Indian labour and American machinery, the road, covered by the Chinese divisions, was at this time, the winter of 1943, beginning to nose its way south.

Inadquate railways, shortage of motor transport, few roads and those at the mercy of climate, to say nothing of enemy action, made the movement of men and supplies a constant anxiety. Our immediate worry, however, was not only inadequate transportation but an actual lack of supplies, especially

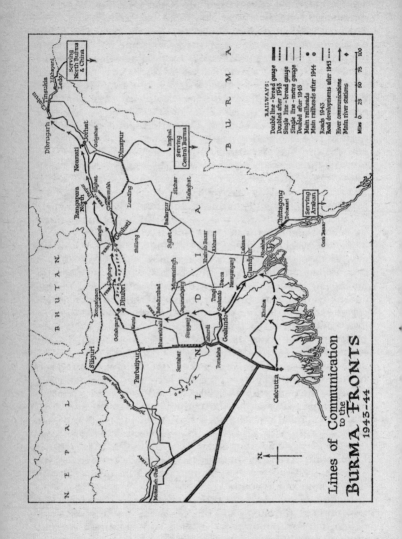

Lines of Communication to the
BURMA FRONTS
1943-44

RAILWAYS:
▬▬▬ Double line - broad gauge
▭▭▭ Doubled after 1943
━━━ Single line - broad gauge
──── Single line - metre gauge
╌╌╌ Doubled after 1943
● ● Main railheads after 1944
Main railheads 1943
╌╌╌╌ Road developments after 1943
→ River communications
◆ Main river stations

Miles 0 25 50 75 100

N

Serving North Burma & China

Serving Central Burma

Serving Arakan

NEPAL

BHUTAN

BURMA

INDIA

Rangoon

Ledo
Tirhapani
Tinsukia
Dibrugarh
Jorhat
Gogabat
Neamati
Dimapur
Imphal
Rangapara North
Sibsagar
Gauhati
Amingaon
Rangia
Dhubri
Bengaigaon
Goalpara
Shillong
Badarpur
Sibsagar
Silchar
Karaghat
Lumding
Chaparmukh
Mymensingh
Jagannathganj
Tungi
Goalundo
Khulna
Serajganj
Sara
Kaunia
Bhaurakhali
Bahadurabad
Bhairab Bazar
Pacca
Narayanganj
Dacca
Akhaura
Laksam
Chandpur
Chittagong
Dohazari
Coxs Bazar

Silguri
Parbatipur
Samahar
Santahar
Toroisha

Goldinghat
Bhalukpong
Mangaldai

Mokameh Ghat

Calcutta

G a n g e s

B r a h m a p u t r a

of certain items. Our ration strength was well over half a million, mainly, of course, Indian. Only a fraction of the total were fighting men, the larger proportion were the labour, administrative, technical, and noncombatant units, unavoidable in a country where every road, airfield, and camp had to be made from virgin jungle or rice field. We were a very mixed party, and Snelling's problems were not simplified by there being some thirty different ration scales in the Fourteenth Army. Among the Indians, these were based partly on religion, partly on district of origin, and partly, in such cases as the Indian Tea Association labour, on the special contract of their service. These scales were all reasonably adequate—the question was, 'Were the men, especially in the forward areas, getting them?' The answer was, as I had suspected, 'No.'

Meat is one of the main items on which a soldier fights. The British soldier without it cannot fight. Even the Indian, who in his village is often almost a vegetarian for economic reasons, as a soldier needs a regular ration of meat twice a week if he is to reach his full physical and intellectual vigour. Meat was one of our greatest difficulties. On the Assam front, owing to the complete lack of cold-storage facilities and of insulated wagons, the British troops in Imphal were receiving only half an issue a week of fresh meat; those forward of Imphal, that is, almost the whole of the fighting troops, got none. Instead, they received bully beef, a good enough food in itself, but terribly monotonous and very unattractive in hot weather when it flows half molten from the tin. There were no stocks of alternatives to bully beef, no tinned or dehydrated meat, and no combined meat and vegetable rations, such as were available in other theatres. To make matters worse, except for a rare issue of tinned herrings or bacon, there were no 'breakfast meats' at all. No animals could be purchased locally, there were no sheep or goats, and the only cattle were needed for the plough. To have slaughtered those would have given only a momentary relief and would have left us with another starving population on our hands. As a result, the average British soldier on the Assam front went month after month without tasting fresh meat. In Arakan, where the transport difficulties for live goats were not so impossible and where there were some local slaughter cattle, the British soldier was better off and received one or two fresh meat issues a week. For the rest, like his comrade in the north, he had to be content with bully beef.

The Indian soldier fared much worse. Near railheads and in Arakan he got up to two issues of meat a week, but forward of that he got none. The sepoy, whether Hindu or Mohammedan, does not eat tinned meat and, therefore, when fresh was not obtainable he went without meat altogether. This would not have been so serious were the authorized substitutes, additional issues of milk, and *ghi* (clarified butter), available. They were not. In Assam the total stock of *ghi* allowed for only thirteen days of normal issue, the arrival of further supplies was uncertain, and obviously no extra issues could be made. For milk it was much the same. Our stocks of tinned milk were very low. One reason for this is interesting. To guard against disruption of milk supplies by bombing in the United Kingdom the government had wisely laid in large stores of tinned milk in various parts of the country. The tins were sent from America in cardboard cartons. When demands for large quantities of milk for India were received the crisis in England was not so acute, and the food controller very sensibly decided to take the opportunity of turning over his store. So the milk was shipped to India. The cartons, already weakened by long storage and handling, rapidly deteriorated during the tropical voyage around the Cape, the tins rusted, and the cartons turned into pulp, making it impossible to pack them safely for the long rail journey across India with its interminable bumping and shunting. The wagons when opened on their final arrival at advanced railheads contained often a heap of battered, rusted tins and disintegrated cardboard. The unhappy supply officer was lucky if he rescued half in a still usable state, but, even so, gone was his chance of issuing a substitute for the non-existent meat.

Vegetables ranked with meat as an almost insoluble problem. Fresh vegetables could be grown in great quantity in Bengal and around Shillong in Assam, but the week or more's journey in lorries and steel railway wagons in great heat resulted usually in a putrid mass on arrival that could not be thrown away quickly enough. It was of course a little better in the cold weather, and again the troops in Arakan fared better, being nearer the sources of supply, but the almost complete lack of fresh vegetables in so many men's diets had a serious effect on health. The substitutes should have been tinned vegetables, tinned fruit, dried fruit, or dehydrated vegetables, but there were practically none of these in the forward supply depots. Stocks even of such basic commodities as rice and *atta* (Indian whole-meal flour) were a cause for anxiety. On the main front at Dimapur we should have had 65,000 tons of supplies for the troops already based on that depot, even without regard to the increased numbers expected. The actual stock, I found, was only 47,000 tons, a deficiency of 27 per cent. This was bad enough, but made much worse by the unbalanced state of the reserves with their almost complete lack of certain essential commodities. The supply situation was indeed so serious that it threatened the possibility of any offensive.

Although General Giffard had already set up his 11th Army Group Headquarters in Delhi, he had not yet had time nor had he the staff to take over administration from India. I, therefore, seized the opportunity of a visit by General Auchinleck to my headquarters to represent the dangers of the supply situation to him. He had only recently taken over in India and its seriousness was new to him. He summoned me to a conference with him and his principal supply officers in Delhi. On November 3, 1943, this meeting took place. Snelling was with me, armed as usual with all the facts and figures.

It appeared that to a large extent the Indian peacetime system of financial control still operated in the procurement of supplies. For example, when large quantities of dehydrated vegetables were ordered from Indian contractors, demands placed on the United Kingdom for tinned vegetables were, in accordance with peacetime rules, cancelled. The scale of issue of dehydrated vegetables is one-quarter that of tinned, so, for every hundred tons of dried ordered in India, four hundred tons of tinned ordered in England were cancelled. The quantities ordered in India and the deliveries promised were hopelessly optimistic so when the dehydrated failed to appear we were left without any vegetables at all. Again it had been ruled that supplies for formations either being raised or coming into India could not even be ordered until the troops had actually been raised or arrived. Not all our troubles, however, were due to a financial control intended for peace. The alarming shortages in such staples as rice and flour were caused by the failure of the Food Department to deliver as promised, which in turn rose largely because some provincial governments could not supply their quotas.

Whatever the causes, it was clear that the supply situation was critical, and equally obvious that something vigorous would have to be done to avoid disaster. Luckily, General Auchinleck was the man to do it. There was a considerable and prompt injection of ginger into the Indian administrative machine, military and civil. Even at the beginning of 1944 the results of Auchinleck's drive began to show. Gradually, with now and then a temporary setback, our rations and our reserves climbed up and up. It was a good day for us when he took command of India, our main base, recruiting area, and training ground. The Fourteenth Army, from its birth to its final victory, owed much to his unselfish support and never-failing understanding. Without him and what he and the army in India did for us we could not have existed, let alone conquered.

Our shortages were, unfortunately, not limited to supplies. In ammunition, for instance, we fell seriously below even the modest reserves calculated for jungle warfare, and they were much below those of any other theatre. Some typical shortages were:

Rifle	26 per cent
Sten- and tommy-gun	75 per cent
2- and 3-inch mortar	25 per cent
25-pounder H.E.	42 per cent
5.5-inch H.E.	86 per cent

Generally speaking, the ammunition we needed was in India, but that was a thousand miles from where we wanted it, and to bring it forward was a slow and laborious business. It was rather irritating, too, to find that some people had the habit of reckoning ammunition as on our charge the moment an order for its issue from an arsenal in India left Delhi, irrespective of the fact that it would be several months before it reached the Fourteenth Army depots. We were not only deficient of the ammunition but also of the guns to fire it. We were below our needs in most forms of equipment, notably vehicles, wireless sets, ambulances, and medical stores. In fact, we were short of everything.

Snelling's task was an immense one, and, having discussed it fully with him and selected the key men to work under him, I gave him a very free hand to carry it out. Soon, under his energetic direction, there were signs of improvement, and, while my anxieties on the supply side remained, I could see for myself wherever I went that our difficulties were being grappled with throughout the army and that we were getting increasing understanding and help from India.

My second great problem was health. In 1943 for every man evacuated with wounds we had one hundred and twenty evacuated sick. The annual malaria rate alone was 84 per cent per annum of the total strength of the army and still higher among the forward troops. Next to malaria came a high incidence of dysentery, followed in this gruesome order of precedence by skin diseases and a mounting tale of mite or jungle typhus, a peculiarly fatal disease. At this time the sick rate of men evacuated from their units rose to over twelve per thousand per day. A simple calculation showed me that in a matter of months at this rate my army would have melted away. Indeed, it was doing so under my eyes.

In anxious consultation with Snelling and my senior medical officers I reviewed our resources. To start with, I discovered that for some reason the medical establishments of the Fourteenth Army were lower than those of other British armies in Africa or Europe, and that actual strengths were gravely below even this reduced establishment. We were short of units, doctors, nurses, and equipment. Our hospitals had been of necessity expanded to take 25 per cent more patients than they were designed to hold. We now had twenty-one thousand hospital beds, all occupied. To nurse these seriously sick or wounded men we had a total of four hundred and fourteen nursing sisters, less than one nurse to fifty beds throughout the twenty-four hours, or in practice one to one hundred beds by day or night.

Demands for more nurses from home met with the answer that there were none to spare from other fronts and that, anyway, India should provide the nurses for Indian troops who formed the bulk of my army. We might just as well have been told that India must provide the aircraft for the air force. Aircraft were not made in India; nor were nurses. The Indian Military Nursing Service, struggling heroically against prejudice and every kind of handicap, was in its infancy and could only grow very slowly. In spite of all our efforts, and although General Auchinleck milked the hospitals of India to danger point to help us, it was clear that any increase in our medical strength would be grievously slow.

I knew we had to beat Germany first. I was even ready to accept the fact that the Fourteenth Army was the Cinderella of all British armies, and would get only what her richer sisters in Africa and Europe could spare. I would not grumble too much if we came last for men, tanks, guns, and the rest, but I would protest, and never cease from protesting, that we should be at the bottom of the list for medical aid. That was not fair, nor, I believe, wise.

However, as we had long ago discovered, it was no use waiting for other people to come to our help. Nor was it much use trying to increase our hospital accommodation; prevention was better than cure. We had to stop men going sick, or, if they went sick, from staying sick. We tackled this problem on four main lines :

(i) The practical application of the latest medical research.
(ii) The treatment of the sick in forward areas instead of evacuation to India.
(iii) The air evacuation of serious casualties.
(iv) The raising of morale.

The prevention of tropical diseases had advanced immensely within the last few years, and one of the first steps of the new Supreme Commander had been to get to Southeast Asia some of the most brilliant research workers in this field. Working closely with medical officers who had had experience of practical conditions, they introduced new techniques, drugs, and methods of treatment. Gradually the new remedies became available, although for long we lagged behind in their supply. Sulphonamide compounds, penicillin, mepacrine, and DDT all appeared later than we liked but still in time to save innumerable lives. Without research and its results we could not survive as an army.

It was, however, forward treatment that brought the first visible results. Up to now, when a man contracted malaria, he had been transported, while his disease was at its height, in great discomfort hundreds of miles by road, rail, and boat to a hospital in India. Before he reached there he had probably been reinfected several times, and while his first bout would be over he was booked for a relapse. In any case, he would not return over the congested line of communication for, on the average, at least five months; often enough he was employed in India and never returned. To avoid all this we organized 'MFTUS,' Malaria Forward Treatment Units. They were, in effect, field hospitals, tented or more often in *bashas*, a few miles behind the fighting lines. A man reached them within twenty-four hours of his attack of malaria and he remained there for the three weeks or so it took to cure him. He was back fit with his unit again in weeks instead of months, the strain on the line of communication was lightened, and he avoided the often terrible discomforts of the long journey. MFTUS had one other advantage. When morale was not high some men welcomed malaria and took no precautions to avoid it, reasoning that a bout of malaria was a cheap price to pay for getting away from the Burma front. If it only took them half-a-dozen miles from the front and brought them briskly back it was not so attractive.

For the wounded, forward surgical teams were introduced on an increasing scale. Working almost in the midst of the battle, specially selected surgeons, including some of the leading professors of our medical schools, performed major operations within a few hours of a man being wounded. Their work was brilliant, but it should be remembered that where the surgeon saved the individual life, the physician, less dramatically, saved hundreds by his preventive measures. We also sent nurses—when we had them—farther into the battle area than had been usual. There were some diseases, such as mite typhus, for which we had then no proved treatment, in which the patient's chance of survival depended more on the nurse than on the doctor. The extra danger and hardship these nurses cheerfully endured were repaid in lives many times over.

Air evacuation, in the long run, probably made the greatest difference of all to the wounded and sick. Only those who have suffered the interminable anguish of travel over rough ground or tracks by stretcher or ambulance and the long, stifling railway journey for days on end, with broken limbs jolting and temperatures soaring, can realize what a difference quick, smooth, cool transport by aircraft can mean. In November 1943 we had for all transport purposes, other than the maintenance of the 81st West African Division in Arakan, only some one hundred and twenty air sorties a month, but the number was rapidly growing and with it our technique of air evacuation. Later, light planes of the Moth, Auster, or L5 type picked up the casualties on air strips hurriedly cut out of jungle or rice field within a mile or two of the fighting. Each little aircraft carried one lying or two sitting patients and flew them to the supply strip, anything from ten to forty miles farther back. Here the casualties were transferred to Dakotas returning empty from the supply run and flown direct to a general hospital. There were, I remember, heated arguments as to where these hospitals should be situated. Roughly, there was the choice between putting them in such hot, sticky places in the plains as at Comilla or in the cool of the hills as at Shillong. I plumped for the plains, because there we could have an air strip almost alongside the hospital; to reach the hills would have meant long and trying road journeys. So our casualties went almost direct from the battlefield to the hospital and later as convalescents by road from the plains to the hills. There was some shaking of heads among the more orthodox, but the results justified it. One such hospital took in during 1944 and 1945 more than eleven thousand British casualties straight, in their filthy, blood-soaked battledress, from the front line. The total deaths in that hospital were twenty-three. Air evacuation did more in the Fourteenth Army to save lives than any other agency.

Good doctors are no use without good discipline. More than half the battle against disease is fought, not by the doctors, but by the regimental officers. It is they who see that the daily dose of mepacrine is taken, that shorts are never worn, that shirts are put on and sleeves turned down before sunset, that minor abrasions are treated before, not after, they go septic, that bodily cleanliness is enforced. When mepacrine was first introduced and turned men a jaundiced yellow, there was the usual whispering campaign among troops that greets every new remedy—the drug would render them impotent—so often the little tablet was not swallowed. An individual medical test in almost all cases will show whether it has been taken or not, but there are a few exceptions and it is difficult to prove for court-martial purposes. I, therefore, had surprise checks of whole units, every man being examined. If the over-all result was less than 95 per cent positive I sacked the commanding officer. I had to sack only three; by then the rest had got my meaning.

Slowly, but with increasing rapidity, as all of us, commanders, doctors, regimental officers, staff officers, and N.C.O.s, united in the drive against sickness, results began to appear. On the chart that hung on my wall the curves of admissions to hospitals and Malaria Forward Treatment Units sank lower and lower, until in 1945 the sickness rate for the whole Fourteenth Army was one per thousand per day. But at the end of 1943 that was a long way off.

My third great anxiety, intimately involved with health as with every aspect of efficiency, was morale. There was no doubt that the disasters in Arakan, following an unbroken record of defeat, had brought morale in large sections of the army to a dangerously low ebb. Morale was better in the forward combat formations, as most of the shaken units from Arakan had been withdrawn. IV Corps in the centre, and, I flattered myself, XV Corps in the south were staunch enough. It was in the rear areas, on the lines of communication, in the reinforcement camps, amid the conglomeration of administrative units that covered the vast area behind the front that morale was really low. Through this filter all units, drafts, and individuals for the forward formations had to percolate, and many became contaminated with the virus of despondency. In the summer of 1943 there was a depressingly high incidence of desertion from drafts moving up the line of communication. Right back into India rumours were assiduously spread picturing the Japanese as the super bogey-men of the jungle, harping on their savagery, their superior equipment and training, the hardships our men suffered, the lack of everything, the faults in our leadership, and the general hopelessness of ever expecting to defeat the enemy. Such stories were brought even by drafts from England. It was an insidious gangrene that could easily spread. Whether morale went up or down, and with it hope of victory, was an issue that swayed in the balance.

On our side we had the somewhat phoney propaganda that followed Wingate's raid and the more solid influence of General Giffard's character. Against us was that record of defeat, the lack of even elementary amenities, the discomfort of life in the jungle, and worst of all the feeling of isolation, with all the heartsickness of long separation from home. The British soldier, especially, suffered from what he felt was the lack of appreciation by his own people and at times of their forgetfulness of his very existence. The men were calling themselves a

'Forgotten Army' long before some newspaper correspondent seized on the phrase. It was an understandable one. After all, the people of Britain had perils and excitements enough on their own doorsteps, and Burma was far away. Its place in the general strategy was not clear, nor did what happened there seem vital. Much more stirring news was coming out of Africa. It was no use belly-aching because the Fourteenth Army was not in the headlines of the home papers; so far, we had not done anything to put us there. When we had won a victory or two we should be in a better position to complain. All the same, this feeling of neglect, of being at the bottom of all priority lists, had sunk deep. There was a good deal of bitterness in the army, and much too much being sorry for ourselves.

So when I took command, I sat quietly down to work out this business of morale. I came to certain conclusions, based not on any theory that I had studied, but on some experience and a good deal of hard thinking. It was on these conclusions that I set out consciously to raise the fighting spirit of my army.

Morale is a state of mind. It is that intangible force which will move a whole group of men to give their last ounce to achieve something, without counting the cost to themselves; that makes them feel they are part of something greater than themselves. If they are to feel that, their morale must, if it is to endure—and the essence of morale is that it should endure— have certain foundations. These foundations are spiritual, intellectual, and material, and that is the order of their importance. Spiritual first, because only spiritual foundations can stand real strain. Next intellectual, because men are swayed by reason as well as feeling. Material last—important, but last— because the very highest kinds of morale are often met when material conditions are lowest.

I remember sitting in my office and tabulating these foundations of morale something like this:

1. *Spiritual*
   (*a*) There must be a great and noble object.
   (*b*) Its achievement must be vital.
   (*c*) The method of achievement must be active, aggressive.
   (*d*) The man must feel that what he is and what he does matters directly towards the attainment of the object.

2. *Intellectual*

(a) He must be convinced that the object *can* be attained; that it is not out of reach.

(b) He must see, too, that the organization to which he belongs and which is striving to attain the object is an efficient one.

(c) He must have confidence in his leaders and know that whatever dangers and hardships he is called upon to suffer, his life will not be lightly flung away.

3. *Material*

(a) The man must feel that he will get a fair deal from his commanders and from the army generally.

(b) He must, as far as humanly possible, be given the best weapons and equipment for his task.

(c) His living and working conditions must be made as good as they can be.

It was one thing thus neatly to marshal my principles but quite another to develop them, apply them, and get them recognized by the whole army.

At any rate our spiritual foundation was a firm one. I use the word spiritual, not in its strictly religious meaning, but as belief in a cause. Religion has always been and still is one of the greatest foundations of morale, especially of military morale. Saints and soldiers have much in common. The religion of the Mohammedan, of the Sikh, of the Gurkha, and of the fighting Hindu—and we had them all in the Fourteenth Army—can arouse in men a blaze of contempt for death. The Christian religion is above all others a source of that enduring courage which is the most valuable of all the components of morale. Yet religion, as we understand it, is not essential to high morale. Anyone who has fought with or against Nazi paratroops, Japanese suicide squads, or Russian commissars, will have found this; but a spiritual foundation, belief in a cause, there must be.

We had this; and we had the advantage over our enemies that ours was based on real, not false, spiritual values. If ever an army fought in a just cause we did. We coveted no man's country; we wished to impose no form of government on any nation. We fought for the clean, the decent, the free things of life, for the right to live our lives in our own way, as others could live theirs, to worship God in what faith we chose, to be free in body and mind, and for our children to be free. We fought only because the powers of evil had attacked these things. No matter what the religion or race of any man in the Fourteenth Army, he *must* feel this, feel that he had indeed a worthy cause, and that if he did not defend it life would not be worth living for him or for his children. Nor was it enough to have a worthy cause. It must be positive, aggressive, not a mere passive, defensive, anti-something feeling. So our object became not to defend India, to stop the Japanese advance, or even to occupy Burma, but to destroy the Japanese Army, to smash it as an evil thing.

The fighting soldier facing the enemy can see that what he does, whether he is brave or craven, matters to his comrades and directly influences the result of the battle. It is harder for the man working on the road far behind, the clerk checking stores in a dump, the headquarter's telephone operator monotonously plugging through his calls, the sweeper carrying out his menial tasks, the quartermaster's orderly issuing bootlaces in a reinforcement camp—it is hard for these and a thousand others to see that they, too, matter. Yet every one of the half million in the army—and it was many more later—had to be made to see where his task fitted into the whole, to realize what depended on it, and to feel pride and satisfaction in doing it well.

Now these things, while the very basis of morale, because they were purely matters of feeling and emotion, were the most difficult to put over, especially to the British portion of the army. The problem was how to instil or revive their beliefs in the men of many races who made up the Fourteenth Army. I felt there was only one way to do it, by a direct approach to the individual men themselves. Not by written exhortations, by wireless speeches, but by informal talks and contacts between troops and commanders. There was nothing new in this; my corps and divisional commanders and others right down the scale were already doing it. It was the way we had held the troops together in the worst days of the 1942 retreat; we remained an army then only because the men saw and knew their commanders. All I did now was to encourage my commanders to increase these activities, unite them in a common approach to the problem, in the points that they would stress, and in the action they would take to see that principles became action not merely words.

Yet they began, as most things do, as words. We, my commanders and I, talked to units, to collections of officers, to headquarters, to little groups of men, to individual soldiers casually met as we moved around. And we all talked the same stuff with the same object. Whenever I could get away from my headquarters, and that throughout the campaign was about a third of the time, I was in these first few months more like a parliamentary candidate than a general—except that I never made a promise. One of the most successful of British commanders once told me that you could make an appeal to these higher things successfully to officers, but not directly to the rank and file. He underestimated his countrymen, and he had forgotten history. His dictum was not true of the England of the Crusades, of Cromwell, of Pitt, nor of Churchill. It was not true of my army, of either the British, Indian, Gurkha, or African soldier. I made a point of speaking myself to every combatant unit or at least to its officers and N.C.O.s. My platform was usually the bonnet of my jeep with the men collected anyhow round it. I often did three or four of these stump speeches in a day. I learned, or perhaps I had already learned in XV Corps, the various responses one got from the different nationalities. Even the British differed. A cockney battalion saw the point of a joke almost before it came, a north country unit did not laugh so easily, but when it did, the roar was good to hear. All responded at once to some reference to their pride in the part of Britain they came from or in their regiment. A lot more could be made of this local pride; it is a fine thing. All the British were shy of talk of the spiritual things. This was most marked in the English; the Welsh and Irish had fewer inhibitions on these subjects, and the Scots, who are reared more on the romance of their history, least of any. While Indian races differed in almost everything, they all were more ready than the British to respond openly to direct appeals on these more abstract grounds. They had not only a greater feeling for personal leadership, but their military traditions, their local patriotisms, and their religions were much more part of the everyday fabric of their lives than such things are with us. Their reaction was immediate and often intense. The Gurkha, bless him, made the most stolid of all audiences. He had a tendency to stand or sit to attention and his poker face never changed its expression until it broke into

167

the most attractive grin in Asia at a rather broad jest. With the African I was handicapped by language but, speaking without deep knowledge, I should say that, allowing for his greater lack of sophistication, he responded much as an Indian.

Language was a difficulty. The Indian Army now contained many recruits who had not had time to learn Urdu, and some units such as the Madras ones had hardly any Hindustani speakers. However, I managed somehow, although it was only the innate good manners of the Indian soldier that on many an occasion prevented laughter at some gaffe I made. I remember one day I spoke to a Gurkha battalion, drove a mile or so, and addressed an Indian one. My talk in substance was the same to both of them. When I had finished what I thought was a particularly eloquent Urdu harangue to the Indians, I turned to my A.D.C. and said with some pride, 'That was a pretty good effort, wasn't it?' 'Quite, sir,' he replied crushingly, 'but I suppose you know that after the first two sentences you relapsed entirely into Gurkhali!'

I learned, too, that one did not need to be an orator to be effective. Two things only were necessary: first to know what you were talking about, and, second and most important, to believe it yourself. I found that if one kept the bulk of one's talk to the material things the men were interested in, food, pay, leave, beer, mails, and the progress of operations, it was safe to end on a higher note—the spiritual foundations—and I always did.

To convince the men in the less spectacular or less obviously important jobs that they were very much part of the army, my commanders and I made it our business to visit these units, to show an interest in them, and to tell them how we and the rest of the army depended on them. There are in an army, and for that matter any big organization, very large numbers of people whose existence is only remembered when something for which they are responsible goes wrong. Who thinks of the telephone operator until he fails to get his connection, of the cipher officer until he makes a mistake in his decoding, of the orderlies who carry papers about a big headquarters until they take them to the wrong people, of the cook until he makes a particularly foul mess of the interminable bully? Yet they *are* important. It was harder to get this over to the Indian subordinates. They were often drawn from the lower castes, quite illiterate, and used to being looked down upon by their higher-caste fellow townsmen or villagers. With them I found I had great success by using the simile of a clock. 'A clock is like an army,' I used to tell them. 'There's a main spring, that's the army commander, who makes it all go; then there are other springs, driving the wheels round, those are his generals. The wheels are the officers and men. Some are big wheels, very important, they are the chief staff officers and the colonel sahibs. Other wheels are little ones, that do not look at all important. They are like you. Yet stop one of those little wheels and see what happens to the rest of the clock! They *are* important.'

We played on this very human desire of every man to feel himself and his work important, until one of the most striking things about our army was the way the administrative, labour, and non-combatant units acquired a morale which rivalled that of the fighting formations. They felt they shared directly in the triumphs of the Fourteenth Army and that its success and its honour were in their hands as much as anybody's. Another way in which we made every man feel he was part of the show was by keeping him, whatever his rank, as far as was practicable in the picture of what was going on around him. This, of course, was easy with staff officers and similar people by means of conferences held daily or weekly when each branch or department could explain what it had been doing and what it hoped to do. At these conferences they not only discussed things as a team, but, what was equally important, actually *saw* themselves as a team. For the men talks by their officers and visits to the information centres which were established in every unit took the place of those conferences.

It was in these ways we laid the spiritual foundations, but that was not enough; they would have crumbled without the others, the intellectual and the material. Here we had first to convince the doubters that our object, the destruction of the Japanese Army in battle, was practicable. We had to a great extent frightened ourselves by our stories of the superman. Defeated soldiers in their own defence have to protest that their adversary was something out of the ordinary, that he had all the advantages of preparation, equipment, and terrain, and that they themselves suffered from every corresponding handicap. The harder they have run away, the more they must exaggerate the unfair superiority of the enemy. Thus many of those who had scrambled out of Burma without waiting to get to grips with the invader or who had been in the rear areas in 1943, had the most hair-raising stories of Japanese super efficiency. Those of us who had really fought him believed that man for man our soldiers could beat him at his own jungle game, and that, in intelligence and skill, we could excel and outwit him.

We were helped, too, by a very cheering piece of news that now reached us, and of which, as a morale raiser, I made great use. In August and September 1942 Australian troops at Milne Bay in New Guinea had inflicted on the Japanese their first undoubted defeat on land. If the Australians, in conditions very like ours, had done it, so could we. Some of us may forget that of all the Allies it was Australian soldiers who first broke the spell of the invincibility of the Japanese Army; those of us who were in Burma have cause to remember.

But all this could not be convincingly put over by talking and education alone. It had to be demonstrated practically. This is what my predecessors had tried in Arakan, but they had been, among other things, too ambitious. A victory in a large-scale battle was, in our present state of training, organization, and confidence, not to be attempted. We had first to get the feel through the army that it was we who were hunting the Jap, not he us.

All commanders, therefore, directed their attention to patrolling. In jungle warfare this is the basis of success. It not only gives eyes to the side that excels at it, and blinds its opponent, but through it the soldier learns to move confidently in the element in which he works. Every forward unit, not only infantry, chose its best men, formed patrols, trained and practised them, and then sent them out on business. As was to be expected, the superior intelligence of our officers and men told. These patrols came back to their regiments with stories of success, of how the Japanese had walked into their ambushes, how they had watched the enemy place their observation posts day after day in the same place, and then had pounced on them, how they had followed their patrols and caught them asleep. Our men brought back a Japanese rifle, an officer's shoulder straps, a steel helmet. Sometimes they brought back even more convincing exhibits, as did the Gurkhas who presented themselves before their general, proudly opened a large basket, lifted from it three gory Japanese heads, and laid them on his table. They then politely offered him for his dinner the freshly caught fish which filled the rest of the basket. The buzz went round each unit, 'Have you heard about Lieutenant Smith's patrol? Cor, they didn't 'alf scrag the Nips...!' 'We rushed them as they were cooking, Havildar Bhupsingh bayoneted three....' 'Rifleman Gingerbir crept up *luki-luki* behind him with his *kukri*. The yellow-belly's head bounced three times before it stopped rolling!' The stories lost nothing in the telling, and there was no lack of competition for the next patrol. It went out with new men but under an experienced leader, and came back with more tales of success. Even if it returned with little to report, it had stalked its quarry without finding him, and that is one way to whet a hunter's appetite. In about 90 per cent of these tiny patrol actions we were successful. By the end of November our forward troops had gone a long way towards getting that individual feeling of superiority and that first essential in the fighting man—the desire to close with his enemy.

This recovery had already been accomplished to a very large extent in the two divisions, the 17th and 23d, which held the Assam front during the monsoon of 1943, before I took over command of the whole Burma front. All I did was to see that this became an army method and was carried on in all formations.

Having developed the confidence of the individual man in his superiority over the enemy, we had now to extend that to the corporate confidence of units and formations in themselves. This was done in a series of carefully planned minor offensive operations, carried out as the weather improved, against enemy advanced detachments. These were carefully staged, ably led, and, as I was always careful to ensure, in greatly preponderating strength. We attacked Japanese company positions with brigades fully supported by artillery and aircraft, platoon posts by battalions. Once when I was studying the plan for an operation of this kind submitted by the local commander, a visiting staff officer of high rank said, 'Isn't that using a steam hammer to crack a walnut?' 'Well,' I answered, 'if you happen to have a steam hammer handy and you don't mind if there's nothing left of the walnut, it's not a bad way to crack it.' Besides, we could not at this stage risk even small failures. We had very few, and the individual superiority built up by successful patrolling grew into a feeling of superiority within units and formations. We were then ready to undertake larger operations. We had laid the first of our intellectual foundations of morale; everyone knew we could defeat the Japanese, our object *was* attainable.

The next foundation, that the men should feel that they belonged to an efficient organization, that Fourteenth Army was well run and would get somewhere, followed partly from these minor successes. At the same time the gradual but very noticeable improvements that General Giffard's reorganization of the rear areas and Snelling's and the line of communication staff's almost incredible achievements within the army itself were making themselves felt. Rations did improve, though still far below what they should be; mail began to arrive more regularly; there were even signs of a welfare service.

An innovation was to be the publication of a theatre newspaper—*Seac*. One day I was told its editor designate was touring the army area and had asked if I would see him. A hefty-looking second-lieutenant was ushered into my office and introduced as Frank Owen. I had strong views on service newspapers, and sat the young man down for ten minutes while I explained to him exactly how his paper should be run and what were an editor's duties. He listened very politely, said he would do his best, saluted, and left. It was only after he had gone that I learned he had been one of the youngest and most brilliant editors in Fleet Street and had characteristically thrown up his job to enlist at the beginning of the war. *Seac* under his direction—and Admiral Mountbatten wisely gave him complete editorial freedom—was the best wartime service journal I have seen. It—and Owen himself—made no mean contribution to our morale.

One of the greatest weakeners of morale had been the state of the rest and reinforcement camps. In these camps on the line of communications all reinforcements to the various fronts were held often for weeks until required or until transport was available to take them forward. Almost without exception I found these places depressing beyond words. Decaying tents or dilapidated *bashas*, with earth floors, mosquito ridden and lacking all amenities, were the usual accommodation; training and recreation were alike unorganized; men were crowded together from all units. No wonder spirits sank, discipline sagged, and defeatist rumours spread. Worst of all, the commandants and staffs, with a few notable exceptions, were officers and N.C.O.s who were not wanted by units or who preferred the rear to the front. This lamentable state of affairs had to be taken in hand at once. The first step was to choose an officer with energy, experience, and organizing ability to take over-all charge. I found him in Colonel Graddige of the Indian Cavalry. The next was to select really good officers to command and staff the camps. Fighting unit C.O.s were naturally reluctant to spare their best, but when the need was explained, and in some cases a little pressure applied, they produced them. General Giffard was the first to appreciate the need and he gave us every possible help from the still meagre equipment and resources he had. Each camp was allotted to a forward division. That division provided its officers and instructors; the divisional flag was flown and its sign worn. Divisional commanders were encouraged to visit their camps, and from the moment a man arrived he was made to feel that he belonged to a fighting formation in which he could take pride. Training became real, discipline was reasserted, and in a few months the Fourteenth Army reinforcement camps, although still on a scale of accommodation and amenities much below what I could wish, were clean, cheerful, active parts of the army. Although Graddige controlled on an average fifty thousand men I was never allowed to give him even the acting rank of brigadier. Few colonels did more for the success of the Fourteenth Army than he.

Behind these camps Generals Auchinleck and Giffard had established two training divisions, the 14th and 34th, who drew their commanders and instructors from battle-experienced officers and N.C.O.s of the Fourteenth Army. Here recruits who had completed their elementary training passed on to practical jungle work. Within a few months the quality of the reinforcements reaching us from these divisions through the camps had completely changed, not only in skill but, above all, in morale.

In the main, as always, the men judged the efficiency of their show by the qualities of their leaders. Corps and divisional commanders had their men's confidence to the full; they were capable, experienced, and above all they were known to their troops. Our brigadiers and unit commanders had been carefully weeded and were an active, tough bunch of professional fighting soldiers. We kept them such. I was often throughout the campaign pressed to take straight into appointments as brigadiers or battalion commanders, sometimes even as divisional commanders, officers from home or India without war experience in command. I always resisted this. I would take them as seconds-in-command of brigades or battalions for a period of trial and instruction, but it would not have been fair, whatever their peacetime or training records, either to the men they were to command or to the officers themselves, to have thrust them raw into a jungle battle. Let them win their spurs. Most of them did, but some did not. It was as well to find out first.

The setting up of Southeast Asia Command, divorced from India, was itself a promise of better things, of new drive, new resources. When Admiral Mountbatten, the new supreme commander, appeared these hopes were confirmed. Youthful, buoyant, picturesque, with a reputation for gallantry known everywhere, he talked to the British soldier with irresistible frankness and charm. To the Indian he appealed equally. The morale of the army was already on the upgrade; he was the final tonic.

I met him for the first time on the brick-floored airfield at Barrackpore near my headquarters. He was an hour or so late, and I sat in my car, chatting to an American air general. There had been some confusion between the markings on Japanese aircraft, the single round red blob, and on our own, the R.A.F. red, white, and blue roundel, with its red centre. As a result the R.A.F. in the Burma theatre had repainted their markings to do away with their red centre and we had issued orders that an aircraft with any red on it was an enemy and could be shot at. The first thing I noticed, as Mountbatten's large transport aircraft came in to land, was the conspicuous red centres of the roundels on its wings and fuselage. Luckily no one was trigger happy, and he landed without incident.

His visit was very brief. He came to our headquarters, met the commanders and staff of the R.A.F., the U.S.A.A.F., and my chief staff officers, and gave us a short speech on what he intended to do. It seemed a lot, but we were all for it. I gathered from this talk and from the few minutes we had together that ideas of taking Burma from the north were off. The main offensive was now to come from a landing in the south. This seemed to be eminently sensible. It had often been discussed before, but was hopeless until we got the necessary naval covering forces and landing craft. When I asked him if these would be forthcoming, 'We're getting so many ships,' he told us, 'that the harbours of India and Ceylon won't be big enough to hold 'em!' We saw him off in his aircraft for Delhi—the red roundels would not matter much inside India—and went back to our work all the better for his visit and with confidence that the Burma front was at last moving up the priority list. We began to feel that we belonged to an efficient show, or what was going to be one, and that feeling spread.

A most potent factor in spreading this belief in the efficiency of an organization is a sense of discipline. In effect, discipline means that every man, when things pass beyond his own authority or initiative, knows to whom to turn for further direction. If it is the right kind of discipline he turns in the confidence that he will get sensible and effective direction. Every step must be taken to build up this confidence of the soldier in his leaders. For instance, it is not enough to *be* efficient; the organization must *look* efficient. If you enter the lines of a regiment where the quarter guard is smart and alert, and the men you meet are well turned out and salute briskly, you cannot fail to get an impression of efficiency. You are right; ten to one that unit *is* efficient. If you go into a head-quarters and find the clerks scruffy, the floor unswept, and dirty tea mugs staining fly-brown papers on the office tables, it *may* be efficient, but no visitor will think so.

The raising of the standard of discipline throughout the army, which, especially in many of the newly formed units, had deteriorated, was taken vigorously in hand by all com-manders. We tried to make our discipline intelligent, but we were an old-fashioned army and we insisted on its outward signs. In the Fourteenth Army we expected soldiers to salute officers—and officers to salute in return—both in mutual con-fidence and respect. I encouraged all officers to insist whenever possible, and there were few places where it was not possible, on good turnout and personal cleanliness. It takes courage, especially for a young officer, to check a man met on the road for not saluting properly or for slovenly appearance, but, every time he does, it adds to his stock of moral courage, and whatever the soldier may say he has a respect for the officer who does put him up. I would have made only one exception to the rigid enforcement of saluting. I would have declared Calcutta a nonsaluting area. That city was crowded with officers and men on leave; they had no mufti clothing, and to walk down Chowringhee, Calcutta's main street, was a weariness for all of us. Either one saluted every five steps or one was constantly checking soldiers for failing to salute. However, I was not successful in persuading my superiors to accept this innovation.

With growing confidence in the possibility of defeating the Japanese, the lift that the establishment of Southeast Asia Command gave to our hopes, and the rapid improvement in discipline, the intellectual foundations of morale were laid. There remained the material. Already the greater backing we were getting from Auchinleck's India, the steady improvements in transportation, and the general toning up of all rearward services were having their effect. Material conditions, though lamentably low by the standards of any other British army, were improving.

Yet I knew that whatever had been promised to the Supreme Commander from home, it would be six months at least before it reached my troops. We would remain, for a long time yet, desperately short. In my more gloomy moments—and in private I had plenty—I even doubted if we should ever climb up the priority list. There was only one thing to do if the hearts of my men were not to be sickened by hope deferred—admit to them the shortages, already only too obvious, but impress on them that:

(i) The Germans in Europe had to be beaten first. The Germans had a much higher scale of equipment than the Japanese. In fairness and common sense, therefore, the armies fighting them, however hard it was on us, should have first call on new equipment.

(ii) Within this limit every responsible commander would do his utmost to get what we needed.

(iii) If we could not get everything we wanted issued to us, we would either improvise it ourselves or do without.

(iv) We should be short of many things but I would not ask the troops to do anything unless there was at least the minimum of equipment needed for the task.

These things were frankly put to the men by their commanders at all levels and, whatever their race, they responded. In my experience it is not so much asking men to fight or work with inadequate or obsolete equipment that lowers

176

morale but the belief that those responsible are accepting such a state of affairs. If men realize that everyone above them and behind them is flat out to get the things required for them, they will do wonders, as my men did, with the meagre resources they have instead of sitting down moaning for better.

I do not say that the men of the Fourteenth Army welcomed difficulties, but they grew to take a fierce pride in overcoming them by determination and ingenuity. From start to finish they had only two items of equipment that were never in short supply: their brains and their courage. They lived up to the unofficial motto I gave them, 'God helps those who help themselves.' Anybody could do an easy job, we told them. It would take real men to overcome the shortages and difficulties we should be up against—the tough chap for the tough job! We had no *corps d'élite* which got preferential treatment; the only units who got that were the ones in front. Often, of course, they went short owing to the difficulties of transportation, but, if we had the stuff and could by hook or crook get it to them, they had it in preference to those farther back. One of the most convincing evidences of morale was how those behind—staffs and units—accepted this, and deprived themselves to ensure it. I indulged in a little bit of theatricality in this myself. When any of the forward formations had to go on half rations, as throughout the campaign they often did, I used to put my headquarters on half rations, too. It had little practical effect, but as a gesture it was rather valuable, and it did remind the young staff officers with healthy appetites that it was urgent to get the forward formations back to full rations as soon as possible.

The fair deal meant, too, no distinction between races or castes in treatment. The wants and needs of the Indian, African, and Gurkha soldier had to be looked after as keenly as those of his British comrade. This was not always easy, as many of our staff officers, having come straight from home, were, with the best will in the world, ignorant of what these wants were. There were a few, too, who thought that all Indian or African troops required was a bush to lie under and a handful of rice to eat. The Indian soldier's needs are not so numerous or elaborate as the Britisher's, but his morale can be affected just as severely by lack of them.

In another respect we had no favourites. I was frequently asked as the campaign went on, 'Which is your crack division?'

I always replied, 'All my divisions are crack divisions!' This was true in the sense that at some time or other every division I ever had in the Fourteenth Army achieved some outstanding feat of arms, and it might be any division that at any given period was leading the pack. The men of each division believed that their division was the best in the whole army, and it was right they should, but it is very unwise to let any formation, however good, be publicly recognized as better than the others. The same thing applies to units, and this was especially important where we had fighting together battalions with tremendous names handed down from the past, newly raised ones with their traditions yet to make, men of recognized martial races, and others drawn from sources that had up to now no military record. They all got the same treatment and they were all judged by results. Sometimes the results were by no means in accordance with accepted tables of precedence.

The individual, we took pains to ensure, too, was judged on his merits without any undue prejudice in favour of race, caste, or class. This is not always so easy as it sounds or as it ought to be, but I think promotion, for instance, went by merit whether the officer was British or Indian, regular or emergency commissioned. In an army of hundreds of thousands many injustices to individuals were bound to occur, but, thanks mainly to officers commanding units, most of the Fourteenth Army would, I believe, say that on the whole they had, as individuals, a reasonably fair deal. At any rate we did our best to give it them.

In these and in many other ways we translated my rough notes on the foundations of morale, spiritual, intellectual, and material, into a fighting spirit for our men and a confidence in themselves and their leaders that was to impress our friends and surprise our enemies.

BOOK III: THE WEAPON IS TESTED

CHAPTER X

THE BEST-LAID PLANS

Having set things in motion to deal with the three great internal problems of supply, health, and morale, I next turned my attention to the location of my own headquarters. As a place, I intensely disliked Barrackpore. Its sordid slums depressed me, as did the faded splendours of the pre-Mutiny buildings in which we worked and lived. The distractions of Calcutta were on our doorstep and were not good for us or for our work; worst of all, it was too far from the fighting areas. Air travel, the only practicable way of getting around the fronts, reduced time, but it by no means annihilated distance. By air Barrackpore to Imphal was about four hundred miles, the fighting was from one hundred to one hundred and fifty miles beyond that, and the northern Chinese front farther still. It was as if I were controlling from London a seven-hundred-mile battle front in the Italian Alps, only the roads and railways of Europe did not exist and the telegraphic and wireless communications were comparatively rudimentary. It was obviously necessary from every point of view to get my headquarters moved forward and, if possible, more centrally placed.

Our choice fell on Comilla, a largish town some two hundred miles east of Calcutta. For Bengal, its road and rail communications were good, it could be developed into an air centre, and being the capital of a district, it contained a number of large administrative buildings. A Bengali town, its walls mildewed and stained by past monsoons, is invariably depressing, but Comilla had a side line in melancholy all its own—its most noticeable features were the memorials erected to British civil and police officers, who, with monotonous frequency, had been murdered in the town by Bengali terrorists. My office windows would give me a good view of one such monument.

My next task was to get around my front. Arakan could wait. I was well acquainted with it and with what was going on there, but the main front in Assam I had not visited since June 1942, so I went there first. A lot had happened since the Retreat, not so much in the way of fighting as in administrative development. I found Lieutenant-General Geoffry Scoones, who commanded on that front, a little worried about the dispersion of his corps on a two-hundred-mile stretch. However, I felt that if the local situation on the Japanese side remained much as it was, if our intentions continued offensive, and, above all, if plans for a major amphibious operation were going to be realized, we need not be unduly anxious about the rather scattered dispositions of IV Corps.

From the Assam front I was called to Supreme Headquarters to attend conferences on the forthcoming general offensive. It was a sudden change from the jungle *bashas*, bivouacs, and worn green battle dress of IV Corps to the decorative interiors of New Delhi, thronged by every known, and some unknown, types of Allied uniform, male and female.

The conferences themselves were impressive affairs. They took place in the red sandstone secretariat building, where, as a junior staff officer, I had worked fifteen years before. The room in which they were held was large, and it was full. I had never seen so many people at a planning conference, but then, I reminded myself, I had never before seen a planning conference on this level. At the head of a very long table flanked by big windows sat the Supreme Commander, Admiral Mountbatten; down each side were ranged his commanders in chief and his principal staff officers, while at the foot a scurry of secretaries of two nations and six services ran a note-taking marathon. On ranks of chairs filling the rest of the room were American generals, Chinese admirals, British air marshals, Dutchmen, Indians, and what seemed to me a very large number of officers of all ranks and kinds.

The men who impressed me most in these gatherings were General Wheeler, the American chief administrative officer, obviously a man of great ability, and, what was even more important, experienced common sense, and my own commander in chief, General Giffard, who, although not at his best in debate of this sort, kept to the fore the element of practical soldiering. I was surprised to find that the conference often occupied itself with minor matters of equipment, moves of units, and a dozen things that might have been thrown to staff officers to handle. A good many hares were put up and enthusiastically chased. At times we seemed to be thinking more of the effects of our proposed action on Whitehall and Washington than on Tokyo. The truth was I had not been accustomed to the large staffs that had become popular in Europe and Africa, nor did I make allowances for the inevitable teething troubles of a great headquarters.

This was the first conference I had sat through at S.E.A.C. Headquarters, and I found it a little bewildering. I attended many in the next two years, and it was interesting to see how rapidly they became more business-like and effective as Admiral Mountbatten learned the job of supreme commander. Because he had to learn it. No Englishman ever got much opportunity to practice high command in peace, and none to be a supreme commander. Admiral Mountbatten's career as a naval officer, his command of a destroyer flotilla, and later an aircraft carrier with the quick-thinking, instant decisions and direct control of men that such tasks call for, were the finest possible training for tactical command. His period as chief of Combined Operations gave him an insight into the organization and working of the other two services that was of tremendous value to him; but the tactical planning of combined operations involves, more than any other, attention to and concentration on detail, in contrast to the broader, long-term considerations that are the province of the supreme commander. It was a member of the Chiefs of Staffs Committee for Combined Operations, where he came into contact with the wider direction of the war as a whole, that he served his apprenticeship for supreme command.

His comparative youth—he was ten years younger than I and twenty years younger than Stilwell—was something of a stimulant to most of us, and certainly to our troops. There may have been a few in the Navy, where they are more stripe conscious, who found it hard to forget that they were admirals when he was a commander, but in the Army we are more tolerant in these matters. We are too accustomed to the vagaries of acting and temporary rank. My substantive rank when I became army commander was still colonel, but I do not think that bothered anyone very much. From the very start no one could fail to like the Supreme Commander—even Stilwell, in a picturesque phrase, once admitted that to me

—and his quick brain, backed by a remarkable memory and tireless vitality, enabled him to grasp the intricacies of the whole vast organization of which he was the head. He came more and more to concentrate on essentials and to look farther ahead, until he was in every sense a real supreme commander.

I found Supreme Headquarters a fascinating place to wander through. It was full of interesting people, not least persuasive young men interested in selling short cuts to victory, of which they held the rights of way. These 'racketeers,' as I called them, were of two kinds, those whose acquaintance with war was confined to large nonfighting staffs where they had had time and opportunity to develop their theories, and tough, cheerful fellows who might be first-class landed on a beach at night with orders to scupper a sentry post, but whose experience was about the range of a tommy gun. I liked talking to them, and they were very willing to oblige me. Few of them had anything really new to say, and the few that had usually forgot that a new idea should have something to recommend it besides just breaking up normal organization.

While the new headquarters was quickly getting into its stride there arose in Delhi one disturbing feature—a growing danger of serious friction between Supreme Headquarters, Southeast Asia, and General Headquarters, India. Many of the newly arrived staff had no knowledge of India, its limitations or its capabilities, and sometimes they showed the arrogance of ignorance. The old hands at Indian Headquarters, in their turn, were too ready to resent their displacement in control of operations and to be sensitive to criticism of their past efforts. It was only the admirable good sense of the commanders themselves that avoided the catastrophe of a split into two factions, the pro-Mountbatten and the pro-Auchinleck. They set their faces firmly against any encouragement of this rivalry, and, in spite of the many real difficulties, cooperated fully and unselfishly. Had they not, success in Southeast Asia would have been longer delayed.

All this time, planning was proceeding at high pressure, and in what might justly be termed two camps—the 'Sac' and the 'Cic,' the Supreme Allied Commander's planners and the commanders in chief's planners. It was rather like a game of tennis. One set of planners tossed up a plan and served it to the others, who amended it and sent it back over the net. These returns went on for quite a time, until Sac or Cic eventually ended the rally by a triumphant smash that bounced the unfortunate plan right out of court. Early in the proceedings the Supreme Commander himself became aware of this, and it was not long before he organized a machine that really worked by the simple expedient of placing the commanders in chief's planners and his own in one joint body under the chairmanship of his senior planner.

The first directive from the Combined British and American Chiefs of Staff laid down two tasks for the Allied Forces in Southeast Asia. First, they were to engage the Japanese as closely as possible so as to divert enemy formations from the Pacific theatre, where the Americans were staging an offensive, and, second, they were to expand our contacts with China by developing the air route and by building a road through North Burma to connect with the old China–Burma route. Full advantage was to be taken of our increasing superiority at sea and in the air to seize some area which would induce a powerful reaction from the enemy. Mr. Churchill had for this purpose strongly urged an amphibious operation against Sumatra, and the first task of the planners had been to consider this. It was, however, decided that, with the resources available, it could not be undertaken. This was reported to the chiefs of staff, who replied that no more could be sent to Burma at this stage of the war. There was then no alternative but to abandon the Sumatra project.

Nothing daunted, the planning teams set to work to discover something less ambitious in the way of an amphibious operation. The Andaman Islands were obviously a second choice, but the best within the scope of the forces available. The capture of these islands, combined with operations in Burma itself, would, it was hoped, fulfil the directive. By the end of November these plans had crystallized into a series of connected offensives which were to take place in 1944. They were:

(i) The capture of the Andaman Islands by XXXIII Corps in an amphibious operation.

(ii) The occupation of the Mayu Peninsula in Arakan by XV Corps, as a preliminary to an amphibious assault on Akyab.

(iii) An advance across the Chindwin by IV Corps on the central front, with the object of drawing off the main

184

Japanese forces from (iv).

(iv) An advance by General Stilwell's Chinese from Ledo to Myitkyina to cover the building of a road to China.

(v) To help Stilwell's advance, a long-range penetration operation behind the Japanese opposing him, by Wingate's Special Force.

(vi) An airborne operation by the Indian Parachute Brigade and an Indian division to seize the Rail Indaw area, first to help Stilwell's advance and, second, to cooperate with (vii).

(vii) An offensive by the Chinese Yunnan armies into the Lashio–Bhamo area.

This programme, in addition to the Andamans assault, entailed a widespread offensive over the whole of the Burma front. The operations proposed were within the compass of the land forces and strategically well integrated. Obviously, however, as they included one major and one lesser amphibious operation, and at least two large airborne or air-supplied campaigns, to say nothing of other air transport commitments, the whole plan depended for its practicability on large numbers of naval landing craft and considerable air transport formations being available. Everyone at S.E.A.C. Headquarters appeared confident that these forces would be forthcoming from those already in or firmly allotted to the theatre. I had the pleasant feeling that now we really were on the map in Whitehall and Washington.

The first difficulty that arose was over command of the operations in Burma. It had originally been intended that Stilwell would command the Ledo advance and the Chinese Yunnan forces as soon as they entered Burma. At this time, November 1943, his command was in effect only a small corps, but it was hoped to bring in more Chinese divisions to join the Ledo force, and, when the large but amorphous Yunnan armies were added, Stilwell would have under him the rough equivalent of an army. The other Burma operations, in Arakan, on the central front, and the two airborne landings behind the Japanese would be under Fourteenth Army. Stilwell and I would each act as army commanders, under General Giffard, the commander in chief of 11th Army Group, who would thus have two fairly well-balanced armies in his group. This would have been the logical and militarily sound organ-

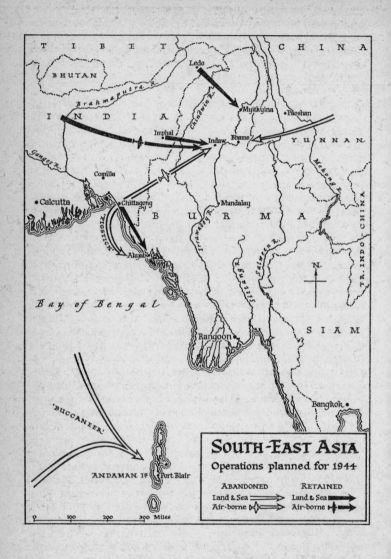

SOUTH-EAST ASIA

Operations planned for 1944

ization of the command. Stilwell, however, bitterly resisted it, and when that old man resisted anything it was a dour business. Dour, yet not without its humorous side. To watch Stilwell, when hard pressed, shift his opposition from one of the several strong points he held by virtue of his numerous Allied, American, and Chinese offices, to another, was a lesson in the mobile offensive-defensive.

Finally, to settle this matter of command, the Supreme Commander held a conference—wisely not so large a one as usual. There were present, besides the Supreme Commander and his chief staff officers, American and British, Generals Giffard, Stilwell, and myself. The proceedings opened by Admiral Mountbatten very politely suggesting that as he had a military commander in chief for an army group, and as his own headquarters was not designed to deal direct with subordinate formations, Stilwell should come under General Giffard's command. Stilwell at once pointed out that, as commander in chief of the Chinese forces in Burma, he had to obey the Generalissimo's order that these formations must remain under his direct command, subject only to the over-all control of the Supreme Commander. After some brisk argument around this contention, Stilwell came out as the commanding general of the American China–Burma–India Theatre. Giffard, he said, was not an Allied but a British commander in chief, and, as an American general, he had not the President's authority to put himself or his forces under a purely British commander. A good deal more time was occupied in arguing that. Then the redoubtable old man changed hats again and appeared in another role. As deputy Supreme Commander he was, anyhow, senior to any group commander and could not, therefore, fittingly be put under General Giffard! The more Admiral Mountbatten, showing infinite patience, reasoned with him, the more obstinate and petulant the old man became. The real trouble lay in the unfortunate personal antipathy that had existed between Giffard and Stilwell from their first contacts. While each had basic qualities that should have appealed to the other, they were such poles apart in manner, upbringing, outlook, and methods that neither could or would conceal his opinion of the other.

The temperature of the meeting rose. Stilwell fell back on a surly obstinacy that showed him at his worst. I, of course, said nothing, as I was only there to accept such decision as would be reached; neither did General Giffard who, in spite of considerable provocation, behaved, as he always did, with dignity. The American officers were in a peculiarly uncomfortable position—and they looked it—for, although of Admiral Mountbatten's staff, they realized clearly that Stilwell was very much the senior American general, and the Americans have a respect for seniority only equalled by our Navy. He would have been a brave American who would have stood up to Joe Stilwell to his face. Admiral Mountbatten was growing, understandably, more and more exasperated. He had, as one of the powers granted him by both the American and British Chiefs of Staff, the right to remove any Allied officer in his command if he thought fit, and thus held the final card if he cared to use it. It looked as if there could be no solution to the deadlock but a flat order from the Supreme Commander to his deputy.

Suddenly, with one of those unexpected gestures that I had seen him make more than once, Stilwell astonished everyone by saying, 'I am prepared to come under General Slim's operational control until I get to Kamaing!' With great relief, this surprising solution was hastily seized upon as a way out of the impasse. Actually it created an even more illogical situation. By it, I took command of all land operations on the Burma front, but I was responsible to my army group commander for only the Fourteenth Army portion of my force. For Stilwell's formations I was theoretically responsible only to the Supreme Commander, thus bypassing my own commander in chief. Rather rashly, Admiral Mountbatten inquired how Stilwell and I proposed to work this military nonsense. With one accord we asked to be allowed to discuss that together. The conference broke up, and Stilwell and I went straight to his Delhi headquarters, where he functioned as commanding general of the American China–Burma–India Theatre. He was, while determined on certain things, by no means uncompromising. Luckily he and I were determined on the same things—to get more Chinese divisions for the Ledo force, to push hard for Myitkyina, and to use Wingate's Chindits to aid that push. After my experience with Sun's 38th Chinese Division in the Retreat, I had always agreed with Stilwell that his Chinese, given a fair chance and a superiority in numbers, could beat the Japanese, and that he was the man to see they did. Tactically we were in agreement and, wisely, we avoided strategic discussion. He told me how he proposed to launch his

188

offensive and what his objectives were. I assured him that, as long as he went on those lines, he would not be bothered by a spate of orders and directives from me, that Wingate's force would be used to help him, and that my operations on the Assam front would keep the main enemy strength engaged. We shook hands; he went back to his headquarters and I to mine.

In practice, this illogical command set-up worked surprisingly well. My method with Stilwell was based on what I had learned of him in the Retreat—to send him the minimum of written directions, but, whenever I wanted anything, to fly over and discuss it with him, alone. Stilwell, talking things over quietly with no one else present, was a much easier and more likeable person than Vinegar Joe with an audience. Alone, I never found him unreasonable or obstructive. I think I told him to do something he did not approve of on only two or three occasions, and on each he conformed, I will not say willingly, but with good grace.

I was told that the command organization, especially the fact that Stilwell was under my operational control, was not to be made public. Whether this was face saving for Stilwell, on the lines of our Chinese allies, or to avoid the criticism that such an illogical set-up was bound to provoke, I do not know— both, probably. In any case, it did not affect me, and I was careful at all times to observe the condition. Generalissimo Chiang Kai-shek had at the end of November agreed to Stilwell and his Chinese army coming under my control, but had made it clear that this was a concession that applied only and personally to me. As he had never seen me, I cannot help thinking that, had Stilwell held other views, he might as easily have persuaded the Generalissimo to accept General Giffard.

After these conferences I returned to Comilla where Army Headquarters, on much the same organization as I had used for XV Corps, was now working smoothly. I never adopted the 'Chief of Staff System,' under which the chief general staff officer not only coordinates the work of the whole staff, but is the mouthpiece of the commander to the other principal staff officers and the heads of services, interpreted to them his intentions and wishes. I stuck to the old method of myself dealing directly with my principal staff officers. It is not that one system is better than another. Command is the projection of the commander's personality and whichever enables him best to instil his will into every part of his force is, for him, the better. The danger to be avoided is that generals may slavishly model their organization and even their behaviour on those of some outstandingly successful commander when they are quite unlike him in character, mental qualities, and perhaps appearance. Imitations are never masterpieces.

In Fourteenth Army, while I relied on my brigadier general staff to coordinate the complex working of the headquarters, my senior staff officer was actually my major-general in charge of administration. For an army engaged in a campaign in Burma this was logical, as adminstrative possibilities and impossibilities would loom large, larger than strategical and tactical alternatives.

The principles on which I planned all operations were:

(i) The ultimate intention must be an offensive one.

(ii) The main idea on which the plan was based must be simple.

(iii) That idea must be held in view throughout and everything else must give way to it.

(iv) The plan must have in it an element of surprise.

My method of working out such a plan was first to study the possibilities myself, and then informally to discuss them with my brigadier general staff, major-general administration, and my opposite number in the Air Force. At these discussions we would arrive at the broadest outline of possible alternative courses of action, at least two, more often three or four. These alternatives the B.G.S. would give to our team of planners, especially selected but comparatively junior officers, representing not only the general and administrative staffs, but the air staff as well. They would study the practicability, advantages, and disadvantages of each course and were at liberty to make new suggestions of their own or devise permutations and combinations of our originals. The results came to me and to the air commander as a short paper on which the two of us would reach a broad agreement. Thanks to the unselfishness of the air commanders, American and British, with whom I was lucky enough to work, we always did. The intelligence officer who represented the Japanese Command at my headquarters —a key appointment—then gave his idea of what the enemy reaction would be. I intentionally waited until I had selected my plan before considering the enemy response to it, because I intended them to conform to me, not me to them. There followed a meeting with all my principal staff officers at which I put over the plan, met or overrode any difficulties they might have, and sent them off to get things moving in their own spheres. The B.G.S. and the senior air staff officer then together dovetailed the land and air aspects and produced the operation orders or directives for subordinate commanders.

The wording of these orders I left to them, with the exception of one paragraph, the shortest, which I invariably drafted myself—the Intention. This gives, or should give, exactly what the commander intends to achieve. It is the dominating expression of his will by which, throughout the operation, every officer and soldier in the army will be guided. It should, therefore, be worded by the commander himself.

The next step was to take the operation order myself to the subordinate commanders who were to act on it. On principle, in the field, it is better to go forward to them than to call them back; to give them their orders at their headquarters rather than at your own. That applies whether you command a platoon or an army group.

In November 1943 about two-thirds of the Allied air squadrons operating in Burma were British, the rest American, but while the British preponderance always remained, the numbers of American transport squadrons rapidly increased until there they were greatly in the majority as cargo carriers. Much against Stilwell's wishes, Admiral Mountbatten had integrated the two air forces, with Air Chief Marshal Pierce of the R.A.F. as air commander in chief. Under him Major General Stratemeyer, U.S.A.F., at Eastern Air Command, controlled all Allied air formations in Burma. His command, thus, as long as I commanded all land forces on the Burma front, corresponded to mine on the ground. Under Stratemeyer, Air Marshal Baldwin commanded the Third Tactical Air Force with:

(i) The American Northern Air Sector, whose task was to support Stilwell and protect the air route to China.

(ii) 221 Group, R.A.F., cooperating with IV Corps on the main front, and

(iii) 224 Group, R.A.F., with XV Corps in Arakan.

Stratemeyer's headquarters was set up in a huge jute mill near Barrackpore, while Baldwin's Third Tactical Air Force Headquarters was alongside mine at Comilla. Brigadier-General Old, the commander of the joint American and British Troop Carrier Command, also established his headquarters there. In actual practice we, Fourteenth Army, Third T.A.F., and Troop Carrier Command, worked to a considerable extent as a joint headquarters. We pooled intelligence resources, our planners worked together and, perhaps most effective of all, the three commanders and their principal staff officers lived in the same mess. We even reached the stage when the Americans contracted the tea-sipping habit and the British learned to make drinkable coffee. With this intimate contact between Baldwin, Old, and myself and our staffs, direct references to Eastern Air Command from Fourteenth Army became less frequent, although occasionally Stratemeyer and I issued joint directives. I also found it less cumbersome to place demands on Brigadier-General Davidson's Strategic Air Force through Baldwin, who in effect became my opposite number in the air. Fourteenth Army owed an especial debt to Third Tactical Air Force, to Troop Carrier Command, to the Strategic Air Force and to their commanders. We grew into a very close brotherhood, depending on one another, trusting one another, and taking as much pride in each other's triumphs as we did in our own. The difficulties overcome and the successes obtained on the Burma front were a joint achievement.

Life at the headquarters followed a daily routine. At six-thirty I got up; at seven, saw the important messages received during the night; at seven-thirty to eight, breakfasted with the air commanders and our principal staff officers. I attended the joint air and land intelligence conference, known as 'morning prayers' at eight-thirty, when the events of the past twenty-four hours were related and commented on and those for the next described to a considerable audience by British and American army and air officers. I then dealt with any urgent matters with my B.G.S. and Major-General Administration, and saw to the multifarious business that comes to an army commander for decision. We all met again at lunch and usually talked shop through the meal. I left my office at about three, read a novel for an hour, had tea, and went for a walk in the cool with one of my staff; dined at seven-thirty, talked at the bar of the mess till half past nine, visited my operations' room for a final look at the latest reports, and was in bed by ten. If, between then and six-thirty, when my faithful Gurkha orderly, Bajbir, roused me, anyone disturbed me for anything short of a real crisis, he did so at his peril. I had seen too many of my colleagues crack under the immense strain of command in the field not to realize that, if I were to continue, I must have ample leisure in which to think, and unbroken sleep. Generals would do well to remember that, even in war, 'The wisdom of a learned man cometh by opportunity of leisure.' Generals who are terribly busy all day and half the night, who fuss round, posting platoons, and writing march tables, wear out not only their subordinates but themselves. Nor have they, when the real emergency comes, the reserve if vigour that will then enable them, for days if necessary, to do with little rest or sleep.

I had not long been back at my headquarters when events began which threatened to upset some, and then most, of the plans I had brought with me from Delhi. The seven offensive operations, scheduled for 1944, had been approved by the Combined Chiefs of Staff at the Cairo Conference at the end of November 1943. Only a week later, however at Teheran, Marshal Stalin promised to enter the war against Japan if all Anglo-American efforts were directed first to defeating Germany. Roosevelt and Churchill accepted the condition, and, as part of this concentration against the main enemy, more than half the amphibious resources of Southeast Asia were ordered back to Europe. As this rendered impossible the sea assault on the Andaman Islands, it was planned to use what remained for a landing behind the Japanese in Arakan. The Generalissimo had made the move of his Yunnan armies into Burma conditional on the Allies carrying out an amphibious operation against the Japanese in Southeast Asia. When he was informed that the contemplated attack on the Andamans had been abandoned but that a smaller landing would be carried out, he refused to regard this as fulfilling the agreement made at Cairo and withdrew his orders for the advance of the Yunnan force. This, in turn, would make the airborne landing of an Indian division in the Indaw area to cooperate with the expected Chinese advance from Yunnan useless, and indeed likely to be disastrous. So *that* operation, too, had perforce to be cancelled. In spite of this, plans and preparations for the Arakan landing were pushed on, but at the end of December, the Chiefs of Staff informed the Supreme Commander that, as the General-·issimo did not accept the Arakan landing as a substitute for the attack on the Andamans, amphibious operations in South-east Asia would be cancelled and *all* landing craft returned forthwith either to England or the Mediterranean. So that was that.

As our schemes, one by one, each with its picturesque code name, went the way of the ten little nigger boys, the planners worked manfully, and at times frantically, to adjust projects to melting resources. It was no fault of theirs or of the supreme commander's, who had been subjected to such sudden and violent cuts in the forces firmly promised, that our operations were thus whittled away. We tried to take these disappointments and all the wasted effort they entailed, philosophically and good-humouredly. Even the poor planners, in a whirl of feverish activity, could laugh at themselves, and one of them found time to put into verse something of the turmoil of plans, modifications, substitutes, cancellations, and code names in which they existed as:

> *Plan followed plan in swift procession.*
> *Commanders went; commanders came,*
> *While telegrams in quick succession*
> *Arrived to douse or fan the flame.*

The practical result of all this was that the projected operations in Southeast Asia for 1944 were reduced from seven to four all under Fourteenth Army.

(i) The overland advance of XV Corps in Arakan.

(ii) The advance of Stilwell's Chinese on Myitkyina.

(iii) A long-range penetration operation by Wingate's force to help Stilwell.

(iv) An advance on the main front in Assam by IV Corps to the Chindwin.

The correct strategy, that of a landing in southern Burma, had thus perforce to be abandoned, and we fell back on this four-pronged invasion. As I thought over the coming campaign, I was confirmed in my belief that, in spite of this, it should be possible to re-enter and reconquer Burma from the north; but there were disturbing features in our latest plan. The Japanese, we knew, were being steadily reinforced. On both the northern front, as more Chinese divisions came into action, and on the southern in Arakan, with its shorter and easier communications, we could count on concentrating superior strength to the enemy. In Assam, however, on the central front, where the decisive battles would have to be fought, the most optimistic calculations cast doubt on our ability to move and maintain, over so precarious a line of communication, forces even equal to those the Japanese could muster against us. To be frank, too, at this stage, much as our troops had improved in training and morale, I did not want the first big clashes to be on equal terms, division for division. I wanted superior strength at the decisive point for the opening of the struggle; after one victory to confirm the spirit of the Fourteenth Army, I should not worry so much about the odds against us.

I racked my brains and bullied my administrative staff to discover some means of getting even one more division on to the central front, but without avail. With the transportation we had at that time, and with the vast numbers of noncombatants needed to build roads and airfields for an advance, to squeeze in another fighting formation would have been to take a grave administrative risk. It was a risk, however, which I think I should have insisted upon, but I did not. Had the campaign taken place as planned we should have suffered from my failure to do so. I became a better judge of administrative risks later.

There was, of course, an attractive alternative by which the odds could be turned in our favour. If we could somehow seriously weaken the Japanese Army *before* we plunged into Burma, the whole picture would be changed. The only way this could be done was, at an early stage, to entice the enemy into a major battle in circumstances so favourable to us that we could smash three or four of his divisions. The thought of how to do this constantly nagged at my mind, but my generalship was not enough to find a way to provoke such a battle. I devoted myself, therefore, to ensuring that our offensive as planned should be successful.

Three of my commanders, Stilwell, Scoones, and Christison, had already discussed their plans with me, and had them vigorously in hand. There remained only the plans for Wingate's operation in support of Stilwell to be finally settled. Wingate and I, in Delhi and elsewhere, had discussed at length the principles on which his force should be used, its training, its composition, and his plan for its use. On the whole, Wingate and I agreed better than most people expected, perhaps because we had known one another before or perhaps because we had each in our own way arrived at the same conclusions on certain major issues, the potentialities of air supply, the possibility of taking Burma from the north, and in our estimates of the strengths and weaknesses of the Japanese. Of course we differed on many things. It was impossible not to differ from a man who so fanatically pursued his own purposes without regard to any other consideration or person.

His force, known for deception reasons as the 3d Indian Division, had in it British, Gurkhas, Burmese, and Africans, but no Indians. It had finished its training in India, and was now placed under my command. I called Wingate to Comilla to clear up several matters about the forthcoming operations on which there might be misunderstanding, and to give him his orders.

The proposed employment of Wingate's force had, like that of all others in the theatre, to be repeatedly modified and changed as resources available waxed and waned. He was, however, fortunate compared with others, in that while for them there was more waning than waxing, his resources had, thanks to the power and brilliance of his advocacy in Whitehall and Washington, greatly increased. He had, first of all, taken over complete the 70th British Division that had formerly been part of my XV Corps at Ranchi. This was done after the separation of Fourteenth Army from India, when the division, which had remained behind, was no longer under my command. I was not, therefore, consulted on the change; had I been I would have opposed it as strongly as I could. I was convinced—and nothing I saw subsequently caused me to change my mind—that a battle-tried, experienced, well-knit British division, like the 70th, would have more effect against the Japanese than a special force of twice its size. Moreover, the 70th Division was the only British formation trained in jungle warfare. It was a mistake to break it up. With it Wingate's force now had an infantry strength of over two divisions and an elaborate staff and administrative set-up. In addition it had the unique luxury of its own air force. Admiral Mountbatten, fired by Wingate's burning enthusiasm, had in turn persuaded General Arnold, head of the United States Army Air Force, to provide the 3d Indian Division with an American force, known as No. 1 Air Commando, containing not only fighters and light bombers for close support, but transport aircraft, gliders, light planes for intercommunication and evacuation of wounded, and the necessary maintenance organization. The pilots were carefully chosen and the commando raised and commanded by Colonels Cochrane and Alison, both outstanding fighting aces, and, what is not always the same thing, first-class organizers and leaders. One of the first difficulties that Wingate's force posed was this very air component. It was represented very strongly by the air staffs, American and British, that it was uneconomical permanently to lock up what was an appreciable proportion of our total air strength in Burma in support of one subsidiary operation. While I agreed in principle with this argument—private air forces are no less wasteful than private armies—I felt strongly that the air commando must remain part of Wingate's force. It had been generously given with that intention, it had wholeheartedly identified itself with the force, and to take it away now, apart from provoking heated squabbles with all sorts of people, would depress and upset the men just as they were about to embark on a most hazardous and arduous venture.

The next difficulty was with Wingate himself. I do not think he ever confided his intentions or ambitions fully to anyone, certainly not to his own staff or to his superior commanders, and it was evident to me from our discussions that there had been a considerable development in his views. His original idea had been that of a force, which, penetrating behind the enemy lines, would operate in comparatively small, lightly-equipped columns to harry his communications and rear establishments, while our main forces struck the decisive blows elsewhere. From this, as he increasingly appreciated the possibilities of air supply and transportation, he had gradually swung to the view that the main force should be the penetrating one, the subsidiary forces those that would remain, comparatively static, on what might be called the perimeter. This entailed, first, a great increase in the penetrating force, and, second, demanded for it a much heavier scale of armament as it would be required, not only to hold landing-ground bases against major attacks, but to assault strongly defended positions. As usual, I found Wingate stimulating when he talked strategy or grand tactics, but strangely naïve when it came to the business of actually fighting the Japanese. He had never experienced a real fight against them, still less a battle. The Japanese, unlike the Italians, with whom he had dealt in East Africa, were not to be frightened into a withdrawal by threats to their rear; they had first to be battered and destroyed in hard fighting. Wingate's men were neither trained nor equipped to fight pitched battles, offensive or defensive. The strategic idea that a penetration formation, operating behind the enemy, could be the decisive force was by no means new or unsound—I used it myself in the great Mandalay–Meiktila battle of 1945—but what would have been unsound was to attempt it with his present force and with our present air resources. At one stage of Southeast Asia planning, when it was intended to fly in a standard Indian division to the Indaw area where it would form the central core of an advance by the Yunnan Chinese, we were approaching the idea; but even when that operation had been abandoned, Wingate still hankered after a large force. I did not blame him; all commanders do.

His first demand to me was that I should give him Lomax's 26th Indian Division, which had originally been earmarked and trained for the Indaw landing. I refused. He already had more troops than we should be able to lift and supply by air. The division was the only reserve I had in my whole army; it would have been madness to break it up on the off-chance that Wingate might use it next year. Besides, I knew that if there were ever the chance of the decisive battle I hoped for, the division would be vitally needed.

However, Wingate was, as all good commanders should be, a most determined and persistent fellow, and he had set his heart on expanding his command. When he found argument failed, he turned to sterner measures. Such had been his romantic success with the Prime Minister that he claimed the right to send him messages direct, with his views and recommendations, irrespective of whether Admiral Mountbatten or any other superior commander agreed with them or not. I had been told this extraordinary arrangement existed, so when Wingate began by saying that, while he held a personal loyalty to me, there was a loyalty above that to an immediate commander, I knew what was coming. I asked him to whom it was. He replied, 'To the Prime Minister of England and to the President of the United States.' He went on to say that they had laid on him the duty of reporting direct to them whenever any of his superiors, in his opinion, were thwarting his operations. With the greatest regret he felt that this was such an occasion, and he must, whatever the consequences to me, so report to the Prime Minister. I pushed a signal pad across my desk to him, and told him to go and write his message. He did not take the pad but he left the room. Whether he ever sent the message I do not know, nor did I inquire. Anyhow, that was the last I heard of his demand for the 26th Division.

Next day we resumed our study of Wingate's operations. His original plan had been that three of his brigades should cross the Chindwin and reach their operational areas inside Burma by long jungle marches. After some two or three months the next wave of three brigades would go in on foot and relieve the first. At one stage Wingate proposed that a brigade should be flown in to Paoshan in China and enter Burma from the east. I had, however, come to the conclusion, with which Scoones agreed, that the Japanese were so strong along the Chindwin that it would be impossible to get brigades across without their being intercepted and probably stopped. Finding that, in spite of other air-supply commitments, we could, by supplementing No. 1 Air Commando at peak periods from the meagre resources of Troop Carrier Command, lift two brigades in March and two later, we decided that in each wave two brigades should fly and one march. Wingate, of course, knew that the fly-in of the 26th Division to Indaw was no longer contemplated, and I made it quite clear that I could allot him no more aircraft and no more troops, beyond an extra Gurkha battalion and some artillery that I gave him.

Wingate was dissatisfied with the rate of fly-in, and so was I. Still, as it was impossible to increase it without cancelling operations already begun, which I would certainly not do, or by taking aircraft off the Hump route to China which even the Supreme Commander had not the power to do, I had to stand firm on that, too. He made one last attempt to make me change by saying he could not accept the order I had drafted. I gave him an unsigned copy of the draft, told him to take it away, sleep on it that night, and come back at ten o'clock the next morning, when I would give him the same order signed. I told him I had never had a subordinate officer refuse an order, but if one did, I knew what to do. General Giffard happened to be visiting my headquarters, and I asked him to be in my office next day when Wingate came. I rather expected trouble, but, as soon as Wingate was seated in the chair on the other side of my desk, I passed the signed order across to him and, with a slightly wry smile, he accepted it without comment.

We set up Wingate's headquarters at Imphal alongside that of IV Corps. He was now developing his 'stronghold' technique, the method by which air strips as bases for his columns would be held. This demanded ever increasing scales of defensive equipment, artillery, anti-aircraft guns, mines, machine guns, sandbags, and the rest. I went over with him his ideas of the defence of one of these strongholds and found that he had little appreciation of what a real Japanese attack would be like. I told him to get Scoones's ideas on the 'floater model' of defence as practised in IV Corps, by which each garrison had a satellite mobile column to operate against the rear of an enemy-attacking formation. Scoones must have been a little amused to find this appear as a new Wingate method of defence. Meanwhile the first wave of the Special Force, as we usually called the 3d Indian Division, moved up into the forward areas from which it would fly or march into Burma.

Thus for the moment ended our orgy of planning, but in war it is not only one side that plans. I had throughout been conscious that, improving as our intelligence was since 1942, it was far from being as complete or accurate as that in other theatres. We never made up for the lack of methodically collected intelligence or the intelligence organization which should have been available to us when the war began. We knew something of the Japanese intentions but little of the dispositions of their reserves, and practically nothing about one of the most important factors that a general has to consider—the character of the opposing commanders. I had all the information I could obtain about Lieutenant-General Kawabe, my opposite number, who as commander in chief, Burma Army Area, controlled all Japanese land and air forces in Burma, but it did not amount to much on which to build up a picture of how his mind would work. At this time, from what I had seen of his operations, I could only expect him to be, like most Japanese commanders I had met, a bold tactical planner of offensive movements, completely confident in the superiority of his troops, and prepared to use his last reserves rather than abandon a plan. Many years before, when I was working for the Staff College examination, I had studied the Russo-Japanese War, and one thing about the campaign I had always remembered. The Russians never won a battle. In almost every fight they accepted defeat while a considerable portion of their forces, in reserve, was still unused. On the other hand, the Japanese were prepared to throw in every man, and more than once tipped the scales of victory with their very last reserves. The Japanese generals we were fighting had been brought up on the lessons of that war, and all I had seen of them in this convinced me that they would run true to form and hold back nothing. This was a source of great strength to them, but also properly taken advantage of might, in conjunction with their overweening confidence, be a fatal weakness.

I did, however, manage to get a photograph alleged to be that of Kawabe. It showed what might have been a typical western caricature of a Japanese; the bullet head, the thick glasses, and prominent teeth were all there. To these attractions he added a long waxed moustache, extending well beyond his cheeks. I pinned this picture to the wall of my office, opposite my desk. When I needed cheering I looked at it and assured myself that whichever of us was the cleverer general, even I was, at any rate, the better looking.

At the end of December I visited Stilwell's Northern Combat Area and his base at Ledo. I found the old man in good heart, as he had every reason to be. His advance, after some initial stickiness by the Chinese which he had overcome with characteristic vigour, had gone well. I saw a number of my old American and Chinese friends and left well satisfied with their progress and with my admiration for Stilwell's drive and power of personal leadership confirmed.

Then, my other fronts well under way, I turned my attention to Arakan, where I expected the first really serious clashes of the campaign to occur.

CHAPTER XI

PATTERN FOR VICTORY

As our wider visions of amphibious operations on the Arakan coast faded with the withdrawal of the resources necessary for them, we were thrown back on our original plans. These were certainly modest in their scope—a limited advance down the Mayu Peninsula to secure, first, the tiny port of Maungdaw and then the road running from it, through the central spine of the Mayu Range, to Buthidaung in the valley of the Kalapanzin River. Having got these we could, by using the Naf River and Maungdaw, supply our forward formations in Arakan largely by sea, while the road would give us the essential lateral communications to support forces on the east of the range. Thus firmly established on both its sides we should be in a position later to stage a more formidable offensive with Akyab and beyond as its objective.

We were careful in our plan to guard against the fatal errors of the 1943 campaign—attacks on narrow fronts and the neglect of an enemy outflanking counterstroke. The plan was for the 5th Indian Division to advance on the west of the Mayu Range and along its spine, while the 7th Indian Division kept pace with it on its eastern side. At the same time, the newly-arrived 81st West African Division (two brigades only) would move down the Kaladan Valley still farther to the east, and would, I hoped, be, in its turn, a threat to the Japanese flank and to their west-to-east communications. The 26th Indian Division would pull back into Army Reserve at Chittagong.

During November XV Corps completed its assembly for the advance. The West Africans cut themselves a jeep track for seventy-five miles and debouched at Daletme on the Kaladan River, building air strips along the river as they were to be the first normal formation to rely completely on air supply. It was not until January that they began to move down the valley and on the 20th they overran an enemy post in their first engagement. Showing great dash in the attack, they pushed steadily south towards Paletwa against stubborn resistance from small enemy detachments.

I was determined that this time the main Arakan advance should have adequate armoured support. Thanks to the drive, pertinacity, and ingenuity of Colonel Persse of the Indian Armoured Corps, and in spite of lack of landing craft, weak bridges, tidal creeks, swamps, quicksands, jungle, and Japanese aircraft a regiment of Lee-Grant medium tanks, the 25th Dragoons, was ready in time to go with the leading infantry.

Nor were tanks our only anxiety. The demands on air supply, many of which called for a high proportion of dropping, as distinct from landing, supplies were now in the Fourteenth Army very great. We needed vast numbers of parachutes. Then just as the 81st Division was committed I got the unwelcome news that the despatch of parachutes from India would be much less than we had been led to expect, and would indeed fall far short of our requirements. It was useless to hope for supplies from home. We were bottom of the priority list there for parachutes as for everything else. The position was serious. Our plans were based on large reserves of parachutes for supply dropping; if we had not got them we risked if not disaster, at least a drastic slowing up and modification of those plans. I went for a walk in the comparative cool of the evening and did some hard thinking.

Next morning I assembled Snelling and one or two of his leading air supply staff officers and explained the position. If we could not get proper parachutes of silk or other special cloth we must make them of what we could get. I believed it possible to make a serviceable supply-dropping parachute from either paper or jute. There are great paper mills in Calcutta; all the jute in the world is grown in Bengal and most of it manufactured there. I despatched officers forthwith to Calcutta to explore possibilities. The paper parachute, although I still believe it quite practicable, we could not obtain, because the manufacturers could not produce in time the kind of paper required. With jute we were more fortunate. My assignment officer visited some of the leaders of the British jute industry in Calcutta, told them our difficulty, and asked their help. He warned them that to save time I had sent him direct and that my need was my only authority. I hoped they would be paid, but when or how I could not guarantee. The answer of these Calcutta businessmen was, 'Never mind about that! If the Fourteenth Army want parachutes they shall have them!'

And have them we did. Within ten days we were experimenting with various types of 'parajutes,' as we called them. Some fell with a sickening thud; others had a high percentage of failure. By trial and error we arrived at the most efficient shape and weave for the cloth. In a month we had a parajute that was 85 per cent as efficient and reliable as the most elaborate parachute. It was made entirely of jute—even the ropes—and was of the simplest design. It dispensed with the vent at the top of the normal parachute as the texture of the jute cloth was such that the right quantity of air passed through it to keep the parajute expanded and stable. Instead of having one large vent it had innumerable tiny ones. It would have been risky to drop a man in a parajute, or a particularly valuable or fragile load such as a wireless set, but for ordinary supplies it worked admirably. It had, in addition, another advantage. The cost of a parajute was just over £1; that of a standard parachute over £20. As we used several hundred of thousands of parajutes we saved the British taxpayer some millions of pounds, and, more important even than that, our operations went on. My reward was a ponderous rebuke from above for not obtaining the supply through the proper channels! I replied that I never wanted to find a more proper channel for help when in need than those Calcutta jute men.

At this time the Japanese had one division, the 55th, in and in front of Akyab and another, the 54th, just moving into Arakan. Thus to deal with, at the most, two enemy divisions we were concentrating three (less a brigade) with one in near reserve. This gave us the preponderance needed for attack and in any case I did not intend to take more risks than I had to at this stage. All my plans were based on ensuring a superiority in numbers and force at the decisive points.

The maintenance of the 7th Division east of the Mayu Range was by mule and porter columns by bridle path over the steep Goppe Pass and then by boat on the Kalapanzin River. To supplement this laborious and precarious method we introduced yet another form of transportation to carry loads to the top of the pass—a rope way, last used in the Khyber on the northwest frontier of India. Creaking at every joint, the old rope way tugged valiantly away and saved the situation—

another and ancient monument to the versatility of Fourteenth Army engineers.

On the last night of November 1943 Christison began his advance. Pushing in the Japanese forward defences, he gained contact with their main positions in front of the Maungdaw–Buthidaung road, which midway between the two villages passed literally through the Mayu Range, more than a thousand feet high here, by means of two tunnels, relics of a light railway built to link Maungdaw with the rice fields of the Kalapanzin. This line had been bought out and dismantled by a river steamer company, who much preferred trade to follow rivers rather than go burrowing from one valley to another. The road followed the formation of the old railway and provided the only lateral communication fit for wheels until the Tangup–Prome road was reached, nearly two hundred miles to the south. The Japanese positions in the precipitous jungle hills covered the road continuously, but in three places they grew to an elaborateness and strength that justified the term fortresses. These were, first, at the tunnels themselves, and then in two great buttresses, one each side of the range at Letwedet on the east and Razabil on the west, which thrust forward to guard the approaches. All three positions were of the greatest strength. The Japanese had tunnelled far into the hills, with living accommodation, storerooms, and dugouts 20 or 30 feet below the surface. There were innumerable mutually supporting machine gun posts and strong points subterraneously linked. The extent of their preparation and the extreme formidableness of the defences were not, of course, then fully known to us, but it was obvious that they would be hard nuts to crack.

It now became necessary, if an attack on Letwedet was to be made, to pass vehicles, guns, and tanks across to the 7th Division. A footpath crossed the range, some five miles north of the Maungdaw–Buthidaung road, through the wild and winding Ngakyedauk Pass. It had been declared that this route could not in any conceivable circumstances be converted into a road, but a road there had to be and, poor as it was, this pass was the only hope of making one. Luckily the path was in our hands. On his first arrival Messervy, seeking a better way than the Goppe Pass by which to move and maintain his division, had told one of his brigadiers, Roberts, to find, if possible, an alternative. Roberts, who had an excellent eye for country, decided the Ngakyedauk was the only answer. He took measures at once to strengthen our hold on the pass, and when, soon after, the Japanese, realizing its importance, attacked, a detachment of Punjabis of his brigade were ready for them, and in an all-night fight beat them off. Had it not been for Brigadier Roberts' initiative, the story of Ngakyedauk might have been very different. While other troops held the enemy in his positions just to the south, the 7th Divisional Engineers set about driving their road. With the exception of two or three bulldozers they had only the field equipment of divisional engineers, but in an incredibly short time, right under the snub noses of the Japanese, they built, first a jeep track, and then, before Christmas, a real road, unmetalled of course, but capable of taking tanks and medium artillery. Over this pass, christened the 'Okeydoke' by the British soldiery, flowed the vehicles, stores, and equipment needed for the 7th Division's assault on Letwedet fortress. We, too, now had our lateral road connecting directly the 7th Division on the east of the range and the 5th on the crest and to the sea.

The assault on Razabil began. The Japanese positions were in a series of low but steep hillocks grouped round a main horseshoe-shaped hill known as Tortoise. On the last day of 1943 the artillery preparation began, but it took a week to reduce the outlying positions—a week of hard, fierce fighting. Then our troops slipped past Tortoise and took Maungdaw. I visited what was left of the village next day—a tangle of burned beams, riddled galvanized-iron sheeting, and smashed dock equipment, the whole overgrown with grass and weeds and plentifully laced with mines and booby traps. Loofah plants had spread everywhere and there were enough of these useful bathroom adjuncts to furnish us for years. The 'docks,' never much to boast about, looked incapable of restoration, but by the time the troops had cleared the mouth of the Naf River of Japanese snipers, the 5th Divisional Engineers, emulating their brethren in the 7th, had the 'port' cleared of mines, a couple of steamer berths prepared, and were ready to unload ships. Although the mouth of the river was still under long-range enemy artillery fire, the little coastal steamers crept past in the dark. Many familiar faces from the old Sunderbans flotilla of happy memory appeared, and Maungdaw sprang once more to life as much of the maintenance of XV Corps rattled over its ramshackle wharves.

With Maungdaw safely in the bag, Briggs and his 5th Indian Division set about the keep of Razabil fortress—the Tortoise. This was the first time we had assaulted an elaborate, carefully prepared position that the Japanese meant to hold to the last, and we expected it to be tough. It was. The attack was preceded by heavy bombing from the strategic air force and dive-bombing by R.A.F. Vengeances, directed by smoke shells from the artillery. After this pounding, which left the Japanese apparently unmoved, medium and field artillery took up the task and pumped shells from their accumulated dumps into the smoking, burning, spouting hillsides. Then the guns suddenly ceased and the Lee-Grant tanks roared forward, the infantry, bayonets fixed, yelling their Indian war cries, following on their tails. The Dismal Jimmies who had prophesied, one, that the tanks would never get to the line, two, that they could never climb the hills and, three, if they did the trees would so slow them up that the Japanese anti-tank guns would bump them off as sitting targets, were confounded. The tanks, lots of them—'the more you use, the fewer you lose'—crashed up the slopes and ground over the dug-in anti-tank guns. All was going well, but as the infantry passed ahead of the armour for the final assault the guns of the tanks had to cease firing for fear of hitting our own men. In that momentary pause the Japanese machine gunners and grenadiers remanned their slits and ratholes. Streams of bullets swept the approaches and a cascade of bombs bounced down among our infantry.

The attacks of the first three days shaved the Tortoise bare and cost us many casualties, but they did not shift the Japanese, burrowed deep into the hill, with their cunningly sited, wonderfully concealed, and mutually supporting machine guns. It was the old problem of World War I—how to get the infantryman on his enemy without a pause in the covering fire that kept his enemy's head down. It was solved in Arakan—and copied throughout the Fourteenth Army—by the tanks firing, first, surface-burst high explosive to clear the jungle, then delay-action high explosive to break up the faces of the bunkers thus exposed, and lastly solid armour-piercing shot as the infantry closed in. With no explosion, the last few yards were safe, if you had first-class tank gunners and infantrymen with steady nerves, who let the shot whistle past their heads and strike a few feet beyond or to one side of them. We had such tank gunners and such infantrymen—and they had the confidence in one another, even when of different races, that was needed. Gradually, bit by bit, Tortoise was nibbled away, until only in its very heart a few desperate Japanese, with a courage that, fanatical or not, was magnificent, still held out.

At this stage Christison swung his punch to the other side of the Mayu Range. Over the Ngakyedauk Pass tramped a brigade of the 5th Division to relieve the right brigade of the 7th Division and thus provide Messervy with a larger striking force. With it came the tanks of the Dragoons and a regiment of medium artillery. Where the Ngakyedauk road sank into the valley, a maintenance area for the 7th Division was laid out, with dumps, vehicle parks, and dressing stations—the famous 'Administrative Box.'

Christison and I were quite sure that, before they lost the Tunnels fortress, the Japanese would launch a counterattack. Signs were now becoming clear that this would be much more than a local affair in Arakan but rather something of the nature of a general offensive in Burma.

While our resources had been reduced by recalls to Europe, the Japanese were greatly increasing their Burma forces. Their 54th Division arrived from Java, their 31st from Malaya. In November the 15th was, we heard, marching from Siam, and there were indications of other formations being transferred from the Pacific. From mid-1943 the enemy total had risen from four divisions to seven by January 1944, with strong air reinforcements and, of course, considerable numbers of administrative and garrison units.

These increases from the global strategy aspect were satisfactory as we were fulfilling the Combined Chiefs of Staff directive to draw off enemy forces from other theatres and to prevent their reinforcing their Pacific front. From my point of view, however, it looked as if I were not the only commander in Burma staging offensives. My opposite number General Kawabe was not likely to have his army doubled for defensive purposes.

In Arakan our patrols and minor enterprises grew bolder and developed an especial skill in raiding small Japanese headquarters. From these operations we pinpointed enemy locations and learned that not only had a new Army Headquarters, the 28th, under Lieutenant-General Sakurai Seizo, been formed to control the Arakan front but that a formation of the Indian National Army, the force raised from Indian civilians and prisoners of war by Bose's puppet government, had been brought up close to the front. This indicated an intention to penetrate into India where the renegades would be used in the attempt to arouse rebellion.

I spent several days going round the Arakan front, watching the operations of both divisions, inspecting the Administrative Box, and discussing the future with Christison and his commanders. It was clear that the enemy counterstroke in Arakan would not be long delayed, and, while it was difficult to judge in what strength it would come, we both agreed it would take the form of an outflanking attack on the 7th Division's left. Christison was beginning the transfer of his weight to the east of the range at the time. This reinforcing of the 7th Division suited well with our ideas of the enemy's intentions and it was continued. At the same time Christison warned the V Force posts screening the left to be particularly alert, and for patrolling on that flank to be intensified to obtain warning of any hostile moves. Christison and I agreed that if any XV Corps troops were cut off they would stand fast. I promised that, when necessary, they would be supplied by air and that they would be relieved by our counterattacking forces, with whom they were to cooperate by taking the offensive themselves at the first opportunity.

When I left Messervy's headquarters east of the range, and drove through the Ngakyedauk Pass on my way to the air strip at XV Corps Headquarters at the end of my visit, Japanese fighters were beginning to come over in formations of up to a hundred at a time. This challenge to our air force was clearly the opening move of the enemy counterstroke. It was heartening to see how our fellows took it up. Our Spitfires, much inferior in numbers, fairly laced into the Zeros and began most effectively to knock them out of the sky. While these whirlwind dogfights streaked about high in the clear air, our reconnaissance Hurricanes kept up their steady patrols.

At Chittagong I warned Lomax and his 26th Division that they would probably be needed—and needed in a hurry. Then on to my headquarters at Comilla to meet General Giffard on his way, in his turn, to visit Arakan. I found him in complete agreement with my estimate of the situation and the measures we were taking. He also cheered me very much by telling me that he would order the 36th British Division from Calcutta into Chittagong to replace the 26th Division if I had to move it south. He went on to Christison and I checked over with Snelling, my chief administrative officer, Old, commanding the Troop Carrier Command, and Baldwin, of the 3d Tactical Air Force, the arrangements for air supply to XV Corps, should it be required. The joint air force and army organization which had been supplying the 81st West African Division had already been adjusted to meet possible new demands. Snelling quietly warned the air supply units and organizations at the Comilla and Agartala air strips to go full out on the pre-arranged packing programme and to stand by for twenty-four hours a day working. The supply units were reinforced by Indian Pioneers who took over most of the nontechnical work, additional transport was allotted to airfields, British reinforcement camps were told to earmark men to help supervise packing, and we called for volunteers to fly with the aircraft as 'kickers-out,' whose task it was to push the stores out of the aircraft. The complete maintenance of over a division for several days, everything that it would require, from pills to projectiles, from bully beef to boots, was laid out, packed for dropping, at the air strips. We were as ready as we could be.

Yet when the Japanese struck I am ashamed to say it was a surprise. On February 1, Frank Festing, the commander of the 36th British Division, arrived at my headquarters just ahead of his division. On the 2d General Giffard returned from his tour of Arakan and left again for Delhi next day. He had had a narrow escape when shot up by Zeros in the Ngakyedauk Pass. On the morning of the 4th, not feeling too bright myself, as I had just had my ninth daily ematine injection for dysentery, I was out at a reinforcement camp a few miles from Comilla watching a demonstration of the, to us, new lifebuoy flame thrower, when a motorcycle despatch rider roared up with a message. It told me that the Japanese had suddenly swept down out of the blue and rushed Taung Bazaar, five or six miles in rear of the 7th Division. The situation was obscure, said the signal, but it was clear that the enemy were in considerable strength.

The only thing I can think of more depressing than the effect of a series of ematine injections is the receipt of a message such as this. I had expected ample warning of the Japanese move, but this meant they had passed right around the 7th Division unobserved, and were within two or three miles of the Ngakyedauk Pass and the Administrative Box, which I knew was prepared for nothing more than raids. I was angry and disappointed that all our precautions had failed to give warning of the enemy move, but, trying not to look as anxious as I felt, I quickly got back to headquarters and telephoned Christison. He could tell me little more, except that Messervy's reserve brigade was engaged in heavy fighting somewhere south of Taung Bazaar. It was a real Japanese break-through and looked nasty. This was not cheerful news. I rang up Lomax at Chittagong and warned him to be ready to move at short notice. Meanwhile, my principal staff officers had assembled and I gave them the news, reminding them that things are never so bad—or so good—as they are first reported.

On February 5 I gave Lomax orders to move to join Christison at Bawli Bazaar and General Giffard flew to my headquarters. Some commanders in chief I would not have welcomed at such a moment, but General Giffard had the invaluable knack of not interfering, yet making one feel that he was there, calm, helpful, and understanding, if required. Early on the 6th I flew to Chittagong, saw Lomax just off to Christison, and watched the last of the 26th Division, workmanlike and cheerful, moving out. Then I saw Festing of the 36th Division, the brigadier commanding the Chittagong area of the line of communication, and Air Commodore Gray, commanding 224 Group of the R.A.F. Everything was working smoothly, there was no flap, and 36th Division was taking the 26th Division's place in Army Reserve. Next day, after a conference with Baldwin and Old of the Troop Carrier Command and a talk on the phone with Christison, I told Snelling to put the 7th Division on to air supply. The switchover, as far as I was concerned was simple, thanks to the preparation that Fourteenth Army, Third Tactical Air Force, and Troop Carrier Command together had made—it required only the word 'Go!' I made one attempt to interfere with Snelling's arrangements. 'Wouldn't it be a good idea,' I said, 'to put a case of rum in every fourth or fifth plane so as to make sure that when the stuff is shoved out the chaps will really search for it?' Alf Snelling looked at me in the slightly pitying way professionals look at amateurs. 'Sir,' he said, 'I have *already* given orders that a case of rum should be put in *every* plane!'

It might not have been so simple. The first flight of Dakotas had to turn back to avoid enemy fighters. Old himself at once took the pilot's seat in the leader of the next flight and led it in to drop on the 7th Division. The Spitfires and Hurricanes of the 3d T.A.F. swept up, the Zeros tumbled out of the sky or scuttled back. Air supply for XV Corps was on, and, as long as needed, never faltered. Snelling himself, and in turn his administrative staff officers, flew with the supplies. When an unfortunate crash during taking off destroyed three Dakotas and killed several of the British soldiers who were kickers-out, it only brought a new rush of volunteers. The pilots, American and British, flew three or four sorties a day, or more usually at night, as most of the supply dropping was done after dark to avoid the Japanese fighters, who still occasionally slipped in between our air cover. Day and night the army supply units continuously packed for dropping whatever was required, delivered it on the air strips, and loaded it into the aircraft. All around the clock, in the sunshine or by the light of flares and car lamps, the ground crews, snatching their broken rest on the air strip, worked to turn round the Dakotas.

On the 8th I flew down to Christison's headquarters, which had been subjected to several jitter raids by parties of infiltrating Japanese. With my approval he pulled his headquarters back a couple of miles to Bawli Bazaar behind the river, where it was easier to protect. He was going to have a tough battle to fight, and it would not help if he and his staff were standing to alarm posts half the night. I knew only too well what that meant.

The situation was now fairly clear. Thanks to the Japanese habit of carrying orders and marked maps into action, we had an almost complete picture of their general plan. It was, as we would expect from them, tactically bold and based on their past experience of the effects of cutting our communications. They intended to destroy XV Corps and capture Chittagong as, it seemed, the first stage of an invasion of India.

The Japanese 55th Division, reinforced, and with detachments of the Indian National Army under its command, had been divided into three parts. The first or main striking force under Colonel Tanahashi, who had proved himself the most formidable of the enemy leaders in our 1943 Arakan disasters, was formed round his 112 Regiment and was about seven thousand strong. Its task was to move secretly through the jungle, between the left of our 7th Division and the right of the 81st West African Division, and seize Taung Bazaar from the east. It was then to turn south, overrun the Administrative

Box and cut the Ngakyedauk Pass, thus isolating the 7th Division. The second smaller force, a battalion group under Colonel Kubo, was to move even wider than Tanahashi, block the track south from Goppe Bazaar and, turning west over the

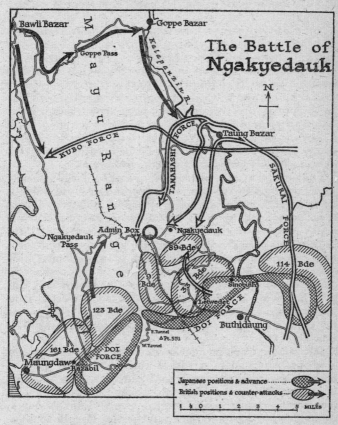

The Battle of Ngakyedauk

range, cut the main road to Maungdaw just south of Bawli Bazaar. This would isolate our 5th Division. The outflanking operations were under the direct command of Major-General Sakurai Tohutaro, the commander of the infantry of the 55th Division, not to be confused with the Lieutenant-General Sakurai Seizo, 28th Army commander. The third Japanese force, known as Doi Force, consisting of the remainder of the 55th Division and some other troops, was to put in holding attacks from the south on both our 5th and 7th Divisions. Over-all command of the whole Arakan offensive was in the hands of Lieutenant-General Hanaya, commander of the 55th Division.

The basic idea was that the British divisions, when thus cut off, would behave as they had in the past, and, deprived of all supplies turn to fight their way back to clear their communications. The 7th Division would be destroyed as it tried to scramble to safety through the Ngakyedauk Pass. All the Japanese forces would then turn on the wretched 5th Division and annihilate it as it struggled to escape across the Naf River. Chittagong would be the next stop for the victorious Sakurai. There the local population, rallied by the Indian National Army, would rise, and Bengal would lie open to the invader. The much heralded 'March on Delhi' had begun.

The operation was planned to a strict timetable under which the total destruction of the British forces was billed to be completed in ten days. The Japanese administrative arrangements were based on capturing our supplies and our motor transport by that time, and thence onward using them. So confident of success were they that they brought with them, in addition to a considerable artillery, units of gunners without guns to take over ours. None of our transport was to be destroyed; it was all wanted intact for the march on Delhi. The Japanese radio had evidently been issued a copy of the programme, as for the first ten days of the battle it announced the destruction of our forces strictly in accordance with the timetable.

Sakurai's outflanking operations began smoothly enough. With its local guides, Tanahashi Force, large as it was, succeeded in evading our posts and patrols, and in the early morning of February 4 burst into Taung Bazaar, scattering a few administrative troops located there. Sakurai's supply column, following up, was not so fortunate. The 7th Division, caught it as it tried to get by, destroyed its escort, captured a considerable quantity of gun ammunition, much rice, and a complete field ambulance, so that the Japanese supply arrangements, already rather sketchy, were further imperilled. The porters of this column were Arakanese Mohammedans and Mughs. All dropped their loads and the Arakanese made off into the jungle, but the Mughs, two hundred of them, preferred, wisely, to be captured rather than have their throats cut by the local Arakenese as they attempted to escape. These prisoners, fed off the supplies they had been carrying, made and maintained an air strip from which, during the operations, American L5 aircraft evacuated more than two hundred badly wounded men. They also did most of the picking up of airdrops for one of our brigades.

Having gained Taung Bazaar, without pause Tanahashi turned on the rear of the 7th Division, but here the Japanese met the second hitch in the great plan. When 9 Brigade of the 5th Indian Division had been sent through the pass a few days before to free the 7th Division for its attack on Buthidaung and Letwedet, a brigade (89) of the latter with the 25th Dragoons had been taken into divisional reserve. Messervy at once launched this brigade and the tanks in a counterattack to the north against Sakurai Force. The attack, especially the tanks whose presence east of the range had not been expected by the enemy, severely jolted the exultant Japanese, but it did not stop them. They swept on around its flanks and, wading through the breast-high dawn mist of the 6th, overran Messervy's divisional headquarters. A fierce dogfight ensued among the camouflaged tents and dugouts of the headquarters and along the jungle paths through it. Clerks, orderlies, signallers, and the staff officers threw back yelling rush after rush, but when the Japanese mortars made the area untenable, Messervy gave the order for the whole headquarters to fight its way through the Japanese to the Administrative Box. After destroying equipment, ciphers, and documents, they broke out in several groups, one led by the general himself. Casualties were numerous, but the bulk reached the Box, and Messervy had a reduced headquarters working and himself in control of his division again by the evening. The enemy swarmed around the Administrative Box, and to strengthen it Messervy called inside its perimeter two additional infantry battalions from certain outlying positions, for use as counterattack troops. The brigades of the 7th Division and 9 Brigade of the 5th Division, in accordance with the orders given for such a situation, dug in for all-round defence on their position, and beat off attacks, frontally from Doi Force and in rear from Tanahashi's troops. On the 7th patrols of the 7th Division moving up the Ngakyedauk Pass from the east were ambushed and had to turn back.

On the 8th patrols of the 5th Division from the west found a well-dug-in road block across the road, for on that day Doi Force and Sakurai's men had joined hands. The 7th Division was surrounded.

Meanwhile Kubo Force pushed north towards Goppe Bazaar, and, dropping a detachment to close the road south, turned directly west to cross the Mayu Range. There was no track; the ridge was almost precipitous for a thousand feet. The Japanese, ant-like, dragged their mortars and machine guns up the cliff and lowered them on the other side, until they burst out on the main Bawli–Maungdaw road, much to the surprise of certain administrative units peacefully pursuing their daily tasks. Bridges were blown up, camps fired on, XV Corps Headquarters harried, and for forty-eight hours the 5th Division was, like the 7th, cut off from all access by road. Well might Sakurai congratulate himself on the success of his blow, while Tokyo Rose crooned seductively on the wireless that it was all over in Burma.

Actually it was just starting. The leading brigade of Lomax's 26th Division, which I had placed under Christison, crossed the Goppe Pass into the Kalapanzin Valley, reoccupied Taung Bazaar, and began to press on Sakurai's rear. On the same day the rest of the division, relieved in the Bawli area by Festing's 36th British Division, followed. Briggs, with the 5th Division, although he had only two of his three brigades left, thinned out along his front, in spite of Doi Force demonstration attacks, and began to push up the Ngakyedauk Pass towards the 7th Division. At the same time, hurriedly organized forces from the 5th Division and corps reserve attacked from both sides the road block that Kubo Force had established south of Bawli Bazaar.

The Japanese knew they *had* to destroy the 7th Division in the next few days and they were going to spare nothing to do it. As their reinforcements arrived they flung them to the attack on the Administrative Box or against our entrenched brigades. The fighting was everywhere hand to hand and desperate. The Administrative Box was our weak spot. Commanded from the surrounding hills on all sides at short range, crowded with dumps of petrol and ammunition, with mules by the hundred and parked lorries by the dozen, with administrative troops and Indian labour, life in it under the rain of shells and mortar bombs was a nightmare. Yet the flimsy defences

domestic items as spare clothing, bedding, razors, soap, tooth-brushes, and the rest. All these items were replaced within forty-eight hours, and would have been delivered earlier had not the first drop unfortunately gone to the Japanese. One item, however, even Snelling could not replace. Messervy's red-banded general's hat had been left behind and not another of the size was available. However, even that loss was recovered a couple of weeks later, when in a party of Japanese, ambushed while trying to escape, one was found to be wearing the general's hat! It was duly returned, the temporary wearer hav-ing no further use for a hat of any kind. When I congratulated Snelling on the excellence of his organization he told me he regarded the Arakan show as merely a rehearsal for bigger things. How right he was!

By the middle of February the Japanese had shot their bolt; a week later Hanaya accepted defeat and, too late, attempted to pull out his disorganized units. Under cover of suicide de-tachments, who hung on to the last, Sakurai Force broke up into small groups and took to the jungle. But our 7th Divi-sion had already passed to the offensive, the 5th was battering through the Ngakyedauk Pass, which was fully opened on the 24th, and from the north swept down, on both sides of the ridge, the 26th and 36th Divisions. The hammer and the anvil met squarely, and the Japanese between disintegrated. Kubo Force, among the cliffs and caves of the Mayu Range, was destroyed to the last man in a snarling, tearing dogfight that lasted days, with no quarter given or expected. Of Sakurai's seven thousand men who had penetrated our lines more than five thousand bodies were found and counted, many more lay undiscovered in the jungle; hundreds died of exhaustion be-fore they reached safety; few survived. The march on Delhi via Arakan was definitely off!

The spirit and cohesion of XV Corps were shown when it quickly resumed its general offensive. In spite of the enemy reinforcements hurriedly brought up and the fact that air supply had to be drastically reduced to meet other calls, Buthidaung, a shattered shambles of a village, was taken on March 11. Then the reduction of the formidable Letwedet fortress was begun and achieved, bit by bit, in savage fighting. The Japanese made one desperate bid to hold up this attack. A suicide party, four hundred strong, infiltrated almost to the Administrative Box, but the troops in reserve quickly and with relish liquidated the lot.

West of the range Briggs's 5th Division rushed the last defenders of Razabil fortress and bayoneted them as they crouched deep in the hillsides. It was then the turn of the British 36th Division to attack the remaining enemy position, the Tunnels fortress. Reinforced, the Japanese fought and counterattacked every step, but Festing's men were not to be denied.

On March 27 a Welsh battalion supported by tanks assaulted the defences of the western tunnel. In the melee a tank fired a shell directly into the tunnel mouth. Ammunition stored inside blew up in a series of stunning explosions, and in the confusion the Welshmen rushed the enemy and the tunnel was ours. On April 1 another battalion, the Gloucesters, attacked the eastern tunnel positions and took a beating; but, with true West Country doggedness, they had another go on the 4th. This time the Japanese had had enough and did not wait for them. The tunnel itself was taken on April 6.

The final step to clear the Tunnels area and to free the road for our use was the capture of the dominating hill known as Point 551, which overlooked a stretch of the road. It was under attack throughout April, during which the 26th Division delivered three separate assaults on it. Its capture on May 3, at the fourth attempt, was the toughest fighting of the whole Tunnels battle. I was glad it fell to Lomax and his 26th Division, for it was here in 1943 that the bottom had fallen out of our box and of our plan to hold the Maungdaw–Buthidaung road. It was the first time we had won a battle on a spot where we had previously lost one; later we were to do this again and again, and it always gave me an especial satisfaction. Revenge *is* sweet. The XV Corps had now achieved all the tasks I had set it.

In the Kaladan the 81st West African Division had by a rapid advance captured Kyauktaw and Apaukwa. The Japanese, realizing the danger to their communications, delivered a sudden and brilliant counterattack with four battalions under a Colonel Koba who, for it, was rightly promoted major-general. The West Africans, thrown into some confusion, were pressed back and finally withdrew to near Taung Bazaar.

It was now clear that the main enemy offensive was about to fall on the central front in Assam. Both my reserve divisions, the 26th and the 36th, were committed in Arakan, and it was therefore imperative to form a new reserve. I ordered Christison to begin to withdraw, first, the 5th Indian Division and later the 7th for transfer to Assam if needed. Meanwhile, although the 25th Indian Division had come to Arakan as a replacement, I decided to pull back the forward troops in Buthidaung, which was unhealthy and low lying, to a line avoiding the worst areas and capable of being held by a minimum of troops. A firm hold was kept on Taung Bazaar, the high ground overlooking Buthidaung, the Tunnels area, Maungdaw, and the mouth of the Naf River.

This Arakan battle, judged by the size of the forces engaged, was not of great magnitude, but it was, nevertheless, one of the historic successes of British arms. It was the turning point of the Burma campaign. For the first time a British force had met, held, and decisively defeated a major Japanese attack, and followed this up by driving the enemy out of the strongest natural positions that they had been preparing for months and were determined to hold at all costs. British and Indian soldiers had proved themselves, man for man, the masters of the best the Japanese could bring against them. The R.A.F. had met and driven from the sky superior numbers of the Japanese Air Force equipped with their latest fighters. It was a victory, a victory about which there could be no argument, and its effect, not only on the troops engaged but on the whole Fourteenth Army, was immense. The legend of Japanese invincibility in the jungle, so long fostered by so many who should have known better, was smashed. I could not help feeling an especial pride that it had been my old XV Corps that had done it. Under Christison's leadership they earned at least one of the three V's I had taken as its badge.

CHAPTER XII

THE NORTHERN FRONT

The northern was the most isolated of the Burma fronts. To reach it by rail—there was no road—you left Dimapur and continued your seemingly interminable journey through the tea-garden area of Assam. As you crept northward, it was impossible to avoid a growing feeling of loneliness, which even the sight of the increasingly busy airfields of the Hump route, strung along the line, failed to dissipate. At last Tinsukia, the junction for the Assam oil fields, was reached, and your train turned wearily into the branch for Ledo. Ledo, in December 1943, seemed rather like the end of the world. Instead, it was the start of the road to China, the road that, if it ever were built, would replace the one from Rangoon, so effectively closed in early 1942.

Many people at this time, Americans no less than British doubted if the Ledo road *could* be built. They doubted if the Chinese divisions would ever be able to drive back the Japanese and clear the route. They doubted if the Ledo railway would carry and maintain the troops, labour, equipment, and material required. They doubted if any road builders could overcome the monsoon climate combined with the extreme difficulty of the terrain. Many, even of those who believed it possible, did not think that the Ledo road would ever repay the expenditure in men and resources that would have to be devoted to it. Indeed, at this time Stilwell was almost alone in his faith that, not only could the road be built, but that it would be the most potent winning factor in the war against Japan. His vision, as he expounded it to me, was of an American-trained and -equipped Chinese force, of some thirty divisions to begin with, maintained, except for what was available in China, by the road from Ledo. This new model army under his command would drive through China to the sea and then with the American Navy strike at Japan itself.

I agreed with Stilwell that the road could be built. I believed that, properly equipped and efficiently led, Chinese troops could defeat Japanese if, as would be the case with his Ledo force, they had a considerable numerical superiority. On the engineering side I had no doubts. We had built roads over country as difficult, with much less technical equipment than the Americans would have. My British engineers, who had surveyed the trace for the road for the first eighty miles, were quite confident about that. We were already, on the central front, maintaining great labour forces over equally gimcrack lines of communication. Thus far Stilwell and I were in complete agreement, but I did not hold two articles of his faith. I doubted the overwhelming war-winning value of this road, and, in any case, I believed it was starting from the wrong place. The American amphibious strategy in the Pacific hopping from island to island would, I was sure, bring much quicker results than an overland advance across Asia with a Chinese army yet to be formed. In any case, if the road was to be really effective, its feeder railway should start from Rangoon, not Calcutta. If it had been left to me, on military grounds, I would have used the immense resources required for this road, not to build a new highway to China, but to bring forward the largest possible combat forces to destroy the Japanese army in Burma. Once that was accomplished, the old route to China would be open; over it would flow a much greater tonnage than could ever come via Ledo, and the Allied forces in Burma would be available for use elsewhere.

This became the fundamental difference between the American and the British outlook in Burma. To the Americans the reconquest of Burma was merely incidental to the reopening of land communications with China, and need be pursued only to the limited extent necessary for that purpose. To the British the reoccupation of Burma was not only an end in itself—the liberation of British territory—but, by the capture of Rangoon, the best means of opening up a really effective link with China. Both points of view were understandable and, with national backgrounds, almost inevitable. Unfortunately, they could easily be distorted, until some Americans could accuse the British of hoping to regain by the efforts of the Americans the empire they had lost, and the British could retaliate by alleging that several Chinese divisions and great logistical resources, devoted to an unsound and largely political American objective, were being held by one Japanese division, while the British fought the main enemy forces. These differences of approach had no serious effect on the relations between the troops, but they did lead in 1943 and early 1944 to a mutual lack of appreciation of their respective efforts.

The main trouble as far as we, the fighting formations, were concerned was due, more than anything else, to the segregation of the various fronts. The British could not see the Americans and Chinese fighting and enduring in the Hukawng Valley, any more than the Americans could see us waging desperate battles in Imphal and Arakan. Actual contact between the troops of both nations would have soon cured it. Indeed it did. It was noticeable that, when the American light aeroplane pilots began to help in the fly-out of thousands of British and Indian wounded, and the American Field Service Ambulance units were attached to our divisions, a strong sense of comradeship grew up between these magnificent Americans, who never spared themselves in their work of mercy, and our troops. Squabbles between allies are hard to avoid, especially when both have suffered disaster as we did in 1942, but, as the tide of war turned and the fronts drew closer together, the troops forgot them, and rejoiced in one another's successes.

In fact, more actual and determined opposition to Stilwell's strategic ideas came from Americans, who, like Chennault, thought all resources should be devoted to building up a great American air force in China rather than to creating a powerful Chinese army. Their theory was that the Japanese in China could be defeated by air power, with such support as local Chinese forces could provide. Stilwell, for personal and military reasons, bitterly opposed this idea. As soon as the American air force became a real nuisance to the Japanese, he affirmed, they would retaliate by an advance against its airfields. Then, unless there were a well-found Chinese army to protect them, they would be overrun and the air force put out of action. Stilwell was undoubtedly right, but the controversy inflamed the rivalry and jealousy between the two leading Americans. Their enmity did not help the Allied cause; still less did the activities of their publicity merchants.

However, it was not for me to decide the merits or demerits of the Ledo road. The Anglo-American Combined Chiefs of Staff had told Admiral Mountbatten to make the road, and so, in every way possible, even to devoting half the total transport lift and large British ground forces to the northern front, we in Fourteenth Army got down to helping Stilwell in what we knew was a tough assignment.

Before he came under my operational control, Stilwell had received orders from Admiral Mountbatten to occupy northern Burma up to the Mogaung–Myitkyina area, so as to cover the building of the road, and to increase the safety of the air route to China. The Chinese 22d and 38th Divisions, under Liao and Sun, had already reached Ledo from India, and their 30th Division with a three-battalion American regiment was to follow. In addition Stilwell had a Chinese light tank group, an irregular force of American-officered Kachin tribesmen, and I had given him the Fort Hertz detachment of a battalion of Burma Rifles with local levies. For air support he had the considerable American Northern Sector Air Force. The whole of this Chinese–American–British force was known, rather clumsily, as Northern Combat Area Command. Further, Wingate's Special Force of several brigades was to be put, mainly by air, in rear of the Japanese opposing Stilwell to cut their communications. Facing the Northern Combat Area Command was the 18th Japanese Division with two of its regiments in depth in the Hukawng Valley and the third held back as a possible reserve for the 56th Division watching the Yunnan Chinese. Stilwell should, therefore, even if the whole 18th Division were used against him, have a comfortable superiority in every respect. I was anxious that he should, as some of the first clashes of the new campaign would come here and a lot would depend on their result.

Stilwell held a multiplicity of offices and when he announced that he would personally take command of Northern Combat Area Command in the field there were not wanting those who thought that, instead of acting as a corps commander, he should have delegated that to some more junior general and placed himself at Supreme Headquarters, where he might properly perform at least some of his other functions. Personally, I think he was right. The most important thing of all was to ensure that the American-trained Chinese not only fought, but fought successfully. No one could do that as well as Stilwell himself. Indeed, he was the only American who had authority actually to command the Chinese. At that time, while there were several able American staff officers in S.E.A.C., I do not think there was one sufficiently experienced to take command of a corps in battle. From my point of view, too, I much preferred to have Stilwell himself under me. I knew that any other American officer would refer all instructions to him, wherever he was, and I did not want a repetition of the Chinese Command set-up of 1942.

In October 1943 the 38th Chinese Division began the advance from Ledo against slight opposition, but early in November the Japanese defence stiffened, and the Chinese, reverting to their old methods, sat down and dug in. Stilwell was away at the Cairo Conference, and Boatner, his deputy, in despair at failing to get them to move, sent a signal to Delhi reporting that the Chinese refused to advance. This had a depressing effect in headquarters from Delhi to Cairo, and produced a good many 'I told you so's' from both British and Americans. I was very disappointed when I heard, but consoled myself with the twofold thought that most troops are a bit sticky at times and that Stilwell was on his way back. He reached the N.C.A.C. front on December 21. On the 22d and 23d he toured the Chinese positions, injected ginger into the senior officers, both Chinese and American, and laid on an attack in superior force on the Japanese detachment blocking the way. On the 24th he saw the attack go in and stayed with the troops until the 30th, by which time the enemy had been completely cleaned up. On the 31st Stilwell flew to Delhi for the conference at which he placed himself under my operational control, and was back again a few days later to repeat the performance at the next holdup. After two or three of these minor successes, the Chinese began really to get their tails up. For the first time they were attacking and defeating a modern enemy—something that had never before happened in the history of China.

The Chinese were now firmly established at Shingbwiyang in the Hukawng Valley, and pushing for their next objective, Shaduzup, at the head of the Mogaung Valley. By December 27 the road had reached Shingbwiyang, a hundred and three miles from Ledo—a magnificent achievement by the American engineers under Brigadier-General Pick and the heterogeneous labour force of Indians, Kachins, and Nagas they controlled. To get this far, the road had been driven over the formidable Pataki Mountains, the most difficult section of the whole route. At Shingbwiyang the Chinese struck the fair-weather road the Japanese had built and this was, of course, a tremendous help in the construction of the new road, which generally followed the Japanese trace.

By February 1 the 38th Chinese Division had, after a series of small actions, occupied Thipha Ga, while a regiment of the 22d Division, moving wide on the right flank, cleared the Japanese from the Taro Valley, which lay on the east bank of the Chindwin, separated from the Ledo road in the Hukawng Valley by a range of rugged jungle hills. This was the 22d Division's entry into the campaign, and they did well. In all these actions Stilwell had kept a close hand on the Chinese troops, steadying them when they faltered, prodding them when they hesitated, even finding their battalions for them himself when they lost them. He was one of the Allied commanders who had learned in the hard school of the 1942 retreat. His tactics were to press the Japanese frontally while the real attacks came in through the jungle from the flank, with probably a road block well behind the enemy. In this way, by a series of hooks around and behind the Japanese, he pushed forward. He also was an advocate of the sledge hammer to crack a walnut at this stage. He saw to it that if a Japanese company was to be liquidated, it was attacked by a Chinese regiment.

At the beginning of March I visited Stilwell at Thipha Ga just as he was launching up to then his biggest attack for the capture of Maingkwan, a large village and the capital of the Hukawng Valley. Besides his two Chinese divisions, he now had with him the American Long-Range Penetration Regiment. Stilwell had changed its original commander for Brigadier-General Merrill, whom I had known well and liked. After him, the regiment was christened 'Merrill's Marauders.' Merrill was a fine, courageous leader who inspired confidence, and I congratulated myself that I had restrained my Gurkha orderly, that day in 1942, when he would have tommy-gunned a jeepload of men wearing unfamiliar helmets. If he had, the Marauders would have had another commander, and that would have been a pity.

Stilwell met me at the airfield, looking more like a duck hunter than ever with his wind jacket, campaign hat, and leggings. As always, he told me fully what was going on tactically, and explained his plan. Like most commanders I have known on the eve of a battle, he was concealing a certain jumpiness. He had had bad luck with the weather recently;

there had been unseasonably heavy showers. Rain now would make things very difficult. He was depending, too, on coordinated timing between Chinese forces and, as he knew better than I did, there was risk in this. But the plan was sound, the Chinese in good fettle, and the Americans out to mark their entry into the campaign. In addition to his dispositions for the immediate battle, Stilwell surprised me by showing me on a map his idea for a sudden dash at Myitkyina, which he thought might be brought off by an outflanking march over the Naura Hyket Pass and sudden descent on the town from the northwest, while the Japanese were concentrating on the defence of Mogaung. Naturally he could not forecast a date for this. As he said, it depended on how things went and when he got Shaduzup, his next objective after Maingkwan. This was the first I had heard of anything approaching a plan for the seizure of Myitkyina, and I do not know whether he had even discussed it with his staff. At any rate, he asked me very solemnly not to speak of it to *anyone*, and made it quite clear that that included not only my staff but my superior commanders. He gave as his reason that if his intentions got to Delhi there would be leakage, and that would be fatal to his plan. Actually there was, judging by experience, much more likelihood of leakage through Chinese channels than through S.E.A.C. or Eleventh Army Group, and I thought the real reason was that, if the operation did not come off or misfired, he did not want anyone to be able to say he had had a failure. I understood this feeling and, as the project depended on a good many intervening ifs, I gave him my assurance I would mention it to no one.

In any case I had not come to discuss the tactical conduct of Stilwell's campaign—I had every confidence in his handling of that and it was his business, not mine. The fly-in of Wingate's Special Force, due to commence on March 5, was intended primarily to help the American–Chinese advance, and I wanted to make sure he was completely familiar with the final arrangements.

Stilwell was always rather prickly about Wingate's force. To begin with, Mountbatten and Wingate between them had persuaded the American Chiefs of Staff to send United States troops, even if only a regiment, to the Burma front, when he himself had failed to get them. Further, he felt passionately that all American troops in the theatre should be under his direct command, and had been angered when they were allotted to Wingate. Stilwell had pressed for them to be transferred to him, and confessed quite frankly to me that he had been very surprised when Mountbatten yielded to his request. Nevertheless, he did not seem particularly grateful to the Supreme Commander and some bitterness remained. Nor did he approve of Wingate's long-range penetration methods; he preferred the short-hook tactics. He now professed doubts as to the value of Wingate's operation, but had to admit, when I put it to him, that if he were the commander of the Japanese 18th Division and suddenly found ten thousand troops sitting across his rear, cutting his communications, he would not feel too happy about it. At last he grinned at me over his glasses, and said, 'That'll be fine if Wingate does it and stays there; if he goes in for real fighting and not shadow boxing like last time.' I told him that my only doubt was, not that Wingate's people would shadow box, but that with his new stronghold technique they might get too pinned down. I promised that whatever happened we would cut the Japanese line of communication for him and keep it cut for quite a time. No commander could ask more than that.

I was struck, as I always was when I visited Stilwell's headquarters, how unnecessarily primitive all its arrangements were. There was, compared with my own or other headquarters, no shortage of transport or supplies, yet he delighted in an exhibition of rough living which, like his omission of rank badges and the rest, was designed to foster the idea of the tough, hard-bitten, plain, fighting general. Goodness knows he was tough and wiry enough to be recognized as such without the play acting, for it was as much a bit of stage management as Mountbatten's meticulous turnout under any conditions, but it achieved its publicity purpose. Many people sneer at generals who wear quaint headdress with too many or too few badges, carry odd sticks, affect articles of civilian attire in uniform, or indulge in all sorts of tricks to make themselves easily recognizable to their troops or to anybody else. These things have their value if there is a real man behind them, and, for the rest, his countrymen should forgive almost anything to a general who wins battles. His soldiers will. Stilwell, thank heaven, had a sense of humour, which some who practice these arts have not, and he could, and did, not infrequently laugh at himself.

The Maingkwan–Walawbum battle, while it did not, as we had hoped, destroy the Japanese 18th Division, was a triumph for the Chinese and a personal one for Stilwell. Merrill's Marauders duly captured Walawbum, thus cutting off the Japanese main force, but during the slow and overcautious Chinese advance the Americans were pushed out again and the bulk of the 18th Division extricated itself from the trap. The operation just missed complete success because Stilwell could not be everywhere at once, and at this time his actual presence was the only thing that would impart real drive to his troops. But we had now won a battle handsomely on each flank of the Burma front.

From the Northern Combat Area Command I flew back to my Comilla headquarters for a day, and then on to Lalaghat and Hailakandi where the two brigades of the first wave of Wingate's Special Force were ready to fly into Burma. Of this wave, 16 Brigade which was to march in was already well on its way. Starting from Ledo on February 8, it had pushed steadily southward, supplied by air through extremely difficult hill and jungle country, to the Chindwin near Singkaling Kamti. Here the rafts the troops had built were supplemented by rubber boats dropped by No. 1 Air Commando, and the brigade crossed to continue its arduous march through almost uninhabited country. In response to a request from Stilwell, the brigade raided Lonkin, some fifty miles south of Maingkwan, but found it practically empty of enemy. No opposition except a Japanese-led Burmese patrol or two was encountered. Passing the great Indawgyi Lake by the end of March, 16 Brigade had established itself in a stronghold christened 'Aberdeen,' some twenty-five miles from the Rangoon–Myitkyina railway, which was the main supply route for the Japanese 18th Division fighting Stilwell, and their 56th Division watching the Yunnan Chinese. The brigade had covered four hundred and fifty miles of about the most difficult country in the world in just more than six weeks—a magnificent feat of endurance.

On the morning of Sunday, March 5, I circled the landing ground at Hailakandi. Below me, at the end of the wide brown air strip, was parked a great flock of squat, clumsy gliders, their square wing tips almost touching; around the edges of the field stood the more graceful Dakotas that were to lift them into the sky. Men swarmed about the aircraft, loading them, laying out towropes, leading mules, humping packs, and

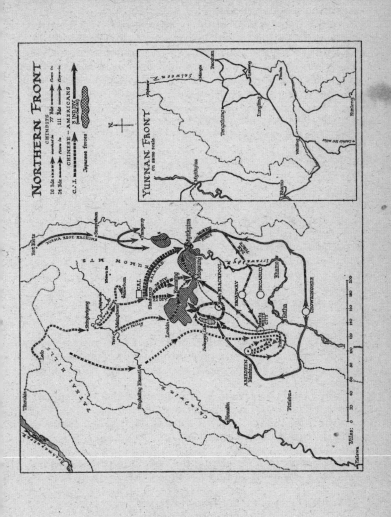

moving endlessly in dusty columns, for all the world like busy ants around captive moths.

I landed and met Wingate at his temporary headquarters near the air strip. Everything was going well. There had been no serious hitch in the assembly or preparation for the fly-in, which was due to begin at dusk that evening. For some days previously our diversionary air attacks had been almost continuous on Japanese airfields and communication centres to keep his air force occupied. Meanwhile, ostentatious air reconnaissances over the Mandalay district had been carried out in the hope of convincing the enemy that any airborne expedition would be directed against that area. The attacks on airfields were useful in keeping Japanese aircraft out of the sky, but the false reconnaissances, as far as I ever discovered, had little effect.

Just a month earlier, on February 4, Stratemeyer, the American commander of the Eastern Air Command, and I had issued a joint directive to Wingate and Cochrane, the American commander of No. 1 Air Commando. In this, Wingate's force was ordered to march and fly in to the Rail Indaw area (*Rail* Indaw to distinguish it from another Indaw not on the Mandalay–Myitkyina railway), and from there to operate under direct command of Fourteenth Army, with the objects of:

(i) Helping the advance of Stilwell's Ledo force on Myitkyina by cutting the communications of the Japanese 18th Division, harassing its rear, and preventing its reinforcement.

(ii) Creating a favourable situation for the Yunnan Chinese forces to cross the Salween and enter Burma.

(iii) Inflicting the greatest possible damage and confusion on the enemy in North Burma.

The tactical plan for getting the force into position behind the enemy was based on four assembly places:

'Aberdeen,' 27 miles northwest of Indaw.
'Piccadilly,' 40 miles northeast of Indaw.
'Broadway,' 35 miles east-northeast of Indaw.
'Chowringhee,' 35 miles east of Indaw.

These places were all away from roads and uninhabited. They were selected because there was enough flat ground to make the building of an air strip possible in a short time and because there was water in the immediate vicinity. They were, in fact, fancy names written on the map within striking distance of Indaw.

It was intended that in the first wave 16 Brigade should march to Aberdeen, 77 Brigade fly in two halves to Piccadilly and Broadway, and 111 Brigade land at Chowringhee. The remaining three brigades, 14, 23, and 3 West African, were to be held for the second wave, which it was expected would be required to relieve the first in two or three months.

As the afternoon wore on the atmosphere of excitement and suspense at Hailakandi grew—the old, familiar feeling of waiting to go over the top, intensified by the strangeness and magnitude of this operation. Everyone, even the mules, moved about calmly, quietly, and purposefully. Except perhaps for those patient beasts, it was, all the same, obvious that everyone realized that what was, up to this time, the biggest and most hazardous airborne operation of the war was about to begin.

During the morning the gliders had been loaded with supplies, ammunition, engineer equipment, signalling stores, and men's kits. In the late afternoon the first wave, 77 Brigade Headquarters, the leading British and Gurkha infantry, and a small detachment of American airfield engineers emplaned. Each Dakota was to take two gliders. This was a heavy load, and, as far as I know, never before had these aircraft towed more than one. There had been a clash of opinion among the airmen themselves on its practicability. Cochrane, in charge of the gliders, was confident it could be done; Old, whose Combat Cargo planes would provide the tugs, maintained it was unsound. Various airmen, British and American, took sides, and argument was heated. Eventually, after experiments, Wingate agreed with Cochrane, and then Baldwin and I accepted the double tow. Now as I watched the last preparations I was assailed by no doubts on that score. The Dakotas taxied into position. The towropes were fixed. Everyone was very quiet as the roar of engines died down and we waited for zero hour. I was standing on the air strip with Wingate, Baldwin, and one or two more, when we saw a jeep driving furiously towards us. A couple of American airmen jumped out and confronted us with an air photograph, still wet from the developing tent. It was a picture of Piccadilly landing ground, taken two hours previously. It showed almost the whole level space, on which the gliders were to land that night, obstructed by great tree trunks. It would be impossible to put down even one glider safely. To avoid suspicion no aircraft had reconnoitred the landing grounds for some days before the fly-in, so this photo was a complete shock to us. We looked at one another in dismay.

Wingate, though obviously feeling the mounting strain, had been quiet and controlled. Now, not unnaturally perhaps, he became very moved. His immediate reaction was to declare emphatically to me that the whole plan had been betrayed— probably by the Chinese—and that it would be dangerous to go on with it. I asked if Broadway and Chowringhee, the other proposed landing places, had been photographed at the same time. I was told they had been, and that both appeared vacant and unobstructed.

Wingate was now in a very emotional state, and to avoid discussion with him before an audience, I drew him on one side. I said I did not think the Chinese had betrayed him as they certainly had no knowledge of actual landing grounds, or, as far as I knew, of the operation at all; but he reiterated that someone had betrayed the plan and that the fly-in should be cancelled. I pointed out that only one of the three landing grounds had been obstructed, and that it was the one which he had used in 1943 and of which a picture with a Dakota on it had appeared in an American magazine. We knew the Japanese were nervous of air landing and were blocking many possible landing sites in North and Central Burma; what more likely than they should include a known one we had already used, such as Piccadilly? He replied that, even if Broadway and Chowringhee were not physically obstructed, it was most probable that Japanese troops were concealed in the surrounding jungle ready to destroy our gliders as they landed. With great feeling he said it would be 'murder.' I told him I doubted if these places were ambushed. Had the Japanese known of the plan I was sure they would either have ambushed or obstructed all three landing grounds. Wingate was by now calmer and much more in control of himself. After thinking for a moment, he said there would be a great risk. I agreed. He paused, then looked straight at me. 'The responsibility is yours,' he said.

I knew it was. Not for the first time I felt the weight of decision crushing in on me with an almost physical pressure. The gliders, if they were to take off that night, must do so within the hour. There was no time for prolonged inquiry or discussion. On my answer would depend not only the possibility of a disaster with wide implications on the whole Burma campaign and beyond, but the lives of these splendid men, tense and waiting in and around their aircraft. At that moment I would have given a great deal if Wingate or anybody else could have relieved me of the duty of decision. But that is a burden the commander himself must bear.

I knew that if I cancelled the fly-in or even postponed it, when the men were keyed to the highest pitch, there would be a terrible reaction; we would never get their morale to the same peak again. The whole plan of campaign, too, would be thrown out. I had promised Stilwell we would cut the communications of the enemy opposing him, and he was relying on our doing it. I had to consider also that one Chindit brigade had already marched into the area; we could hardly desert it. I was, in addition, very nervous that if we kept the aircraft crowded on the airfields as they were, the Japanese would discover them, with disastrous consequences. I knew at this time that a major Japanese offensive was about to break on the Assam front, and I calculated on Wingate's operation to confuse and hamper it. Above all, somehow I did not believe that the Japanese knew of our plan or that the obstruction of Piccadilly was evidence that they did. There was a risk, a grave risk, but not a certainty of disaster. 'The operation will go on,' I said.[1]

Wingate accepted my decision with, I think, relief. He had by now recovered from his first shock and had realized that the obstruction of one landing site need not hold all the implications he had imagined. We walked back to the group of officers and, with Baldwin's concurrence, I announced that the fly-in

[1] In an account of this incident written shortly afterward, but which I did not see until after his death, Wingate reversed his role and mine. In it he stated that he used these arguments to urge that the fly-in should go on and that I accepted them and agreed. That is not my recollection of his first reactions, nor in accordance with my notes made nearer the time. In any case, the point is of little consequence, as whether Wingate persuaded me, or I him, the responsibility for ordering the operation to continue and for all its consequences could not be his, but must be Baldwin's and mine.

would proceed, adding that as Piccadilly was obviously out, it was for Wingate as the tactical commander to decide what changes should be made. He stated the case for continuing the operation clearly and calmly, and directed that the troops allotted to Piccadilly were to be diverted to Chowringhee. Although this was strictly Wingate's business and not mine, I very much doubted the wisdom of this. Chowringhee was on the east of the Irrawaddy; the railway and road to be cut were on the west. Before the troops could be effective, therefore, they had to cross the river, and I questioned if this could be done as quickly or as easily as Wingate thought. I asked Calvert, the commander of 77 Brigade, and I found him strongly against Chowringhee. Cochrane also opposed it for the very sound reason that the layout there was quite different from Piccadilly and Broadway and there was little time to rebrief pilots. Baldwin, who as commander of the Third Tactical Air Force, had the over-all responsibility for the air side of the operation, was emphatic that Chowringhee could not be used by Piccadilly air crews, and that settled it. Wingate saw the force of these opinions and accepted that the fly-in would take place as originally planned, with the exception that the troops for Piccadilly would go to Broadway.

Cochrane collected the Picadilly Dakota and glider pilots, whose destination was now changed, to rebrief them. Curious to see how he would break the news of the alter. ion and a little anxious lest so obvious a hitch at the start might have a rather depressing effect on them. I followed to listen. Cochrane sprang on to the bonnet of a jeep. 'Say, fellers,' he announced, 'we've got a better place to go to!'

The leading Dakota, with its two gliders trailing behind, roared down the runway just after six o'clock, only a few minutes behind scheduled time. The moment one was clear the next followed at about half-a-minute intervals. The gliders took the air first, one or two wobbling nervously before they took station behind, and a little above, the towing aircraft. More than once I feared a Dakota would overrun the strip before the gliders were up, but all took off safely and began the long climb to gain height to cross the hills. The darkening sky was full of these queer triangles of aircraft labouring slowly higher and higher into the distance. Eventually even the drone of engines faded and we were left waiting.

And an unpleasant wait it was. Sixty-one gliders had set off.

The full complement for Broadway and Piccadilly had been eighty, but we had agreed that sixty was about the most we could hope to land on one strip in the hours of darkness, so the rest had been held back. I sat in the control tent, at the end of the air strip, to which all messages and signals came. At the rough table with its field telephones was Tullock, Wingate's chief staff officer, who proved himself quick, reliable, and cool in crisis, and Rome, another admirable staff officer. As the moon came up, in spite of hurricane lanterns and one electric lamp, it was almost lighter outside than within. There was a pause. Then came a report of red flares, fired from the air a few miles away. That meant a tow in distress—ominous if difficulties were beginning so soon. I took a turn outside and thought I saw a red Very light fired high up in the distance. I returned to the tent to find more rumours of gliders down or tows returning before they had crossed our lines. Not so good. Then another long wait. We looked at our watches. The leading aircraft should be over Broadway now with the gliders going in. We ought to get the first wireless message any minute. Still it did not come. Wingate prowled in and out, speaking to no one, his eyes smouldering in a pallid face. Tullock sat calmly at the phones. A garbled report over the telephone from another airfield told us that a tow pilot had seen what looked like firing on the Broadway strip. It was the time when doubts grow strongest and fears loom largest. Then, just after four o'clock in the morning, the first signal from Broadway, sent by Calvert, came in plain language, brief, mutilated, but conveying its message of disaster clearly enough—'Soya Link.' The name of the most disliked article in the rations had been chosen in grim humour as the code word for failure. So the Japanese *had* ambushed Broadway! Wingate was right and I had been wrong. He gave me one long, bitter look and walked away. I had no answer for him.

Then more signals, broken, hard to decipher, but gradually making the picture clearer. Gliders had crashed, men had been killed, there were injured and dying lying where they had been dragged to the edge of the strip—but there was no enemy. There had been no ambush. A great weight lifted from me as I realized that this was going to be like every other attack, neither so good nor so bad as the first reports of excited men would have you believe. We had to recall the last flight, as Broadway was too obstructed by smashed gliders to accept them. The situation was still far from clear to us as I left the control tent after dawn, but I was confident that if only the Japanese did not locate them for the next twelve hours, the Chindits would have the strip ready for reinforcements by nightfall.

Of the sixty-one gliders despatched only thirty-five reached Broadway. The airmen who said that one Dakota could not tow two gliders had been right. In practice the steep climb to cross the mountains, so close to the start, put too great a drag on the nylon ropes and many parted. It also caused overheating in the aircraft engines and unexpected fuel consumption, with dire results. Many gliders and a few aircraft force landed, some in our territory, nine in Japanese. There was a brisk battle near Imphal between the Chindits of a crashed glider, convinced they were behind the enemy lines and determined to sell their lives dearly, and our own troops rushing to their rescue. Gliders by chance came down near a Japanese divisional headquarters and others beside a regimental headquarters far from Broadway. These landings confused the enemy as to our intentions and led to a general alert for gliders and parachutists through all his units.

Long afterwards we discovered that it was not the Japanese who had obstructed Piccadilly but Burmese tree fellers, who had, in the ordinary course of their work, dragged teak logs out of the jungle to dry in the clearing. The firing reported at Broadway was a nervous burst from a shaken glider pilot.

Even without the enemy, that night at Broadway was tragic and macabre enough. One or two of the leading gliders, circling down to a half-seen gap in the jungle, had crashed on landing. The ground-control equipment and its crew were in a glider that failed to arrive so that, until a makeshift control could be improvised, it was impossible to time landings. Some gliders hurtled into the wrecks, others ran off the strip to smash into the trees or were somersaulted to ruin by uneven ground concealed under the grass. Twenty-three men were killed and many injured, but more than four hundred, with some stores, and Calvert, the brigade commander, landed intact. Most of the engineering equipment did not arrive, but the small party of American engineers, helped by every man who could be spared from patrolling, set to work with what tools they could muster to drag the wreckage clear and prepare the ground. Never have men worked harder, and by evening a strip was fit—but only just fit to take a Dakota.

Next night the fly-in continued. Fifty-five Dakotas landed at Broadway and the first flights reached Chowringhee, where also there was no sign of the enemy. By March 11 the whole of Calvert's 77 Brigade and half Lentaigne's 111 Brigade were at Broadway. Lentaigne's Brigade Headquarters and the other half with 'Dah-force,' a body of Kachins with British officers for use in raising the local tribes, were safely at Chowringhee. Between March 5 and 10 one hundred glider and almost six hundred Dakota sorties flew in nine thousand troops and eleven hundred animals. In addition, Ferguson's 16 Brigade had reached Aberdeen after its long march, so that Wingate now had nearly twelve thousand troops well placed, as he put it, 'in the enemy's guts.'

It was clear that the initial operation had been a success and, as a minor consequence, there was the usual fuss about publicity. I was in favour of saying nothing and letting the Japanese find out what they could for themselves, but that was quickly overruled. A fierce controversy then arose as to whether Wingate's name should be mentioned. It was decided not to, on what grounds I was never quite clear, but to Wingate this was *Hamlet* without the Prince of Denmark, and he was furious. He protested, with a good deal of reason, that all formations wanted, if possible, to see their names in the papers, and that to refer to his Chindits as 'troops of the Fourteenth Army' would gain nothing and miss a chance of giving their morale a boost. I agreed because I thought the Japanese were much more likely, if Wingate's name were given, to take this expedition as merely a repetition of his minor and ineffective raid of 1943, and not be too urgent in concentrating strong forces against it. What we wanted was no interference until we were well established. After a certain amount of the silly temper on both sides that such matters always seem to evoke, Wingate's name was announced.

The Japanese reaction to the landings was surprisingly slow. It is true they had been nervous of airborne attack, but not in the rather inaccessible places we had chosen. Their major offensive towards Imphal was on the point of being launched and all troops were, as we had calculated, either massed on the eastern border for this or moving towards it. The number of our aircraft passing over, night after night, must have been some indication of the size of our force, but Kawabe and his army commanders decided—and kept to the decision—not to divert any considerable number of troops from the main Imphal battle. They took some time collecting and organizing into scratch formations a number of lines of communication and other odd units to deal with the Chindits. The only action taken against the landings was an air attack on Chowringhee on March 10, a couple of hours after Lentaigne had marched off, leaving only derelict gliders behind him. Three days after thirty enemy fighters attacked Broadway, which was humming with activity. The Japanese pilots met with a surprise. By that time not only was a troop of light anti-aircraft artillery in position, but a flight of Spitfires from 221 Group R.A.F. was stationed on the strip—the first time an operational airfield had been established *behind* the enemy. The Japanese lost from guns and Spitfires more than half their strength.

The slowness of the enemy reaction gave Calvert's 77 Brigade the chance to strike first. On March 16, destroying a Japanese detachment, Calvert established an air strip and a stronghold near Mawlu on the Mandalay–Myitkyina railway, christened 'White City,' from the supply parachutes that soon draped the trees. Thus in eleven days Special Forces' first task was accomplished—the main road and rail communications to the Japanese fighting Stilwell had been cut. The enemy could not ignore this. From the 53d Japanese Division now arriving in Burma, an improvised force, never much exceeding six thousand in strength, delivered a series of ferocious assaults by day and night on White City, where in hand-to-hand fighting of the bloodiest kind British and Gurkhas beat them back. The Japanese withdrew badly shaken.

Another column of Special Force cut the important Bhamo–Myitkyina road while Lentaigne's brigade moved to the west of Indaw. These operations, to my disappointment, did not seriously affect Japanese communications to the Assam front, although they did for a couple of months delay a few units of the enemy 15th Division on their way to take part in the offensive against Imphal.

This Japanese offensive was now obviously the dominating and decisive factor in the Burma campaign. It at once confronted me with two problems in Wingate's operations: whether to send his second wave to relieve or reinforce his first and, more important, whether I should change his object from that of helping Stilwell to helping Imphal. Although the situation there was anxious and Stilwell, having a considerable numerical and material superiority over the Japanese opposing him, was in no dire need of help, I decided to adhere to my original plan. I ordered Wingate's 14 Brigade and his West African Brigade to be flown in and his main effort to be directed north rather than west, towards Stilwell rather than towards Imphal. I was wrong. I should have concentrated all available strength at the decisive point, Imphal. I fell into the same error as so many Japanese commanders: I persisted in a plan that should have been changed.

No sooner had these decisions been taken than Special Force suffered a tragic loss. Wingate, flying from Imphal to his new headquarters at Lalaghat in a Mitchell bomber, crashed by night in the wild tangle of hills west of Imphal. He, and all with him, were instantly killed. The cause of the accident cannot be definitely stated. The wreckage was eventually found on the reverse side of a ridge, so it was unlikely that the aircraft had flown into the hill. The most probable explanation is that it had suddenly entered one of those local storms of extreme turbulence so frequent in the area. These were difficult to avoid at night, and once in them an aeroplane might be flung out of control or even have its wings torn off.

I was at Comilla when the signal came in that Wingate was missing. As the hours passed and no news of any sort arrived, gloom descended upon us. We could ill spare him at the start of his greatest attempt. The immediate sense of loss that struck, like a blow, even those who had differed most from him—and I was not one of these—was a measure of the impact he had made. He had stirred up everyone with whom he had come in contact. With him, contact had too often been collision, for few could meet so stark a character without being either violently attracted or repelled. To most he was either prophet or adventurer. Very few could regard him dispassionately; nor did he care to be so regarded. I once likened him to Peter the Hermit preaching his crusade. I am sure that many of the knights and princes that Peter so fiercely exhorted did not like him very much—but they went crusading all the same. The trouble was, I think, that Wingate regarded *himself* as a prophet, and that always leads to a single centredness that verges on fanaticism, with all its faults. Yet had he not done so, his leadership could not have been so dynamic, nor his personal magnetism so striking.

There could be no question of the seriousness of our loss. Without his presence to animate it, Special Force would no longer be the same to others or to itself. He had created, inspired, defended it, and given it confidence; it was the offspring of his vivid imagination and ruthless energy. It had no other parent. Now it was orphaned, and I was faced with the immediate problem of appointing a successor. This was one of those cases in which seniority should not be taken much into account. To step into Wingate's place would be no easy task. His successor had to be someone known to the men of Special Force, one who had shared their hardships and in whose skill and courage they could trust. I chose Brigadier Lentaigne. He not only filled all the requirements, but I knew him to be, in addition, the most balanced and experienced of Wingate's commanders. It is an interesting sidelight on a strange personality that, after his death, three different officers each informed me that Wingate had told him he was to be his successor should one be required. I have no doubt at all that they were speaking the truth.

While all this was going on the Chindits had not slackened their activity. Ferguson's 16 Brigade from Aberdeen attempted to seize Rail Indaw by surprise, but was compelled to abandon the attempt and fall back. Exhausted by this abortive effort after their long march, there was nothing for it but to fly them out. However, Lentaigne still had three mobile brigades, considerable numbers of 'stronghold' troops, and the Japanese communications both road and rail to their 18th Division were effectively cut. The enemy, refusing to divert any formation from the vital Assam front, swept up more odds and ends, including part of a regiment of his newly arrived 2d Division, to add to Take Force. In May the concentration against White City grew too threatening, and the Chindits slipped away to establish another stronghold at 'Blackpool,' just north of Hopin.

Meanwhile, Stilwell to the north of them had been pushing his Chinese southward. Using Merrill's Marauders in short hooks behind the Japanese, after a tough fight at Jambu Bum, on March 19, his sixty-first birthday, he broke into the Mogaung Valley leading to the town of that name.

The old warrior was well pleased with his progress and he had cause to be. Not only were the Chinese, under his skilful prodding, fighting well, but, reinforced by Admiral Mount-

would say.

To give a feeling of security to the American airfields, as I could not spare troops for the purpose, he would send a regiment of one of his new divisions to Dinjan where, in addition, it would be well placed for a fly-in if Myitkyina were taken. I asked him if he still had his plan for seizing Myitkyina and when he would do it. He replied that he had, and, if all went well and there was not too much rain, he hoped to be there about May 20. He again asked me to tell no one of his plan or of the proposed date of its execution. I agreed I would not. After all, everyone knew he had been ordered to take Myitkyina, and whatever his motives in this secrecy I was prepared to humour him. After lunch Admiral Mountbatten, Lentaigne, Stopford, and others arrived and the Supreme Commander held a conference at which he approved the instructions I had given Stilwell.

Meanwhile the small force of Burma Rifles and British-officered Kachin levies, isolated far out on Stilwell's left, had struck south from Fort Hertz and seized Sumprabum, the first great triumph of their little private war. The main Chinese forces were pressing hard towards Kamaing and, if Stilwell was to get Myitkyina before the monsoon, his dash for it could not be long delayed. In great secrecy he organized his striking force. It consisted of the three battalions of American Marauders, each joined with two Chinese battalions, to form three mixed brigades. On April 28 Merrill set out on his hazardous expedition; and hazardous it was. He had to lead his men nearly a hundred miles through the wildest country; to cross a mountain range six thousand feet in height by tracks that had to be hacked out of the hillsides before the pack mules could pass over. Then at the end he would have to attack an enemy whose strengh could not be accurately assessed.

No sooner had the striking force started than it rained, trebling the difficulties of their march and tormenting Stilwell with anxiety. Luckily it was not the monsoon, but merely warning storms, and the weather cleared again. On May 14, Merrill reported he was within forty-eight hours of his objective; on the 15th, within twenty-four, and the follow-up Chinese were warned for the fly-in.

On May 17 Merrill's force, brushing aside slight opposition, rushed the airfield at Myitkyina. The surprise had been complete, and the Japanese with a total strength of about eight hundred withdrew into the town itself. During the afternoon the fly-in of the first of the Chinese reinforcing regiments began, followed quickly by another. The Marauders and the Chinese who had marched in with them were exhausted with their effort, much as Ferguson's Chindits had been after a similar march, and, thinking that the enemy in Myitkyina were in strength, contented themselves with consolidating about the airfield. Actually the Japanese garrison in Myitkyina was small, consisting as it did of the headquarters of 114 Regiment of the 18th Division, two very weak battalions, some aerodrome defence troops, and about three hundred administrative details. In addition there was the 18th Divisional Field Hospital, containing several hundred patients, many of whom, in accordance with Japanese custom, were at once turned out to fight.

The newly arrived Chinese regiments attacked the town on the 19th. They were going into action for the first time, and they were not very well led, nor had they had much time, since getting out of their planes, to orientate themselves. After a little progress they were held up. In the confusion one body of Chinese fired into another, panic ensued, and the attack fell back in disorder. The Japanese reacted quickly to the threat to Myitkyina by calling in to its help all units in the neighbourhood. By the end of May there were in the town elements of both the 18th and 56th Divisions, which with the hospital patients, line of communication and administrative troops, made up a strength of some three thousand five hundred men. Colonel Maruyama of 114 Regiment was in command until Major-General Mizukami, from the 56th Division, reached the town on June 2 and took over from him. Both these officers proved themselves to be of outstanding courage and determination, while the heterogeneous garrison fought with fanatical desperation.

Unfortunately, Merrill had collapsed soon after arrival at Myitkyina, and the officers sent to replace him were inexperienced and unaccustomed to the strain of actual command in the field. The fact was that Stilwell had no one, at this time, except himself, on whom he could rely either to direct or push through an operation, and he could not be in two places at once.

Reinforcements continued to pour into the original Myitkyina airfield and the other strips that were quickly made near

columns of Lentaigne's men were collecting. The rain had made it impossible to keep earth air strips in action and there seemed little hope of getting out the increasing number of sick and wounded that were being laboriously brought in by their comrades. The R.A.F. found the answer in two Sunderland flying boats, which, as a change from submarine hunting in the Indian Ocean, flew from Colombo to this fifteen-by-five miles stretch of water in the heart of Burma. Working throughout some of the worst monsoon weather, they flew out nearly six hundred casualties.

During the first weeks of June Stilwell's Chinese had kept up their drive down the Mogaung Valley. Fighting with increasing confidence and boldness, they destroyed the Japanese who tried to bar their way at Shaduzup and Laban. Then on June 16 the Chinese 22d Division took Kamaing, and on the 20th Calvert's 77 Brigade of Lentaigne's force stormed Mogaung, just ahead of the Chinese 38th Division coming from the north. By this time, too, the great battles around Imphal had definitely turned against the Japanese. Such reinforcements as he could scrape up, Kawabe, the enemy commander in chief, was sending there to cover his withdrawal. His two northern fronts were crumbling and there was little he could do to bolster them up. He was by now plainly reduced to fighting merely a delaying campaign in North Burma.

Negotiations had been going on between Admiral Mountbatten and Generalissimo Chiang Kai-shek for Wei Li Huang's Yunnan armies to come under Southeast Asia Command when they crossed the Burma border. As seemed inevitable, however, where Chinese were concerned, there was considerable mystification about the command of these troops. To begin with, the Sino-Burmese frontier was not marked in these outlandish hills. British maps showed it in one place, the Chinese several miles farther west. In any case, whatever the line, it was likely that at times some parts of the same Chinese formation would be on each side of it—a hopeless complication. The Generalissimo kept a tight hand on these Yunnan troops, and Stilwell's control, exercised through an American mission, was, I gathered from him, pretty nebulous. Still, whether he commanded them or not, Stilwell's own force now amounted to about seven divisions and the agreement had been that when Kamaing was taken he should pass from my command. It was only logical to regard him as an army commander on the same footing as myself and place him, like me, under Eleventh Army Group, but once again Stilwell refused to serve under General Giffard. He insisted on coming directly under Admiral Mountbatten, although there was no organization at Southeast Asia Command Headquarters to deal direct with an army.

When I visited Stilwell on his passing from my command he said, with his frosty twinkle, 'Well, General, I've been a good subordinate to you. I've obeyed all your orders!' That was true enough, but so was my retort, 'Yes, you old devil, but only because the few I did give you were the ones you wanted!'

The long-drawn-out siege of Myitkyina was a great disappointment to Stilwell, and it was at this period that he really lived up to his nickname, Vinegar Joe. He was extremely caustic about his unfortunate American commanders, accusing them of not fighting, and of killing the same Japanese over and over again in their reports. He was equally bitter against the Chindits, complaining that they did not obey his orders, had abandoned the block at Hopin unnecessarily, and had thus let strong Japanese reinforcements into the Kamaing–Myitkyina area. He asked for British parachute troops to restore the situation, but, apart from the fact that the small parachute formation available was already in the thick of the fighting at Imphal and could not have been extricated, there was no doubt he took a much too alarmist view of the position on his front. Lentaigne retaliated to the accusations hurled at him by complaining that Stilwell was demanding the impossible and that, by continually setting simultaneous tasks for all his columns, was making it impossible to give any part of his force the time essential for reorganization and evacuation of casualties without which they could not operate effectively. Relations between the two commanders became strained, and finally, at the end of May, Stilwell asked Admiral Mountbatten to withdraw Special Force. As a result, early in June, although I was no longer in command of this front, I was sent to N.C.A.C. to adjudicate between Stilwell and Lentaigne and to attempt to heal the breach.

I found Stilwell bitter and Lentaigne indignant, both obviously and very understandably suffering from prolonged strain. One of the troubles was that Stilwell, in his then mood, would not meet Lentaigne and really discuss things with him. There was too much of the Siege of Troy atmosphere, with commanders sulking in their tents. However, with me, Stilwell, after one or two outbursts, was reasonable and explained his charges against the Chindits. I had already seen Lentaigne and heard his version. Stilwell's orders on the face of it were sound enough and it was quite obvious that the Chindits had not carried out all of them. It was equally clear that in their present state of exhaustion, after the casualties they had suffered and in the rain which made movement so difficult, unless given some chance of reorganization they were physically incapable of doing so. Stilwell replied to this by pointing to his Marauders who, he said, were still operating effectively. Without belittling their efforts, I pointed out that Lentaigne's men had endured the strain of being actually behind the enemy's lines for longer periods than Merrill's and that their incidence of battle casualties, as compared with sick, was much higher. As far as his complaints against Morrisforce on the east of the river were concerned, I told him I thought it was a bit hard to reproach a few hundred men for not doing what thirty thousand had failed to do on the other bank. Finally, looking at me over the top of his glasses, he said, 'What do you want me to do?' I said, 'See Lentaigne, talk things over with him, give his columns a chance to get out their casualties and reorganize, and keep his force on until Myitkyina falls.' He agreed, and I returned to headquarters.

I had hoped that Myitkyina would fall by the middle of June, but at the end of the month it was still apparently as far from capture as ever. It then became obvious that the remains of Special Force were not fit to continue operating throughout the monsoon. Admiral Mountbatten himself this time visited Stilwell and an arrangement was made by which two of Lentaigne's brigades that had been longest in the field should be medically examined and all unfit men flown out at once—the remainder to operate for a short time further and then follow them. The last of Special Force would remain until the 36th British Division, which was refitting at Shillong in Assam, began to come into Stilwell's command, when they, too, would be taken out.

Actually it would have been wiser to take the whole of the Chindits out then; they had shot their bolt. So, too, for that matter had the Marauders, who a little later packed in completely. Both forces, Chindits and Marauders, had been subjected to intense strain, both had unwisely been promised that their ordeal would be short, and both were asked to do more than was possible.

On the afternoon of August 3, after a siege of two and a half months, Myitkyina fell. Some days before Mizukami, the Japanese commander, had ordered what was left of the garrison to break out. He had then committed suicide. Maruyama, the original commander, had again taken over, and under his leadership the Japanese attempted to escape by night on rafts down the river. Most of them were intercepted and killed, but Maruyama himself and a couple of hundred did get away.

The capture of Myitkyina, so long delayed, marked the complete success of the first stage of Stilwell's campaign. It was also the largest seizure of enemy-held territory that had yet occurred. Throughout the operations on the northern front the Allied forces, Chinese, British, and American, had been vastly superior to the Japanese on the ground and in the air, even without including the Chinese Yunnan armies. This superiority was achieved only because the main Japanese forces were held locked in the vital Imphal battle, and any reinforcements they could rake up were fed into that furnace. The Japanese had the advantage of position and communications, but even their desperate courage and defensive skill could not hold back such a numerical preponderance. Yet, when all was said and done, the success of this northern offensive was in the main owing to the Ledo Chinese divisions—and that was Stilwell.

BOOK IV: THE TIDE TURNS

CHAPTER XIII

HOW IT WAS PLANNED

The great encounter that loomed over the Central Assam front in early 1944, and which was fought out with relentless fury around Imphal and Kohima from March to July in that year, was the first of the two decisive battles of the Southeast Asia campaign. Tarauchi, the Japanese Supreme Commander, and Kawabe, their commander in chief in Burma, both meant it to be decisive—and so did we.

Their daily mounting shipping losses in the Pacific were beginning to tell on the Japanese. Unless they could score some far-reaching strategic success, their armies, strung out on a vast perimeter of conquest, faced slow strangulation. It was to Burma that their slit eyes turned hopefully. Here was the one place they could stage an offensive that might give them all they hoped. If it succeeded, the destruction of the British forces in Burma would be the least of its results. China, completely isolated, would be driven into a separate peace; India, ripe as they thought for revolt against the British, would fall, a glittering prize, into their hands. They were right in thinking that victory in Assam would resound far beyond that remote jungle land; it might, indeed, as they proclaimed in exhortations to their troops, change the whole course of the world war. Burma, for a space, no longer a sideshow in the global struggle, would hold the centre stage.

Kawabe, knowing this, concentrated his forces to achieve a breakthrough in Assam. To him, the fighting in Arakan was aimed at absorbing and holding our reserves from the vital theatre; on the northern front, where he could afford to yield ground, he would use the barest forces to slow up the Chinese advances.

For us, too, it was our great chance. Lack of landing craft compelled us to enter Burma overland from the north where the terrible country so limited the forces we could maintain that any invasion, unless we could first wear down Japanese strength, would be a gamble. I wanted a battle *before* we went into Burma; it looked as if I should get it.

Lieutenant-General Scoones, an informed, thoughtful soldier with a clear analytical mind, was commanding IV Corps on the Assam front. His appreciations could be reread after the event and found uncannily accurate, and he had, too, a steadiness in crisis that was, for the coming battle, to be invaluable. He had, in accordance with the over-all plan for the theatre, been preparing for an advance, and the whole layout of his area and the dispositions of his fighting formations were designed with this idea.

The Imphal Plain, some forty by twenty miles in extent, is the only considerable oasis of flat ground in the great sweep of mountains between India and Burma. It lies roughly equidistant from the Brahmaputra Valley and the plains of Central Burma, a natural halfway house and staging place for any great military movement in either direction between India and Burma. The aspect of the Imphal Plain had greatly changed since we had sought there in vain for rest and shelter after the Retreat. Instead of the dripping trees, sodden ground, bombed-out buildings, and muddy tracks that had greeted us, there were now orderly *basha* camps, hutted hospitals, supply dumps, ordnance depots, engineer parks, and wide tarmac roads. Camps of every kind and sort were dotted over the six hundred square miles of the plain, but most were clustered around the villages of Imphal itself and Palel twenty-five miles south. These administrative establishments had all been sited, as was natural, in the most suitable and accessible spots for their various purposes, with the idea of protection from the air by dispersion, but with no thought of defence against attack by land. As a result they were spread over large areas and were almost invariably overlooked by high ground at point-blank range. In these camps, and scattered along the roads leading north into India and south into Burma, were some sixty or seventy thousand Indian noncombatants, mostly labour. The sprawling railhead base that had been hacked out of the jungle at Dimapur, one hundred and thirty miles north of Imphal, was similarly laid out and manned. As long as our intentions remained offensive and those of the Japanese defensive, Imphal and Dimapur were suitably organized; should the roles be reversed, these widespread bases would become a terrible embarrassment.

Our whole situation on this central front had another grave tactical disadvantage. Our only line of communication was the road our engineers had so magnificently built from railhead at Dimapur up the hill to Kohima, and on to Imphal. This now forked and we were laboriously extending the two prongs, one down the valley of the Manipur River and the other into the Kabaw Valley. All of these roads ran of necessity north and south, parallel to the Japanese front, and at no great distance from it. Thus, whether we took the offensive or remained on the defensive, they exposed a classic military weakness to an enemy peculiarly fitted and experienced to exploit it to the full.

IV Corps had one division at the end of each of the roads to the south; the 17th, veterans of the Retreat, on the right about Tiddim in the Chin Hills, and the 20th, which had been with me in Ranchi, on the left in the Palel–Tiddim area. There was an eighty-mile gap of jungle mountains between them but, with a two-hundred-and-fifty-mile front, rather than try to close it, Lieutenant-General Scoones, commanding the IV Corps, had kept his third division, the 23d, in Imphal as a striking force. With it was 254 Indian Tank Brigade, two regiments only, equipped with Lee-Grant and light Stuart tanks, all obsolete and long outmoded in other theatres. But Cinderella was still bottom of all priority lists.

During and after the 1943 monsoon the 20th Division had pushed steadily forward; the Kabaw Valley was re-entered and the Chindwin reached and crossed by patrols. It was on the 17th Division front that progress fluctuated. There, beyond Tiddim, among a chaos of jungle-matted, knife-edged ridges with peaks up to eight thousand feet, the division waged a small-scale but bitter private war against its old opponent, the Japanese 33d Division. Well matched, they took it in turns to ambush, raid, attack, and counterattack one another. On the whole, the Japanese had the better of it, holding our men from their goal at Kalewa on the Chindwin and even forcing them back in places. On the front the Japanese had chosen for their decisive blow there were thus two widely separated divisions forward and a third many miles behind.

We knew the offensive was coming, for throughout January and February, besides the general reinforcement of the Burma theatre by fresh Japanese formations, there were increasing local indications on IV Corps front. I had not at my disposal the sources of information of the enemy's intentions that some more fortunate commanders in other theatres were able to invoke. We depended almost entirely on the intelligence gathered by our fighting patrols, and the superiority we had developed in this form of activity now paid a high dividend. In spite of the fact that our patrols were finding it more difficult to cross the Chindwin, the newly-arrived 15th Japanese Division was identified along the river.

Enemy activity and strength all along IV Corps front were noticeably increasing. Documents, diaries, marked maps, and even operation orders taken from Japanese killed in these patrols clashes were being brought in almost daily. We had luck and a good haul of documents in one or two bold raids on minor headquarters. All these clues, painstakingly fitted into the mosaic of our intelligence at Corps and Army Headquarters, began to give us a general picture of the enemy's intentions. In spite of our air superiority, the nature of the country and the Japanese habit of moving by night limited the value of air reconnaissance. We did, however, get three very significant items of news from this source. Our pilots reported that the enemy were developing the roads towards the Chindwin from Central Burma. Then they saw large numbers of logs being collected at various places on the east bank of the river and many camouflaged rafts concealed in the lower reaches of the Uyu River opposite Homalin, due east of Imphal. Equally significant, they located great herds of cattle, each several hundreds in number, south of the Uyu and near Thaungdut on the Chindwin. We knew that the Japanese had seized all cattle belonging to the local inhabitants, and it was evident that these herds were being driven to the river as supplies for considerable forces. Our 'V' Force agents also brought us stories of the massing of transport, mechanical and animal, even of elephants.

Piecing all this together, Scoones and I agreed that the Japanese Fifteenth Army under Lieutenant-General Mutuguchi would begin the offensive about March 15 with three divisions, the 15th, 31st, and 33d, with probably another in reserve. His objectives would be, first, Imphal and, second, to break through to the Brahmaputra Valley, thus cutting off the northern front and disrupting the air supply to China. We expected an attempt by the 33d Division to get behind our forward divisions, while some two enemy divisions would cross the Chindwin near Homalin and Thaungdut, making for Imphal via Ukhrul. A regiment, three battalions, we thought would advance against Kohima to cut the road north of Imphal and threaten our Dimapur base. Having made our forecast—broadly accurate it proved—we now had to consider what to do to meet it.

Our two forward divisions were an invitation to destruction in detail; our third could go to the help of only one, and in doing so would leave Imphal wide open. There remained three broad alternatives:

(i) To anticipate the enemy offensive by crossing the Chindwin and attacking him first.

(ii) To hold the Japanese 33d Division in the Tiddim area and fight with all available forces on the line of the Chindwin, hoping to destroy the enemy as he crossed the river, with part of his forces on each bank.

(iii) To concentrate IV Corps in the Imphal Plain and fight the decisive battle there on ground of our own choosing.

The first alternative—to forestall the enemy and attack ourselves—had all the glamour of boldness. Indeed, there were not wanting senior visiting officers who urged me 'to fling two divisions across the Chindwin.' I am afraid they left my headquarters thinking I was sadly lacking in the offensive spirit, but somehow I have never had great confidence in generals who talk of 'flinging' divisions about. 'Fling' is a term for amateurs, not professionals. Besides, I noticed that the farther back these generals came from, the keener they were on my 'flinging' divisions across the Chindwin. Had I accepted their advice the enemy could easily have concentrated, along good communications, a force greatly in excess of any we could maintain east of the Chindwin. We should have fought superior numbers with the dangerous crossing of a great river behind us and with our communications running back through a hundred and twenty miles of the worst country imaginable. Similarly, but to a somewhat lesser extent, if we decided to fight at Tiddim and on the west bank of the Chindwin, we still had this difficult and precarious line of communication behind us. Whatever success we had in those conditions we were unlikely to achieve a decisive result—and it was a decisive success I wanted.

At this stage of the campaign against an opponent as tough as the Japanese and one whose morale was still as high as his was, to gain a decisive success I must concentrate against him a force superior both in numbers and armament. I therefore decided to adopt the third course—to concentrate IV Corps in the Imphal Plain, and fight a major battle there to destroy the Japanese Fifteenth Army. I was tired of fighting the Japanese when they had a good line of communications behind them and I had an execrable one. This time I would reverse the procedure. An important consideration, too, in all my calculations, was that the enemy, if he was to avoid destruction, must win his battle before the monsoon set in. If he had failed by then to occupy the Imphal area he would be in an impossible supply position. Another factor was, of course, our supremacy in the air and the ability it gave me to use air supply. It should be remembered, however, that this would be dependent during the monsoon on the possession of all-weather airfields. The only ones we had were Imphal and Palel; there were none, nor could we construct them in time, on the east bank of the Chindwin.

I realized that from the point of view of morale a withdrawal was not the best opening for a decisive battle. It would be unpopular with commanders and troops alike. Both the 17th and 20th Divisions were at the time confident, with good cause, that they could not only hold their positions but also drive back the enemy. The abandonment of so much British territory would depress our friends and exult our enemies all over the world. It would spread alarm and despondency in India, our base. Yet it was not the hundreds of square miles of jungle mountains that mattered, but the chance to destroy the enemy's forces. That done, territory could easily be reoccupied. I was sure, too, that if commanders explained the design to their men, they would see its soundness, and morale would not suffer.

In war it is all-important to gain and retain the initiative, to make the enemy conform to your action, to dance to your tune. When you are advancing, this normally follows; if you withdraw, it is neither so obvious nor so easy. Yet it is possible. There are three reasons for retreat: self-preservation, to save your force from destruction; pressure elsewhere which makes you accept loss of territory in one place to enable you to transfer troops to a more vital front; and, last, to draw the enemy into a situation so unfavourable to him that the initiative must pass to you. It was for this third reason that I now voluntarily decided on a withdrawal. Here was the contrast between the forced retreat of 1942, whose object became merely the preservation of our troops as an intact force, and that of 1944, which was carefully calculated to lead inevitably to our regaining the initiative. Yet so many scrambles to escape have been described as 'withdrawals according to plan' that I was not surprised to find it hard to convince many, especially highly placed civil officials, that it was possible to fight defensively and even to retreat, yet keep the initiative.

Scoones and I discussed the alternatives and we both came independently to the same conclusions—to fight at Imphal. It would be very largely his battle and it was important to have his agreement with the basic ideas on which I wanted it fought. General Giffard also approved my reasoning, and it was a great satisfaction to me to know that his judgment supported me. The plan for what we knew would be the decisive battle was first for Imphal Plain to be put into a state of defence. This entailed the concentration of the scattered administrative units and headquarters into fortified areas, each of which would be capable of all-round defence and completely self-contained in ammunition and supplies for considerable periods. The two all-weather airfields at Imphal and Palel, vital to the defence both for supporting air squadrons and for air supply, became the main strong points or 'keeps' in the defence scheme. The garrisons of these fortified areas and keeps were to be found mainly by the administrative troops themselves, so that the fighting units and formations would be free to manoeuvre in an offensive role. These preparations were put in hand and throughout February went on at an increasing tempo. Almost every unit in the Imphal Plain moved; a large number of strongly defended localities were dug, wired, and stocked. The evacuation of noncombatant and labour units began, while the training of the remaining administrative troops in a fighting role for the defence of their own localities was intensive.

A most important part of the plan was the provision of reinforcing formations for Assam. Within the army I proposed to pull the 5th Division out of Arakan and move it by air and rail from Chittagong to Dimapur and Imphal. General Giffard had arranged to send a division from India to replace it, and, when, that arrived, I contemplated sending the 7th Division from Arakan after the 5th. I also asked for another division to be railed from India to Dimapur, but here there was a differ-ence of opinion between me and the administrative staffs at Eleventh Army Group, who, with considerable mathematical justification, declared that the already over-burdened Assam railway would not be able to compete with the added strain of transporting and then maintaining so large a reinforcement. General Giffard compromised by sending me the Indian Para-chute Brigade of two battalions and by putting in hand arrangements to move the 2d British Division if it became urgently necessary to do so.

The IV Corps tactical plan was for the 17th Division to move rapidly back from Tiddim to the Imphal Plain, drop-ping one brigade group some forty miles south of Imphal to block the Japanese advance. The remainder of the division would be in Corps Reserve. The 20th Indian Division was to withdraw from its forward positions in the Kabaw Valley, con-centrate in the Moreh area, and, when all 'soft' units on the line of communication had been cleared to Imphal, to fall back slowly on Shenam, which would be held at all costs. The 23d Indian Division, leaving one brigade group in the Ukhrul area, was to form with the 17th Division, the Indian Parachute Brigade, when it arrived, and the 254 Indian Tank Brigade, the corps offensive reserve. The Japanese would thus be al-lowed to advance to the edge of the Imphal Plain, and, when comm_....ed in assaults on our prepared positions, would be counterattacked and destroyed by our mobile striking forces, strong in artillery, armour, and aircraft.

The plan that Scoones and I had hammered out was, I was sure, the right one. It only remained to decide when it should be put into force. The essence of all military planning is timing. A brilliant plan wrongly timed, put into operation too early or too late, is at the best a lame thing and at the worst may be a disaster. When and by whom was the order for the 17th and 20th Divisions to retire on Imphal to be given? It was here I made a mistake. I was, in my own mind, convinced that a Japanese offensive on a large scale against Imphal was com-ing, and I judged it would begin about March 15. On the other hand, it was impossible to be absolutely certain that it would come then, or even that it would come at all. If we pulled back to Imphal and it did not come, not only would we look foolish, but we should have unnecessarily jeopardized the preparations for our own offensive, abandoned much territory, and done nothing to help the Chinese advance in the north. The effect on morale could not but be bad. I therefore decided that all preparations to put the plan into force should be made, but that the word to start the withdrawal to Imphal should be given by the local commander, Scoones, when he was sure that a major Japanese offensive was imminent. What I should have done was to act on my own judgment and give a definite date early in March on which the withdrawal should begin, and another, some days later, by which the two divisions should be in their new positions. To put the responsibility on local commanders was neither fair nor wise. I was in a better position to judge when a real offensive was coming for I had all their information, and, in addition, intelligence from other sources. Local commanders were bound to be reluctant to retreat without at least a trial of strength; all the hesitations that could assail me would inflict them threefold. There was thus a real risk, that I did not appreciate, of the withdrawal being started too late. Instead of being carried out without interference, it might degenerate into a series of fights to break through involving our reserves and disorganizing the whole plan of battle.

Happily oblivious of the cardinal error I had made and of its possible consequences, I continued preparations to meet the expected onslaught. I was confident that our plans were sound, and I was supported by the knowledge that General Giffard was preparing to send me, should need arise, reinforcements from India, These, added to the formations I proposed myself to transfer from Arakan, would give me the superiority in strength that I wanted to make sure that the invading divisions were not only repelled but destroyed. It seemed that the enemy was about to play into my hands and give me the opportunity I had always hoped for, to cripple his army *before* we re-entered Burma. It was in this rather complacent mood that I awaited the battle. I should have remembered that battles, at least the ones I had been engaged in, very rarely went quite according to plan.

CHAPTER XIV

HOW IT HAPPENED

The story of the prolonged and hard-fought battle of Imphal–Kohima that developed from the plans of Japanese and British commanders is not easy to follow. It swayed back and forth through great stretches of wild country; one day its focal point was a hill named on no map, the next a miserable, unpronounceable village, a hundred miles away. Columns, brigades, divisions, marched and countermarched, met in bloody clashes, and reeled apart, weaving a confused pattern hard to unravel. Yet the whole battle can be divided into four reasonably clear phases:

(i) *Concentration*—as each side strained every sinew to bring its forces into the fight.

(ii) *Attrition*—as week after week in man-to-man, hand-to-hand fighting, each strove to wear down the other's strength and to break his will.

(iii) *Counteroffensive*—as gradually, but with increasing momentum, the British passed to the attack, and

(iv) *Pursuit*—when the Japanese broke and, snarling and snapping, were hunted from the field.

The opening moves of the Imphal battle began in the first days of March 1944. About Tiddim, Cowan's 17th Indian Division was, with increasing success, systematically recapturing lost ground when the conditions of his local war changed completely.

On March 6, the 214 Regiment of the Japanese 33d Division suddenly violently attacked our detachment at the bridge over the Manipur River near Tonzang, twenty miles north of Tiddim and to secure this vital position in his rear Cowan despatched his 63 Brigade. Meanwhile, on the 8th, another Japanese regiment (215), circling our positions, moved north

by tracks through the hills. In thick jungle neither air reconnaissance nor patrol could keep touch with it or estimate its
strength, but on the 13th came ominous news. The Engineer
camp at Milestone 109, nearly sixty miles north of Tiddim,
containing practically no fighting troops but a large number
of noncombatants, including five thousand Indian labourers,
reported a large Japanese force in the hills a few miles to the
west. A detachment of Indian machine gunners, the only combat troops within reach, was hurriedly diverted to the camp
which, scattered and low-lying, was most difficult to defend.

These alarming events had been reported to Scoones who, at
0240 hours on March 13, ordered Cowan to withdraw his division to the Imphal Plain; at 2200 hours Cowan issued orders
for the withdrawal next day.

It was a long column that began to wind through the hills
on the afternoon of the 14th. The whole division went on foot
for, although it took with it great numbers of vehicles and
animals, transport was reserved for stores, ammunition, supplies, and wounded. The first day it covered twenty miles
while the Japanese cautiously followed; with sound tactical
sense they were concentrating on cutting in ahead and blocking the road. This, by the 14th, they had done in two places,
just north of Tonzang and at the unhappy Milestone 109
Camp, where the tiny garrison, hampered by a mass of noncombatants, was quickly in difficulties. The Gurkhas of the
17th Division, on the 16th, dealt swiftly and effectively with
the first block, sweeping the enemy from their position with
bayonet and *kukri*. The road was now open—but only to
Milestone 109.

Nor was the Tiddim road the only sector from which danger
threatened. On the night of March 15–16, the Japanese 15th
and 31st Divisions, poised along the east bank of the Chindwin, moved in earnest. The 15th Division crossed the river in
three columns about Thaungdut with orders 'to advance
through the hills like a ball of fire,' to isolate Imphal from the
north, and then capture the town. Moving swiftly, by March
18 one column was pressing our 20th Division's flank near
Myothit and others, already only fifty miles from Imphal, were
approaching Ukhrul. At the same time the 31st Japanese Division, in eight columns, crossed the Chindwin on a forty-mile
front from Homalin to the north, and pushed west like the
probing fingers of an extended hand. As far as we could judge,

some of these columns were to aid the 15th Division in taking Ukhrul and Imphal, while others cut the main road north of Imphal, and still more streamed through the hills towards Jessami, southeast of Kohima. Then the hand would close and, as the Japanese commander described it, 'at one fell swoop fall on Kohima and annihilate the British on that front!' Full of confidence in themselves and contempt for their enemy, they plunged forward.

In Imphal I was impressed by the steadiness of commanders and troops. Scoones, in control of the tactical battle on the whole Assam front, had been faced with a difficult and momentous decision. The fog of war had descended. He was deluged with reports and rumours of Japanese columns which seemed to flit in and out of the jungle, now here, now there; little was definite and nothing certain. Two things, however, were clear: first that the 17th Division was cut off, second, that a strong threat to Imphal itself from the east was developing. Time was short. The commander of IV Corps had to make up his mind, there and then, whether he would hold his reserve, the 23d Division, to meet the thrust at Imphal or send the bulk of it towards Tiddim to help out the 17th Division. Calmly he balanced the risks of each course. Rightly he decided to hold to our plan for the battle and to follow the course which would, if successful, more quickly concentrate his corps in the Imphal Plain. He therefore sent, first one brigade, and then a second of the 23d Division to fight down the road towards the 17th Division.

On how fine a margin the success or failure of these decisions depended can be seen from the history of the Japanese thrust at Imphal from the east. On March 19 part of the enemy 31st Division surged against the two Indian Parachute Battalions and one battalion of the 23d Division, dug in to cover Ukhrul. For two desperate days the fight went on, then the brigade was pushed back and Ukhrul fell to the enemy. The three battalions, now considerably weakened, stood again at Sangshak, nine miles to the south. There, from the 21st to the 25th, they resisted desperate night attacks, which were closely supported by the Japanese artillery, while by day snipers and shelling took their toll. With the Japanese came the Jiffs, as we called members of the Indian National Army, who were employed not in direct attacks but in unavailing attempts to confuse and suborn our Indian troops. On the morning of March 26 the enemy put in an all-out daylight assault. Our losses and theirs were heavy in hand-to-hand fighting. The main positions held, but unfortunately one of the two meagre water-supply points was lost. Throughout the action the R.A.F. had kept up the closest support, and they

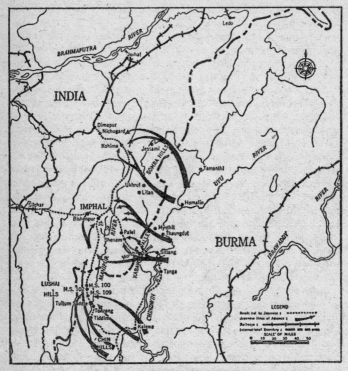

JAPANESE INVASION ROUTES, BURMA 1944

now attempted, in spite of heavy fire from the ground, to deliver water, but the area held by our troops was so restricted that most of the drops were lost. Almost without water, it was impossible to hold on any longer, and after dark on March 26, what was left of the brigade was ordered to break out and make for Imphal. The ten days' delay and the heavy casualties this small force and the R.A.F. who supported them had inflicted on the enemy were of inestimable value at this critical stage of the battle.

While this savage fighting was going on at Litan, about ten miles to the southwest, a newly-arrived battalion of the 5th Division, hurriedly digging in to close the road, was attacked by superior forces on the night of March 24–25. It suffered heavily and, in spite of counterattacks, lost its forward positions, being in danger of encirclement. But now, in the nick of time, troops of the 5th Division flown from Arakan came into action straight from their aircraft. The 123 Brigade pushed up the road, clearing it for six miles and immediately behind it came 9 Brigade, just landed. The Japanese advance from Ukhrul direct on Imphal was roughly handled and in a week of clashes was held. But another Japanese thrust, that against the Kohima–Imphal road, broke through. On March 30, the enemy blew up a bridge and established strong road blocks thirty miles north of Imphal; except for the Silchar track to the west, Imphal was now cut off.

While all this was going on, the 23d Indian Division, less one brigade, left for the defence of Imphal, had begun its fight on the Tiddim road towards the 17th Division. Major-General Ouvry Roberts, who commanded the 23d Division, was a good man for such a job. Years before, when I had taught him at the Staff College, he had been marked as likely to become not only a first-class staff officer but a successful commander. He had been my chief staff officer in the 10th Indian Division in Iraq in 1941. There he had done what I have always considered to be one of the best single-handed jobs any officer of his then rank had performed in the war. The Iraq Army was besieging the Royal Air Force base at Habbaniyeh, and, in spite of the gallantry of the pilots of the flying school, in their obsolete machines, and of Assyrian Levies and airmen on the ground, it looked as if it might fall. At the most critical moment of the siege we flew in Roberts. By his energy, by the direction he imparted to the operations, and by the confidence he inspired, he transformed a somewhat bewildered defence into a successfully aggressive one. Had Habbaniyeh fallen, the results would have been disastrous to the whole Middle East. Now he had transferred those qualities to the command of a division.

The leading units of Roberts's 37 Brigade, with a few light tanks, moving rapidly, drove off a Japanese force which was besieging a small detachment of ours at Milestone 100 on the Tiddim road. Before our troops could push on to the relief of the camp at Milestone 109 the enemy, infiltrating through the jungle, had established a series of road blocks behind them. They were thus forced to turn and clear the road towards Imphal while the second brigade of the 23d Division fought south towards them. The situation on the Tiddim road was now for a time as it had once been in the Arakan coast—a Neapolitan ice of layers of our troops alternating with Japanese—but in both training and morale our men were much better fitted to deal with such a confused and harassing business than they had been in 1943.

With relief thus delayed, the situation at Milestone 109 grew critical. On the night of March 16–17, the noncombatants were skilfully led through the enemy by jungle paths to join the 23d Division; the handful of fighting troops hung on for two days more and then followed them. The Japanese, swarming in to seize abandoned supplies and vehicles, at once set to work to build powerful defences to deny passage to the 17th Division.

Cowan, advancing north with his main force on the road, wisely sent infantry high on the ridges to each side. While these columns cleared the crests, 48 Brigade, with R.A.F. fighter-bomber support, broke through a desperately defended position astride the road and, after another hard fight on March 25, retook the camp itself, recovering intact most of the lost stores and vehicles. As the head of the 17th Division thus effectively dealt with the Japanese 215 Regiment, the rear guard was nightly beating off fierce attacks from a reinforced 214 Regiment. A final all-out assault on March 24, when several enemy tanks were knocked out, was repulsed. Two days later the rear guard, blowing up the bridge across the Manipur River, withdrew, and the whole division moved on again. The back of the Japanese obstruction had been broken and, after some minor engagements, the 17th and 23d Divisions met at Milestone 102. Leaving two brigades of the 23d Division to cover this approach, the 17th Division reached Imphal complete on April 5.

During the later stages of its withdrawal the division had been maintained by supply dropping from the air but the Japanese Air Force made only one major attempt to attack the long, retreating column and that without serious effect. The enemy's inactivity in the air at this critical time is a measure of what the 17th Division owed to 221 Group R.A.F. Had not our fighters maintained continuous cover and given quick support at call, the withdrawal, if it could have been carried out at all, would have been a much grimmer and more protracted affair, with serious consequences to the main battle around Imphal.

This action on the Tiddim road was, in itself, a considerable success. The 17th Division was now in the Imphal Plain, intact with all its transport and wounded. It and the air forces supporting it had inflicted heavier losses on the Japanese than it had suffered. It had beaten them on every occasion in stand-up fights, and, as I saw for myself when I met the division just outside Imphal, its morale was correspondingly high. The 23d Division had similarly shared in these successes and, in addition, took a slightly mischievous pride in the fact that it had had to come to the rescue of the redoubtable 17th. Yet, looked at from the over-all picture of the battle, the fact that the 17th Division had been delayed, and still more that the bulk of Scoones's reserve had of necessity been drawn away at a critical time, might have had tragic consequences.

The other forward division of IV Corps, Gracey's 20th, in the Tamu area and at the head of the Kabaw Valley was never in so difficult a situation as the 17th, and its withdrawal went much more according to plan. To deal with it, the Japanese had assembled in the Kabaw Valley, under Major-General Yamamoto, around a nucleus of five battalions of their 33d Division, considerable bodies of the Burma Traitor Army and of Jiffs. To this rather mixed force, because the Sittaung–Palel –Imphal road was the most direct and easiest way to bring heavy equipment into the Imphal Plain, they entrusted a large part of their medium artillery, most of their one tank regiment, and a great deal of their mechanical transport.

On March 12, covered by a confusing screen of Jiffs and Burmans, the Japanese advanced. The 20th Division's rear guard repulsed all their attacks and it withdrew at its own pace. In these exchanges the division took its first prisoners, an officer and two men, all wounded. By this time, however, other Japanese forces which had crossed the Chindwin began to threaten our flank, and the order to fall back to the defended locality of Moreh, two miles north of Tamu, was given. On the 20th one of the few tank versus tank engagements of the campaign took place between a troop of the 3d Dragoon

Guards and Japanese medium and light tanks. The enemy armour was routed, four of their tanks destroyed, and another, to the great satisfaction of the Dragoons, captured and brought back. After dark, on March 22, the Japanese heavily attacked Moreh but were repulsed with the loss of more tanks.

By now the pressure of the main Japanese advance on Imphal from the east was growing more menacing, and Scoones was compelled to look for a reserve to replace the brigades of the 23d Division that had gone to the rescue of the 17th. He could find this only by drawing on the now heavily pressed 20th Division, and to provide it he had to order Gracey to evacuate Moreh and come back to Shenam and Tengoupal, about nine miles from Palel. On April 2, 32 Brigade was, therefore, withdrawn into Corps Reserve, leaving only two brigades to cover Palel and hold the southeastern approaches to the plain.

Within a week of the start of the Japanese offensive, while the 17th Division was still fighting its way out, it became clear that the situation in the Kohima area was likely to be even more dangerous than that at Imphal. Not only were enemy columns closing in on Kohima at much greater speed than I had expected, but they were obviously in much greater strength. Indeed it was soon evident that the bulk, if not the whole, of the Japanese 31st Division was driving for Kohima and Dimapur. I had been confident that the most the enemy could bring and maintain through such country would be one regimental group, the equivalent of a British brigade group. In that I had badly underestimated the Japanese capacity for large-scale, long-range infiltration, and for their readiness to accept odds in a gamble on supply. This misappreciation was the second great mistake I made in the Imphal battle.

It was an error that was likely to cost us dear. We were not prepared for so heavy a thrust; Kohima with its rather scratch garrison and, what was worse, Dimapur with no garrison at all, were in deadly peril. The loss of Kohima we could endure, but that of Dimapur, our only base and railhead, would have been crippling to an almost fatal degree. It would have pushed into the far distance our hopes of relieving Imphal, laid bare to the enemy the Brahmaputra Valley with its string of airfields, cut off Stilwell's Ledo Chinese, and stopped all supply to China. As I contemplated the chain of disasters that I had invited, my heart sank. However, I have always believed that a motto for generals must be 'No regrets,' no crying over spilt milk. The vital need was now to bring in reinforcements, not only to replace the vanished reserve in Imphal but, above all, to ensure that Dimapur was held. To achieve this I bent all my energies.

I at once ordered the 5th Indian Division to begin flying from Arakan to Assam but, with the demands already on them, the four British and four American Dakota squadrons of Troop Carrier Command could not possibly lift the division at the rate I demanded. It would then have been madness not to divert for a battle on which the fate of China might depend, some aircraft from the large numbers on the Hump route, but only the American Chiefs of Staff in far-off Washington had authority to do that. Baldwin and I pressed the vital need on Admiral Mountbatten and, seeing the urgency, on his own responsibility he ordered thirty Dakotas to join Troop Carrier Command—a decision which earned my gratitude and had a major effect on the coming battle.

Between March 17 and 18, headquarters and two brigades (9 and 123) of the 5th Division deplaned in Imphal—just in time. The third brigade (161), much as I disliked splitting up a division, I sent to Dimapur where the menace to Kohima made immediate help imperative. I also warned Christison in Arakan to have the 7th Indian Division ready with all speed to follow to Assam and to send the two commandos of 3 Special Service Brigade by rail to Silchar from where, by the Bishenpur track, they could threaten any Japanese move around the west of Imphal.

At my request, too, General Giffard, always a tower of strength in emergency, sent Wingate's 23 Brigade from India to Jorhat where I could use it to cover the Ledo railway to Stilwell and, if necessary, to take in flank a hostile move against Dimapur. He also sent, mainly by sea, the new 25th Indian Division to Arakan to replace those I had withdrawn. With General Auchinleck he had already begun to prepare the move to Assam from India of Headquarters, XXXIII Corps and the 2d British Division; I now asked that they should be sent as quickly as possible. On March 18 General Giffard ordered their move to Dimapur to begin and on March 23 Lieutenant-General Stopford, XXXIII Corps commander, reported to me.

There was among the administrative staffs understandable anxiety as to whether we should be able to supply these considerable reinforcements, but I declared my willingness to accept the risk. We were evacuating noncombatants and labour at thousands a week by every returning air, road, and rail vehicle; besides, I have found that British administrative staffs work to such safety margins that there is always quite a lot in hand. I was sure that, even if we went short for a bit, we would manage.

Time, in fact, made me more anxious than supply—time was so short. It was a race between the Japanese onrush and the arrival of our reinforcements. As I struggled hard to redress my errors and to speed by rail and air these reinforcements I knew that all depended on the steadfastness of the troops already meeting the first impetus of the attack. If they could hold until help arrived, all would be well; if not, we were near disaster. Happily for the result of the battle—and for me—I was, like other generals before me, to be saved from the consequences of my mistakes by the resourcefulness of my surbordinate commanders and the stubborn valour of my troops.

Pushed out some thirty miles to the east, to cover the approaches to Kohima, was one battalion, the newly-formed Assam Regiment, with detachments of the Assam Rifles, the local armed police. The main weight of the enemy advance fell on this battalion, in the first battle of its career. Fighting in its own country, it put up a magnificent resistance, held doggedly to one position after another against overwhelming odds, and, in spite of heavy casualties, its companies, although separated, never lost cohesion. The delay the Assam Regiment imposed on the 31st Japanese Division at this stage was invaluable.

Behind this screen, desperate efforts were in hand to make Kohima Ridge into a great road block to bar the way to Dimapur. Noncombatants and hospital patients had already been evacuated, and, under the energetic and determined leadership of Colonel Richards, commanding Kohima, the men in the convalescent depot, some five hundred of them, were issued arms, organized into units, and allotted to the defences. Every man who could be scraped up from administrative units was roped in to fight. More trenches were dug, dressing stations prepared, defences manned, but it was a very miscellaneous garrison of about a thousand who stood to as the covering troops were forced slowly back, and it was a grim prospect they faced as fifteen thousand ravening Japanese closed in on them.

I flew into Dimapur and at once realized that, with Imphal likely to be cut off and our affairs there going by no means according to plan, I could not expect Scoones to control a tactically separate battle at Kohima. I, therefore, placed all operations in the Kohima–Dimapur–Jorhat theatre, until the arrival of III Corps, under General Ranking, who commanded the base and rear areas of Assam, known as 202 Line of Communications Area—a sudden plunge for him from peaceful administrative duties to the stresses of a savage battle against desperate odds. And it would be against odds. His fighting troops were the Assam, a raw Nepalese, and part of a Burmese battalion. I asked the brigadier commanding the Dimapur Base what his ration strength was. 'Forty-five thousand, near enough,' he replied. 'And how many soldiers can you scrape up out of that lot?' I inquired. He smiled wryly. 'I might get five hundred who know how to fire a rifle!' As I walked around with him, inspecting bunkers and rifle pits, dug by noncombatant labour under the direction of storemen and clerks, and as I looked into the faces of the willing but untried garrison, I could only hope I imparted more confidence than I felt.

During the last days of March 161 Brigade of the 5th Indian Division completed its fly-in from Arakan, and never was reinforcement more welcome. The whole Japanese 31st Division was reported ten to twenty miles from Kohima and our problem was whether to give up Kohima and hold the vital Dimapur or send 161 Brigade to hold the enemy on Kohima Ridge until the 2d Division came to the rescue. If we had not enough troops to hold Kohima, we certainly had not enough to hold sprawling Dimapur, and as long as we clung to the ridge we covered the arrival of reinforcements. When I held a conference of officers at Dimapur, I was not surprised to see some apprehensive faces, but I gave them three tasks:

1. To prepare Dimapur for defence and if attacked to hold it at all costs.

2. To reinforce Kohima with 161 Brigade and hold it to the last.

3. To prepare for the rapid reception and assembly of the large reinforcements now on the way.

As always happens on these occasions, as soon as everybody was given a clear task into which he could throw himself, spirits rose and even I began to feel a little better. I took Warren, who commanded 161 Brigade, outside and walked him up and down the path while I gave him, without any attempt to minimize the hazardous task he was being set, a fuller view of the situation, and especially of the time factor. I told him I calculated that the enemy could reach Kohima by April 3 and, even if we held there, might by-pass our garrison and be attacking Dimapur by the 10th. I could not expect more than one brigade of the 2d Division to have arrived by that time, or the whole division before the 20th. Actually the Transportation Services materially improved on these timings. Steady, unruffled, slow-speaking Warren heard me out, asked a few questions, and went quietly off to get on with his job. I hope I had as good an effect on him as he had on me.

After my talk with him, Warren took his brigade to Kohima on March 29, and such was his energy that the next day one of his battalions was in action with the enemy, more than twenty miles south, while the rest of the brigade was disposed to cover the withdrawal of the Assam Battalion. I had meanwhile left Dimapur and sent Ranking my written directive, in which I stressed that his main task was to safeguard Dimapur base. There were at this time reports and rumours of Japanese forces within striking distance of Dimapur, and he decided that the situation necessitated troops for the close defence of the base if he was to carry out this task. He therefore, much to Warren's annoyance, ordered 161 Brigade back to the Nichugard Pass, eight miles southeast of Dimapur, to be in position there by the evening of March 31. In taking this action Ranking was, I think, influenced understandably by the stress I had laid on his primary task—the defence of Dimapur base. The reports proved untrue, and the withdrawal of the brigade was an unfortunate mistake. Had it remained south of Kohima, Warren would almost certainly have at least delayed the Japanese advance on Kohima for several days. That would have put a very different aspect on the battle that followed.

Japanese pressure towards Kohima was mounting. With the withdrawal of 161 Brigade, the covering troops were in grave difficulties as the enemy outflanked and enveloped them. The Assam Battalion, still fighting stubbornly and losing heavily, was split in two. Half of it, about two hundred strong, made its way into Kohima and joined the garrison; the rest evaded encircling Japanese and, in good order but exhausted, reached the main Dimapur road behind 161 Brigade.

I have spent some uncomfortable hours at the beginnings of battles, but few more anxious than those of the Kohima battle. All the Japanese commander had to do was to leave a detachment to mask Kohima, and, with the rest of his division, thrust violently on Dimapur. He could hardly fail to take it. Luckily, Major-General Sato, commander of the Japanese 31st Division, was, without exception, the most unenterprising of all the Japanese generals I encountered. He had been ordered to take Kohima and dig in. His bullet head was filled with one idea only—to take Kohima. It never struck him that he could inflict terrible damage on us without taking Kohima at all. Leaving a small force to contain it, and moving by tracks to the east of Warren's brigade at Nichugard, he could, by April 5, have struck the railway with the bulk of his division. But he had no vision, so, as his troops came up, he flung them into attack after attack on the little town of Kohima. I have said I was saved from the gravest effects of my mistake in underestimating the enemy's capacity to penetrate to Kohima by the stubborn valour of my troops; but it needed the stupidity of the local enemy commander to make quite sure. Unfortunately, at the time, I did not know this was to be supplied, or I should have been saved much anxiety. Later, when it was evident, I once found some enthusiastic Royal Air Force officers planning an air strike on Sato's headquarters. They were astonished when I suggested they should abandon the project as I regarded their intended victim as one of my most helpful generals! But the time to indulge in such frivolities was not yet.

Lieutenant-General Montague Stopford, commander of XXXIII Indian Corps, with some of his staff, had reached my headquarters at Comilla on March 23. I knew him and had every confidence in him as a commander, but his Corps Headquarters had not previously operated and, indeed, had done little training. They would have to shake down and gain experience as they fought—never an easy thing to do. The success and speed with which they overcame their teething troubles were a measure of their ability and their commander's leadership.

I had at first considered Silchar at the location for XXXIII Corps Headquarters. It was central, had certain advantages in approach to Imphal and in communications; but the unexpected seriousness of the threat to Dimapur made it imperative to get not only the bulk of the reinforcements but Corps Headquarters also into that area. I also decided that Kohima at this stage must have priority over Imphal. Stopford himself urged this and I agreed with him. I gave Stopford as his objects:

1. To prevent Japanese penetration into the Brahmaputra or Surma valleys or through the Lushai Hills.
2. To keep open the Dimapur–Kohima–Imphal road.
3. To move to the help of IV Corps and to cooperate with it in the destruction of all enemy west of the Chindwin.

These tasks were not changed throughout the battle, and remained the over-all directive for XXXIII Corps. I gave him tactical freedom in the methods he chose to carry them out, and he, therefore, deserves the credit for accomplishing them.

On April 3 Stopford arrived at Jorhat on the Assam railway, some sixty-five miles north-northeast of Dimapur, and established his headquarters there. Next day he took over control of operations from Ranking. In the ten days that had passed since Stopford had received his original orders the Kohima situation had developed, but not, alas, to our advantage, and I decided that his immediate tasks had now become:

(i) To cover the concentration of his corps as far forward as practicable.
(ii) To secure the Dimapur base.
(iii) To reinforce and hold Kohima.
(iv) To protect, as far as possible without jeopardizing (i) to (iii), the Assam railway and the China route airfields in the Brahmaputra Valley.

The XXXIII Corps plan to achieve these ends was:

(a) To concentrate the corps as it arrived northeast of Dimapur. This would avoid its becoming immediately involved in an enemy attack on the base and would place it advantageously to deliver a counterstroke. It would also automatically protect the railway to Ledo.

(b) To send forward the first brigade of the 2d Division as soon as it arrived to hold the Nichugard Pass, eight miles southeast of Dimapur, thus covering the base against a direct Japanese advance.

(c) To reinforce Kohima with 161 Brigade of the 5th Indian Division at once.

(d) To use 23 Brigade (Chindits), expected about April 12, to strike south on Kohima and to the east of it, with the double object of checking Japanese infiltration towards the railway and of cutting the enemy line of communication to the Chindwin.

(e) To cover the western end of the Silchar–Bishenpur track with another Nepalese battalion which I had made available until the arrival of 3 Special Service Brigade.

(f) To continue to use the newly-formed Lushai Brigade to prevent an enemy advance into the Lushai Hills.

Wasting no time, on the evening of April 4, Stopford ordered 161 Brigade to move again to Kohima. It left Nichugard the next day, and its leading unit, the 4th Battalion, The Royal West Kent Regiment, joined the garrison late the same day, just after the first Japanese night attack had overrun some of our positions. The rest of the brigade, warned of the congestion in Kohima, halted and dug in for the night. Early on the morning of the 6th a company of Rajputs got into Kohima and one platoon of it brought out two hundred walking wounded and noncombatants. During the morning, however, the Japanese closed around the town, and the brigade was unable to gain the ridge. The road behind was soon afterwards cut by a strong enemy detachment who established a block between the brigade and Dimapur. The situation at Kohima was thus: its garrison of about three thousand men closely invested by superior forces, 161 Brigade cut off five miles to the north, a detachment holding the Nichugard defile southeast of Dimapur, and the base itself in no state to resist a serious attack. A decidedly unpleasant situation, but there were not wanting more hopeful signs.

At the end of March the 2d British Division had been dispersed in training in southern India. Such was the rapidity of its move, carried out by the Movement Staffs of General Headquarters India and of General Giffard's headquarters, that on April 2 its leading elements were arriving at Dimapur, two brigades and the Divisional Headquarters were on the way by air, and one brigade by rail. A regiment of tanks and later 268 Indian Motorized Brigade were also thrown in for good measure by General Auchinleck.

As I shuttled between Dimapur, Imphal, and my headquarters at Comilla, I was beginning to see light. We had hard days ahead of us, but everywhere our troops, unperturbed by events, were steady and full of fight. We had lost nothing vital.

CHAPTER XV

ATTRITION

On the Assam front the first week of April had been an anxious one. Thanks to my mistakes the battle had not started well; at any time crisis might have slipped into disaster—and still might. We were in tactical difficulties everywhere. The Japanese were pressing hard on the rim of the Imphal Plain; they still threatened the Dimapur base, while the Kohima garrison was in dire peril; and they had cut the Kohima–Imphal road, which was certainly no part of *my* plan. Yet for their gains they had paid a higher price in dead and wounded, and, above all, in time, than they had calculated on in *their* plan. Now our air forces, tireless and bold, dominated the skies. Under their wings our reinforcements were flowing in more smoothly and rapidly than I had hoped. As I watched the little flags, representing divisions, cluser round Imphal and Kohima on my situation map, I heaved a sigh of relief. As the second week of April wore on, for all its alarms and fears I felt that our original pattern for the battle was reasserting itself.

By the beginning of April Scoones should have the best part of four divisions at Imphal, enough to turn the tide there. It was on the Kohima side of the picture that I looked more anxiously, and I decided that, even at the cost of skimping Scoones, I must nourish Stopford. Luckily Sato continued to limit himself to frontal attacks on Kohima, first by day and then, as the toll exacted by the garrison and by the swift retaliation of our aircraft in daylight proved too high even for Japanese stomachs, by night. Throughout the day and in the intervals between these night attacks the enemy artillery, mortars, and machine guns hammered relentlessly at our positions on Garrison Hill. British and Japanese trenches were within yards of one another, every move brought a shot, rest was impossible. Sheer exhaustion rather than the enemy threatened to vanquish our men. Then came the worst blow of

all. During the night of April 5–6 the Japanese gained possession of the water supply, and thirst was added to the other
horrors. The R.A.F., regardless of fire from the ground, swept
over at treetop level to drop motorcar inner tubes filled with
water. By good fortune a small spring was found inside our
lines, yet, even with this to supplement the air force contribution, the water ration dropped to less than a pint a man and a
little more for the wounded. Gradually the area we held was
squeezed until, from a rough square with sides of a thousand
yards, it became a meagre five hundred by five hundred. Into
this confined space the enemy rained down a pitiless bombardment; against its haggard, thirsty garrison they hurled attack
after attack.

But help was at hand. By April 11 headquarters and two
brigades of the 2d Division had reached Dimapur; the third
was following close behind, and next day the Chindit 23 Brigade arrived at Jorhat. We had thus drawn about level with
the Japanese in numbers, and, as soon as the 7th Indian Division, now under orders from Arakan, could be got in we
would be on the way to superiority.

Stopford at once sent the leading brigade of the 2d Division
up the road towards 161 Brigade, still held up short of
Kohima. Every few miles Japanese positions barred the advance but, one by one, they were stormed in stiff fighting, the
enemy counterattacking time and again. On April 15, the two
brigades joined hands and 161 Brigade was able to resume its
assault astride the road and along a ridge on its right. The
Japanese reacted fiercely and progress was at first slow, but on
the 18th Warren's men finally broke through to the hard-
pressed garrison, clinging grimly to its smoking hilltop.
Kohima was relieved.

After dark the wounded were brought out, and next day,
although the road remained at times under fire, Kohima was
restocked, while 161 Brigade fought to gain a little more space.
In the dark, early on April 20, 6 Brigade of the 2d Division
relieved the rest of the garrison, and Colonel Richards handed
over the command he had so gallantly held. Then he and his
men left the dust, din, and stench of death in which they had
lived for eleven days.

They had endured much. Forced into an ever-contracting
circle by the relentless assaults of vastly superior numbers,
their casualties had been severe. There had been no evacua-

tion for the wounded, and men were hit again and again as they lay in the casualty stations. Thirst was not the least of the trials of these devoted men. Sieges have been longer but few have been more intense, and in none have the defenders deserved greater honour than the garrison of Kohima.

Although the small force that had been cut off on Garrison Hill had now been relieved, most of Kohima Ridge itself remained in hostile hands. With their centre on the town, the Japanese held an immensely strong position, some seven thousand yards long, astride the main Imphal–Limapur road. The natural defensive strength of a succession of steep, wooded ridges had been improved by the Japanese genius for inter-supporting fieldworks and concealment, until it was as formidable a position as a British army has ever faced. Its flanks, extending into high and most difficult country, were protected by inaccessibility. The enemy also had detachments dug in well forward on tracks which led through dense jungle to the main road and railway. There was thus the constant threat of infiltration and of movements against our rear. It was always a wonder to me why Sato did not attempt a bold stroke of this kind. It would háve been typically Japanese, and he had, even at this stage, enough troops for it if he cared to take some risk at Kohima itself.

Our own build-up was proceeding rapidly. The 2d British Division was almost complete—too complete as far as its generous scale of motor transport was concerned. However, an attack by twelve Oscars on a mass of these useless vehicles, jammed into a village, added point to my exhortations to XXXIII Corps to get them out of the area. Relieved of excessive transport, the division found, like others in Burma, that it could move faster without it. The leading brigade (33) of the 7th Indian Division had also arrived by air from Arakan and columns of 23 Chindit Brigade were successfully engaged and moving in the direction of Jessami.

Stopford energetically urged the 2d Division to advance, but the terrain and type of warfare were strange to British troops, while Grover, its commander, was hampered by the piecemeal arrival of his formations. In spite of this, the division went forward on April 21. Its left brigade (5), in an attempt to outflank the Japanese, climbed two thousand feet to a ridge running due north from Kohima, but then, its further advance, delayed by rain on the slippery ascent, was held up, a few days later, well short of its final objectives. Nor did the right brigade, similarly handicapped by rain and supply difficulties among the ridges on that flank, make the progress expected.

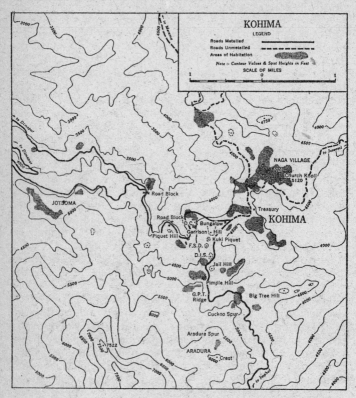

KOHIMA

LEGEND

Roads Metalled
Roads Unmetalled
Areas of Habitation

Note :- Contour Values & Spot Heights in Feet

SCALE OF MILES

The centre brigade (6) was, on the night of April 22–23, heavily attacked on the shambles of Garrison Hill. In fierce hand-to-hand fighting the Japanese were beaten off, but for the next two days our men were under constant pressure and bombardment, much as the original garrison had been. On the 22d an attempt with infantry and tanks to relieve the pressure failed, as the tanks were held up by difficult ground. Then, on the night of the 27th a more formidable assault—the first of a series of attacks and counterattacks—was launched on the deputy commissioner's bungalow. This had once been a charming house in a delightful garden but was now a heap of rubble with only one chimney standing, black and twisted, against the sky. This attack, after desperate fighting, succeeded in reaching and holding, not only the site of the house but the bluff in the garden, which overlooked the Kohima crossroads and denied them to the enemy—a very valuable tactical success. On the night of the 29th–30th the Japanese made a final attempt, in an all-out counter-attack, to regain possession, but failed with heavy loss. Each side was left holding part of the garden, with the tennis court as a no-man's land between them, and with hand grenades shuttling back and forth in the place of tennis balls.

As neither flank brigade could make the progress hoped for and as the centre brigade was hard pressed opposite Kohima itself, the divisional plan was changed. The wider turning movements were abandoned, and it was decided to deliver a more concentrated attack on the Japanese position so that all three brigades could act in close tactical combination and in turn have the full support of the divisional and corps artillery.

This setback was disappointing, but the 7th Indian Division was coming in well and would be followed by 268 Indian Lorried Brigade, giving me the two-to-one superiority that was my aim at both Kohima and Imphal. The 2d British Division, while as brave as troops could be, was inexperienced and so, while I continued to divert to XXXIII Corps resources badly needed elsewhere, I did not nag Stopford to hurry. I had no intention of yielding to urgings from a distance to break through at all costs and relieve Imphal. Imphal was in no danger of falling and General Giffard increased my debt to him by the firmness with which he stood between me and such pressures.

The battle of Kohima was a bloody one. The first full-scale assault by the 2d Division under the new plan, much delayed by rain, went in on May 4. The brigade on the right (4), whose objectives were G.P.T. Ridge and Jail Hill, succeeded only in taking part of the first, where by nightfall the enemy and our own men were inextricably mingled. The centre brigade failed to take Kuki Piquet and, although with tanks our infantry reached F.S.D. Ridge, they were unable, under the devastating enfilade fire that met them, to dig in on more than a portion of the ridge. Here again at the end of the day the enemy positions and ours were mixed together. The left brigade (5) at first succeeded in taking Naga Village, but during the night heavy counterattacks pushed us back to the western edge of the village. The Treasury area remained firmly in enemy hands. Both sides were now exhausted; the Japanese unable to counterattack while we could only secure minor adjustments at the cost of considerable casualties. Even when Stopford handed over his reserve, 33 Brigade of the 7th Indian Division, it failed after a gallant attempt to dislodge the enemy from Jail Hill.

After four days' bitter fighting with heavy casualties, the assault had little to show. While the 31st Japanese Division certainly lacked initiative, it had all the enemy's fanatical stubbornness in defence. Our troops were again discovering that it was one thing to reach a Japanese bunker, another to enter it. Nor had artillery bombardment and accurate attacks by Hurricanes and Vengeance bombers on the limited areas engaged had much result. The most effective weapon proved to be the tank, firing solid shot at point-blank range; but the wooded terrain, its steepness, and the wet that made tanks churn everything into liquid mud restricted their use. It was clear that the battle would be prolonged and savage.

The attack was resumed on the night of May 10–11, when two brigades of the 2d Division attempted to seize G.P.T. and F.S.D. Ridges, with the object of preventing the attack on the main objectives, Jail Hill and the D.I.S. Area, by 33 Brigade of the 7th Division being enfiladed as had previously happened. The advance of the 2d Division was only partly successful; the enemy at dawn still held the reverse slopes of G.P.T. Ridge and a strong point on F.S.D. Ridge, but 33 Brigade fared better. At dawn, in spite of heavy casualties, they were in possession of most of Jail Hill and all the D.I.S. area, but as they tried to dig in they came under accurate automatic fire from the parts of G.P.T. and F.S.D. Ridges still in enemy hands. They hung on with great determination in rain and mud, losing men fast, until relieved by a heavy smoke screen put down by our artillery for several hours. During the night of the 12th they cleared a mine field, thus enabling tanks to join them, and by the morning of the 13th had put such pressure on the Japanese that both the key points of Jail Hill and D.I.S. Area fell completely to us. Seeing this, the enemy abandoned

G.P.T. Ridge, F.S.D. Ridge, and Kuki Piquet, all of which the 2d Division occupied.

While this considerable action was going on, our other positions all along the front were being cleared up and extended by local operations. Typical of the Japanese resistance was the last phase of the prolonged struggle for the deputy commissioner's bungalow, where, although cut off, some enemy in deep bunkers continued to fight stubbornly. Sappers made a track up which a tank could climb, and the Dorsets then attacked with its support. Each bunker was engaged in turn by the tank's 75-mm. guns, whose effect at thirty yards was decisive. Japanese attempting to escape were bayoneted or shot; none tried to surrender. The few remaining bunkers were demolished by pole charges thrust through their loopholes and, by the afternoon of May 13, the deputy commissioner's bungalow, his garden, and tennis court, which had acquired an almost ritual significance, were all finally in our hands at remarkably low cost in casualties.

Treasury Hill was the next objective of 33 Brigade. A Gurkha battalion was concentrated on Garrison Hill during the 14th for a deliberate attack next day, but from patrol reports the brigadier concluded that most of the enemy were pulling out and he ordered an infiltrating attack in the dark. By first light on the 15th the Gurkhas, meeting practically no resistance, had occupied the whole of Treasury Hill.

The gains thus made in a few days since May 10 changed the whole picture around Kohima. The most satisfactory feature was the failure of the Japanese anywhere to counterattack— evidence of their increasing disorganization under these heavy blows. There followed on this part of the battlefield a short lull while both sides regrouped themselves for a renewal of the struggle.

Meanwhile, on the Imphal front fighting as bitter but more diffuse had been claiming my attention. It was not without its moments of anxiety, for Scoones was being hard pressed.

Like unevenly spaced spokes of a wheel, six routes converged on to the Imphal Plain to meet at the hub, Imphal itself:

 (i) From the north, the broad Kohima road.
 (ii) Also from the north, the footpath down the Iril River Valley.
 (iii) From the northeast, the Ukhrul road.

(iv) From the southeast, the tarmac Tamu–Palel road.
(v) From the south, the rugged Tiddim highway.
(vi) From the west, Silchar–Bishenpur track.

It was by these that the Japanese strove to break into the plain. The fighting all around its circumference was continuous, fierce, and often confused as each side manoeuvred to outwit and kill. There was always a Japanese thrust somewhere that had to be met and destroyed. Yet the fighting did follow a pattern. The main encounters were on or near the spokes of the wheel, because it was only along these that guns, tanks, and vehicles could move. The Japanese would advance astride the route, attack our troops blocking it, and try to outflank or infiltrate past them. We should first hold, then counterattack, and the struggle would sway a mile or two, one way and the other. All the time our airmen, who played so vital a part in these battles, would be daily in sortie after sortie delivering attacks at ground level and hammering the enemy's communications right back into Burma. Gradually we should prevail, and, driven from the spokes of the wheel, the Japanese would take to the hills between them. Relentlessly we would hunt them down and when, desperate and rabid, they turned at bay, kill them. This pattern repeated itself along each of the spokes as, on one after the other, we passed from defence to offence.

Our casualties in this kind of fighting were not light. The infantry, as usual, suffered most and endured most, for this was above all an infantry battle, hand to hand, man against man, and no quarter. Our heaviest losses were among the officers, not only in the infantry who in this close fighting could not fail to be conspicuous, but among the artillery observation officers who to give accurate support pushed on with the leading troops, and among the young tank commanders who regardless of safety, kept their turrets open or moved on foot so that they could guide their tanks through the jungle.

To deal briefly with the events on each spoke of the wheel is probably the clearest way to give a picture of this battle, but it should be remembered that encounters on all the spokes were going on simultaneously. At no time and in no place was the situation either to commanders or troops, as clear even as I can make it now. Into Scoones's headquarters, from every point of the compass, day and night, streamed signals, messages, reports, announcing successes, setbacks, appealing for reinforcements, demanding more ammunition, asking urgently for wounded to be evacuated, begging for air support. His was the task of meeting or withstanding these appeals, of deciding which at the moment was the place to which his by no means overgenerous reserves should be allotted. It was impossible for him to satisfy all his commanders. It needed a tough, cool, and well-balanced commander to meet, week after week, this strain. Luckily Scoones *was* tough, cool, and well balanced.

To take first the actions on the Iril Valley and Ukhrul road spokes. In the first days of April the leading troops of the 5th Division, straight from their aircraft, had pushed back the Japanese threat developing from Ukhrul. The enemy then attacked Nungshigum, a great hill, which not only dominated the Imphal Plain and gave direct observation at a range of five miles over the main air strip, but threatened the rear of our troops on the Ukhrul road. Nungshigum has two peaks; the original Japanese assault drove out men from the northern, but we clung to the southern. After five days of enemy attack we lost that, too. Next day we retook it, only to lose it again, but on the following day, the 13th, while Hurribombers, their guns blazing, dived almost into the treetops, and tanks, winched up incredible slopes, fired point-blank into bunker loopholes, our infantry stormed both peaks—and held them. The last Japanese, still fighting, were bayoneted in their last fox holes. So difficult was the country and so dense the jungle that our tanks went into action with turrets open so that the commanders could see to help the infantry. These young officers and N.C.O.s unhesitatingly took this risk and, alas, a high proportion of them were killed.

With Nungshigum secure, the 5th Division proceeded to clear the Iril Valley, and for three weeks a struggle went on to eject the Japanese from the commanding Mapao Spur between the Iril Valley and the Imphal–Kohima road. Here we drove the enemy from his southern positions, but he still held grimly to the rest of the spur. Meanwhile, two brigades of the 23d Division combed the hills south of the Ukhrul road, chased the headquarters of the 15th Japanese Division, and pushed the enemy back to within fifteen miles of Ukhrul. By the middle of May the situation both in the Iril Valley and on the Ukhrul road could be considered stabilized.

On the Palel road spoke of the wheel at the beginning of April the 20th Division, having lost one brigade taken for Corps Reserve, was with the two remaining brigades, 80 and 100, holding a twenty-five-mile front running from Tengoupal, ten miles southeast of Palel, through Shenam to Shuganu, fifteen miles southwest of Palel. The country is a crisscross of steep ridges and deep *nullahs*, all tree covered, with in parts dense jungle. Gracey's troops could not, of course, maintain a continuous line; they had to content themselves by holding the most important heights and the passes by which the main road and the most usable tracks approached Palel and the Imphal Plain. Between these tactical points they strove to dominate the country and prevent Japanese infiltration by constant and aggressive patrolling. In this, luckily, they had already obtained something of a mastery over the enemy, but it was a long and vulnerable front which, through this phase of the battle, was a source of anxiety to Scoones.

The Japanese commander here, Major General Yamamoto, was under great pressure from his superiors to break into the Imphal Plain. The tanks and artillery which constituted a large part of his force were urgently wanted by Mataguchi, the army commander, to reduce our defences around Imphal. So Yamamoto launched attack after attack to crash through the 20th Division defences on the Shenam Pass. These assaults, supported more heavily than usual for the Japanese by armour and artillery, were constant throughout April.

The bitterest and most obstinate fighting was around Tengoupal, covering the main road up which Yamamoto was trying to blast his way. Between April 4–20, assaults, usually by night and often with tanks, were almost continuous. In attack and counterattack ridges, shorn bare of their trees, changed hands again and again, and our men, never very thick on the ground, were becoming exhausted. At last, on April 22, after very heavy fighting, parts of our position were overrun, but the enemy had suffered too severely to continue and we still held him.

A brigade of the Indian National Army was on this front, and Japanese patrols, accompanied by these Jiffs masquerading as our sepoys, constantly infiltrated towards Palel. It was impossible in such country to intercept every hostile group and one small Japanese party actually reached Palel Keep, where it was wiped out, a stout-hearted attempt, in contrast to the halfhearted, ineffective effort a few days later by a large group of Jiffs which left considerable gangs of these unfortunate Jiffs wandering about without object or cohesion. Large numbers surrendered but our Indian and Gurkha soldiers were not too ready to let them do so, and orders had to be issued to give them a kinder welcome. The Jiffs took no further appreciable part in operations and the Japanese in disgust used those left mainly as porters.

However, Japanese patrols were in the hills north and east of Palel and might interfere with the regular use of the airfield, so Scoones was forced to divert a brigade (48) from the 17th Division and later replace it by the one from the 23d Division that chased the Headquarters of the Japanese 15th Division. This hostile infiltration towards Palel coincided with Yamamoto's final effort to break through on the main road. For six days and nights he resumed attacks on Tengoupal, gradually pushing us back until on May 12 a most gallant counterattack restored an anxious situation here, leaving both sides so spent that neither could seriously revive the battle. The two brigades of the 20th Division had withstood heavy assaults and continuous pressure for more than two months, and Scoones now relieved them on this front by Roberts's 23d Division with all its three brigades; on this spoke of the wheel, too, by mid-May we could consider the situation stabilized.

It was along the Tiddim road and the Silchar–Bishenpur track, the southern and western spokes of the wheel, that some of the heaviest fighting of this Battle of Attrition took place. When the 17th Division reached Imphal after its withdrawal along the Tiddim road, Scoones left behind it, to hold off the Japanese 33d Division which was pressing towards Imphal, two brigades, 37 and 49, of Roberts's 23d Division. The 37 Brigade was quickly recalled to join its division, and 49 Brigade on April 9 was attacked in its positions south of Bishenpur at Milestones 30 and 35 on the Tiddim road. These attacks were repulsed and a Japanese detachment that had audaciously inserted itself between the forward battalion and the rest of the brigade was completely destroyed. In the short lull that followed, Scoones pulled out 49 Brigade so as to complete the 23d Division and replaced it by his Corps Reserve, 32 Brigade of the 20th Division. The brigadier of 32 Brigade, realizing the danger of encirclement from the west that threatened the old 49 Brigade position, decided to pull back to Bishenpur, where he commanded both the Tiddim road from the south and the Silchar track from the west.

It was well that he did so. Repulsed on the Tiddim road, the enemy, reverting to his favourite tactics, concentrated in the jungle west of the road, and made for the Bishenpur–Silchar track, hoping to break into the Imphal Plain from the west. In the second week of April, Japanese patrols reached the track and encountered ours, but by then our 32 Brigade was in position covering Bishenpur. On the night of April 14–15 the Japanese 33d Division, which had now received reinforcements, attacked towards Bishenpur, but was again repulsed. While this attack was developing the enemy succeeded in blowing up the bridge at Milestone 51 on the Silchar track. This was a three-hundred-foot suspension bridge over an eighty-foot deep gorge and its destruction made a complete break in the track. The demolition was a typical Japanese suicide operation. While skirmishing was going on in darkness near the bridge, three Japanese eluded the engineer platoon guarding it and placed the explosive charges. One Japanese jumped to his death in the gorge; the other two went up with the bridge. Having failed to dislodge our troops covering Bishenpur, the enemy then attempted to pass a strong column into the plain around the northwest of the village. Heavy fighting lasting several days resulted, and there were alarms and excursions throughout the area as Japanese detachments probed forward towards Imphal.

The threat from the west had caused Scoones to pull back the 17th Division, which had been operating north of Imphal, and give it the task of securing this line of approach. He also left under Cowan's Command 32 Brigade, now fully engaged and under heavy pressure. On April 19, just in time, the leading troops of the 17th Division began to arrive and went straight into action northwest of Bishenpur. To the south of that village the enemy occupied the straggling hamlet of Ninthoukhong in force. A first attempt by 33 Brigade to eject them failed on April 23, and so did a second by troops of the 17th Division two days later. In these attacks we suffered heavily and lost seven medium tanks. The valour of our troops had been equalled by the tenacity of the Japanese. Very bitter fighting continued and cost both sides many casualties; the Japanese advance into the plain was halted, but they held the village and remained a dangerous threat.

Again the fighting on the Silchar track west of Bishenpur flared up. The Japanese were under orders to break through at all costs and 32 Brigade from the 20th Division was under equally emphatic orders to prevent them. The savage struggle surged backward and forward along the track and across it. Our casualties were alarmingly heavy, especially in British officers of the Indian Army who could not fail to be picked out in such close fighting. These officers, many of them in their early twenties, made me proud to belong to the same army. One young lieutenant-colonel, commanding a battalion that had already lost three-quarters of its officers and who had himself been severely wounded in the stomach by grenade fragments, was again hit while leading his men. When asked why at this second wound he had not gone back at least as far as the field ambulance to have his wounds properly dressed, he admitted that the grenade in the stomach was a nuisance as it made getting about rather difficult, but he could still keep up with his men so there was no need to go back. As to the second wound, 'The bullet,' he explained, 'has passed straight through my shoulder so it causes me no inconvenience!' No wonder the Japanese never broke through. When, a little time afterwards, I wished to promote this very gallant officer to command of a brigade, I found to my grief that he had been killed later in the battle.

Heavy attacks on April 26 were thrown back, although our forward troops remained cut off from Bishenpur for some time until the track was reopened. Fighting continued, and, having failed in direct assaults, the enemy resorted to large-scale infiltration. In the first half of May, too, the Japanese air force made some of its rare appearances in strength. Besides bombing and strafing our airfields, about twenty-five Zeros attacked Bishenpur on the 6th and again on May 10. On the latter day our anti-aircraft guns took heavy toll and the visits were not repeated. The Japanese had managed to get into Potsangbam—the 'Pots and Pans' of the British soldier—only two miles south of Bishenpur. Potsangbam, like many villages in the plain, was intersected by high banks and belts of trees, which hampered tank movement and provided admirable positions for defence. Heavy fighting by 32 and 63 Brigade was needed, with lavish air support from the fighters of 221 Group and the bombers of Strategic Air Force, before our men were able on May 15 to winkle the enemy out. We lost twelve tanks, and it was here for the first time that the Japanese used their ten-inch mortars, one of which we captured. The situation around Bishenpur was still confused. The Japanese 33d Division was living up to its reputation for being always dangerous, but it had suffered heavily. Deserters who came in reported that at the end of April one of its regiments was reduced from some three thousand to a strength of only eight hundred. The fact that even two or three deserters had appeared was a new and encouraging sign. We believed, however, that the division had since received further reinforcements and would again attempt something. It was not possible to say here, as we could on other sectors of the Imphal front, that the situation was stabilized.

On the Imphal–Kohima road, the last and most important of the Imphal spokes, the Japanese 31st Division had cut the road thirty miles north of Imphal on March 30. While some of the enemy turned north and moved on Kohima, a strong detachment of their 15th Division came south towards Kanglatongbi, where we had a large supply depot. This was rather hurriedly evacuated but most of the arms and ammunition there were got out, although stores and clothing fell to the enemy when they occupied it. A brigade of the 17th Division, newly arrived in Imphal from Tiddim, was rushed north and, helped by tanks which to the enemy's surprise climbed steep ridges, began to push back the Japanese. The severe fighting on the Silchar track recalled this brigade to its division and it was relieved at Kanglatongbi by the 5th Division. Briggs, its commander, using one brigade to hold the Mapao Spur on the east of the road, another to deliver a series of short hooks behind the enemy on the west, and his third to push straight forward astride the road, after brisk fighting, on May 21 retook Kanglatongbi and continued to push north. The situation on this spoke was well in hand.

By the middle of May 1944, therefore, my worst anxieties were over. At Kohima the Japanese had been thrown definitely on the defensive; on the Imphal–Kohima road our advance had begun; around Imphal Scoones could feel assured that, unless the enemy were greatly reinforced, danger from the north and east was unlikely. The Japanese 15th Division had been well hammered and was losing cohesion. To the south and west, where the redoubtable 33d Japanese Division was being reinforced from both their 53d and 54th Divisions, there was still the prospect of a last attempt by the enemy. Our command of the air over the whole battlefield was virtually unchallenged and, thanks to this and to the daring of our patrols, the enemy supply system was falling into confusion. Most significant, too, the monsoon was almost upon us.

The more satisfactory turn that events had taken did not pass unnoticed in other circles than Fourteenth Army. The number of visitors at my headquarters notably increased. In the opening stages of the battle most of my visitors had been rather gloomy, a state of mind perhaps understandable, as India was full of rumours of disaster. Now, except that they believed Imphal was starving, they tended to optimism. They were particularly anxious that I should 'relieve Imphal before it was too late.' Neither General Giffard nor I was as anxious as they appeared about Imphal's power to hold out; we knew that IV Corps would shortly take the offensive. The supply situation there, though tight—certain rations had already been reduced—would not become difficult until about the middle of June and not desperate until at least a month later. I therefore stuck to my date, the date I had consistently given for the opening of the road, the third week in June. There were not wanting suggestions from many sources as to how the relief of Imphal might be hastened. They did not all show a practical realization of the problem. One staff officer, not on my head-quarters, proposed that I should push an armoured column, escorting supply lorries, rapidly along the road to replenish Imphal 'as the Royal Navy had revictualled Malta.' I replied that to send a convoy of merchantment, escorted by destroyers, down a canal both banks of which were held by the enemy and in which at frequent intervals, there was no water—for the bridges on the road would be down—should not, I thought, appeal to naval tacticians, however gallant.

All the same, the time had now come for the Fourteenth Army to pass from the vigorous offensive–defensive it had been conducting to a full offensive on the Assam front. Although the road would have to be opened within the next five or six weeks, the immediate object of this offensive would be not so much the relief of Imphal—that would be incidental—but the destruction of the Japanese Fifteenth Army. No one could have been more eager to launch this offensive than my two corps commanders.

The problem for Scoones was whether to make this offensive

IMPHAL AREA

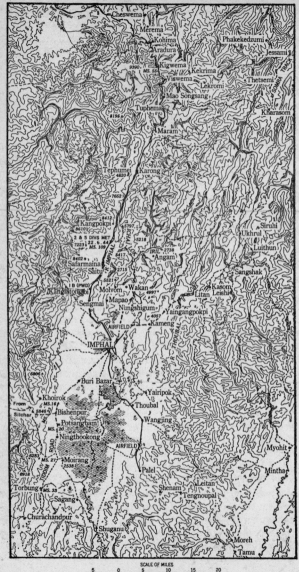

Cheswema
Merema
Kohima
Aradura
Phakekedzumi
Jessami
Kigwema
Kekrima
5990 MS. 55
Viswema
Lekromi
Thetsemi
Mao Songsang
Tuphema
Kharasom
Maram
8156
Tephumei 4820
Karong
7652
2412
Kangpokpi 8610
5797
Siruhi
Ukhrul
5218
2 & 5 DIVS MET 22. 6. 44
7223 MS. 109
Luithun
2738
IRIL
Angam
8402
Safarmaina
4417
Saitu
2715
1 B (PWD)
5521
Kanglatongbi
Molvom
Wakan
Kasom
Leishi
Litan
Sangshak
Mapao
4997
Sengmai
Nungshigum
Yaingangpokpi
4057
Kameng
AIRFIELD

IMPHAL

6806
Buri Bazar
Yairipok
Thoubal
Khoirok
MS. 16
Bishenpur
5846
Wangjing
Potsangbam
MS. 20
Ningthoukong
6283
AIRFIELD
6918
Moirang 2538
Palel
Torbung MS. 33
Myohit
Shenam
Leitan
Sagang
Tengnoupal
Churachandpur
Mintha
Shuganu

Moreh
Tamu

SCALE OF MILES
5   0   5   10   15   20
Contour Interval 1000 feet

on all sectors of this front simultaneously or to strike first on one and then on another. He would have found it difficult to stage large-scale attacks all around the plain because, not only was he limited in ammunition and I had cut him heavily in petrol to save air lift, but the amount of animal transport that would be needed in such extensive operations could not be provided. The monsoon was also upon us. When this came, although it would handicap the enemy more than us, it would, as far as we were concerned, halve the rate of movement off the few main roads and make air supply hazardous. Our offensive could, therefore, be on only part of IV Corps front. Scoones decided, with my full agreement, to launch it against the weakened Japanese 15th Division in the north and north-east, with his 5th and 20th Divisions, while he continued for the moment the wearing-down process on the Palel and Bishenpur fronts, with the 23d and 17th Divisions. This plan had the advantage that not only did it attack the enemy in his weakest link, but by operating along the Kohima road it helped to reopen our line of communication to Dimapur.

On the Palel sector of IV Corps, where the 23d had relieved the 20th Division, the Japanese again attacked during the latter half of May and throughout June, trying continuously to break through at the Shenam Pass and at Shuganu. In hand-to-hand fighting the line swayed back and forward, but the Japanese suffered heavily, and as July came we had pushed them back until they could no longer annoy us by intermittently shelling Palel airfield with their medium artillery. Activity here died down but, as a farewell gesture, on the night of July 3–4 a Japanese officer and seven men penetrated to the air strip itself, destroyed eight aircraft, and escaped unscathed—a very fine effort.

Around Bishenpur and across the Silchar track the struggle between Cowan's 17th and the Japanese 33d Division went on unabated. As might have been expected, each of these old adversaries was plotting a bold surprise stroke against the other. The Japanese planned by a series of sudden thrusts by night to pierce deep into our Bishenpur defences and to disrupt the 17th Division from within; Cowan's plan was not penetration but encirclement. With his 48 Brigade, returned to him from corps reserve, he proposed to swing wide on to the Tiddim road behind the 33d Division and then crush it between this brigade and the rest of the division.

Moving rapidly, 48 Brigade cut the Tiddim road at Milestone 33 on May 17. The Japanese at once attacked with troops hurriedly collected and, when this failed, two days later sent units of their 15th Division to try again. Both assaults were repulsed with heavy loss including several tanks and the brigade, according to plan, moved north. After two days fighting it took Moirang. It was now that the main body of 17th Division should have pressed south, but the advance did not materialize and 48 Brigade fought its way north until on May 30, it rejoined the division. It had swept right through the Japanese, inflicting heavy losses on them at little cost to itself, but the movement had failed in its object—the destruction of the 33d Division.

The reason was that on the night of May 20 the enemy penetration attacks on Bishenpur had begun. One strong hostile column broke through to within a few hundred yards of the 17th Division's headquarters. Cowan, stoutly refusing to move, was saved by a small Indian piquet which for several days held a hilltop against fanatical assault, but he had to call off his own plan and ask for help. Scoones quickly organized a force of about a brigade and sent it to the rescue. The enemy was pinned down and in five days hand-to-hand fighting they were almost annihilated, a few only escaping back into the hills to the west. Visiting the site of the battle a little later, I was struck by the way in which several Japanese gun crews had obviously been shot and bayoneted while serving their pieces in the open at point-blank range. While this was going on, another party of the enemy in darkness broke into 63 Brigade area at Bishenpur and entrenched themselves in the mule lines. Our troops surrounded them and, with the help of tanks in several days' fighting, wiped them out. The slaughter of Japanese, and unfortunately, of mules also was heavy. Bulldozers had to be employed to bury both.

It was here that some Gurkhas were engaged in collecting Japanese corpses from corners inaccessible to bulldozers when one Japanese, picked up by a couple of Gurkhas, proved not to be as dead as expected. A Gurkha had drawn his *kukri* to finish the struggling prisoner when a passing British officer intervened, saying, 'You mustn't do that, Johnny. Don't kill him!' The Gurkha, with his *kukri* poised, looked at the officer in pained surprise. 'But, sahib,' he protested, 'we can't bury him *alive*!'

A third, but minor, Japanese attempt was made in a suicidal attack on our guns just north of Bishenpur. The enemy party was killed to a man. These penetration attacks were remarkable in their boldness and in the desperation with which the enemy fought to the death. They failed in their object—to break through the 17th Division into the Imphal Plain—and they lost heavily, but they did prevent us from reaping the results of our turning movement. There can have been few examples in history of a force as reduced, battered, and exhausted as the 33d Japanese Division delivering such furious assaults, not with the object of extricating itself, but to achieve its original offensive intention.

The order, signed by Major-General Tanaka, on which the 33d Division launched these forlorn hopes is worthy of reproduction, showing, as it does, the attitude of the Japanese commanders and the stark way in which they dealt with their troops:

Now is the time to capture Imphal. Our death-defying infantry group expects certain victory when it penetrates the main fortress of the enemy. The coming battle is the turning point. It will denote the success or failure of the Greater East Asia War. You men have got to be fully in the picture as to what the present position is; regarding death as something lighter than a feather, you must tackle the task of capturing Imphal.

For that reason it must be expected that the division will be almost annihilated. I have confidence in your firm courage and devotion and believe that you will do your duty, but should any delinquencies occur you have got to understand that I shall take the necessary action.

In the front line, rewards and punishments must be given on the spot without delay. A man who does well should have his name sent in at once. On the other hand, a man guilty of any misconduct should be punished at once in accordance with the military code.

Further, in order to keep the honour of his unit bright, a commander may have to use his sword as a weapon of punishment, exceedingly shameful though it is to have to shed the blood of one's own soldiers on the battlefield.

Fresh troops with unused rifles have now arrived and the time is at hand—the arrow is ready to leave the bow.

The infantry group is in high spirits: afire with valour and dominated by one thought and one thought only—the duty laid upon them to annihilate the enemy.

On this one battle rests the fate of the Empire.

All officers and men fight courageously!

Whatever one may think of the military wisdom of thus pursuing a hopeless object, there can be no question of the supreme courage and hardihood of the Japanese soldiers who made the attempts. I know of no army that could have equalled them.

On the east and north sectors of IV Corps front we had now passed to the offensive. The 20th Division from Palel, still only two brigades strong as one of its brigades remained at Bishenpur, was on June 3 ordered to advance to destroy the enemy east of the Iril River and to take Ukhrul. It was soon discovered that the Japanese, whether to resume an offensive or to secure their communications, had built up a considerable concentration with much animal and mechanical transport about Ukhrul, and the advance by one brigade (100) of the 2d Division was promptly counterattacked by two reinforced regiments of the enemy 15th Division. However, after severe local fighting our troops had, by the middle of June, pushed them back and there were definite signs of their resistance cracking.

Meanwhile, the other brigade of the 20th Division (80) had pushed north from Nungshigum up the Iril Valley, and in spite of continuous rain, flooded streams, and deep mud that made all movement a desperate labour, had, by June 20, reached a point some thirty miles north of Imphal where it was astride the main enemy lateral communications to the Chindwin. The Japanese 15th Division, its replenishment routes cut, its supplies dwindling, and the monsoon rendering alternative tracks impassable, was in a bad way. On this sector the IV Corps offensive was going well and with increasing momentum.

On the main Imphal–Kohima road the 5th Division had also made progress. After taking Kanglatongbi, hooking behind the Japanese positions, they had clawed their way along the road and at the beginning of June were preparing in rain and mud for a further push to reach Karong some thirty-five miles north of Imphal. Here we must leave them and move to the other end of the road, to Kohima, where great things were happening.

After our successes in mid-May and the short pause that followed for reorganization, the Kohima battle entered on its second phase. Although we now had the initiative, our situation was not a particularly good one. We had the town, or rather where the town had been, for the whole area in mud and destruction resembled the Somme in 1916; but the Japanese on the left were still holding the dominating Naga Village position and the surrounding hills, while on the right they were along the great Aradura Spur. From both these they commanded Kohima at close artillery range and of course dominated and closed the Imphal road. Brigades 4 and 5 of the 2d British Division were, therefore, ordered to press on and capture the Japanese positions on both flanks. These were formidable tasks, but it was hoped that after their defeat on May 13 the enemy resistance would be crumbling. These hopes were dashed. The second phase of the battle was to be as hard fought as the first. The capacity of the ordinary Japanese soldier to take punishment and his fanatical will to resist were unimpaired. It was in the enemy higher control that weaknesses were first to appear.

During the five days of reorganization, units had some short periods of rest, and 268 Indian Brigade took over part of the forward area. Patrolling and minor attacks by both sides were constant. On May 19, 5 Brigade made its final attempt to clear Naga Village. After initial success the attack was held up by the usual skilfully concealed Japanese bunkers and by mortar fire from reverse slopes. Casualties were heavy and the attack was called off.

While this attack was in progress the headquarters of the 7th Indian Division and its remaining brigade (114) joined its two brigades (33 and 161) already in Kohima area, and the division took over the left sector of the front, which was now about equally divided between the 7th and 2d Divisions. The 7th Division advance took up the attack on Naga Village where the 2d had left off, and after a fortnight of extremely severe fighting the Japanese gave them best and abandoned the village, leaving large numbers of dead in shattered bunkers and fox holes. Progress had also been made north of the village, and the northern half of the Japanese Kohima position was now in our hands.

The attack of the 2d Division on the right against the formidable Aradura Ridge did not at first meet equal success. The scramble up rain-sodden slopes for 3,000 feet was almost as much an ordeal as the enemy fire, skilfully arranged and effective as that proved, and by the end of May a stalemate had been reached amid these slippery jungle ridges. Now, however, with Naga Village in our hands, Stopford could transfer the attack on Aradura Ridge from its western and northern to its eastern slopes. Our troops at the second attempt took Big Tree Hill, nearly a mile and a half northeast of Aradura, and advancing to the west of the road cut the Japanese supply routes to their position high up on the Ridge. This ended resistance; the enemy pulled out and Aradura Ridge was ours.

These successes of our 2d and 7th Divisions had been greatly helped by the skilful and mobile operations of 23 L.R.P. Brigade in difficult and roadless Naga country on the left of XXXIII Corps. The brigade's columns, circling the right flank of the Japanese, took Kharasom, a nodal centre of enemy supply tracks, about twenty-five miles due east of Kohima, against considerable opposition. The action of these columns achieved a threefold success. They cut the main northern Japanese supply route at the most awkward time for him, they constituted a threat to his rear whose strength he found it difficult to assess, and they stimulated the active support of the local tribesmen. These were the gallant Nagas whose loyalty, even in the most depressing times of the invasion, had never faltered. Despite floggings, torture, execution, and the burning of their villages, they refused to aid the Japanese in any way or to betray our troops. Their active help to us was beyond value or praise. Under the leadership of devoted British political officers, some of the finest types of the Indian Civil Service, in whom they had complete confidence, they guided our columns, collected information, ambushed enemy patrols, carried our supplies, and brought in our wounded under the heaviest fire—and then, being the gentlemen they were, often refused all payment. Many a British and Indian soldier owes his life to the naked, head-hunting Naga, and no soldier of the Fourteenth Army who met them will ever think of them but with admiration and affection.

It was clear now, at the beginning of June, that on the Kohima front the enemy was breaking and pulling out as best he could. While he still fought stubbornly as an individual, the cohesion of his units and the direction of his forces were obviously failing. The time had come to press on and destroy what was left of the 31st Japanese Division. The Supreme Commander, on June 8, issued a directive that the Kohima–Imphal road was to be opened not later than mid-July, and I was grateful to him for not being stampeded by more nervous people into setting too early a date. I intended that the road should be open well before mid-July, but I was now more interested in destroying Japanese divisions than in 'relieving' Imphal.

So was Stopford. He launched his whole corps in pursuit; the 2d Division astride the Imphal road, the 7th Division on its left, and still farther out 23 L.R.P. Brigade. We thus exploited the special qualities of each: the hitting power of the 2d Division group, the ability of the 2d Division to operate on pack away from roads, and the extreme mobility of 23 Brigade on air supply. Yet, in spite of its now superiority in strength, the jungle, hills, single road and pelting rain made deployment of XXXIII Corps' full power slow. Small rear guards delayed our advance while larger bodies slipped away, but only in great disorganization and with the loss of most of their equipment and all their transport. Apart from stubborn rear guards it was typical of our advance that on one day along the road our engineers had to clear three landslides, five artificial road blocks, lift a minefield, and replace two sizeable bridges.

The first serious resistance was met at Viswema, where a great ridge across the road, covered by mine fields, artillery, and interlocking machine guns barred the way. It took us a week of probing and attacks to break through and it was not until June 15 that we halted in front of the most formidable position of all—Mao Songsang. Here, on the crest of the watershed between Kohima and Imphal, the enemy had prepared a position of great strength which we knew from reports he intended to hold in a final attempt to halt our advance. We were preparing to crack this very tough nut when, to everyone's surprise, the enemy abandoned his position—the first time in the campaign that he had done so without a fight.

Simultaneously the 7th Division had also advanced, pressing the retreating enemy hard and collecting guns, mortars, and equipment of all kinds. Delayed by a stern struggle with a strong rear guard on Kekrima Ridge, the division on June 16 reached and cut the main enemy east-west supply line, the

Tuphema–Khorasom–Somra track, and threatened Mao Song-sang from the rear. This undoubtedly caused the Japanese to abandon the position there. The maintenance of the 7th Division was now becoming most difficult so it was concentrated about Mao Songsang to operate by small columns against the enemy supply tracks, while 23 Brigade continued its dislocation of the Japanese line of communication farther east.

To my great annoyance at this time I was laid up in hospital in Shillong for some days by an attack of malaria with some unpleasant complications. My annoyance was twofold. First, because I could not visit the front at this very interesting moment, second, because I had always preached that to get malaria was a breach of discipline. I had delivered what I felt to be some very effective exhortations to the troops on this theme and now it would be a little difficult to repeat them. In fact, I had only proved on my own body the truth of my contention. Troops were forbidden to bathe after sunset and I had disobeyed my own orders. Returning very muddy and dirty late one evening, I had washed in the open and been well and deservedly bitten by mosquitoes. However, I was attended while in hospital by my American deputy chief of staff, Colonel Burton Lyons, and a small tactical headquarters. With his usual cheerful efficiency he soon had everything organized, and I was closely in touch from my bed with all that went on.

It was indeed going very well. Torrential rain was slowing up operations on all sectors of the Assam front, but in spite of it by June 18, IV Corps' 5th Division was, by attacks along the Kohima road and short hooks to each side of it, slowly approaching Kangpokpi. Although Scoones had ordered this division to advance to Karong. I had later told him not to let it go beyond Kangpokpi. I did this because reports were then coming in of considerable reinforcement of the Japanese forces south and east of Imphal. I expected, even at this stage, some further trouble from them, and I did not wish the 5th Division to get too far away from the 17th. Besides, XXXIII Corps was making satisfactory progress south. I should, I think, have been wiser, instead, to have urged Scoones to push on along the Kohima road as far and as fast as he could. I exaggerated the danger of the renewed attacks on Imphal, and, by what was in effect slowing up the 5th Division, I allowed a considerable number of Japanese to escape between it and XXXIII Corps towards Ukhrul and the Chindwin. It was largely because of this that Ukhrul proved later to be so well defended.

By June 18 the spearheads of my two corps were some forty miles apart on the Kohima road, the 2d Division approaching Maram and the 5th nearing Kangpokpi. Although he had given up the much stronger defences of Mao Songsang, the enemy attempted to hold against the 2d Division another rear-guard position at Maram, about eight miles farther south. The weight of our artillery preparations and air strike, combined with the rapidity of the 2d Division's deployment and infantry attack, was such that, instead of holding for the ten days ordered, this rear guard was overrun and mostly destroyed in a matter of hours. This was the last serious attempt the enemy made to delay the advance of XXXIII Corps. It was now evident that the 31st Japanese Division was disintegrating and the enemy higher command no longer controlled the battle. In Karong, for instance, our troops captured the almost complete equipment, maps, and documents of the 31st Divisional Infantry Headquarters and at Milestone 92 the double-span bridge, although prepared for demolition, was rushed before the enemy sappers could fire the charges.

On June 22, after a brush with fleeing enemy at the Kangpokpi Mission Station—a Japanese headquarters as it had been mine two years before—the tanks of the 2d Division met the leading infantry of the 5th Division at Milestone 109. A convoy, which was waiting for this moment, was at once sent through, and IV Corps had its first overland supply delivery since the end of March.

The Imphal–Kohima battle, the first decisive battle of the Burma campaign, was not yet over, but it was won.

CHAPTER XVI

PURSUIT

At Fourteenth Army we were now out for much more than the mere expulsion of the invaders, or even their destruction. Evidence was coming in to me daily of the extent of the Japanese defeat, of their losses in tanks, guns, equipment, and vehicles, and of the disorganization of their higher command. In spite of the enemy reinforcements that were being sent into Burma, I calculated that after the defeats he had suffered on all three Burma fronts, Kawabe, the Japanese commander in chief, would desperately need time to regroup and refurbish his battered forces. There was no hope of any considerable amphibious operation against southern Burma; we had not got the landing craft, and, even if we had, the Japanese battle fleet, now returned to Singapore, so dominated the Indian Ocean as to make such attempts too hazardous. I believed, more firmly than ever, in spite of the doubts of so many, that, if we were to regain Burma, it must be by an overland advance from the north. For the first time this now seemed a practical proposition. If we could drive the enemy over the Chindwin, establish bridgeheads on its east bank, and be ready to push a considerable force into the plains of Central Burma immediately the monsoon ended, we could strike Kawabe's main force in front of Mandalay before it had recovered. This now became the object of all our efforts.

General Giffard, with the same thought in mind, had already, in the second week of June, directed me:

(a) To re-establish communications between Dimapur and Imphal.

(b) To clear the Japanese from the area Dimapur–Kohima –Imphal Plain–Yuwa–Tamanthi.

(c) To be prepared to exploit across the Chindwin in the Yuwa–Tamanthi area, i.e., along a stretch of some 130 miles of river.

The first of these three tasks Fourteenth Army had now completed; the second we were about to undertake; the third I had begun to plan as much more than mere exploitation. It was to be a second and final decisive battle. To fight it I must have, by the time the monsoon ended:

(i) The necessary divisions, replenished, trained, equipped, and placed ready to move.

(ii) A vastly improved system of communications to the Chindwin, an adequate land and air transport organization, and enough supplies collected well forward.

(iii) Bridgeheads, firmly held, across the Chindwin.

While Fourteenth Army Headquarters set to work on the colossal administrative labour this entailed, I visited the forward troops to spur them to an all-out pursuit through the terrible monsoon conditions. In this I was asking for the impossible—but I got it.

IV Corps, after cleaning up Bishenpur, pushed south on the Tiddim road but, on XXXIII Corps front, Mutaguchi's Fifteenth Army was being reinforced. Optimistic still, he seemed bent on keeping a foothold in Assam but by July 14, in a fortnight's slogging match in the mud, his last defences about Ukhrul were wiped out. XXXIII Corps continued the advance on Tamu and, fighting all the way, inflicted heavy losses in men, equipment, guns, and tanks, the 23d Division, on July 27, captured Lokchao with its destroyed bridge.

I visited the 23d Division on this day and reached the forward troops, by jeep and on foot, only with difficulty. Whole sections of the road had vanished in landslides; the troops, soaked and filthy, were struggling forward across steep slopes through mud with the consistency of porridge halfway up to their knees. It was campaigning at its hardest, but everyone was cheerful. The litter of the Japanese rout was everywhere; their corpses shapeless lumps in the mud. Luckily our casualties had not been heavy, and devoted efforts were being made to get them back by bearers or jeep ambulances where the road was possible. Their sufferings from wet, cold, and jolting during these interminable journeys were grim, but those I spoke to all assured me in their various languages that they were all right, when quite obviously several of them were, alas, far from it. It struck me then, as so often, that I had very brave soldiers. So had the enemy. A Japanese officer with a horribly shattered leg was brought back roughly bandaged in a jeep ambulance. A British officer was shocked to see the wounded man's hands were bound. He stopped the jeep, and ordered the Indian guards to untie him. They explained that the prisoner had several times torn the bandages from his leg. Even now, with his hands tied, he had attempted to rip them off with his teeth. The Japanese soldier, even in disaster, retained his one supreme quality—he chose death rather than surrender.

After their obstinate defence astride the road, the surviving Japanese, abandoning much equipment, escaped by jungle paths, and a brigade (5) of the 2d Division passed through to occupy Tamu without opposition.

It was always a disappointment in the Burma campaign to enter a town that had been a name on the map and a goal for which men fought and died. There was for the victors none of the thrill of marching through streets which, even if battered, were those of a great, perhaps historic, city—a Paris or a Rome. There were no liberated crowds to greet the troops. Instead, my soldiers walked warily, alert for booby traps and snipers, through a tangle of burned beams, twisted corrugated iron, with here and there, rising among the squalid ruins, the massive chipped and stained pagodas and chinthis of a Buddhist temple. A few frightened Burmans, clad in rags, might peer at them and even wave a shy welcome, but at the best it was not a very inspiring business, and more than one conquering warrior, regarding the prize of weeks of effort, spat contemptuously.

In Tamu he had other reasons for spitting. The place was a charnel house, of a macabre eeriness hard to describe. Five hundred and fifty Japanese corpses lay unburied in its streets and houses, many grouped grotesquely around stone Buddhas which looked blandly out over the sacrifices huddled at their feet. Dozens more, more than a hundred, lay in indescribable filth, dying of disease and starvation, among the corpses. It was not only in Tamu itself that such evidences of the collapse of the enemy administration were found. Along all routes leading to the Chindwin, whether from Ukhrul, Imphal, Tamu, or on the Tiddim road, were found such grisly reminders of the fate of a retreating army. More than once small field hospitals were found where the patients lay on their stretchers, all dead, neatly shot through the head, killed by their comrades who had no means of evacuating them and preferred this—as no doubt the patients themselves did—to their capture. From these and other signs it was increasingly clear that the Japanese Fifteenth Army had suffered an even more disastrous defeat than we had at first realized. The likelihood of our achieving our objects by the end of the monsoon was promising.

With the capture of Tamu the time had come to press on with the regrouping and resting of my formations, which General Giffard had wisely urged on me and which I agreed was necessary if I was to be ready for a major offensive within a few months. I was at this time anxious about the health of the troops. They had endured a great deal and showed it. The infantry especially, who as ever had borne the brunt of the fighting and the worst of the hardships, were very fined down. They were too thin to my mind, a state which was not improved by the jaundice yellow of all our complexions as a result of the daily dose of mepacrine. They were cheerful enough and pleased with themselves, as well they might be, but as fighting died down, sickness rose. I told my doctors to select several battalions, British, Indian, and Gurkha, who had come out to rest, and give them a mass examination. The results perturbed me. A very large proportion of men were sufferering from malnutrition, the disease that had killed thousands of Japanese. It was not that our men had not had enough to eat. Although ration scales had at times been lowered, as at Imphal, and at others had been irregular, there had never, thanks to the efficiency of the supply and transport services and the extreme devotion of the air forces, been a serious shortage. Unavoidably, however, there had been depressing monotony in the diet and practically no fresh meat or vegetables. In addition, I was informed, the constant mental strain of fighting in the jungle had of itself reacted on the metabolism of the men's bodies, so that often food passed through them without the normal amount of nourishment being extracted from it. Obviously rest, freedom from strain, a more varied diet, and some amenities were imperative if these formations were to be keyed up for the winter campaign; and they would have to be, for most of them would be engaged in it.

Headquarters IV Corps with the 17th and 23d Divisions were sent to recuperate in India; 3 Commando Brigade returned to Arakan; and the 2d, 7th, and 20th Division concentrated about Imphal and Kohima, where we did our best to improvise amenities and recreation for them. I am afraid our armies in Europe and Africa would have smiled at our efforts, but the troops made the best of what we could do. Health, appearance, and general well-being improved weekly. The 11th East African Division, under Major-General Fowkes, which impressed me very favourably when I inspected it, but which, I thought, had too many British officers and N.C.O.s, arrived as a replacement.

On August 6, my fifty-third birthday, I sent orders to Stopford, now in control of all operations on the central front:

(a) To pursue the enemy with not less than one brigade group on each of the routes:
    (i) Imphal–Tiddim–Kalemyo–Kalewa.
    (ii) Tamu–Kalewa.
    (iii) Tamu-Sittaung.
(b) To occupy Sittaung and deny the Chindwin to enemy shipping.
(c) If opportunity offered, to sieze Kalewa, and prepare to establish a bridgehead.

In accordance with these instructions the 11th East African Division, having relieved the 23d Division, began a two-pronged advance from Tamu towards Sittaung on the Chindwin, thirty-six miles by road to the east, and into the Kabaw Valley on Kalemyo, some hundred miles south.

A brigade of the East Africans, delayed more by the difficulties of the track than by the enemy, took Sittaung and found it a second Tamu—among hundreds of Japanese corpses only two men were living. On September 10 the Africans formed a small bridgehead on the east bank of the river.

The main body of the East Africans entered the Kabaw Valley of ill omen and, although by no means exempt from malaria, their casualties from disease were less, I think, than other troops would have suffered. Judged by the map, their rate of advance was not rapid, but on the ground it was a real achievement. Rain fell without stopping for three weeks at an average of five inches a day. Mud, water, mosquitoes, and backbreaking labour were the order of the day. A detachment sent eastward, after several attempts had failed, finally drove the Japanese from the vertical cliffs which are a feature of the local landscape, and on November 10 took Mawlaik, a small but valuable Chindwin port. Here the Assam Battalion on loan to the East African Division slipped across the river to establish our second bridgehead.

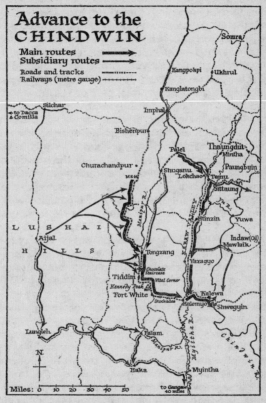

Advance to the CHINDWIN

Main routes →
Subsidiary routes →
Roads and tracks ┄┄┄
Railways (metre gauge) ┄┄┄┄

Miles: 0 10 20 30 40 50

N

Meanwhile, against increasing opposition, the main advance in the Kabaw Valley reached a point five miles west of Kalemyo. On November 13, a patrol met another from the 5th Indian Division, now approaching down the Tiddim road, and the two, sepoys and askaris together, entered the town. This advance of the 11th East African Division in the face of such climatic and natural obstacles would a year earlier have been almost universally proclaimed impossible.

Now to turn to the simultaneous advance of the 5th Indian Division, which had been going on in conditions equally difficult and against stronger opposition. During July, after its drive north to link up with the 2d Division from Kohima, the 5th Division, turning about, joined the 17th Division in pushing back the enemy astride the Tiddim road south of Imphal. By the third week of July the Japanese, after determined resistance, were driven out of the last portion of the Imphal Plain in which they had a footing, and began their long withdrawal. The Japanese retreat on the Tiddim road was under better control than on any other part of the front. The rear guards of the reinforced 33d Japanese Division which had been made up to ten battalions, a tank regiment, artillery, and engineer units, only withdrew under pressure, stubbornly contesting ridge after ridge astride the road. Although our troops inflicted serious losses on them, including the capture of most of their tanks, and the climatic conditions were of the hardest, there was less evidence of disorder such as littered the tracks of the other enemy columns. Again the 33d Japanese Division was living up to its reputation of being the toughest division in Burma.

By the end of July the 17th Division was on its way to a well-earned rest. It had been actively engaged since December 1941, that is, for three years and eight months, and almost all that time in direct contact with the enemy. A record, I should think.

In mid-July the 5th Division took over operations on the Tiddim road and, hooking round stubbornly defended rear-guard positions, was by August 23 eighty-five miles south of Imphal. The weather conditions were appalling—the road disappearing before and behind our troops in frequent land-slides—but several hundred Japanese were killed and tanks, guns, machine guns, and lorries captured. Our troops suffered the inevitable casualties of a monsoon campaign. The figures are instructive; in twenty-six days battle casualties were only ninety-four, but five hundred and seven were lost from sickness.

In these conditions my engineer resources did not permit both the Tiddim and Kabaw Valley roads being maintained. The Kabaw Valley route was capable, as soon as finer weather came, of taking much the heavier traffic so that was chosen for development; the Tiddim road being allowed to disappear behind the 5th Division as it advanced. In the hills no landing strips could be made, and all supply had to be by air-dropping. To make this possible the crews of 221 Group R.A.F. flew over the division on every single day throughout the monsoon—a magnificent display of devotion and determination.

One result of the decision to abandon the road was that casualties could not be evacuated. They must either accompany the division or be dumped in native villages, in either event an unhappy prospect. I was particularly worried about the victims of scrub typhus, a disease that was proving lamentably fatal without really good nursing, so I had asked for a few nurses to volunteer to accompany the division. The only difficulty was to pick the handful required from the numbers who eagerly offered for what could only be a dangerous and hard task. These devoted women not only saved many lives, but were a morale-raiser to the whole division.

It was at this period that a formation that had, up to now, been lurking discreetly in the wings, took the stage in no mean part.

The Lushai Brigade, under Brigadier Marindin, improvised from four Indian battalions and some levies, was in the hills a hundred miles southwest of Imphal. As an orthodox brigade group it left something to be desired; it had little transport or equipment, its signals were improvised, and it had neither engineers nor artillery, but what it lacked in these it made up in initiative. At the end of June I ordered Marindin to take his brigade and 'render the road Tiddim–Imphal, from Tiddim northward, useless to the enemy as a line of communication.' I told him I could give him little or no air support and if he got into trouble he would be too far away for help. As generals always do on these occasions, I wished him luck.

He wasted no time. After difficult marches of from eighty to one hundred and twenty miles across flooded streams and mountains his two northerly battalions were, by the end of July, harrying the road by stealthy ambushes and sudden bursts of fire. More than two hundred enemy were killed, many wounded, and numerous vehicles destroyed, while several hundred Japanese were tied down to picquet the road. All at small cost to us. The third battalion, however, made the biggest bag. It concentrated on an eight-mile stretch where the road, on the east bank of the Manipur, ran through a precipitous gorge. Our men on the west bank, protected by the raging torrent, kept the road under constant fire at close range. All wheeled traffic in this sector ceased.

With his fourth battalion—my old friends the Bihar Regiment, who were so proud of their women—Marindin improved on my orders, and launched them into the Chin Hills to capture the local capitals of Falam and Haka. The Chin levies had with them their families, and, looking like the Children of Israel trekking out of Egypt, they joyfully assisted in liberating their country, dumping the women and children in their own villages as they captured them.

Helped by these actions, the main advance of the 5th Division from the north on the Tiddim road continued. On September 14, the leading troops reached the west bank of the Manipur River, a hundred and twenty-six miles from Imphal. The river, now in flood, was a most formidable obstacle, but one brigade, having turned back through Imphal and Shuganu, marched down the east bank and, as our troops arrived on the west bank, seized the high ground opposite them. The Japanese, in danger of being cut off, abandoned further defence of the river line.

Even with the Japanese driven from its banks, the crossing of the Manipur was no easy operation. The river, one hundred yards wide, was in full spate, flooding through its gorge at a speed of ten to twelve knots, hurling itself against boulders in fountains of spray, and bringing down tree trunks in full career. Its roar, audible for miles, was like that of a great football crowd. Not without difficulty the engineers got a rope across, and a flying bridge—a ferry attached to a cable—was built. The first boat to attempt the crossing was capsized by the fury of the stream. All its occupants were lost. But the cable held and next day the ferry was working, though a crossing was still a hazardous and nerve-testing experience. Ferrying, in these conditions, was a slow business, but by the 19th a road block had been placed behind the Japanese rear guard whose shelling, particularly that of some 155-mm. guns, had been thoroughly unpleasant. Next day the rear guard was attacked. An attempt by the enemy to break through the road block after dark failed, and they took to the jungle, abandoning ninety dead and the objectionable 155-mm. guns.

Without pause Warren, who had replaced Evans, a victim of

climate and exhaustion, in command of the division, pushed on for Tiddim with the troops already across, while tremendous efforts were made to get the remainder of the division over the river as the road behind it collapsed in mud and landslides. The leading brigade (123), in spite of the difficulty of the country, advanced on a wide front so as to overlap the frequent but small Japanese rear guards. By October 1 our troops were in the hills some miles due east of Tiddim, in contact with the enemy who still covered the town and held the main road approach. The advance was a succession of minor engagements in which the Japanese 33d Division still fought well and put in frequent counterattacks. The outflanking tactics of our troops paid, and even the formidable 'Chocolate Staircase' position was turned in this way and abandoned by the enemy after little resistance. Chocolate Staircase was the name given to the Tiddim road where in seven miles it climbed three thousand feet with thirty-eight hairpin bends and an average gradient of one in twelve. The road surface was earth, and marching men, animals, and vehicles soon churned it into ankle-deep mud. The hillside, and with it the road itself, often disappeared in thunderous landslides; then every available man had to turn to with pick and shovel to shape a track again. No soldier who marched up the Chocolate Staircase is ever likely to forget the name of the place. The enemy made several more desperate attempts to block the road to Tiddim but the constant threats to his line of retreat, his fear of losing guns and vehicles, the accuracy of 221 Group's air strikes even in this country, and the unquenched *élan* of our troops in direct attack had their effect. Tiddim was occupied on October 17.

After Tiddim, as the 8,800-foot Kennedy Peak was approached, the Japanese resistance hardened again. While his main force pushed steadily on, Warren staged two wide turning movements, one of which established a road block behind the enemy. In several days' fighting among mist-covered mountains the Japanese were forced to withdraw, and after frantic and costly attempts to break through on the road, they abandoned everything except their small arms and took to the jungle. On November 8 our troops reached Fort White and on the 13th, as already related, the 5th Indian and 11th East African Divisions jointly entered Kalemyo.

The 5th Division thus completed a remarkably fine feat of

arms and endurance. Thirteen hundred and sixteen Japanese bodies were counted on the ground, and fifty-three prisoners were taken; the division's battle casualties in the same period were eighty-eight killed, two-hundred and ninety-three wounded, and twenty-two missing—a measure of the skill now reached in the art of killing Japanese. The division was then flown from Kalemyo to refit in the Imphal Plain.

The Lushai Brigade, operating on the right flank of the 5th Division, during its advance, had pushed on and, infiltrating on a front of a hundred miles, broke into the Myittha Valley with the ultimate object of seizing Gangaw, seventy-five miles south of Kalemyo. By October 19, it had occupied the Chin capitals of Falam and Haka amid great rejoicings and re-unions of the loyalist tribesmen, not a little enlivened by the free distribution of captured rice and stores. By mid-December, when greater events were impending, the Lushai Brigade had patrols on the east bank of the Chindwin, had cleared the whole country west of the Myittha River, and was closing in on the last Japanese foothold in the Myittha Valley at Gangaw.

There is no doubt that the enterprise and dash of this improvised and lighthearted brigade were a very real contribution to the pursuit to the Chindwin. It had operated for six months on pack transport, supplemented by an unavoidably meagre air supply, across two hundred miles of jungle mountains, against the enemy flank and rear. Considering the paucity of its equipment and resources, it gave one of the most effective and economical examples of long-range penetration.

Another independent brigade which had played a less spectacular but nonetheless helpful part was 268 Indian Infantry Brigade, under Brigadier Dyer, a commander whose resource and cheerfulness became renowned throughout the army.

Reconstituted with one Nepalese and three newly-raised Indian Battalions, it energetically cleared the wild jungle country on the west bank of the Chindwin north of Sittaung, capturing many enemy supply dumps. In October it took over from the East Africans at Sittaung and, pushing deeper into the screen the Japanese were building up, enlarged the bridgehead.

While these flank diversions had been going on the 11th East African Division advancing on Kalewa, by a series of assaults, forced its way through the gorge of the Myittha River and on December 2 entered a Kalewa reduced to ruins by our air bombardment. Simultaneously a brigade of the division crossed the Chindwin twelve miles north of Kalewa on tarpaulin rafts, and bore down on the enemy holding the east bank opposite the town. On the night of December 3-4 Fowkes, commanding the East African Division, in spite of opposition, got a brigade across just north of Kalewa, and followed it up with another the next night. Even with the whole division across, it was not until December 8 that the enemy gave way and withdrew towards Shwegyin.

On December 10 our engineers completed a floating Bailey bridge over the Chindwin. Its length was 1,154 feet, then the longest Bailey bridge in the world. The Indian sappers and miners assembled the spans in the Myittha River under cover, floated them in to the Chindwin, and put the bridge in position in twenty-eight hours. It was an obvious target for air attack, and so we brought from Calcutta barrage balloons no longer needed there. Two days later an attack was made on the bridge, but luckily without success, and our anti-aircraft fire brought down two aircraft. For several days the bridgehead was expanded by minor advances and clashes, until on December 13, Shwegyin was occupied, and the area around it cleared. The 11th East African Division by mid-December thus occupied a firm bridgehead east of Kalewa extending to about eight miles by twelve, and the pursuit that had begun at Imphal had now set the stage for the next act.

The Imphal–Kohima battle which now ended was the last and greatest of the series that had been fought continuously during the past ten months on all the Burma fronts. They had achieved substantial results; the Japanese Army had suffered the greatest defeat in its history. Five Japanese divisions (15th, 18th, 31st, 33d, and 55th) had, at any rate temporarily, been destroyed as effective fighting formations, while two other divisions, an independent brigade, and many line-of-communication units had been badly mauled. Fifty thousand Japanese had been killed or died, and their bodies counted on the Arakan and Assam sectors. Allowing only half that number for badly wounded—and a very high proportion of their wounded died or were maimed—the enemy had lost permanently some seventy-five thousand men. Add to this fifteen thousand casualties suffered on the North Burma sector of N.C.A.C., and the total irrecoverable losses inflicted in operations under Fourteenth Army command were some ninety thousand men. The Japanese themselves later estimated their casualties in these battles at this figure. In addition, there were the four or five thousand Japanese accounted for by the Yunnan Chinese.

A most remarkable feature of the fighting had been the few prisoners we had taken. Some six hundred had been captured, and of these I do not believe that more than a hundred and fifty were physically capable of further resistance; the rest were either grievously wounded or in the last stages of exhaustion. This proportion of prisoners to killed, about one in every hundred, is notable compared with that in European or African theatres, and is an indication of the fanatical nature of Japanese resistance.

Japanese losses in equipment were also high. Nearly all the tanks and most of the vehicles that the enemy brought into Assam were destroyed or captured. More than two hundred and fifty guns were taken, besides those thrown into rivers or buried by the Japanese themselves. Of course, given time, these losses both in men and matériel could be made good, and the divisions would fight again; but whether, even if we allowed them that time—and I had no intention of doing so—they would ever become once more the same aggressive, arrogant fighting formations was another matter.

Our own losses, as was to be expected in such fighting, had not been light. The Fourteenth Army, alone, had suffered some forty thousand battle casualties, killed and wounded. Many of the latter would recover and return to fight again, but losses had been heaviest where they were hardest to replace, in the officers and N.C.O.s of the fighting units. We had yielded only a handful of prisoners; of these the wounded had almost invariably been murdered or left to die. We had lost no guns. An area of Burma more than twice the size of Ireland had been liberated. We had done well.

If you are a general, whether your army has won a great battle or lost it, it is hard not to slur over your own mistakes, to blame others for theirs; to say, if you lost, what bad luck you had, and, if you won, how little luck had to do with it. My army had indubitably won *this* battle, and I looked back now on its conduct with considerable personal satisfaction, allowing myself, in the warm glow of success, a good deal more credit, no doubt, than I deserved. Yet the plan of the Imphal battle had been sound and we had adhered to it. Basically it had been to meet the Japanese on ground of our own choosing, with a better line of communication behind us than behind them, to concentrate against them superior forces drawn from Arakan and India, to wear them down, and, when they were exhausted, to return and destroy them. All this we had done in spite of my mistakes in mistiming the withdrawal of the 17th Division from Tiddim and underestimating the strength of the Japanese thrust at Kohima. These errors would have been disastrous but for the way in which, supported by the Supreme Commander and General Auchinleck, General Giffard sent so speedily to my rescue reinforcements from India. They and the fighting qualities of my troops saved me in the first days of the battle.

We had proved right in our reliance on the air forces, British and American, first to gain control of the air, and then to supply, transport, and support us. The campaign had been an air one as well as a land one. Without the victory of the air forces there could have been no victory for the army, and, when it came, the shares of the soldier and the airman were so intermingled that it was a joint victory. Air supply and close support by fighters and bombers had been carried out with precision and effect in full view of the army, but far beyond the range of its sight the enemy's line of communication and administrative installations had been kept under almost constant attack by the Allied bombers. The cumulative effect of this was immense; his river craft, his motor transport and railway trains slunk along haltingly only at night. The air forces never stopped him moving his formations, but they slowed them up, destroyed their vehicles, and disrupted their communications. In future we knew it would be safe to put even greater reliance on our air arm.

Our estimate of the Japanese mentality and generalship had also proved right. Kawabe and his subordinates showed the overboldness, the rigidity, and the disregard of administrative risks that I had expected and which gave me my opportunity. We had learned how to kill Japanese; how to use tanks in any country that was not a swamp; how to build roads and airfields with little equipment and strange materials. Our troops had shown themselves steadier, more offensive, and better trained than ever before. They did not now accept any country as impassable, either for the enemy or themselves. They refused to be jittered by encirclement; they were as ready as the enemy to strike out into the jungle and to infiltrate. We had by degrees become better in the jungle than the Japanese. Most important of all, every British, Indian, African, and Chinese division that had served under Fourteenth Army had met picked Japanese troops in straight, bitter fighting and had beaten them. Our troops had proved themselves in battle the superiors of the Japanese; they had seen them run. This was the real and decisive result of these battles. They had smashed for ever the legend of the invincibility of the Japanese Army. Neither our men nor the Japanese soldier himself believed in it any longer.

Shortly after we had recaptured it, I visited Shwegyin. There, still lying in the amphitheatre of hills on the riverbank, were the burned-out and rusted tanks that I had so reluctantly destroyed and abandoned in the Retreat two and a half years before. As I walked among them, resavouring in imagination the bitter taste of defeat, I could raise my head. Much had happened since then. Some of what we owed we had paid back. Now we were going on to pay back the rest—with interest.

BOOK V: THE DECISIVE BATTLE

CHAPTER XVII

APPROACH TO THE IRRAWADDY

It often happens that, when the first phase of a hard-fought campaign has been successfully completed and the second is in full swing, the commander will be as much occupied in preparations for the next stage as with the actual fighting in progress. This was so with me during the pursuit to and over the Chindwin. My mind and my time were largely filled with plans and preparations for the great battles that must follow the establishment of our bridgeheads over that river.

Nor was I the only one so employed. As the Imphal battle drew to a victorious close an orgy of planning broke out at all levels. Admiral Mountbatten and his staff were examining various alternatives, and I told him I considered that an offensive would require no greater manpower than would be needed to hold a defensive line. I would, I said, be ready to begin the advance on November 1.

The Chiefs of Staff in London had issued a directive for further operations in Burma, giving as our objects:

To develop, broaden, and protect the air link to China, in order to provide maximum and timely flow of POL (Petrol, Oil, Lubricants) and stores to China in support of Pacific operations. So far as is consistent with the above, to press advantages against the enemy by exerting maximum effort, ground and air, particularly during the current monsoon season, and in pressing such advantages to be prepared to exploit the development of overland communications to China. All these operations must be dictated by the forces at present available or firmly allocated to S.E.A.C.

This directive was plainly a compromise between British and American views, with the American predominating. To me it seemed much too modest. I believed that the best and quickest way to secure worth-while communications with China was to clear the enemy out of Burma, and use Rangoon. The extent of the Japanese defeat at Imphal, which did not seem to have been appreciated, made this now feasible. I was sure that Admiral Mountbatten would be more ambitious in his plan. I, therefore, set my staff to work on plans for the capture of the Mandalay area, but always with the intention that this would at once be followed by an advance south on Rangoon. Indeed, we ran an unofficial private Fourteenth Army plan to effect this, which my chief of staff, Tubby Lethbridge, christened 'Operation Sob'—Sea or Bust.

Meanwhile, above us in S.E.A.C. Headquarters three alternative plans were being prepared:

Plan X. Stilwell's N.C.A.C., reinforced by more British and Indian divisions from Fourteenth Army, to be the main striking force, and to secure up to the line Katha–Mongmit–Lashio, while the Yunnan Chinese pushed to join up with them about Lashio. The reduced Fourteenth Army to conduct a limited offensive across the Chindwin.

Plan Y. The Fourteenth Army to be the main striking force, and to secure the Mandalay area. The N.C.A.C. and Yunnan Chinese to stage an offensive from the north, and join up with Fourteenth Army about Maymyo.

Plan Z. The capture of Rangoon by an amphibious and airborne operation, followed by a drive to meet our forces coming from the north.

I was heartily in favour of Plan Y. Apart from the fact that it allotted the major role to my army, it seemed to me to offer the best prospect of making the Japanese fight a battle with their main forces on ground favourable to us, and so giving us a chance of really smashing them before the next monsoon. I did not at this stage favour Plan Z. It was strategically most attractive, but I doubted if we could get in time either the equipment or forces that would be required for an amphibious attack on a defended Rangoon. I thought our 'Operation Sob' would get us there at least as quickly.

However, from the Supreme Commander's directive we discovered that both Plans Y and Z were to be attempted. The new plan (Capital) was:

(i) An advance across the Chindwin up to the Irrawaddy and the capture of Mandalay by the Fourteenth Army.

(ii) A complementary advance by N.C.A.C. and the Yunnan Chinese to the line Thabeikyin–Mogok–Lashio.

(iii) A limited advance in Arakan by XV Corps.

(iv) A sea and airborne assault (Dracula) on Rangoon about March 1945.

I had doubted our ability to carry out Plan Z (Dracula) with the forces we had and thought to attempt Y and Z together would be to fall between two stools, unless, of course, fresh forces were to come from Europe, but optimistic views on the imminent collapse of Germany were fading. I was relieved, therefore, when at the end of July General Giffard told me Plan Z depended on whether such reinforcements would be available, and meanwhile I was to get on with Plan Y in three phases:

(i) The occupation of the Kalewa–Kalemyo area by a land advance and an airborne operation.

(ii) Overland and airborne operations to secure the Shwebo Plain.

(iii) The liberation of Burma as far south as Pakokku–Mandalay and a juncture with N.C.A.C. about Maymyo.

This was in essentials our existing Fourteenth Army plan; the only difference being that I proposed to omit the airborne operations and use all available aircraft for supply. Not only did I think I should advance faster and inflict greater losses on the Japanese this way but it would reduce roadmaking to something practicable. General Giffard accepted this, but I had to admit I should not now be ready to advance until November 15. One reason for this was that reinforcements from home were not nearly enough to keep my British units up to strength, and in spite of converting several thousand anti-aircraft artillerymen into infantry, I was being compelled more and more to substitute Indian for British battalions in my divisions.

As the autumn of 1944 turned to winter, one by one, we established our bridgeheads—at Sittaung, east of Tamu, at Mawlaik fifty miles south, and at Kalewa. The first phase of General Giffard's directive had been completed and, to my great satisfaction, without an airborne operation. There was no doubt about the troops' keenness to close with the enemy—

the hallmark of high morale; I grew increasingly confident.

The Japanese higher command had played into our hands. We had inflicted on them in the Imphal battle the major defeat that I had always felt would be necessary *before* we could with assurance break into Central Burma and meet their main army on its own ground. The extent of that defeat became clearer from the sights that greeted our pursuing troops on the heels of the Japanese, abandoned guns and tanks, bogged-down vehicles, scattered equipment, and everywhere corpses lying singly beside the track, sitting grotesquely in cars, propped against trees, huddled together in miserable huts, floating in every stream—the whole horror of retreat in the monsoon, the ultimate beastliness of war. It is true that we had crushed only a portion of Kawabe's Burma army, but it would be disorganized, diseased, and almost starving remnants of some of his best divisions that would scramble across the Chindwin. He would need time to reform and re-equip these shattered formations.

It is of interest that our estimates of enemy casualties in the Imphal–Kohima battle were, as we discovered after their final surrender, very close to the figures the Japanese themselves calculated. These were:

	Strength		
	Before	After	
Formation	Battle	Battle	Losses
15th Division	20,000	4,000	16,000
31st Division	20,000	7,000	13,000
33d Division	25,000	4,000	21,000
Army troops			
Administrative units	50,000	35,000	15,000
Totals	115,000	50,000	65,000

Our battle casualties at Kohima–Imphal were more than fifteen thousand, but to these must be added a much larger number evacuated sick during the monsoon campaign and pursuit. Including these we had probably a rather higher total than the Japanese, but the great bulk of our casualties recovered; most of theirs died on the retreat from lack of medical care, exposure, and exhaustion.

The more I considered the enemy situation and our own,

the more I was sure that here was our opportunity. My orders were to drive the enemy out of a considerable part of northern Burma and take Mandalay, but more important than the occupation of any area or any town was the destruction of the Japanese Army. A second great defeat for that army, properly exploited, would disrupt it and leave, not Mandalay, but all Burma at our mercy. It therefore became my aim to force another major battle on the enemy at the earliest feasible moment.

I had already handed back the N.C.A.C. and, to allow me to concentrate my attention on the vital central front, General Giffard, as I wished, relieved me not only of the Arakan front but also of the vast line-of-communication area that had made me look back almost as often as forward. I was now free to devote myself to the innumerable tactical and administrative problems of the offensive, all of which were dominated by three questions:

(i) Where should we bring the enemy main forces to battle?

(ii) What maximum force could we maintain east of the Chindwin?

(iii) What would be the Japanese strength?

I wanted to fight the battle on ground where our superiority in the air and in armour would have its greatest scope, that is, in comparatively open country. The obvious place was the Shwebo Plain, a great loop of land enclosed between the Irrawaddy and the Chindwin, immediately northwest of Mandalay. This is part of the 'Dry Belt,' the central plain of Burma. Here the country is generally flat or undulating, covered in cultivation with some scrub patches, easily passable, sprinkled with villages, crisscrossed by many cart tracks and some roads. Over considerable areas it is so open and, except in the rainy season, so dusty as to offer something like desert conditions. It would suit us admirably.

But it was one thing to decide we would like to fight there, another to persuade the Japanese to do so. If they did, the enemy commander would know full well what disadvantages he was accepting. He would fight with the river loop around him—difficult when all his supplies would have to be brought over it under air attack, disastrous if he had to retreat. Yet I was quite sure he *would* fight in the Shwebo Plain. I relied on my knowledge of the Japanese and on the mentality of their high command as I had known it. I knew there had been changes in that command. In October reports had reached me that Kawabe had been sent back to Japan in disgrace and replaced by a General Kimura, of whom not a great deal was known, except that he was regarded by the Japanese as one of their best men. Even so, I expected him to conform to type, to be overbold, inflexible, and reluctant to change a plan once made. In spite of the Imphal lesson, he would, I thought, be confident that he could beat me on his own ground and, even if he were not, he would never dare to lose face by giving up territory without a struggle. He would see the Chindwin behind us, not the Irrawaddy behind him. I did not believe it was in the Japanese nature to let Mandalay go, or even be brought into the front line, without a pitched battle. He might try to hold us on the Chindwin or even to throw our bridgeheads into the river, but he had largely lost his chance to do that. In fact, I was prepared to back my judgment that he would choose to fight a defensive battle, with his main strength, north of Mandalay. If he won this, he could then leave the difficulties of maintenance in the monsoon to force us to withdraw; he might even hope to restage an offensive of his own into India after the rains. The Japanese were always military optimists.

We must, therefore, get as many divisions and as much armour as possible quickly into the Shwebo Plain and there fight an army battle. The problem, as almost all in Burma were, was one of supply and transport. I had available for the battle six and two-thirds divisions and two tank brigades, and I could, if I could use them, get another division, perhaps two, from India. But we should be four hundred miles from railhead; two hundred and fifty miles of that distance only fair weather road, unless we could rebuild it before the monsoon. After much discussion I had been given a firm allotment of supply aircraft on which to plan, but our airlift would come mainly from Comilla and Chittagong, at the extreme limit of practical range; even Imphal was two hundred miles away and not served by rail. Scheme as we might, take risks to the limit of reason, we could not maintain trans-Chindwin more than four and two-thirds divisions and the two tank brigades.

What were they likely to meet? As far as we then knew, the

total enemy strength in Burma was ten infantry divisions, two independent brigade groups, one tank regiment, and one hundred thousand line-of-communication troops. There were, in addition, two Indian National Army divisions and the Burma National Army. Of this considerable force I relied on N.C.A.C. and the Yunnan Chinese to hold two Japanese divisions in the north; XV Corps to keep one and a third in Arakan, and fear of amphibious attack to tie down a further one and a third in the south. This would leave against me five and one-third Japanese divisions, one independent brigade, the tank regiment, some thirty or forty thousand communication troops and, for what they were worth, the two I.N.A. divisions. By taking risks on other Burma sectors, the enemy might increase his forces about Mandalay; he might possibly even bring formations from Siam and Indo-China. American successes in the Pacific made it not only unlikely that serious reinforcements could come from Japan or overseas but that it would be hard for the enemy to replace any further losses in Burma.

All the same, four and two-thirds British and Indian divisions, a river behind them and at the end of this precarious line of communication, was not the odds I should have liked with which to attack five and a third Japanese divisions in their own selected positions. A year ago I would not have looked at the proposal. Even now, it was not so much our advantage in the air, in armour, in greater mobility in the open, which gave me confidence to go on with my plan, but the spirit of my troops, my trust in their experienced commanders and in the high fighting value and hardihood of them all.

It will be noted that my plan was based on three foundations:

(i) The firm intention of the enemy commander to fight with his main forces north of Mandalay.

(ii) The ability of other sectors of our Burma front to hold off from us during the battle some four or five Japanese divisions.

(iii) A definite air and road maintenance lift on which I could rely.

The first was a matter of my own judgment in which, perhaps rashly, I had at that time considerable faith. The second, I thought, should be safe enough. Both XV Corps in Arakan, with four and two-thirds divisions and a tank brigade, and N.C.A.C. in the north, with the equivalent of five or six divisions, were much superior to any Japanese likely to oppose them. Indeed these flank forces might seem out of balance with my army on the vital front. Yet it was not a question of numbers but of ability to maintain them; I already had all I could supply. To reduce XV Corps would not help, as it was maintained by sea and by road and rail links separate from mine. The help I looked for from Christison would be, not only to hold down some Japanese forces but, as I advanced south of Mandalay out of range of our present air-supply bases, to provide nearer ones. To support large operations these would have to be served by either sea or rail; no possible sites were accessible by rail, but the islands of Akyab, Cheduba, and Ramree, all in Japanese hands off the Arakan coast, would provide excellent airfields within the necessary two hundred and fifty miles of most of South Burma. I therefore urged that XV Corps should take these islands quickly and establish on them our air supply bases. A reduction in N.C.A.C. could have benefited me only if the airlift thus saved were transferred to Fourteenth Army, but it was much more likely to go to China. The Chinese divisions could, however, take a big weight off me if they would push hard, east of the Irrawaddy, to the south of Lashio. I hoped they would.

As we in Fourteenth Army Headquarters worked hard at our plans, and as our divisions reorganized, regrouped, and began to move into their assembly areas, above us in Supreme Headquarters change and reorganization were in the air. In mid-October Stilwell was recalled. The Generalissimo had insisted on it, and, in spite of pressure from Washington and from Admiral Mountbatten, had refused to yield. The only thing that was surprising was that the open breach had not come sooner. Stilwell, although Chiang's chief of staff, had never bothered to hide his contempt for 'The Peanut,' as he usually called him in private and in public. The American had no confidence in the Chinaman's military judgment or political integrity, and announced it. He believed that the Generalissimo was more interested in using American lend-lease money and equipment to secure his own personal position in China than in fighting the Japanese. Stilwell, who overestimated his own indispensability to Chiang and the extent to which the American government would go in his support, was surprised and deeply hurt. In Fourteenth Army and, I think, throughout the British forces our sympathies were with Stilwell—unlike the American 14th Air Force who demonstratively rejoiced at his downfall. To my mind he had strange ideas of loyalty to his superiors, whether they were American, British, or Chinese, and he fought too many people who were not enemies; but I liked him. There was no one whom I would rather have had commanding the Chinese army that was to advance with mine. Under Stilwell it *would* advance. We saw him go with regret, and he took with him our admiration as a fighting soldier. He was replaced by three generals who divided between them his half-dozen jobs. The command of N.C.A.C. went to his loyal second-in-command Lieutenant-General Dan Sultan, whom I already knew and liked. Wedemeyer, Admiral Mountbatten's American deputy chief of staff, replaced Stilwell in China as Chiang Kai-shek's adviser, but I gathered that the idea of building up a great American-led Chinese army to march to the sea vanished with Stilwell. General Wheeler became Deputy Supreme Commander, an excellent appointment.

One advantage did come from Stilwell's departure. It became easier to set up a reasonable land command in Southeast Asia in the place of the, to say the least, illogical organization that had been tried up till then. Admiral Mountbatten at last was able to persuade the Combined Chiefs of Staff to accept an Allied Land Forces commander with an integrated Anglo-American Headquarters. Allied Land Forces Southeast Asia (A.L.F.S.E.A.), would control Fourteenth Army, N.C.A.C., XV Corps and Line-of-Communications Command. We welcomed this, but a sad blow fell on Fourteenth Army when we learned that General Giffard was not to continue to command. He had seen us through our efforts to become an army and through our first and most desperate battles. Fourteenth Army owed much to his integrity, his judgment, his sound administration, his support in our darkest hours, and to the universal confidence he inspired among us. We saw him go with grief. I and others built on the foundations he laid. He was succeeded on November 12, 1944 by Lieutenant-General Sir Oliver Leese, who had commanded the Eighth Army in Italy.

General Leese, whom I had already known when he was an instructor at the Quetta Staff College, I found easy to serve under. His military judgment was eminently sound. Indeed, in this I differed from him only once—on the need for a sea and airborne operation against Rangoon—and then he was right and I was wrong. His staff, which he brought with him and which replaced most of our old friends at General Giffard's headquarters, had a good deal of desert sand in its shoes and was rather inclined to thrust Eighth Army down our throats. No doubt we provoked them, for not only were my people a bit sore at losing General Giffard, but, while we had the greatest admiration for the Eighth Army, we also thought that the Fourteenth Army was now quite something. However, almost all the new men were experienced and able staff officers—some such as Bastyan, the chief administrative officer, were outstanding—and our staffs soon settled down to working together. The new commander in chief approved the plans which I had worked out under his predecessor and which were in fact already under way.

During September and October there was great activity throughout the Fourteenth Army back areas. For two years our formations had fought in jungles and among hills; they were now about to break out into open country with unobstructed views and freedom of movement away from tracks. Not only would the laborious tactics of the jungle have to be replaced by speed, mechanization, and mobility, but commanders and troops would have to adjust their mentality to the changed conditions. This was especially so in the use of armour and artillery. Instead of one or two tanks, surrounded by infantry, carefully nosing forward along a narrow jungle track, we might hope to use powerful, rapidly moving armoured formations on extended fronts. Artillery would fire at longer ranges, change position more frequently, and have to be ready to answer calls from the air more quickly. In the same way our supporting airmen would have to be ready instantly to come to the help of infantry. In all the divisions not engaged in actual fighting, training to meet these new conditions proceeded vigorously. It says much for the energy and skill of corps and divisional commanders that, in the short time available, and in spite of constant moves, so much was accomplished to fit the troops for their new role.

Under the new command organization the air supply bases from which Fourteenth Army maintenance had come were no longer in its area or under its control. The small joint army,

R.A.F., and U.S.A.A.F. staff which had controlled our air supply was expanded into a new formation, known as Combined Army Air Transport Organization (C.A.A.T.O.). The American Brigadier-General Evans commanded the air and Brigadier Dawson, from my staff, the army portion. Fourteenth Army provided the reception end, Forward Airfield Maintenance Organizations (F.A.M.O.s), and very soon air supply was working better than ever.

In my own army, too, there were some changes. We altered the normal mixed animal and mechanical transport organization of the two divisions in reserve, the 5th and the 17th, to a new one we had invented. In this the whole division, except one brigade group, was completely mechanized; the remaining brigade was made entirely air transportable, i.e., its only vehicles jeeps, its twenty-five pounder guns fitted with narrow axles to wheel into a Dakota aircraft, and its scale of baggage and ammunition drastically reduced. I wanted these divisions available, if necessary in substitution for others, for a very mobile role in Central Burma.

Another change affected me personally very closely. Steve Irwin, who from the formation of Fourteenth Army had been my chief of staff and to whose loyalty, brilliance, and imperturbable common sense I owed so much, was promoted Major-General and left me to be commandant of the Quetta Staff College. If there he turned out staff officers approaching his own standard of devotion and ability, no man could have served his country better, but, selfishly, I was very sorry to see him go. I was again very fortunate, as I was able to get in his place Brigadier 'Tubby' Lethbridge, a sapper who combined the typical clearheadedness of an engineer with a broad humanity that made him a pleasure to work with or under. His sense of humour, which, thank Heaven, all my principal staff officers have had, and, wonderful to relate, retained, was perhaps more rumbustious than Steve Irwin's, but equally unquenchable. He entered at once into the partnership with Snelling on which so much, including myself, depended. The experience he had gained during a long visit to the Australian Army in New Guinea made the conditions of our war familiar to him.

While the 11th East African and the 5th Indian Divisions were battling for Kalemyo, I had moved my headquarters from Comilla to Imphal and begun to assemble IV and

XXXIII Corps for the advance across the Chindwin. IV Corps Headquarters had returned refreshed, but Scoones, who had so stoutly defended Imphal, promoted to a command in India, had been replaced by Frank Messervy of the 7th Division. Messervy had the temperament, sanguine, inspiring, and not too calculating of odds that I thought required for the tasks I designed for IV Corps. To him I allotted his old 7th and the newly-arrived 19th Indian Divisions with 255 Tank Brigade; to Stopford's XXXIII Corps, the 2d British and 20th Indian Divisions, 268 Brigade, and 254 Tank Brigade.

Both corps I ordered to break into the Shwebo Plain; IV Corps through the Sittaung bridgehead and XXXIII Corps from Kalewa as soon as the East Africans had gained a bridgehead there. The Lushai and a new 28 East African brigade would push down west of the Chindwin on Gangaw and thus protect XXXIII Corps' right.

I was anxious to avoid a proposal to take Shwebo by an airborne operation. Apart from the risk, I needed all available aircraft for supply, and I therefore ordered reconnaissances by land and air to discover whether it would be possible to move large forces by certain northern tracks from the Chindwin to the railway. Reports being favourable, I agreed to Messervy committing the 19th Division by these routes, but I told him not to let the 7th Division cross until I saw I should not still have to fly it in.

The Fourteenth Army offensive began on December 3, 1944, when a brigade of the 20th Division of XXXIII Corps crossed the Chindwin thirty miles north of Kalewa. On the next day the 19th Division of IV Corps broke out from the Sittaung bridgehead and made for Pinlebu sixty miles east. It was not until the 18th, however, at Kalewa, where the East Africans had gained their bridgehead, that the rest of the 20th Division, followed by the 2d Division, could begin to cross and advance on Pyingaing, the 'Pink Gin' of the Retreat.

To meet these invading columns the Japanese had, we believed, the 15th, 31st, and 33d Divisions with lines-of-communication troops, all badly mauled in the Imphal battle, but strenuous efforts were being made to bring them up to strength, and they now amounted to some twenty-five thousand. In addition, in the river loop some of the enemy's 53d Division had been identified opposing the 36th British Division, the right formation of Sultan's N.C.A.C., as it advanced down the railway.

As the Japanese made no serious attempt to stop the 19th Division's crossing, I expected them to fight hard to delay us in the passes through the Zibyu Taungdan Range which, a two-thousand-foot-high barrier, run parallel to and twenty-five miles east of the Chindwin.

The 19th Division made surprisingly rapid progress. Two of its brigades followed a northerly track; the third, one roughly parallel but more to the south. Both routes would pass through the Zibyu Taungdan Range to turn south on Shwebo. This was the first time the division had been in action, but the troops, a high proportion of whom were pre-war regulars, advanced with the greatest dash, led literally by their dynamic commander, Peter Rees, known to his British troops as the 'Pocket Napoleon,' a reference to his size and his success in battle. What he lacked in inches he made up by the miles he advanced. Whether he was hallooing on his troops from the roadside or leading them in his jeep, he was an inspiring divisional commander. The only criticism I made was to point out to him that the best huntsmen did not invariably ride ahead of their hounds.

On December 12, Rees's headquarters was forty-five miles northeast of Sittaung, on the 16th he had taken Banmauk, forty-odd miles further east, and pushed a patrol on to Rail Indaw where it met the 36th Division, thus forming, for the first time, a connected front from the Indian Ocean to China. On the same day his southern column captured Pinlebu. The 19th Division was now well through the Zibyu Taungdan, and, while the Japanese rear guards had fought well, the irresistible rush of our men had swept them away.

I had, a week before, begun to suspect that I had misread the Japanese commander's intention. Now I realized I had. If he had meant to fight in the Shwebo Plain, he would undoubtedly have held on to these hills with more determination. Since the beginning of the month, too, I had been getting reports, confirmed by air reconnaissance, that the general direction of Japanese movement in the river loop was back across the Irrawaddy, not forward. Then, too, the defensive positions captured by the 19th Division in the defiles did not seem designed for prolonged resistance, but for delay only. We had surprised the enemy by the speed with which we had mounted our offensive over the Chindwin, and by its strength and swiftness. It was borne in upon me that, either because of this, or because I had all along mistaken the enemy's intention, he was not going to do what I had expected—fight a major battle north of the Irrawaddy. It looked as if this battle, like so many of mine, was not going to start quite as I intended. It was time for me to use a little of that flexibility of mind that I had so often urged on my subordinates.

The fact that the first foundation on which I had built my plan had collapsed was, to say the least, disconcerting. The idea of crowding the whole of Fourteenth Army into the river loop, if the enemy were not going to wait for me there, was obviously not a good one. It could only lead to frontal assaults across the Irrawaddy, with the whole Japanese Army free to dispose itself in superior force to resist, or, if we did get over, to attack us in our inevitably weakened state. My object remained the destruction of the Japanese Army; I could never achieve it that way. Luckily, IV Corps had only one division committed across the Chindwin, so I still retained fluidity; but any major alteration, to be effective, must be quick, and would in any case throw a terrific burden on the administrative staffs. The first thing to do was to discover, or at least re-estimate, what was now the Japanese intention.

After the Imphal battle there had been a great shake-up in the Japanese High Command. A number of senior officers besides the commander in chief, Kawabe, had been removed. I knew that Kimura had replaced him, but, partly through wishful thinking and partly through lack of information about the new man, I had concluded he would have much the same characteristics and faults as his predecessor. In this I was wrong. General Kimura was to prove himself a commander with a much higher degree of realism and moral courage. An artilleryman, regarded with some justification as one of the most brilliant officers of the Japanese Army, Kimura was transferred straight from Imperial General Headquarters in Tokyo to Burma. Within a fortnight of his arrival he had completely recast the plans for the defence of Central Burma. About the time Kimura took over, the Japanese forces in Burma were, to the best of our knowledge, organized in three armies, or, as we should have called them, corps:

(i) *Twenty-eighth Army*, under Lieutenant-General Sakurai, already well known to us, was responsible for the Arakan front and, although we only learned this later the Irra-waddy Valley, up to the Yenangyaung oil fields. It had the 54th and 55th Divisions and the newly-raised 72d Independent Mobile Brigade.

(ii) *Fifteenth Army,* under Lieutenant-General Katamura (late commander of the 54th Division, who had replaced Mutaguchi, removed), consisted of the 15th, 31st, and 33d Divisions and, we thought, 24th Independent Mobile Brigade. It was responsible for the central front, including the Railway Corridor.

(iii) *Thirty-third Army,* under Lieutenant-General Honda, which held the northeastern front, facing N.C.A.C. and the Yunnan Chinese, had consisted originally of the 18th and 56th Divisions, but we had also identified in this area units of the 53d and 2d Divisions. We were not sure if these divisions were complete in the area.

(iv) *Burma Army Area Reserve,* we thought to be the 49th Division in South Burma, about Pegu.

Kimura decided he could not, in their present state, risk the three battered divisions from Imphal in a battle in the open plain. He therefore ordered a gradual withdrawal behind the Irrawaddy, leaving only light covering forces behind to delay our advance while he prepared for what he called the 'Battle of the Irrawaddy Shore.' In that battle, by concentrating his maximum strength against the Fourteenth Army, he hoped, not without reason, to cripple us as we struggled to cross the river, and then, with the help of the monsoon, to destroy us as we limped back to the Chindwin. As part of his preparations he reduced the Thirty-third Army considerably by sending the 2d Division back to Meiktila and transferring the 53d to Fifteenth Army. He also removed 24 Independent Brigade to Moulmein. The 2d Division and 24 Brigade came into his General Reserve which up to now had contained only the 49th Division. This reserve could be moved north again by rail or road when required, and served as a precaution against possible British amphibious operations in southern Burma. Later Marshal Terauchi ordered the removal of the 2d Division to Indo-China and it was en route when our offensive across the Irra-waddy developed. It was an inexplicable order and Terauchi must have reproached himself for it. Kimura was able to make these reductions in his Thirty-third Army and in the Railway

Corridor, as he intended in the northeast to remain completely on the defensive and, if forced, to withdraw slowly before the advance of our 36th Division, Sultan's Chinese, and the Yunnan force.

Of course, the full extent of these alterations in Japanese plans and organization was not known to me for a long time but the 19th Division's advance had brought us the usual harvest of captured Japanese diaries, letters, and orders. From these and air reports we could piece together, reasonably accurately, what the enemy intended. My suspicions were confirmed; it was obvious that, wisely, they had decided to fight behind, instead of in front of, the Irrawaddy. My problem was now to cross the river first and defeat them afterwards—a much harder one than to defeat them and then cross.

My staff and I, before preparing our original plan, had naturally studied several alternatives. Among them had been a project to pass a considerable force up the Gangaw Valley to seize a bridgehead over the Irrawaddy near Pakokku and then, striking east, appear south of Mandalay. This idea I had discarded because I was sure the Japanese would remain north of Mandalay and I should require IV Corps there if I were to defeat their main force. The route to Pakokku was long and most difficult, but after some hard thinking I reverted to this scheme in a modified form.

My new plan, the details of which were worked out in record time by my devoted staff labouring day and night, had as its intention the destruction of the main Japanese forces in the area Mandalay–Thazi–Chauk–Myingyan. It was based on XXXIII Corps, with the 19th Division transferred to it, forcing crossings of the river north and west of Mandalay, thus drawing towards itself the greatest possible concentration of Kimura's divisions. Meanwhile IV Corps, moving secretly south up the Gangaw Valley, would suddenly appear at Pakokku, seize a crossing, and, without pause, strike violently with armoured and airborne forces at Meiktila.

Meiktila, with Thazi twelve miles to the east, was the main administrative centre of the Japanese Fifteenth and Thirty-third Armies. In this area were their chief supply bases, ammunition dumps, hospitals, and depots. There were also five or six airfields. Road and rail routes from the southeast and west converged on Meiktila and Thazi, to spread out again to the north like the extended fingers of a hand whose wrist was Meiktila. Crush that wrist, no blood would flow through the fingers, the whole hand would be paralysed, and the Japanese armies on the arc from the Salween to the Irrawaddy would begin to wither. If we took Meiktila while Kimura was deeply engaged along the Irrawaddy about Mandalay, he would be compelled to detach large forces to clear his vital communications. This should give me not only the major battle I desired, but the chance to repeat our old hammer-and-anvil tactics: XXXIII Corps the hammer from the north againt the anvil of IV Corps at Meiktila—and the Japanese between.

Time was pressing. The more units of IV Corps that crossed the Chindwin the more difficult it would be to get the corps on to its new axis. At a table outside Messervy's caravan, near Tamu, I explained my new plan to both corps commanders. At this conference I made clear my intention that the forthcoming battle would be followed by a dash south to take Rangoon before the monsoon. This project, the taking of Rangoon, had been in all our minds at Fourteenth Army Headquarters for some time, and a good deal of examination and planning for its achievement had been carried out. It was first issued to subordinate formations in the Operation Instruction issued on December 19, after our meeting. In it I gave as my intention:

(i) In conjunction with N.C.A.C., to destroy the enemy forces in Burma.
(ii) To advance to the line Henzada–Nyaunglebin.
(iii) To seize any opportunity to advance from that line and capture a South Burma port.

I did not specify Rangoon because, while Rangoon would ultimately be necessary, I was inclined to consider that Moulmein might be a better initial strategic objective. There would be plenty of time to decide later which we should attempt.

I allotted formations to corps thus:

IV Corps
    7th and 17th Divisions
    255 Tank Brigade (Sherman tanks)
    Lushai Brigade
    28 East African Brigade

XXXIII Corps
2d, 19th, and 20th Divisions
254 Tank Brigade (Lee-Grants and Stuart tanks)
268 Brigade.

The 5th Division, reorganizing on its mechanized and airborne establishment, I held in Army Reserve.

The two corps commanders accepted these changes without fuss and with the determination that, however difficult, the new plan would be made to succeed. Stopford in XXXIII Corps proceeded to revise his plans; Messervy in IV Corps completely to remake his.

For success it was essential that both the blow that was being launched from Pakokku and its strength must be concealed from the enemy until the moment it fell upon him. A scheme was therefore prepared, which, it was hoped, would persuade Kimura that IV Corps was still moving complete into the Shwebo Plain, on the left of XXXIII Corps, and that any movement in the Gangaw Valley was merely a demonstration to distract his attention from our attack on Mandalay from the north. To achieve this a dummy IV Corps Headquarters, using the same wireless channels, had to be substituted at Tamu for the real one when it moved out. All signals from XXXIII Corps to the 19th Division had to be passed through this dummy headquarters. The real IV Corps was to keep wireless silence until control of operations in the Gangaw Valley necessitated breaking it; even then they were limited to simulating only the headquarters of the withdrawn 11th East African Division. 'Indiscreet' conversations in clear between staff officers and operators were arranged, news broadcasts made slightly inaccurate references to formations engaged, and many ingenious devices were employed to mislead the simple Japanese, while the volume of traffic was made to conform to having both corps concentrated in the Shwebo Plain. Operationally this signal deception scheme was a real annoyance to corps and divisional commanders and its enforcement a test of patience and discipline, but it paid an excellent dividend. The enemy was completely deceived.

I had been tempted to make the seizure of Meiktila a wholly airborne operation in its first stages, but I had to abandon the idea, partly for lack of parachute troops, but mainly because the air lift allotted to Fourteenth Army would barely cope with maintenance alone. It was as well I did so. At dawn on December 10 I was awakened in my headquarters at Imphal by the roar of engines as a large number of aircraft took off in succession and passed low overhead. I knew loaded aircraft were due to leave for XXXIII Corps later in the morning, but I was surprised at this early start. I sent somebody to discover what it was all about. To my consternation, I learned that, without warning, three squadrons of American Dakotas (seventy-five aircraft), allotted to Fourteenth Army mainten-ance, had been suddenly ordered to China, where Stilwell's prophecy had been fulfilled, and the Japanese, galled by Chennault's air attacks on shipping, had begun to overrun the forward American airfields. Passing overhead were the first flights bound for China. The supplies in the aircraft, already loaded for Fourteenth Army, were dumped on the Imphal strip and the machines took off. The noise of their engines was the first intimation anyone in Fourteenth Army had of the administrative crisis now bursting upon us.

For it was a crisis. It meant that the second foundation—a firm allotment of air lift—on which all our plans had been based, was swept away. The loss threatened to bring opera-tions to a standstill. The proposed move of IV Corps, which I was then contemplating and on which Fourteenth Army Staffs were already working, was most affected; but even in XXXIII Corps, whose arrangements were less difficult, the buildup of supplies and stores for the advance would now be dangerously slow. What this would mean in additional anxiety and work for all administrative staffs could hardly be exaggerated. I was especially sorry for those of Fourteenth Army and IV Corps Headquarters. They were wrestling with a complete change of plan and the diversion of half the army to Meiktila; now all the calculations of air lift and all timings would, with the loss of seventy-five aircraft, have to be worked out again. When they tackled this problem, their resiliency, ingenuity, and re-fusal to be beaten by anything filled me with admiration.

Thanks to great efforts by A.L.F.S.E.A. and S.E.A.C. and by drastic reductions in XV Corps' air lift the lost tonnage was gradually replaced, but our plans were delayed by a fortnight or three weeks. This gave the Japanese more time to recover and react to our moves and left us less time to complete our tasks before the monsoon. More than ever it was now obvious that the new plan would strain all our resources to the utmost.

The administrative risks were great.

First, we were proposing to move two or three divisions and a tank brigade, for three hundred and twenty miles over the curves and gradients of a rough hill track which in rain' was impassable mud and in dry weather almost impassable dust. Then, at the end of it, we must build up the resources needed for a great river crossing and the dash for Meiktila. Formidable enough undertakings, but to achieve them in two months and without the enemy being aware of what we were doing would require no mean effort of skill and determination—and a little luck.

While the move of IV Corps was in progress it would crowd everything else off the road; even its own maintenance supply would have to be by air. Snelling calculated that we should just have the minimum number of aircraft to meet our bare requirements, provided neither the enemy nor the weather seriously interfered, and if we could in the time build, secretly, the air strips needed for supply aircraft and defending fighters —another huge task.

We had to concentrate on the IV Corps route all possible engineers and road machinery. This meant that many other roads such as those to Tiddim and Sittaung literally disappeared, while ideas of any all-weather construction, except on one vital stretch from Tamu to Kalewa, were abandoned. Even this, from lack of road metal and machinery, would have been impossible had not Bill Hasted, my chief engineer and one of the heroes of the campaign, made a revolution in road building by using 'bithess.' The earth formation of the road was levelled and packed tight, largely by hand labour; deep ditches, with frequent spillways, were dug along each side, and the surface covered by overlapping strips of Hessian cloth dipped in bitumen. As long as no holes appeared in the waterproof cover all was well, and even when, as was inevitable, they did, repairs, like patching a tyre, were quickly and easily made. For more than a hundred miles this novel surface proved able to take a thousand vehicles a day when the monsoon came. All the same, I had some uncomfortable moments when I thought of what depended on this one road.

The Japanese railways which we hoped to take over as we advanced would be badly damaged both by our own bombing and by demolitions. We should be very lucky if we got any serviceable locomotives, although we might pick up a little repairable rolling stock. However, in spite of all our bombing efforts, the Japanese were working their railways, and if they could, we should be able to restore any lengths of line that fell into our hands. We therefore planned to concentrate on getting the lines Alon–Ava and Myingyan–Meiktila into operation at the earliest opportunity. It is not easy to fly in, or bring by road, railway locomotives, but from various sources we collected in India miscellaneous light engines which later we flew in in pieces or even brought whole on tank transporters. For the rest, the incomparable jeep, converted to rail, would have to serve.

In our difficulties we turned our eyes hopefully to water transport. We now held a stretch of the Chindwin and hoped soon to be on the Irrawaddy. Apart from the perils of navigation, especially on the Chindwin, there was one serious obstacle to the use of these rivers as our line of communication—we had no boats. Most of the shipping on the Chindwin we had sunk ourselves during the Retreat and since by air attack; the remainder the Japanese had destroyed or removed downstream to the Irrawaddy. One hot day at the beginning of the advance I took Bill Hasted, my quiet-spoken chief engineer, a little upstream of Kalewa and said, 'Billy, there's the river and there are the trees,' pointing to the great forests within half a mile of the bank. 'In two months I want five hundred tons of supplies a day down the river.' He looked thoughtfully at the river and the trees, and then at me. 'The difficult we will do at once; the impossible will take a little longer,' he quoted from a saying in frequent use in the Fourteenth Army, and added with a grin. 'For miracles we like a month's notice!' 'You're lucky,' I answered. 'You've got two!'

But it was I who was lucky, lucky to have such a chief engineer. A few weeks later, when I revisited the site, along the riverbank, humming with activity, there was a mass-production boatbuilding yard. Hasted's engineers, reinforced by I.W.T. construction companies flown in from India and by local Burmese labour, were turning out boats by the dozen from teak logs dragged in from the forest by 'Elephant Bill's' Fourteenth Army elephant companies. The boats were not graceful craft; they looked like Noah's arks without the houses, but they floated and carried ten tons each. Three of these, lashed together and decked, made a very serviceable raft that would carry anything up to a Sherman tank. Building these dumb barges was no mean achievement—we launched several hundred of them—but the real problem was to provide power craft to tow them. A.L.F.S.E.A. came to our rescue by flying in outboard engines, marine petrol engines, and even small motor tugs in parts which were put together on the riverbank. Tank transporters, borrowed from our armoured units, went back and brought motor launches from railhead at Dimapur—a nightmare drive, described by an indignant tank commander as 'the prostitution of transportation.' Kalewa, its quays rebuilt, was restored to its former position as a considerable river port.

Some of the most spectacular feats of our I.W.T. services were the salvaging, with most inadequate and improvised equipment, of many comparatively large vessels, Japanese landing craft, heavy steel floats, tugs, and even small steamers, from the bottom of the river. These formed a considerable proportion of the tonnage eventually available. My especial pride, however, was the warships we built for the Royal Navy in our Kalewa shipyards. They were two wooden, punt-like vessels, with lightly armoured bridges, which steamed twelve knots, and were armed with one Bofors gun, two Oerlikons, and a couple of double Browning light automatics mounted for antiaircraft fire. I claimed to be the only general who had designed, built, christened, launched, and commissioned warships for the Royal Navy. One I called *Pamela*, after Admiral Mountbatten's younger daughter, and the other *Una*, after our own daughter. The sequel to the double christening, which I effected with a couple of bottles of wine of doubtful quality, came in the form of a dignified rebuke from Their Lordships of the Admiralty who pointed out, more in sorrow than in anger, that only Their Lordships themselves were authorized to suggest names for His Majesty's ships of war. I hope they forgave me, for H.M.S. *Una* and H.M.S. *Pamela* brought the White Ensign, and all it meant to us soldiers, back to the Chindwin and the Irrawaddy. The little ships and their navy crews maintained the real Nelsonian tradition of steering closer to the enemy. They were often in action and both suffered damage from enemy shot. In their day they swept the seas, or at least the rivers. It was fun to have our own navy again.

The line of communication on which Fourteenth Army

operations would, apart from direct air supply, depend as soon as the monsoon began in May, was thus a varied one, and would run:

(a) By the all-weather road from railhead at Dimapur, via Imphal to Tamu—two hundred and six miles. Then by,

(b) the fair-weather road which, by expedients like 'bithess,' we hoped to make all-weather, to Kalewa—one hundred and twelve miles.

(c) Across the Chindwin by Bailey bridge and a fair-weather road to Shwebo; thence by a very bad but all-weather road to Mandalay and XXXIII Corps—one hundred and ninety miles.

(d) The river link, with our home-built or assembled boats, from Kalewa to Myingyan—two hundred miles—serving IV Corps.

(e) Finally, from Myingyan partially by all-weather road, and, it was hoped, rail to Meiktila—fifty-nine miles.

To carry out the opposed crossing of a great river and fight a major battle at the end of such a line of communication, between five hundred and six hundred miles from railhead, would have been difficult enough had we been granted ample time, but the monsoon, to be expected in early May, meant that within five months or less we had to make this line of communication fit for bearing traffic in all weathers. If by that time we had not done so, unless we had the use of a port in South Burma, the Fourteenth Army could hardly hope to maintain itself. We were certainly going to have a busy five months.

As it emerged from the hills, 19th Division's drive gained momentum and the enemy rear guards broke before it. On December 19 our men swept through Wuntho and, having turned south, by the 23d were some twenty-five miles beyond it. This advance of nearly two hundred miles in twenty days was an astonishing feat, not so much because of the opposition overcome—although that was by no means negligible—but because of the difficulty of the country. For most of the distance there was no road; the earth track built through the hills by the Japanese for their invasion of Assam had largely disappeared during the rains. The 19th Division, with very little road-making equipment, had to cut the track anew. Most of the division went on foot, but guns and lorries had often to be winched and man-hauled up steep slopes, and in one place the only way to get the track round a cliff was to cantilever it out on timber supports. It was vastly exhilarating to fly over the division in a light aeroplane. Through gaps in the treetops that screened the hills below I could see on every rough track files of men marching hard with a purposefulness that could be recognized from five hundred feet. Behind them gangs, stripped to the waist, were felling trees and hauling them to make rough bridges across the numberless streams and gullies that cut the route, while guns waited to move on again the moment the last log was in position. Dust rose in reddish clouds as whole companies with pick and spade dug into banks to widen the road and let the lorries pass. These men hacking out a road, dragging vehicles, pushing on with such fierce energy to get to grips with the enemy, were a heartening sight. When I came down on their hurriedly-prepared air strip and talked to them, and to Pete Rees, who was as usual in the van, my spirits soared. The 19th Division had waited long enough to get at the enemy and nothing was going to stop it now.

Also under IV Corps, 268 Brigade had crossed the Chindwin south of Sittaung, and, advancing by jungle paths, had seized Oil Indaw, broken through the hills, and reached the Mu River which flows south into the Shwebo Plain. It was now moving south on the right of the 19th Division. On December 26, in accordance with the new plan, I transferred both 268 Brigade and 19th Division from IV Corps to XXXIII Corps, which from that date became responsible for the tactical direction of all operations on the northern part of Fourteenth Army's front.

While the 19th Division swept south, XXXIII Corps pushed east through Pyingaing and cleared the gorge against Japanese rear guards. A small mechanized column from the 2d Division made a dash which narrowly forestalled a Japanese demolition party at the Kabo weir which controlled the irrigation and indeed the life of the Shwebo Plain. By January 5, the division had seized Ye-u, rushed the lightly-defended Mu River and, from Kabo, made touch with the 19th Division. There ensued between these two divisions a race for Shwebo. The reconstituted Japanese 15th Division was now in full retreat, but a regiment of their 31st Division frought stubbornly to cover the withdrawal. The 19th Division with immense *élan* broke through and entered Shwebo on January 8, beating the 2d Division by a short head. Meanwhile, the 20th Division struck south from Pyingaing, and its forward brigade moving on pack by forest paths, took Budalin in a savage assault and on January 8 was closing in on Monywa.

As XXXIII Corps thus vigorously cleared the Swebo Plain, Messervy's IV Corps was on its long march to Pakokku. Ahead went the Lushai Brigade, with orders to take defended Gangaw, and on its tail trod the new 28 East African Brigade. The Lushai Brigade having been in contact with the enemy in the area for some time and 28 Brigade being easily mistakable for the 11th East African Division, I hoped that the Japanese would believe that our forces here were unchanged and that the whole of IV Corps was still far away on Fourteenth Army's left. Behind these brigades every available man of IV Corps and every engineering resource I could give it strove tirelessly to improve the track for the passage of the 7th Division, which, after a hundred-mile march from Tamu, was now hidden in the forests south of Kalemyo.

The administrative skill of IV Corps staff at this period, and indeed throughout the campaign, was taxed to the utmost. Not only had their complete plan been suddenly changed, when I switched them from the left of the army to its extreme right, but they had to arrange the three-hundred-mile march of the whole corps by a very inferior fair-weather track winding through hills. For miles at a time they had, in fact, to make the track. It was difficult enough to get three-ton lorries over it, but when it came to passing through the tank brigade with its fifty-ton load of tank and transporter coaxing their long wheel bases around tight bends with one edge over a sheer drop, constantly reversing and going forward again, the march became a nightmare in slow motion. The gradients and the dust were at times such that the tanks had to tow their own transporters. Traffic control was a major problem. Imagine the scene if a tank transporter, loaded with a big motor launch, grinding up a hill on the way to Pakokku, met another returning empty, sliding in the dust down the same one-way track above a precipice. That such encounters occurred only at prepared crossing places was one of the things the road control had to watch. How effective that control was can be judged by the fact that there were no major holdups.

The loss of our allotted air-transport squadrons fell heavily on all our moves. What would have gone by air now had to go by road, adding to the congestion and the time. The air forces, British and American, were magnificent. The transport planes that remained to us flew incredible hours. They identified themselves completely with the army. It was as much a point of honour with them as with the soldiers that, not only the troops, but all the thousands of tons of supplies and gear required, should get through in time. Airmen, too, realized as well as we did that the whole success of the coming battle depended on the secrecy of IV Corps' move. A single Japanese reconnaissance plane, investigating too closely a cloud of dust, might sight a line of tanks moving slowly towards Pakokku and realize what that meant. Vincent's 221 Group R.A.F. was responsible that no enemy plane got close enough to do this, and he discharged his responsibility with unsurpassed thoroughness. Throughout daylight his fighters patrolled over the route, and, as far as I know, no Japanese scout ever penetrated his screen without being shot down for his daring. Vincent and his men piled up our debt to them until we could never repay it, and 221 Group R.A.F. had as big a share in our victory, when it came, as any army formation. We were proud to serve them, but I could not help thinking that sometimes the army recognized their achievements more readily than some of the higher Air Force headquarters.

Gangaw proved rather a tough nut to crack. Messervy did not want to deploy too many troops against it, as that would arouse Japanese suspicions. The lightly-armed Lushai Brigade probed hard, but the Japanese, as ever, resisted stubbornly in well-prepared positions. The problem was solved by laying on an 'Earthquake,' that is, a really heavy—for the Burma front—air bombardment. We called in to our aid the bombers of the Strategic Air Force, and a most imposing demonstration of air power was promised. To view it the corps commander, a couple of air marshals, and some other senior officers rather lightheartedly set out with me on January 10 in a flight of light planes for Gangaw. Guided in the leading plane by a most distinguished air officer, we flew low over very attractive country. Neither my pilot nor I was concerned with navigation; we followed our leader. However, I suddenly realized we had been flying for a long time; I consulted my watch and with a start realized that unless we had travelled in a circle, which we did not seem to have done, we must for about the last half-hour have been flying steadily south over Japanese-held territory. I began to take an intense interest in the country below. True enough, we were well beyond Gangaw. I signalled wildly to my companions; my pilot quickly gained height and turned back. The rest followed, we flew north again, and after a little circling we found the Gangaw air strip. Those assembled there to greet us had watched us fly steadily past them to the south, their feelings a mingling of astonishment, alarm, and—I regret to add, among the more junior—amusement. The air marshal's chagrin and the comments on his ability as a navigator were luckily offset by the success of the 'Earthquake.' The airmen dropped several tons of explosive for every Japanese in the position, but, what was better, they dropped them *on* the position. Then cannon and rocket-firing fighters went in just ahead of the assaulting troops, the last wave so close to our men that to keep the enemies' heads down it had to be a dummy run. Gangaw was taken by the air force and occupied by the Lushai Brigade—a very satisfactory affair. Soon afterwards the gallant Lushai Brigade was assembled and I bade its officers and men farewell. They were then flown out to a well-earned rest in India, after a year of the most strenuous and effective long-range penetration operations. Their place was taken by 28 East African Brigade which continued to cover the concentration and screen the advance of the 7th Division close on their heels.

The divisions of the Fourteenth Army were now, in the second week of January, approaching—or, in the case of the 19th Division, were actually on—the Irrawaddy along a front of more than two hundred miles, from Wuntho in the north to Pakokku in the south. The Japanese, as far as we knew, were still unaware of our change in plan and of the stealthy march of IV Corps; their eyes, we hoped, were still fixed on Mandalay, not Meiktila. The stage was set for that most dramatic of all military operations—the opposed crossing of a great river.

CHAPTER XVIII

CROSSING THE IRRAWADDY

The Irrawaddy, which the Fourteenth Army now approached, is one of the world's great rivers. It runs through Burma for thirteen hundred miles, a thousand of them navigable from the sea by sizeable steamers. From time immemorial it has been the main highway of Burma; trade and war have followed its course. The waters of the Irrawaddy rise with the rains from March to September, when they are at their highest, and then subside again, while the river's current, like its width, varies with the season, from one and a half miles an hour to five or six. Thus, in January, the water was low and the current at its slowest.

Nevertheless, as an obstacle the Irrawaddy was most formidable. In the northern part of the Fourteenth Army area, where it confronted the 19th Division, it ran, first through forests and then for twenty-five miles between low hills, which narrowed it to some five hundred yards. As the country flattened out, the river widened to an average of two thousand yards, with a maximum of well over four thousand at its junction with the Chindwin. In the narrower parts the banks shelved steeply; in the broader stretches, through flat, arid country, they were low and the stream was frequently divided and obstructed by islands and sand banks, which changed position with every flood. In many places, as the water had fallen, it had left behind broad stretches of soft sand into which vehicles sank axle deep, thus limiting the approaches to the river. Navigation was always difficult, especially when, as now, the water was low and the selection of a crossing place could be made only after detailed reconnaissance.

The advance of the Fourteenth Army was going well. In XXXIII Corps the 19th Division, reaching the Irrawaddy about Thabeikkyin and finding the enemy on both sides of the river, was vigorously clearing the west bank against considerable opposition; the 2d Division was pushing south from

Shwebo and the 20th sweeping down on Monywa. IV Corps had begun its secret flank march; the 5th Division was in Army Reserve at Jorhat and the 17th reorganizing in India.

On my left, east of the Irrawaddy, Sultan had lost his 14th and 22d Chinese Divisions, flown back to China in answer to appeals for help. Stilwell's forecast had come true: the Japanese there had advanced and already some American airfields had been abandoned, more were threatened. Nevertheless Sultan continued his advance south against weakening resistance. His right-hand division, the British 36th, had, after making contact with my 19th, crossed to the east bank at Katha and now had one column north of Thabeikkyin and another moving parallel farther east up the Shweli River. Still farther east was the 50th Chinese Division, and the 30th and 38th Chinese, having captured Bhamo, were about to gain touch with the Yunnan Forces at Wanting, one hundred and twenty miles east of the Irrawaddy.

To meet this menacing and broad-fronted Allied advance astride the river Kimura had, we believed, regrouped. He had placed Honda's Thirty-third Army (18th and 56th Divisions with temporarily some detachments from the 2d and 49th Divisions) to hold Sultan's forces and the Yunnan Chinese. The four divisions of Katamura's Fifteenth Army he had spread from right to left, with the 15th and 53d Division about Mandalay to oppose our 19th Division; the 31st holding the Sagaing Hills and the Irrawaddy's south bank westward; and, on his left, the 33d Division covering Monywa and Gangaw. The Japanese 54th and 55th Division were in Arakan and South Burma while, in reserve somewhere behind the central front, were most of the 2d and 49th Divisions, two strong, independent brigades and the surviving Indian National Army formations.

The enemy knew we were about to attempt crossings, and, realizing that it was impossible to hold two hundred miles of river line continuously and effectively in strength, he did not attempt to do so. Instead, he wisely concentrated his defences at the most likely crossing places, watched the intervening spaces, and held his reserves, especially artillery and tanks, mobile and well back until our intentions were clearer. He left certain detachments on our side of the river in the Sagaing Hills and around Kabwet, some sixty miles north of Mandalay, to impede our advance, to give him observation, and, if necessary, to form sally ports across the river. He also organized small suicide penetration units to raid on our bank, and, by interfering with our preparations, to delay and confuse us. Generally speaking, Kimura's dispositions to meet our assault from the north were suitable, and after his tour of inspection he probably felt that, while he might not be able to stop us crossing in some places, he should be able to destroy such forces as did manage to get over. His shortage of air support and reconnaissance was, of course, a great handicap, and must have worried him a great deal, but he made arrangements to use what he had more freely and more boldly.

If Kimura was not without anxieties, I certainly had mine. One of the greatest was shortage of equipment. I do not think any modern army has ever attempted the opposed crossing of a great river with so little. We had few power craft, and those we had were small, old, and often damaged by the long journey over execrable roads. Our handful of military boats and rafting stores had seen months, even years, of hard use and rough handling. All our equipment was very much 'part worn.' We were especially weak in outboard engines, on which we should have to rely to a great extent; most, even of those available, were underpowered for their tasks and almost all were unreliable. We tried to eke out our own equipment with a number of captured pontoons, but these were of poor type and really suitable only for bridging. Burmese country boats, of which we obtained a few, were good cargo carriers, but, to the uninitiated, extremely awkward to navigate. We strained every nerve to produce more amphibious equipment, but it was simply not there. My headquarters found all the equipment, technical units, and help it possibly could, but strive as we would, I could not provide my corps commanders with more than a fraction of what I should have liked or of what they might reasonably demand. Apart from its deplorable quality, I could not give them equipment enough to allow of more than one division at a time crossing in each corps, and, even for that one division, far too many trips would be required, the boats and rafts having to ferry back and forth many times. I was, as I said at the time, asking them to cross on 'a couple of bamboos and a bootlace.' They knew the risks quite as well as I did, but neither they nor the divisional commanders made unnecessary protests. They realized no more was available; what was lacking in matériel they made up in ingenuity, skill, organization, and determination. The only equipment my army had in full supply was, as ever, brains, hardihood, and courage.

As the only hope of counterbalancing these shortages, I appealed for increased air power, and Stratemeyer, the American general, commanding Eastern Air Command, responded nobly. He placed the United States 12th Bombardment Group under Vincent of 221 Group R.A.F. and instructed the tenth Army Air Force (U.S.A.A.F.), the Strategic Air Force, and 224 Group R.A.F. in Arakan to give all possible support to the Fourteenth Army on demand. This really formidable strength Vincent handled brilliantly throughout. I had already moved my headquarters to Imphal and soon after to the jungle north of the Kalemyo–Kalewa Road. Vincent's and my headquarters now lived side by side, worked and moved as one. To watch Vincent's chief of staff, the huge 'Tiny' Vass and my stocky 'Tubby' Lethbridge, both stripped to the waist, working out their intricate, dovetailed programmes of reconnaissances, patrols, strafes, supply drops, bridge bustings, and bombardments was a lesson in good temper and interservice cooperation. The enemy's communications were harried all round the clock, his movements by day made perilous and by night delayed. Never was air cooperation closer, quicker, or more effective; never more gratefully appreciated than by the Fourteenth Army and its commander.

My hope was to persuade Kimura to believe that all serious crossings would be north and immediately west of Mandalay; then, when he was committed in desperate fighting there, to catch him off balance with the decisive blow at Meiktila.

Obviously the first crossing should, therefore, take place north of Mandalay. If the 19th Division got over here, it would look as if it was meant to join with the British 36th Division, already on the east bank, in a strong drive on Mandalay from the north. This would draw enemy formations to meet it. The 19th Division was, therefore, ordered to snatch a crossing as quickly as possible, well above Mandalay. There would then, inevitably, be a pause while the rest of XXXIII Corps drew up to the river and prepared to cross. IV Corps, with much farther to go and more unknown perils to meet, might be later in arriving on the river about Pakokku. Would it be better to let the next division of XXXIII Corps cross west of Mandalay before IV Corps farther south? If it did, it should strengthen the idea that our main thrust was in the north and might attract and pin down still more Japanese formations in that area. On the other hand, I was very nervous that Kimura would realize that the southern crossing was in strength. The longer Messervy's divisions hesitated on the bank or were assembled near it, the greater risk of discovery. I decided, therefore, that the first IV Corps crossing should take place as soon as Messervy was in position to launch it. This would mean that it would probably be either simultaneous with, or a little after, the XXXIII Corps crossing west of Mandalay. As soon as possible after the establishment of its bridgehead, IV Corps would deliver the mechanized and airborne blow at Meiktila.

Once these decisions were made, I left it to corps commanders to select the exact locations for their crossings, to choose which divisions should make them, and to prepare the best tactical plans and arrangements that the meagre resources I had allotted them would permit. I really believe that the heroes of this time were the men who kept the wheels turning and the wings flying—the Indian drivers who, two to each three-ton lorry, drove night and day in shifts over hundreds of miles of crumbling roads; the sappers who built up those roads almost between the passing wheels; the R.I.E.M.E. men who worked incredible hours to turn the worn vehicles around again; the Air Force mechanics, stripped to the waist, who laboured in the sun by day and the glare of headlights by night to service the planes. All of them were magnificent to watch. They identified themselves utterly with the troops ahead; they were and felt themselves to be a part, and a vital part, of the team. They had the pride and bearing of fighting men, for they were one with them.

Yet sometimes, even when I was in the midst of these splendid men or with the forward divisions, doubt and fear slunk in upon me. I was asking so much of them—was it too much? In no other theatre would an army have been launched on such a task with so pitiful an equipment. Success depended on what? Luck? A Japanese pilot streaking the treetops in his Oscar, an enemy agent with a wireless set crouched above the track counting tanks, or a prisoner tortured until he talked— and Kimura's divisions would move, the muzzles of his guns swing towards our crossing places. Imagination is a necessity for a general, but it must be a *controlled* imagination. At times I regained control of mine only by an effort of will, of concentration on the immediate job in hand, whatever it was. And then I walked once more among my soldiers, and I, who should have inspired them, not for the first or last time, drew courage from them. Men like these could not fail. God helps those who help themselves. He would help us.

I drew comfort, too, at this time from quite another thought. I had, more than once, in two great wars, taken part in the forcing of a river obstacle, and I had on every occasion found it less difficult and less costly than expected. I had also read some military history, and, although I cudgelled my brains, I could not call to mind a single instance when a river had been successfully held against determined assault. As the time drew near for the first crossings, I hugged this thought to me. Historically, the odds were in my favour.

By January 11, 1945, Rees's 19th Division, probing up and down the river, had got several patrols across by night and was hard at it reducing a well-dug-in and fiercely-defended enemy position at Kabwet on the west bank. Three days later a whole company crossed by stealth near Thabeikkyin, followed each day by another, until the whole battalion was over and had established a small bridgehead, which was further reinforced just in time to throw back a series of savage counterattacks. On the night of January 14-15, the main divisional crossing began near Kyaukmyaung, twenty miles south, where only patrols were encountered. By the time the Japanese realized this was serious the whole of 64 Brigade held a bridgehead and was able in hand-to-hand fighting to repulse several determined attacks. The brigade even was able to press outward and seize a scrub-covered ridge, eight hundred feet high, three miles inland, and a bare peak rising abruptly from the river-bank more than two miles south. These successes denied the enemy observation over the bridgehead and ensured its retention.

The Japanese, confused by numerous feints and patrol crossings elsewhere, had not been quick to decide which were the real crossings, and even then they took some time to concentrate against them. Every hour of this delay was invaluable to the sweating 19th Division ceaselessly ferrying men and supplies across the river on almost anything that would float. Yet, once they had begun to assemble, the enemy reacted swiftly and violently. As I had hoped, Katamura, commander of the 15th Japanese Army, responsible for the river line here, took these crossings to be an attempt to join up with the 36th British Division, as a preliminary to an advance down the east bank on Mandalay by the whole of our IV Corps, which he still thought was on the Fourteenth Army's left. He called up his 15th and 53d Divisions and added artillery units from his other divisions, the 31st and 33d. Kimura, who himself believed, as did his army commander, that this was the expected British IV Corps attack, transferred to Katamura a strong force of additional artillery and some of his few remaining tanks. This was a formidable force with which to overwhelm the two brigades of our 19th Division newly across the river, but Katamura, luckily for us, instead of building up a strong, well-prepared attack, committed the common Japanese error of launching his troops into the assault piecemeal as they arrived. Covered by the heaviest artillery concentration that our troops had as yet endured on so small a front, he put in attack after attack, some by direct suicide assault, some by infiltration. These were kept up almost daily and nightly for three weeks. Gradually, as the enemy dead piled up, the edge was taken from the attack and in the beginning of February, for the first time, there was a lull for two days and two nights. Tanks had now been ferried over, and preparations were begun for the breakout.

I had visited the bridgeheads and seen something of the bitter struggle to retain them. The fighting had been severe, the casualties to our men considerable, and the strain of fighting in these restricted places with their backs to the river no light one. The troops looked fine drawn and thin, but were in good heart. I was able to visit my own old battalion, the 1/6th Gurkha Rifles, in which I had served for many happy years. It was good to see them again and to be told by their divisional commander that they had done well in the bridgehead fighting. I spoke to Gurkha officers whom I had first known twenty-odd years before, when I was adjutant and they were chubby recruits straight from the Nepal hills. Now they were subadars, commanding companies and platoons on a hard-fought field, wise soldiers and real leaders. The British officers whom I had known as junior subalterns—some of the sons of my friends, even as babies—were now seasoned battalion or company commanders, among them General Cowan's son, a most gallant and promising young officer. I felt proud—and a little conscious of my fifty-odd years—as I looked at them.

They were all loud in their praises of Vincent's airmen who supported them. He had moved fighter squadrons to strips within a few miles of the river and the answer to a call for help from the bridgeheads came in a matter of minutes. When I visited these airmen I saw pilots leaving for their fifth or sixth sortie of the day. Their part in holding the bridgeheads was a great one. They became particularly effective in locating and silencing the Japanese artillery, and in shooting up his tanks.

During February our increasing pressure nearer Mandalay prevented the further reinforcement of the Japanese facing the 19th Division. Their attacks became attempts to contain rather than to evict, and as our men gathered strength in the bridgehead, they, in turn, passed to the attack. Steadily, as in bitter local actions they drove the enemy from villages and high ground, the bridgehead grew in area and security.

As the 19th Division fought hard for its footing over the Irrawaddy, the 20th, under Gracey, cleared the approaches to the now-ruined but still fortified Chindwin river port of Monywa. The garrison, part of the 33d Japanese Division, made us pay, as was their habit, for every strong point we took, but on January 22 Monywa was ours.

As soon as Monywa was securely in our hands I moved my Tactical Headquarters there as it was admirably placed to control both my corps. On February 8 my Main Headquarters with the Headquarters 221 Group joined me there, and we set up a complete and very comfortable joint headquarters, partly in the jungle and partly in some of the least-battered houses on the outskirts. The Japanese had left behind a number of booby traps which were disconcerting, but my chief frights came from snakes which abounded in the piles of rubble. They seemed especially partial to the vicinity of my War Room which lacked a roof but had a good concrete floor. It was my practice to visit the War Room every night before going to bed, to see the latest situation map. Once when doing so I had nearly trodden on a krait, the most deadly of all small snakes. Thereafter I moved with great circumspection, using my electric torch, I am afraid, more freely than my security officers would have approved. It seemed to me that the risk of snakebite was more imminent than that of a Japanese bomb. Paying one of my nightly visits, moving slowly, and, as I was wearing rubber-soled shoes, silently, I lifted the blanket which served as a door. On the other side of the room, seated before the situation map, lit by a shaded light, were the officer on duty and a younger colleague who had recently joined the Headquarters. The older officer was speaking in the voice of assured authority. He placed his finger firmly on the map. 'Uncle Bill,' he announced, 'will fight a battle here.' 'Why?' not unreasonably asked the youngster. 'Because,' came the answer, 'he always fights a battle going in where he took a licking coming out!'

On the day Monywa was taken, other troops of the 20th Division, pressing on, reached the Irrawaddy at Myinmu. Near here, a few days later, there was a fight with a large Japanese party attempting to withdraw over the river. Resisting stubbornly, the enemy had been almost annihilated, when the last survivors, in full equipment and with closed ranks, under the astonished eyes of our men, marched steadily into the river and drowned. For the next ten days the division searched for a crossing place. Daring reconnaissances were carried out and our patrols, constantly pushed across the river, maintained a reign of terror and thuggery among the Japanese posts on the southern bank.

The Japanese commander, Kimura, although he had failed to drive the 19th Division into the river, did not waver in his determination, at all costs, to prevent us entering Central Burma. He had as yet no knowledge of our projected stroke at Meiktila, nor of the march of IV Corps; activity towards Pakokku he regarded as minor distractions. His divisions were in strong positions; his 15th to contain our 19th, his 31st to hold Sagaing and the Irrawaddy south bank as far west as Ngazun; his 33d, strengthened by a regiment of the 4th, with additional artillery and the bulk of his remaining tanks to meet the impending crossing of our 20th Division. His 53d Division he placed centrally near Myotha, as his mobile reserve, to strike as the battle developed. He was already bringing troops from Pakokku, northward and followed this by one regiment of his 2d Division from Meiktila itself. He also proposed to withdraw troops from his 18th Division about Lashio to Mandalay. Kimura exhorted his toops to stand firm in what he called 'the decisive battle of the Irrawaddy shore.'

Gracey, meanwhile, searched for crossing places. He had a couple of weeks in which to do this, as at least that time was needed to build up in XXXIII Corps area the supplies and equipment that would be required for the Irrawaddy battle. This buildup was not easy. I gave preference in transport and airlift to IV Corps, who not only had the more difficult and hazardous operation, but would, I hoped, be the decisive factor. This meant some restriction on the operations of XXXIII Corps before the crossings, and a slowing up of its preparations, which were very galling to them, but which were unavoidable if the Pakokku crossing was not to risk discovery. XXXIII Corps, which up to now had been the favoured child in the Fourteenth Army, found some of these things hard to bear, especially as its troubles were added to by some ominous creaking in the new air-transport machine as it got into top gear. However, in spite of several minor crises, the whole forward concentration of the corps, including its tank brigade, and the assembly of the stores and equipment allotted to it for the battle, were completed in time.

The actual 20th Division crossings, covered by several feints, began on the night of February 12–13. There were two—a main one by 100 Brigade just west of Myinmu, and a subsidiary by 32 Brigade about seven miles downstream. Firm ground led down to the water and there was some cover for forming up, but the sites were selected mainly because reconnaissance had shown that there were no Japanese permanently posted to cover them and their patrolling was not frequent. The spot chosen for 32 Brigade crossing was also on the exact boundary between the Japanese 31st and 33d Divisions as shown by captured maps. Experience had taught us that to attack at such a point was always an advantage, as the Japanese rarely seemed properly to interlock their junction points.

At 0400 hours on February 13 the leading flight of 100 Brigade, the Border Regiment, pushed off in silence. The night was dark, but throughout the evening the wind had freshened and it now proved troublesome to heavily-laden and underpowered boats. The river here was one thousand five hundred yards wide, but obstructed by partially submerged sand banks, between which ran strong currents. Several boats grounded, and there was difficulty in getting them off. At first luckily there was no opposition, and it was not until some time after the first troops had landed that light and ill-aimed small-arms and mortar fire was directed against them. Once the first landing had been made, the rest of the brigade followed rapidly, and by eight o'clock the whole of it was over—an excellent piece of organization. A well-directed and heavy air strike on the Japanese artillery that was likely to cover the crossing places had been put down the previous day, and the enemy guns were in process of moving or taking up new positions at the critical time. A few 75 mm. shells burst on the beach with little effect. The landing could be claimed as a complete surprise and practically unopposed. By dusk on February 13, 100 Brigade had established a small bridgehead.

The 32 Brigade had a longer water crossing and suffered greater difficulties from wind, currents, and sand banks. The outboard motors were, as usual, unreliable and very difficult and noisy to start. However, here also the crossing was a surprise, and by dawn the first battalion, the Northamptons, were over and digging in. All ferrying at both crossings stopped at daylight, but neither bridgehead was seriously attacked through the day. Again the Japanese were slow to recognize main crossings and to collect their troops to attack. Real opposition did not begin until the 15th when Japanese aircraft strafed the beaches, damaging a number of boats but inflicting few casualties. This was followed by a heavy night attack on 100 Brigade, during which the Japanese landed by boats behind our men and used flame throwers. The attack was repulsed and, pushing on, our troops extended their bridgehead until it was more than three miles long by half a mile deep.

Fighting now became fiercer as each enemy reinforcement arrived, to be thrown in, as usual, piecemeal. By February 15, in spite of pressure, our bridgehead was six miles by two, so that on the 16th we were able to start ferrying by day and our buildup rapidly increased. There followed a series of suicide attacks, mainly on 100 Brigade, by waves of Japanese infantry supported by tanks, but the two bridgeheads had now joined up and they held firm. The enemy losses were heavy; five of their attacks were in daylight, and on several occasions our aircraft caught them as they assembled for the assault. Rocket-firing Hurricanes proved our most successful anti-tank weapon, and their best day was February 20, when they knocked out thirteen medium tanks. The fiercest fighting with the heaviest casualties on both sides occurred between February 21 and 26. When the Japanese counterattacks were finally thrown back and they recoiled exhausted on one sector of our defences five hundred enemy corpses were buried by bulldozers and on another more than two hundred. The commander of the

Japanese 33d Division, Tanaka, said later that during this period two of his battalions delivered an attack with a strength of twelve hundred men, only to lose nine hundred and fifty-three. By February 27, fighting strongly, the 20th Division had expanded its holding to eight miles by two and a half in depth. Some of the hardest fighting of the campaign had taken place in this narrow bridgehead.

All this time IV Corps had continued its secret march towards Pakokku and, by the 18th, the 7th Division was collected about one hundred and sixty miles from its objective. I had given Messervy, the corps commander, February 15 as the last acceptable date for his Irrawaddy crossing and, fearing in this difficult hill country the delay even small hostile rear guards might inflict, he had, to outflank them, ordered his advance on a wide front. In addition he sent one brigade (89) on pack transport far out by jungle tracks on the left flank to swing in on the main route again at Pauk, only forty miles from Pakokku. The deceptive East Africans still led and the Japanese, not in great strength, relied mainly on mines and obstacles to delay them. In a three-mile stretch through the hills they felled several hundred trees across the path, but with the help of 'Quads,' guntowing vehicles, and ten elephants, our engineers cleared them in one day. There were several minor alarms and clashes but on January 28 the hooking brigade fell on Pauk and, after a skirmish, seized the high ground astride the main track fifteen miles farther on, overlooking the Irrawaddy Valley. Here IV Corps got its first distant view of its objective.

When I saw the troops at Pauk, their jungle-green uniforms and their faces were red from the dust and so was the jungle itself each side of the track, every leaf thick with the red powder. But there was no time for rest. At Pauk the 7th Division took the lead and, on February 3, advanced to take Pakokku, known to be strongly defended. The East African Brigade went south to make feints at crossing opposite Chauk, forty miles downstream. The exact sites of the real crossings would of course have to wait on actual reconnaissance, but Messervy had already decided that they would be in the neighbourhood of Nyaungu, at the narrowest part of the river. He realized that because of this Nyaungu was rather an obvious place, but the slowness and fewness of his power craft and the need to build up quickly on the far bank forced him to choose a short crossing. Even here the river was a thousand yards wide. Deception was essential. He planned to divert the enemy from his real crossing place by having, in addition to that of the East Africans at Chauk, two other demonstrations—a main one at Pakokku itself and another at Pagan, six miles south of Nyaungu. So much depended on these deceptions that they were elaborately and carefully prepared. I longed to be able to give Messervy a battalion or two of parachute troops, who would have simplified his problem a great deal, but we had none.

Daily photographic air reconnaissance along the Irrawaddy, combined with other sources of intelligence, gave us a fairly complete idea of the Japanese dispositions on the sector which IV Corps was approaching. The enemy had no suspicion that a major crossing was about to be attempted here. His troops were strung out along the river. On the west bank in the Letse area, fifteen to twenty miles northwest of Chauk, he had 153 Regiment. The four battalions of 72 Independent Mobile Brigade with the 2d Indian National Army Division, whose strength was variously reported as between five and ten thousand, held a wide stretch from Chauk to Nyaungu. Farther north, about Pakokku, was 214 Regiment. For some fifty miles of river this was not much. The enemy were thin on the ground, and, if we could draw them away from our crossings, we might hope to have a substantial grip on the far bank before they could collect force enough to oust us. One advantage of Messervy's choice was that, like the 20th Division, he was crossing at the junction of two Japanese formations. The 214 Regiment at Pakokku was the extreme left of the Japanese Fifteenth Army and 72 Independent Brigade was the right of Twenty-eighth Army; the boundary between the two ran practically through Nyaungu.

IV Corps' threefold advance to the river was pushed with determination. The 114 Brigade, approaching Pakokku, soon ran into strong opposition eight miles west of the town, where the enemy were well dug in on high ground at the Kanhla crossroads and seemed determined to fight it out. Our first immediate assault failed, and it was not until February 10 that a deliberate attack by the brigade with tanks drove the Japanese out and inflicted severe casualties on them in the open. The brigade was then given the tasks of clearing the west bank of stragglers and preventing any interference with the crossings from Pakokku which appeared to be held in force. The 89 Brigade reached the west bank opposite Pagan, and by night slipped a patrol of Sikhs across, who reported by wireless that the south end of the town was unoccupied. This patrol remained hidden on the east bank and continued to send back most valuable reports of the enemy movements around it. Three or four large country boats with Burmese crews were captured near Pagan, and this, together with the reports of the patrol, decided Evans to turn the feint at Pagan into a subsidiary but real crossing. The plan was for one company to cross silently in the country boats, to be followed by the rest of the battalion. The 28 East African Brigade also reached its objective, Seikpyu, without serious opposition, and began realistically to stage the first moves of a crossing. The 33 Brigade, selected to make the main crossing at Nyaungu, occupied Myitche and under cover of the village made its preparations.

The most thorough reconnaissance possible with the enemy on the opposite bank was made to select the actual crossing places. The water had again dropped in February, and it was found that the river had considerably changed its bed. New sand banks had appeared, and no direct crossing was possible. The oblique courses that had to be followed were from fifteen hundred up to two thousand yards long. In fact, one of those eventually used was just over two thousand, the longest opposed river crossing attempted in any theatre of World War II. Soundings were made by night by men of the Special Boat Section and frogmen who painstakingly charted the only practicable channels. The west bank was low and cultivated with rice fields at practically river level; the east bank, a line of rugged cliffs one hundred feet high, broken by eroded gullies, completely overlooked it. Defences could be seen in places along the cliffs, but as the days passed no increase in them showed on our air photographs. On the other hand, more digging appeared opposite those places where we were making feints.

It had originally been intended to make a daylight crossing with full artillery, air, and tank support to overwhelm opposition, but the shortage of air lift and the difficulties of road transportation made it impossible to dump the ammunition required in the time. The idea of a completely silent night crossing was then explored, but there would be no moon and it was thought that boats would be unable to find the tortuous channels in the dark, and this method was abandoned. Finally it was decided that the first flight would be silent just before dawn and would be followed up immediately by the remaining flights in power craft under all available covering fire. It was calculated that, even if all went well, a brigade could not be ferried over in the equipment available in less than seven hours.

Eventually it was decided that the operation should be in four phases:

(i) An assault crossing, the first flight of which was to be silent and at night, launched from points on the west bank, one and a half to three miles upstream of Nyaungu, to seize four beaches and the cliffs one mile northeast of the village on the east bank. The South Lancashire Regiment was loaned for the assault crossing from another brigade as they had had experience in boat work and had taken part in the landing at Madagascar.

(ii) A rapid follow-up in daylight of the three battalions of 33 Brigade and some tanks, under all available covering fire, to build up the bridgehead.

(iii) A rapid advance from the bridgehead to capture Nyaungu and with it the eastern end of the shortest river crossing, which would be organized and put into operation at once.

(iv) Expansion of the bridgehead to take the 17th Division which would cross as soon as possible by the direct Nyaungu route.

On my visits to IV Corps I had completely approved Messervy's and Evans's plans. I was much impressed by the skill and energy with which they overcame the obstacles that confronted them at every step in their preparations and which would have daunted any but the most forceful commanders. As the moment of this all-important crossing approached, on which the whole fabric of my battle plan rested, I devoted myself mainly to doing what I could to support Messervy.

One of the anxieties I had was to ensure that the 17th Division was ready to cross the moment the bridgehead was gained. For surprise, we must strike at Meiktila without delay. I had taken Cowan, still the divisional commander, and his senior officers now at Imphal, completely into my confidence and explained their role to them. They seized the opportunity to study the country they would operate over and to conduct sand-table exercises based on the forthcoming operations. The move from Imphal to Pauk caused anxiety, as the transport shortage, both road and air, was still acute, but, ferrying itself a part at a time in its own transport, the division, less its airborne brigade which dropped off at Palel, was concentrated in Pauk by February 12—just in time. Much of the divisional artillery and engineers had already gone forward to help the 7th Division in its crossing.

The night chosen for the 7th Division crossing was February 13–14. The engineers could not begin to bring up their equipment until the enemy had been evicted from the Kanhla crossroads, and this did not take place until the 11th. Even after that, movement could be only at night. Time was short. Yet to drag these cumbersome loads along sandy, uneven tracks in complete darkness, with the least possible noise, and to have every trace of the feverish activity of the night hidden before daylight from prying eyes that overlooked every yard of our bank, was not only a vast labour but a great feat of organization. Yet by dawn on February 13 all the troops and the equipment were assembled in concealment within reach of the crossing points. Here they spent a day in final preparations and in a wait for zero hour, that anyone with a glimmer of imaginaion must have found trying.

Six miles downstream the Sikhs of 89 Brigade were similarly and with equal stealth preparing for the subsidiary crossing, while still farther south the East Africans were more openly staging a false crossing.

As soon as darkness fell, equipment, boats, and all the paraphernalia for the main crossing began to move down to the water. Assembly areas were marked and the troops tramped slowly and silently from their bivouacs. The Special Boat Section made a final reconnaissance of the far bank to see if it had been occupied, and in doing so met two Japanese swimming in the river. To prevent their escape they had to be shot, and it is possible that the noise put the enemy on the alert.

The night was pitch dark, a strong wind was blowing, and there was a distinct lop on the water, as at a quarter to four the leading company of South Lancashires got into their boats and started the long paddle across. At last their boats grounded on the opposite bank. With as little splashing as they could, they waded ashore and scrambled up the cliffs, while the boats turned and went back. By five o'clock on the morning of February 14 the company had reached the cliff top, so far without meeting any enemy. There they disposed themselves for defence and awaited the rest of their battalion.

On the west bank the remainder of the South Lancashires moved down according to programme and began to embark just as the first faint light of dawn was tinting the sky. The channels to be followed had been marked behind the first flight and things had indeed gone well, but from that moment they began to go wrong. In spite of their past experience, the Lancashire men fumbled badly at the embarkation, and there was a good deal of delay and confusion. Because of noise, it was not possible to start up the outboard engines until the men were in the boats, and when the time to do so eventually came several motors failed to start. Some of the boats also were found to leak badly, having been damaged in transit. More delay resulted. Eventually the commanding officer, realizing that a start must be made, ordered the boats that were ready to move off, irrespective of whether they were in their correct flights or not. The result was that the reserve company, which should have been last, found itself when daylight came in midstream ahead of the first wave. Even then all might have been well had the boats made straight for the east bank, but the reserve company decided it would circle to take its proper place behind the others. The strong current and the wind were too much for the feeble engines, and the reserve company, in confusion, began to drift downstream. The remaining boats, seeing them go and not realizing what was happening, turned to follow them. At this moment the enemy opened fire with rifles from the cliffs and with machine guns from the water's edge. Two company commanders and the engineer officer were quickly killed, casualties grew, and several boats, including that of the commanding officer, were sunk. The guns on our bank and some of the tanks waiting to embark now opened fire, but owing to secrecy they had not registered, and at first their shooting was perforce slow. Within a short time aircraft from the cab rank were called in, and under this combined cover the boats made back to our bank. The crossing, except for the isolated company, now in great danger, had failed.

Nor was this the only failure. The subsidiary crossing by 89 Brigade had met with initial disaster. The gallant patrol hidden on the east bank in Pagan had during the night reported that the enemy had reinforced the town and the whole of it was now occupied. The assaulting company, however, stout-heartedly decided to set out in its native craft. As they approached the far bank they came under fire and the Burmese boatmen, not unnaturally, panicked. The clumsy boats got out of control and in spite of the Sikhs' efforts were swept downstream. At last the boatmen, urged by the sepoys, regained control and brought them back to the starting point. It would have been suicide to have tried to cross in daylight in these slow, awkward boats, and there the crossing rested.

To watch across the great river as dawn breaks over ancient Pagan is to hold one's breath at so much beauty. Pagan, once the capital of Burma, was in all its glory at the time of the Norman Conquest; now silent, ruined, and deserted, it is still noble—and very beautiful. Its twelve hundred temples, madder red or ghostly white, rise, some like fantastic pyramids or turreted fairy castles, others in tapering pagoda spires, from the sage-green mass of trees against the changing pastel blues, reds, and golds of sunrise. As a foreground flows the still dark yet living sweep of moving water. Yet as the officers of 89 Brigade gazed disconsolately towards Pagan in the chill of early morning, they are to be forgiven if the beauty of the scene was somewhat lost to them. They had other and less pleasant things to think about: their attempt at crossing had definitely failed. Then, suddenly, to their surprise, they saw a small boat bearing a white flag put off from the opposite bank. In it were two Jiffs, who, when they came ashore, said that the Japanese had marched out of Pagan and moved hurriedly up-river, leaving only troops of the Indian National Army to garrison the town. Their one wish, now the Japanese were gone, was to surrender. Quickly a platoon of the Sikhs with a British officer crossed in the only available boats. True to their word, the garrison of Pagan marched out and with smiles laid down their arms. By evening most of the Sikh battalion was established in the outskirts of Pagan. This incident was, I think, the chief contribution the Indian National Army made to either side in the Burma War.

Back at the main crossing, while all this was going on at Pagan, the engineers were working feverishly to repair the returned boats for a new crossing. The South Lancashire Company on the east bank reported it was now firmly dug in and had not so far been attacked. It was therefore decided to make a second effort to reinforce it. The brigadier judged it would take too long to reorganize the South Lancashires, so he ordered a Punjabi battalion to make the crossing as soon as possible. The 4/15th Punjabis, with great calmness and in excellent order, embarked on what promised to be a most hazardous enterprise. At 9:45 A.M. their leading company set out under the heaviest covering fire that could be provided by artillery and air. As the boats chugged slowly across they were hardly fired on at all; it seemed that there were still no Japanese at the actual crossing and that even those downstream, who had taken such toll of the South Lancashires as they drifted past, had withdrawn. Some of the boats grounded on sand banks but the men waded or swam ashore. The whole company reached the beaches intact and swarmed up the cliffs. The curtain of covering fire moved ahead of them and swept their flanks. As soon as the boats were available the rest of the battalion began to cross, and throughout the afternoon heavily-laden craft continued to go to and fro practically unmolested. By nightfall three battalions were over, and ferrying had stopped as the risk of losing boats in the treacherous current in the dark became too great.

The 33 Brigade for the night formed a small but well-defended bridgehead and stood to, expecting savage counter-attacks. None came; only a few jitter parties prowled about the perimeter. We even succeeded in getting a patrol along the riverbank to the Sikhs at Pagan. At dawn on the 15th the crossing was resumed with increasing tempo. All day long men, mules, tanks, guns, and stores poured across, and again no enemy opposed them. By evening the South Lancashires and most of 89 Brigade were in the bridgehead. The Japanese, who had now collected in some strength, were driven into caves near Nyaungu where they held out desperately in a sort of catacomb. Its entrances were blown in and sealed off, the defenders left to die inside. During the day another company of the Indian National Army surrendered. By the 16th Nyaungu Village was in our hands and the main bridgehead, now about four miles by three, had joined up with the Sikhs at Pagan. We were over.

This sudden success after a shaky beginning was something of a surprise as well as a relief. It was owing, first, to the fact that the enemy command was concentrating on the crossings of XXXIII Corps to the north and regarded all riverbank activities from Pakokku southward as mere demonstrations. A captured Japanese intelligence officer later explained that they did not believe that there was more than the East African division in the area, and that it was directed down the west bank towards Yenangyaung. Even when crossings appeared to be threatened, the enemy considered they would not be in force and that if any actual attempts were made they would be at Pakokku and Chauk. They therefore pulled their troops away to meet these threats, leaving only small detachments and the Indian National Army to watch the Nyaungu sector. In fact, as the 7th Division made its crossings the enemy was hasily marching away to the north and south from the sites—a happy result brought about by Messervy's able deception measures.

These deception measures had indeed drawn off the Japanese, as those engaged in them discovered. As 114 Brigade of the 7th Division closed in on Pakokku, the Japanese hurried in reinforcements from the river line and put up a stubborn struggle. Even after being driven out of the town the remnants of the garrison, now convinced that a crossing was about to be attempted here, dug themselves in on an island in the river a little to the south, while other Japanese hurriedly strengthened their positions on the opposite bank. Having cleared the town and west bank, we kept the enemy pinned here by making faces at him, until he realized from the seriousness of the Nyaungu crossing that he was wasting his time.

The feint at a crossing opposite Chauk by 28 East African Brigade was so convincing that it brought prompt and violent retaliation. The Japanese here were able to counterattack in some strength, as they had collected a force on the west bank to meet the expected advance of a division of ours towards the Yenangyaung oil fields. The East African Brigade was driven back some miles and Messervy had to send it reinforcements of all arms to prevent a threat to the route from Pauk to Nyaungu developing. After some sharp exchanges this Japanese counterattack was held at Letse, twenty-five miles south of the road, before any delay to the main operations could be caused.

Meanwhile in the 7th Division bridgehead there was great activity. Patrols and air reconnaissances were pushed out in all directions to give warning of the hourly-expected Japanese attacks. Yet it was not until February 17 that the enemy acted. Several air attacks were delivered on our crossing places and the enemy troops, driven across the river out of Pakokku, marched against the left flank of 33 Brigade's bridgehead at Nyaungu, where they were roughly handled by that brigade as it pushed outward to gain elbow room. On February 19, 89 Brigade, doing the same to the south of Pagan, met troops of 72 Japanese Independent Brigade coming north from Chauk after the withdrawal of the East Africans. Realizing at last that the crossing at Pagan was in strength, but still not appreciating what was in store, the local enemy commander ordered all troops in the neighbourhood to concentrate against it and drive the Allied forces back into the river and annihilate them. As a result, there was delivered against our bridgehead and approaches a series of savage counterattacks.

Messervy's original intention had been to expand the bridgehead sufficiently to hold two divisions before the 17th Division assembled in it, but he shared my anxiety that the blow at Meiktila should not be delayed. He therefore decided to pass over the 17th Division before the bridghead was large enough to receive it, and to let it collect outside. During February 16 and 17 the 17th Division, less the brigade left at Palel, moved by night into the vicinity of the crossing and between the 18th and 21st was ferried over to its assembly areas on the east bank. As soon as any of its units were across, the division began to push out patrols, which had some skirmishes, but as far as could be ascertained the Japanese had no idea that a fresh division was now in the bridgehead.

To turn north again for a moment to XXXIII Corps. The 20th Division crossing, which was a direct threat to Mandalay, had, as I hoped, attracted Kimura's attention from our activities about Pagan, but I could not expect to conceal much longer our strength there. I was increasingly anxious, therefore, to push the 2d Division over the Irrawaddy, still nearer to Mandalay, just as Kimura must begin to realize the threat to Meiktila, and thus make him hesitate to detach troops from the Mandalay front for the new battle. It was not easy to stage the 2d Division crossing in time for this, as the equipment for it had to be collected from that used by the other divisions, a process not helped by the fact that much of it had been damaged and a considerable portion of it had to be left with them as ferries at the crossings already made. However, Stopford and Nicholson, commanding the 2d Division were prepared to attempt the crossing on February 24, a date which suited my plans admirably.

Although the enemy must have been expecting an attempt at crossing by our 2d Division, they had used so many of their troops in the attacks on 20th Division bridgehead and to hold the Sagaing Hills on the north bank, that for the fifteen miles of river to the west of Sagaing they had only a regiment, which could do little more than watch and patrol, with detachments at the most likely crossing places. They had, however, in several places prepared strong defensive positions and they obviously hoped, as soon as our intentions were evident, to occupy these with such reserves as they could muster. A good deal of patrol activity went on as both sides pushed scouting parties across the river and the 2d Division nibbled into the Sagaing defences. On February 21 Stopford, in order to allow the division to concentrate for its crossing, sent 268 Brigade to take over the Sagaing sector of its front. By constant pressure this brigade occupied the Japanese garrison, which could have been much better employed if it could have withdrawn to the southern bank.

On the moonlit night of February 24–25, the 2d British Division began its crossing at the village of Ngazun, about ten miles east of 20th Division's bridgehead. The leading battalion of 6 Brigade pushed off on the fifteen-hundred-yard crossing at 2200 hours; but the enemy were alert, and opened heavy machine gun and mortar fire. Although our casualties were not heavy, many assault boats were holed, others damaged, and some sunk. Of the first battalion, a portion reached an island in midstream and dug in there under fire. A second battalion came under heavy fire in its boats and was forced to return to the north bank. A third battalion, whose boats had been pushed somewhat downstream by the current, succeeded, less a company, in gaining the opposite bank and establishing itself precariously there. The crossing, if not a failure, was near to becoming one. Nicholson and his staff rose to the occasion. In spite of the inevitable confusion on the beaches they reorganized the scattered 6 Brigade, brought up fresh troops, and during the 25th, under cover of smoke from all available guns of XXXIII Corps, disregarding heavy enemy fire, passed a battalion over the river and also completed the battalion on the island. By the morning of February 26, 5 and 6 Brigades were all on the south bank with some tanks. The recovery, after the initial setback, was a fine feat of leadership and organization.

After his first resistance on the beaches, the enemy was strangely passive at this beachhead. Unlike his reaction at the others he delivered little in the way of counterattacks, interfering with our build-up only by shelling and minor air action. Kimura was in fact pausing to regroup for a final effort on the Irrawaddy shore. He did not know it, but the real storm had not yet broken on him.

CHAPTER XIX

THE VITAL THRUST

As the last week of February 1945 began, Kimura could—and did—contemplate the Burma scene, if not with confidence, at least with hope. On his central front, which he recognized as the decisive one, the picture he saw was that both corps of our Fourteenth Army were in the Chindwin–Irrawaddy loop; IV Corps on our left, with a bridgehead forty-five miles north of Mandalay, and XXXIII Corps with a foothold over the river thirty-five miles west of the city. Both these bridgeheads he had so far managed to contain; they were isolated and their build-up should be slow. A third division of ours had just begun another crossing nearer to Mandalay, but this, too, he could hope to hold for a time. The British 36th Division, which he had expected to continue south to join our IV Corps, had, rather surprisingly, suddenly turned east, and was at the moment fighting a desperate battle to maintain the small bridgehead it had gained over the Shweli River at Myitsun. It seemed clear that this division was definitely committed to the American–Chinese drive on Lashio, and need not, for the present, be taken into account in the Mandalay battle.

To Kimura the situation on his northeastern front cannot have been reassuring. Sultan's Chinese divisions, now in touch with the Yunnan Chinese, were fifty miles from Lashio, but the Japanese 56th Division had extricated itself and could be expected to delay the Allied advance while Kimura fought his decisive Mandalay battle. In Arakan, too, his 54th Division had been roughly handled by our XV Corps and a new British landing at Ru-ywa threatened to cut his Arakan force in two. However, in Arakan, as long as the passes into Central Burma at An and Tangup were held, the British could do no vital damage. Our Irrawaddy crossing at Pagan Kimura, thanks to our deception measures and the failure of his air reconnaissance, was considered merely a demonstration by one division to distract him from a main attack by two corps on Mandalay.

In South Burma seaborne invasion did not seem imminent; he might risk reducing the forces held to meet it.

Mandalay, Kimura realized, was the decisive sector. His object must be to collect here the greatest force he could, as quickly as he could, and hurl it against the Fourteenth Army while it was split by the Irrawaddy and its divisions in his bank of the river were isolated. If he could defeat the Fourteenth Army, the loss of Lashio and Arakan would be a trifle and only temporary at that.

Kimura decided that everything must give way to the Battle of the Irrawaddy Shore and that accordingly the bulk of his forces on all other sectors must be withdrawn to be brought against the Fourteenth Army in the Mandalay area. From his northern front he called in the bulk of his 18th Division and a regiment of his 49th, leaving only the 56th Division to face Sultan and the mass of the Yunnan Chinese while one regiment of the 18th delayed the British 36th Division. From Arakan, his 54th Division, dropping rear guards on the two passes, was to move with all speed to the north of Yenang-yaung. From southern Burma were ordered the remainder of the 49th Division, one regiment of the 55th, and a regiment of the 2d Division which was turned back on its way to Siam. The arrival of these formations would give Kimura the equivalent of eight Japanese divisions and one and a third Indian National Army divisions against the estimated British five, straddled across the river. It should be enough. The Battle of the Irrawaddy Shore could yet be won!

Considering our practically complete command of the air, Kimura regrouped by road, rail, and river with surprising speed. I did not, of course, know the full extent of these transfers, but it was soon clear that the odds against me would be heavier than I had calculated. It will be remembered that I had originally based my plan for the battle of Central Burma on the three assumptions that:

(i) The Japanese would fight in the Shewbo Plain north of Mandalay.

(ii) My allotted air-transport lift would not be reduced, and

(iii) Pressure on the other Burma fronts and the threat of sea-borne landings would prevent the Japanese from seriously reinforcing their formations opposing my army.

The first of these the Japanese had disposed of by withdrawing behind the Irrawaddy; the second the Combined Chiefs of Staff in Washington and London had shattered by sending a substantial part of my American squadrons to China; and now the third had gone after the other two. War is like that.

Apart from urging that XV Corps should thrust from Tangup towards Prome and that the 36th British Division should be returned to Fourteenth Army—but only if its American air maintenance could come with it—the only action I could take was to bring in the 5th Indian Division. On paper it could be demonstrated conclusively that it was impossible with our resources to maintain a sixth division. Yet I had to have it. Which risk should I take, the tactical one of losing my battle through lack of troops or the administrative one of the battle collapsing because I was unable to supply them? I ordered up the 5th Division.

Snelling's staff and that of Combat Cargo Task Force, as was their duty, pointed out that all our supply services were already strained. Our air crews had been flying for weeks at intensive rates that according to the book could not be demanded for more than a few days, but once the decision had been made they worked their miracles without even the month's warning. Throughout the battle we were never without acute anxiety on the supply and transport side. Almost daily there was a crisis of some kind. The reserves of some basic ration would fall frighteningly low, guns would be silent for want of ammunition, river craft out of action for want of spares, wounded collecting in some hard-pressed spot with no means of evacuating them. Petrol was always desperately short. Yet we got over all these difficulties and a thousand others by juggling between formations with the limited transport available and by cruelly over-working the men who drove, flew, sailed, and maintained our transport of all kinds. Time and again, and just in time, the bare essentials for their operations reached those who so critically needed them. Very rarely had any formation more than its basic needs. If it had, it meant that some officer in it, with the understandable but selfish desire to be able to say, 'Thanks to me, our chaps are better off than other troops,' had somehow got hold of more than his fair share, while his neighbours, or more probably those ahead of him, went short. It was a natural failing, and the Army staff soon came to know who were the greedy ones, individuals and formations.

I called Warren, now commanding the 5th Division, to my headquarters to explain what would be required of him. As usual, he wasted neither time nor words, or asked for equipment he knew I could not give him; *he* was not one of the selfish sort. When I said good-bye to him, he had strengthened my confidence in success. I never saw him again. Somewhere in the jungle hills between his headquarters and mine he lies with his comrades. He was not easily replaced but I had just appointed Bob Mansergh, the chief artillery officer of the 5th Division, an exceptionally able young officer whom I had marked for advancement, to command the 11th East African Division. I recalled him to the 5th Division where he was well known as divisional commander. As the division, leaving behind its airborne brigade, began to move to the Pakokku area I watched it, full of ardour, pass through Monywa, but by that time the battle for Meiktila was in all its fury.

By February 21 the 17th Division and 255 Tank Brigade, less a regiment left on the west bank, had crossed into the 7th Division bridgehead. The advance on Meiktila began the same day while the last units of the division were still crossing. Resistance was soon met astride the road, but the tanks brushed it aside and in the afternoon a point fifteen miles from the river had been reached. Next day the advance continued in three columns on a broader front with the idea of a pincer movement on Taungtha and of confusing the enemy by a threat to the oil fields. Opposition increased throughout the day but was overcome with the capture of four guns, and the night was spent, under cover of outposts, making a crossing for vehicles over the half-mile wide sandy *chaung* just west of Taungtha. Soon after dawn on February 24, the town was captured in brisk fighting and the whole division moved across country on a broad front, over-running Japanese parties, to an assembly place on the main road and railway to Meiktila. During the early part of the night 'Snipers' Triangle' had to be cleared of enemy suicide squads. More than a hundred snipers were flushed from concealment and killed.

During the 25th Japanese appeared from the north but, leaving one brigade (48) to deal with these and collect a supply drop, the division advanced fifteen miles and took Mahlaing, twenty miles from Meiktila. Next day the brigade with the precious supply drop rejoined, and the tanks rushed Thabutkon air strip, ten miles farther on, where all night work went on to repair damage done by the retreating Japanese. On the 27th, while the tank brigade had to halt for a petrol drop, the fly-in of 17th Division's airborne brigade (99) began, and the division pushed on along the road. Eight and a half miles from Meiktila, at a well-dug-in, wired, and mined position, it encountered the strongest attempt yet made to hold us up. Without pause a brigade (63) made a wide hook to the north and came in behind the enemy, at the same time as the replenished tanks arrived and delivered a simultaneous assault on a wide front. The Japanese seemed quite incapable of dealing with these massed, swift-moving armoured attacks and were hunted out into the open, where there was a good killing and a pursuit to within five miles of Meiktila. Patrols in darkness, probing the western defences of the town, reported that they were strongly held and appeared most formidable. All night explosions could be heard and flames seen at various points over the countryside as the enemy destroyed his supply and ammunition dumps. Cowan and his force of a division and a tank brigade had covered eighty miles over difficult tracks and against opposition. We had arrived before Meiktila; we now had to take it.

Major-General Kasuya, commanding the Meiktila area, as senior Japanese officer, had at the first alarm taken control of all enemy troops in and around the base. These totalled some twelve thousand men, but they were scattered in several detachments, protecting dumps, airfields, and communications. In addition he had about fifteen hundred miscellaneous base troops in Meiktila and a number of hospital patients. Kasuya had only a few days in which to prepare the defence of Meiktila, but he realized its importance and was determined to hold it to the last. He displayed the greatest energy, collecting his adminsitrative units, improvising infantry companies from odds and ends, ceaselessly digging defences and organizing his perimeter into sectors and reserves. Every available man went into the fighting line, including any patient in hospital who could stand, even if only on one leg with crutches. The ordnance depots were opened and automatic weapons with ample ammunition issued to almost every man. Kasuya called in two airfield defence battalions and some anti-aircraft batteries from airfields he knew he must abandon, sighting the guns for anti-tank and perimeter defence. He had one piece of luck.

The bulk of a regiment of the 49th Division had just arrived in Meiktila on its forced march to join Fifteenth Army under Kimura's redistribution plan, and Kasuya held it there.

The actual strength return, later captured, of the Japanese in the town itself showed a total of thirty-two hundred with a large number of guns. Dug in under houses, in the banks of lakes, in concrete and earth-covered timber strong points, sitting among its piled up rice sacks and its ammunition dumps, Meiktila's garrison presented a formidable defence. Much more formidable, in fact, than that of either Myitkyina or Bhamo, smaller towns with smaller garrisons, that had taken so long to overcome. Meiktila had another great advantage for defence : its approaches from the west and south were covered by wide lakes, so that the entry roads there were in effect causeways, easily closed by artillery and allowing no chance for manoeuvre. From these lakes also ran deep irrigation channels and ditches into the surrounding country, which would slow up all movement and greatly restrict that of armour.

We had now reached the critical phase of the battle for the destruction of the Japanese Army. Kimura's great drive against XXXIII Corps, which he believed to be the whole Fourteenth Army, was beginning. From all sides his forces converged on the Mandalay area. Now was the time to seize Meiktila quickly, and then, when he reacted, as he must, to that vital threat, to launch from the XXXIII Corps bridgeheads an all-out offensive. Every division of Fourteenth Army was committed; all except one, the 5th, were engaged in full battle. Our expenditure of petrol and ammunition was rising with the increasing area and tempo of the struggle; our supply line lengthening and becoming more precarious. We were unavoidably, once more, putting heavier demands on our air-transport squadrons, and the administrative side of the battle began to look more like a gamble than I relished. The formidable concentration of enemy strength, the struggle for Meiktila ahead of us, and the need for speed had all narrowed our margins for success.

The 17th Division's drive towards Meiktila was well under way and the 2d Division's Irrawaddy crossing just beginning, when, in the midst of all the anxieties of a savage and fluctuating battle, another was unexpectedly added. On February 23 Marshal Chiang Kai-shek demanded the return, without delay, of all Chinese forces in Burma. He also insisted that, pending their departure, they should in no circumstances advance south of a line eighty miles northeast of Mandalay. I had relied on Sultan's forces cooperating in my advance on Mandalay and Rangoon by moving parallel on my eastern flank. Any hope of that had now gone, but even worse I learned that the American squadrons supplying the Chinese would now be used to fly them out, and that the aircraft already allotted to me would have to take on the supply of the British 36th Division and all the Chinese awaiting transfer. I should also be-

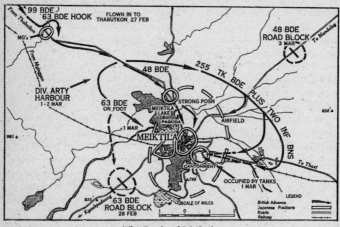

The Battle of Meiktila

come responsible for the protection of the road to China and, obviously, Kimura would be free to transfer almost all the troops on his northern front to mine. In spite of appeals by Admiral Mountbatten, the Generalissimo remained adamant, and with this threat hanging over me I found it hard to maintain before my staff, allies, commanders, and troops that appearance of freedom from anxiety so essential in any army commander. Luckily, on the British Chiefs of Staff representation, the United States chiefs agreed to leave the bulk of their transport squadrons in Burma until either we had taken Rangoon or June 1, whichever was the earlier. Although orders for the withdrawal on the Mars Brigade and the Chinese divisions went out on March 11, and I realized that if my army was caught approaching Rangoon with the monsoon in full blast without the air squadrons we should be in a disastrous maintenance situation, I decided to put all that out of my mind. Sufficient for the day was the evil thereof!

To revert to the 17th Division and 255 Tank Brigade, poised for the attack on Meiktila. The reports Cowan was receiving warned him that the garrison of the town would be stronger than first estimated, and that, while the outer defences extended in an oval some three miles by four and a half all round Meiktila, those on the west, where the two large lakes covered much of the front, would be the most difficult to attack. He knew, also, that considerable bodies of Japanese were roaming the neighbourhood and closing in on the town. The need to seize Meiktila and the airfield on its eastern outskirts, before the enemy could come in strength to the rescue, was urgent. He decided, therefore, to block the main approaches with detachments a few miles out, and using mobility, armour, and air support to the utmost, put in his main attacks from the north and east.

Cowan's moves were bold and flexible. On the morning of February 28, stripped of all but essential fighting equipment, 63 Brigade was in close contact with Meiktila's western defences; a strong road block was placed across the main road from Chauk and the divisional artillery deployed in a position from which it could support attacks on the town from any direction. The 48 Brigade, astride the Thabutkon road, attacked the northern defences, being held up until nightfall by an enemy strong point in a monastery.

The 255 Tank Brigade with two infantry battalions and a battery, after an exhilarating sweep round Meiktila under the bulk of Cowan's artillery and air support, roared, the infantry on their tails, into the eastern defences. This armoured onrush was met by heavy artillery, machine gun, and anti-tank fire from mutually supporting bunkers and fortified houses, while snipers everywhere picked off the foot soldiers. Resistance was fanatical and to the death, yet the attack penetrated well into the town. Even then wounded Japanese and small pockets of survivors still fought on in areas we had overrun. Cowan, fearing for the tanks among the ruins, pulled them out of the town, leaving strong infantry detachments to hold our gains. During darkness the enemy attempted to infiltrate through the houses and a fierce point-blank fight went on all night.

That day I had been on the Mandalay front where the

breakout of XXXIII Corps, led by the 19th Division, was beginning in earnest, and I was anxious that it should be well timed with the IV Corps operation. On my return in the evening to my headquarters at Monywa I studied reports from Meiktila. These gave the impression that the attack was held up, and I decided I ought to go there. We could not risk a second Myitkyina. I would fly in next morning. I was very angry when the R.A.F. informed me, with the utmost politeness but equal firmness, that they would not fly me to Meiktila —it was too dangerous! The air strips had not yet been properly repaired, they were frequently under fire, and Japanese fighters were reported. It was no use pointing out that a whole brigade had been landed on these same air strips, that they were being used every hour of daylight by unarmed R.A.F. and U.S.A.A.F. transports and that if they were being shot up that was not an R.A.F. responsibility, as it was my soldiers who should protect them from ground attack. I was told that the R.A.F. would be delighted to fly any of my staff anywhere at any time, but not me, not to Meiktila, not now. This idea of my value was flattering but extremely annoying. I was about to have it out with Vincent, when luckily, for the sake of our friendship which I valued, I had another idea.

There had just arrived at my headquarters a visiting American general with his own Mitchell bomber. I asked him if he would like to come with me and see something of the Meiktila battle. As I hoped, with characteristic American generosity, he suggested we make the trip in his aircraft. I gratefully accepted and early on the morning of March 1 we set out—I feeling rather like a schoolboy who had dodged his masters and was playing truant for the day. We flew to IV Corps Headquarters on the riverbank opposite Pagan, picked up Messervy, and went on to one of the air strips now in operation near Thabutkon. It was quite peaceful, though there was a little popping not far away and a few dead Japanese on the edge of the field. We were offered a second breakfast, and I ate my first Japanese-provided meal—biscuits and tinned food from a captured store. It was not very good. I gained more mental gratification from it than nourishment. Punch Cowan had sent a couple of jeeps to meet us, and we bounced merrily along the road to his battle headquarters just outside Meiktila. He soon put Messervy, me, and our American friend in the picture of the fight, which, judging by the noise, smoke, and constant zooming of aircraft diving on their targets, was no skirmish. Indeed, this day, March 1, saw the bitterest fighting of the battle. Cowan's troops were slowly biting into Kasuya's defences, tough though they were. The 63 Brigade had begun an attack on Meiktila from the west, and, in spite of restricted approaches, were into the outskirts of the town. The 48 Brigade with some tanks had resumed their assault on Meiktila East from the north, and were making progress against the most resolute opposition. The 255 Tank Brigade and its infantry had seized a steep, heavily defended hill, which rose abruptly to 500 feet on the edge of the South Lake, near the southeast corner of Meiktila, and gave observation over the whole area. Here bitter fighting was going on, as tanks and infantry clawed into the defences of the town itself.

Cowan's conduct of this difficult and divided battle was impressive. With his main attention fixed on the various assaulting brigades, he had at frequent intervals to glance over his shoulder as ground and air reports of Japanese movements in the surrounding country were brought to him. He had, too, all the anxieties of an air supply line, which rested on precariously held landing strips at a time when ammunition and petrol expenditure was at its highest. Not least, he was very short of sleep and remained so for several days. Yet throughout he was alert to every change in the situation on any sector, and swung his air and artillery support to meet and take advantage of it. His firm grip on his own formations and on the enemy never faltered. To watch a highly skilled, experienced, and resolute commander controlling a hard-fought battle is to see, not only a man triumphing over the highest mental and physical stresses, but an artist producing his effects in the most complicated and difficult of all the arts. I thought as I watched what very good divisional commanders I had.

After speaking on the 'blower,' to a brigade commander and listening in on the tank net—always an interesting and often a worthwhile thing to do in an action—I left Cowan conducting his grim orchestra. Assured that the battle was in competent hands at the top, I thought I would go a little closer and see how it was being handled lower down. I chose 48 Brigade, as, at the moment, they seemed to be cracking a particulary tough nut. We went by jeep around the north of the town and then moved forward on foot somewhat more cautiously. We had a word with various subordinate commanders on the way; all very busy with their own little battles and all in great heart. One of them told us the best place from which to see anything was a massive pagoda that crowned a near-by rise. We reached it along a path screened from the enemy by bushes, and, crouching below the surrounding wall, crossed a wide terrace, where already in occupation were some Indian signallers and observation parties. Peering cautiously over the wall, we found on our right the end of the North Lake, placid and unruffled. To our left front, about a thousand yards away, the main road entered Meiktila between close-built houses, now crumbling in the dust, smoke, and flame of a bombardment. We were, I knew, about to assault here, but it was the scene immediately below and in front of us which gripped the attention.

The southern shore of the lake for nearly a mile ran roughly parallel to the northern edge of the town. Between them was a strip about half a mile wide, of rough, undulating country, cut up by ditches and banks, with here and there clumps of trees and bushes. Three hundred yards from us, scattered along water cuts, peering around mounds, and lying behind bushes, were twenty or thirty Gurkhas, all very close to the ground and evidently, from the spurts around them, under fairly heavy fire. Well to the left of these Gurkhas and a little farther forward there was a small spinney. From its edge more Gurkhas were firing Bren-gun bursts. A single Sherman tank, in a scrub-topped hollow, lay between us and the spinney, concealed from the enemy but visible to us. In the intervals of firing we could hear its engine muttering and grumbling. The dispositions of our forces, two platoons and a tank, were plain enough to us, but I could see no enemy.

Then the tank revved up its engine to a stuttering roar, edged forward a few yards, fired a couple of shots in quick succession, and discreetly withdrew into cover again. I watched the strike of the shot. Through my glasses I could see, about five hundred yards away, three low grassy hummocks. Innocent enough they looked, and little different from half-a-dozen others. Yet straining my eyes, I spotted a dark loophole in one around which hung the misty smoke of a hot machine gun; I could hear the *knock-knock-knock*, slower than our own, of its firing. Searching carefully, I picked up loopholes in the other mounds. Here were three typical Japanese bunkers, impervious to any but the heaviest shells, sited for all-round defence and bristling with automatics—tough nuts indeed. The tank intervened again. Without shifting position it lobbed two or three grenades, and a white screen of smoke drifted across the front of the bunkers. One of the Gurkhas below us sprang to his feet, waved an arm, and the whole party, crouching as they went, ran forward. When the smoke blew clear a minute or two later, they were all down under cover again, but a hundred yards nearer those bunkers. A few small shells burst in the water at the lake's edge. Whether they were meant for the tank or the Gurkhas, they got neither, and the enemy gunners made no further contribution.

When I looked for it again, the tank had disappeared, but a smoke screen this time, I think, from infantry mortars, blinded the bunkers again. The Gurkhas scrambled forward, dodging and twisting over the rough ground, until some of them must have been hardly thirty yards from the enemy. Somewhere behind the spinney the tank was slowly and methodically firing solid shot at the loopholes. Spurts of dust and debris leaped up at every impact.

As the fight drew to its climax, we moved out of the pagoda enclosure to a spot a little forward and to the right where, from behind a thick cactus hedge, we had a clearer view. The tank reappeared round the spinney's flank and advanced still shooting. Gradually it worked round to the rear of the bunkers, and suddenly we were in the line of its fire with overs ricochetting and plunging straight at us. One army commander, one corps commander, an American general, and several less distinguished individuals adopted the prone position with remarkable unanimity. The only casualty was an unfortunate American airman of our crew, who had hitchhiked with us to see the fun. As the metal whistled over his head he flung himself for cover into the cactus hedge. He was already stripped to the waist and he emerged a bloodstained pincushion. However, he took his misfortune very well and submitted to what must have been a painful plucking with fortitude.

After this little excitement the tank having, to our relief, moved again to a flank, we watched the final stages of the action. The fire of Brens and rifles swelled in volume; the tank's gun thudded away. Suddenly three Gurkhas sprang up simultaneously and dashed forward. One fell, but the other two covered the few yards to the bunkers and thrust tommy guns through loopholes. Behind them surged an uneven line of their comrades; another broke from the spinney, bayonets glinting. They swarmed around the bunkers, and for a moment all firing ceased. Then from behind one of the hummocks appeared a ragged group of half-a-dozen khaki-clad figures, running for safety. They were led, I noticed, by a man exceptionally tall for a Japanese. Twenty Gurkha rifles came up and crashed a volley. Alas for Gurkha marksmanship! Not a Japanese fell; zig-zagging, they ran on. But in a few seconds, as the Gurkhas fired again, they were all down, the last to fall being the tall man. The tank lumbered up, dipped its gun and, with perhaps unnecessary emphasis, finished him off. Within ten minutes, having made sure no Japanese remained alive in the bunkers, the two platoons of Gurkhas and their Indian-manned tank moved on to their next assignment which would not be far away. A rear party appeared, attended to their own casualties, and dragged out the enemy bodies to search them for papers and identifications. It was all very businesslike.

If I have given more space to this one incident that was being repeated in twenty places in the battle than I have to much more important actions, I plead some indulgence. It was the closest I had been to real fighting since I had been an army commander, and it was one of the neatest, most workmanlike bits of infantry and armoured minor tactics I had ever seen. There is a third reason. The men who carried it out were from a Gurkha regiment of which I have the honour to be colonel.

The assault on Meiktila had not everywhere gone so smoothly as the little fight we had watched. Where every house was a strong point, every water channel had its concealed bunker and every rubble heap its hidden machine or anti-tank gun, fighting was costly and progress slow. Throughout March 1 and its night there was hand-to-hand fighting as savage as any yet experienced in a theatre where close combat was the rule rather than the exception. During March 2 and 3, gradually the enemy was forced from house to house. They died where they fought, until the last fifty Japanese plunged into the lake and were drowned or killed in the water. The slaughter had been great. In one small area alone two hundred by one hundred yards, eight hundred and seventy-six Japanese bodies were collected. Meiktila was a shambles, but by six o'clock on the evening of the 3d it was ours.

The country around Meiktila was crowded with villages and

in them, among them, along ditches, on the butts of a rifle range, and in broken ground enemy parties fought with the same grim fierceness. Nevertheless, the main airfield was in our hands and operating by the 5th, although still under fire at times. The capture of Meiktila in four days and the annihilation of its garrison—for the Japanese admitted that hardly a man escaped—was a magnificent feat of arms. It sealed the fate of the Japanese Army in Burma, and Kimura realized the fatal danger he would be in if he could not quickly retake Meiktila. Unlike many Japanese commanders, he always reacted speedily and boldly to changed situations. He at once abandoned his plan to concentrate all his resources against our XXXIII Corps. Reinforcements moving on Mandalay from every part of Burma were diverted to Meiktila; even some troops already engaged against our Mandalay bridgeheads were put into reverse to meet the new danger.

Lieutenant-General Honda, with his Thirty-third Army Headquarters, was ordered to retake Meiktila and left in no doubt as to its urgency. At least six divisions contributed to his force, which in all should have been the equivalent of a corps of more than two divisions. His plan was to cut the communications of our 17th Division on both sides of the Nyaungu bridgehead east and west of the Irrawaddy. With its vital artery cut, strong Japanese forces would then attack Meiktila. The plan, about as good a one as he could make, like so many Japanese plans, did not take into account certain realities. Honda's forces were arriving piecemeal from all directions; it was difficult to concert their common action, especially as their transport losses mounted daily and we had control of the air. Even so, Honda might have had a chance had not our commanders and troops shown themselves so aggressively active.

From Meiktila, Cowan's 17th Division struck in all directions. Infantry and tanks went out daily to hunt, ambush, and attack approaching Japanese columns of various sizes in a radius of twenty miles of the town. So successful were these actions that attempted enemy concentrations were broken up and large-scale attacks prevented or at least delayed. Nevertheless, the pressure on Meiktila increased as the hostile forces built up. The enemy's chief aim was to take the air strip, some two miles from the town, on which, as the road to the bridgehead was now closed, all our supplies were landed. Could he succeed in denying this to us for any length of time we should be compelled to rely entirely on dropping, and our situation would become precarious. The struggle for the airfield was savage and continuous, but the 17th Division still continued to push out in all directions, killing hundreds of Japanese and capturing many guns.

Cowan had not enough troops to spare for the complete perimeter defence of the airfield, and the enemy by mid-March had dug in so close to the strip that by night our troops disputed with his patrols in the no-man's land of the actual runway. At dawn each day, before aircraft could land, a sweep had to be carried out to drive back enemy infiltration and to clear the ground of mines. The fly-in of the airborne brigade of the 5th Division began and was completed by March 17. The last part of this brigade was landed while the strip was under direct artillery fire, and it says much for the gallantry of the American and British air crews that every sortie, without exception, was completed, even though machines were being destroyed after landing. The losses in troops during this operation were surprisingly small. Only those who have landed in such circumstances can realize how quickly it is possible to empty an aeroplane of passengers.

Soon after the brigade's arrival the Japanese, by a great effort, reached the edge of the airfield. All landings ceased, there was a great reduction in supplies, petrol grew short, reinforcements could not be brought in nor wounded evacuated except by an occasional light plane from a small strip inside the town. Now, for the first time, Cowan found himself cut off in a savage battle. This time to the anxieties of a situation was added a deep personal sorrow. He learned, in the midst of the battle, that his son, the splendid young officer I had met with my old regiment in the 19th Division bridgehead, had died of wounds received in the taking of Mandalay. We lost too many of our generals' sons; the cruellest thing about war is that it takes the best.

It was imperative to regain the use of the main strip. North of it, where the Japanese were dug in, was difficult and broken country, interesected by deep gullies which were tank obstacles. The enemy had brought up many anti-tank guns and was freely using mines which he drew from the many local dumps. When these ran out, he grimly replaced them by human mines. A Japanese soldier with a 100-kilo aircraft bomb between his knees, holding a large stone, poised above the fuse, would crouch in a fox hole. When the attacking tank passed over the almost invisible hole, he would drop the stone—then bomb, man, and it was hoped, tank would all go up together. Luckily the device was not very effective and accounted for more Japanese than tanks. In spite of the fiercest resistance, our infantry, supported where possible by tanks, and almost always by fighter bombers placing their loads within a hundred yards of our troops, gradually forced back the enemy from the airfield. Even then for days after the area near the strip had been cleared Japanese medium artillery dominated it, and it was not until March 29 that the enemy was driven from the last of the broken ground in which his guns were concealed. Beaten in this hand-to-hand fighting, his scattered remnants fell back, leaving behind in our hands nearly all their guns and having suffered disastrous casualties.

While these grim battles were raging, Honda's counterattack to cut our line of communication had regained the hills near Taungtha and closed the road to Meiktila. Messervy's immediate tasks thus became:

(i) To reopen this road.
(ii) To prevent the enemy pressure now building up from the south on both banks of the Irrawaddy from cutting it again.
(iii) To capture Myingyan, essential if we were to use the Chindwin to relieve the strain on our supply routes.

Columns of the 7th Indian Division took Myingyan after four days' house-to-house fighting, against suicide resistance. The enemy losses were heavy, few survivors escaped, and the Japanese 15th Division lost most of its remaining artillery here. Very soon boats from our Kalewa shipyard were unloading at hastily-repaired wharves and an energetic start made to get some traffic running on the Myingyan–Meiktila railway.

Other troops of the 7th Division with a newly arrived brigade of the 5th Division cleared the Taungtha heights and made contact with a column from Meiktila, but their success was threatened when on the Irrawaddy east bank a mixed force of Japanese and Indian National Army attacked the bridgehead. The I.N.A. had little stomach for the fight and fled or surrendered; the Japanese were killed. Simultaneously on the other bank a head-on collision occurred north of Chauk where after being reinforced our troops pushed the enemy slowly back until any threat to the bridgehead was gradually removed.

By the last week in March the battle of Meiktila had been won. It had been intended as the decisive stroke, and I had subordinated everything to its success, yet it had been only half of the great battle of Central Burma. That other half had been fought out simultaneously around Mandalay.

CHAPTER XX

THE BATTLE
OF THE IRRAWADDY SHORE

Before following the course of the battle which, simultaneously with that for Meiktila, was waged about Mandalay, it would be well to glance at events on the flanks of the Fourteenth Army, for these had their effect on the main battle and its subsequent development. On the right, Christison's XV Corps in Arakan and, on the left, Sultan's N.C.A.C., had each been actively engaged.

In Arakan the situation was strategically unsatisfactory, for here we had more than four divisions (25th, 26th Indian, 71st, 82d West African, 3 Commando Brigade, and 50 Indian Tank Brigade) all locked up by the threat of a much smaller Japanese force. The remedy was obvious; push back the enemy until they were no longer in a position easily to restage an offensive, contain them with one division, and use the other three elsewhere. If we took Akyab, secured the mouth of the Kaladan River, and held the Myebon Peninsula we could do this.

Christison began his offensive to achieve these ends December 12. He was supported by 224 Group R.A.F. and by a small naval task force most of whose landing craft had been left in Burma waters as too worn out for use in Europe. Opposing him was Lieutenant-General Sakurai Seizo, commanding the Twenty-eighth Army, who had in Arakan a regiment of the 54th Division and part—at the time we were not sure what part—of the 55th Division. In three days the 82d Division had taken what was left of much-fought-over Buthidaung and re-opened the last few miles of the road to the Kalapanzin. More than six hundred small river craft had been collected at Maungdaw and in five days were carried by road through the tunnels to be launched in the Kalapanzin River to maintain the advance south. Meanwhile, the 81st Division, under Major-General Loftus-Tottenham, advancing for the second time down the Kaladan Valley, converged with the 82d Division on the enemy communication centre at Myohaung and took it on January 25. The Japanese, however, fighting hard, managed to extricate themselves and withdrew. Simultaneously, the 25th Division, under Major-General Wood, supplied from the sea, reached the tip of the Mayu Peninsula, and occupied Kadaung Island, separated from Akyab by only a narrow channel.

The West Africans' advance down the Kaladan Valley had caused the Japanese to send there two of the three battalions garrisoning Akyab. Our intelligence learned of the move of one of these but not of the second. Then on January 2, 1945, an artillery officer flying over the island in a light aeroplane saw local inhabitants making friendly signs; he boldly landed and singlehanded captured Akyab. The last Japanese battalion had pulled out the day before. Our troops, on the point of delivering an all-out assault, ferried peacefully over to the island.

The Japanese were now in orderly retreat down the road which ran along the coast a few miles from the sea, but Christison's command of the air and his landing craft, even if decrepit, gave him power to cut this route ahead of the enemy. This he aimed to do at Kangaw, nearly forty miles from Akyab, but first he had to take the Myebon Peninsula, as it covered the narrow *chaungs* which were the only approaches to Kangaw. The naval difficulties of a landing were extreme. The Arakan coast here was screened by mangrove swamps, cut by muddy, shallow *chaungs*, uncharted, and unpredictable. There were no real beaches, only a few small stretches of soft sand overlooked by jungle hills, where men might wade ashore. Frogmen and small boat parties of the Royal Navy with the greatest daring and skill discovered these places, and on January 12 the Commando Brigade landed by surprise against slight opposition. A brigade of the 25th Division followed, the Japanese hurriedly collecting, counterattacked, were beaten off, and our troops proceeded to clear the whole peninsula.

The next step on January 22 was a second landing near Kangaw. Here the Japanese were more prepared, and so fierce were their attacks on the beachhead that we thought a whole division was against us, when actually their strength was never a brigade. After bitter fighting, at last Kangaw was taken and the Japanese escape route closed. Caught between our block at

Kangaw and the West Africans pressing behind them, the enemy during the first half of February broke and scattered into the hills, leaving behind them more than a thousand dead, sixteen guns, and great quantities of transport and equipment.

Advance in
ARAKAN

Roads & Tracks ———
British advance ⟶

Miles 0 10 20 30 40 50

Less spectacular than the capture of Kangaw, but even more valuable, was the seizure of the islands of Ramree and Cheduba at the end of January. Christison's next task was to develop these islands and Akyab as air bases for the Fourteenth Army. The badly-battered Japanese 54th Division was now in two widely-separated groups collecting, one about An, the other at Tangup. Their 55th Division, which had taken little part in these operations, had already withdrawn to the Prome–Henzada area and the only hope of preventing it being used against me was to put such pressure on the Tangup road as would make it face west again. I therefore asked that XV Corps, in addition to moving on An, should take Tangup and push up the road to Prome. In spite of increasing maintenance difficulties, even after the removal of his 81st Division and the bulk of his tanks, Christison attempted this. I applauded his resolution and urged speed—nothing would embarrass Kimura more than to have XV Corps' spearhead pricking him in the posterior while I punched his nose.

Christison sent his 82d Division up the Dalet Chaung to

approach the An Pass from the northwest while, after a stubbornly opposed landing, the 26th Division took Ru-ywa, only twelve miles west of An. By the first week of March these moves for the encirclement of the enemy at An were in full swing, when, as so often happened in Burma, they had to be called off for reasons beyond the immediate commander's control.

The jungle hills around An compelled all our maintenance to be by air drop and I was at this time clamouring for more aircraft to sustain the Mandalay–Meiktila battle. I could not have it both ways, so wisely General Leese drastically cut the air supply of XV Corps. Inevitably, the operations against An stopped and the troops engaged were withdrawn to Akyab and the coast.

In spite of this disappointment, Christison, with the transport left to him, mainly sea, valiantly attempted the capture of Taungup. A brigade of the 26th Division landed at Letpan, some thirty-five miles north of Taungup and, with another brigade, pushed south until only five miles from the town. Here we were held by strong positions in difficult country and, without air supply for outflanking moves, a stalemate ensued. The Japanese thus remained in firm control of both roads from the coast to the Irrawaddy, free to collect behind these detachments what remained of their Arakan forces and send them to be used against the Fourteenth Army. In actual fact these reinforcements did not amount to as much as I had feared.

At Akyab, Ramree, and Cheduba XV Corps at once began to build airfields and lay in stocks for my army's advance south. Both all-weather and fair-weather strips were built and, as may be imagined, I watched their progress with anxiety which changed to relief as I saw how steadily and rapidly they progressed.

On the Fourteenth Army's other flank, the left, Sultan, although the return to China of all his American and Chinese formations had been demanded and two of his divisions had already gone, continued his advance. But it was necessarily at a slower pace and gave the Japanese the chance, which they took, to retire in good order and to divert troops to oppose the Fourteenth Army. As the action on the N.C.A.C. front was obviously slowing up, I asked General Leese in mid-February to let the 36th British Division revert to my command, so that I could use it in the Mandalay battle. He refused, on the sensible grounds that the loss of this active division would still further upset Sultan's plans and there would be difficulties about bringing its American air contingent with it. However, in an Operation Instruction of February 27, he ordered Sultan to take the Kyaukme–Lashio line, cooperate in the Mandalay battle, and then exploit south towards Loilem. If all that were done, I should be very satisfied.

Meanwhile, Festing was pushing along his 36th Division. On February 9, in the face of determined resistance, he forced the crossing of the five-hundred-yard-wide Shweli River at Myitson, and, with the help of most efficient American fighter and light bomber cover, held his bridgehead against all assaults, including attacks by flame throwers. After nearly a month of these attempts, and having suffered heavy casualties, the Japanese gave up the struggle and fell back south, contenting themselves with attempts to delay. The division went on to clear the Mong Mit area, to take Mogok with its famous ruby mines, and, on March 30, to join up with the American Mars Brigade which had reached Kyaukme.

On April 1 my request for the return of the 36th British Division was granted, and it bade farewell to the N.C.A.C. with whom it had served effectively and in such good comradeship with both Chinese and Americans. Festing and his division, besides a good fighting job, had done a great deal to dispel the cloud of uninformed criticism that at one time threatened to darken Anglo-American relations. Instead of only hearing secondhand and often malicious stories, the soldiers of both nations had now seen one another fighting the enemy. The result was mutual respect. The division was given a great farewell by its American friends as it turned southwest to Maymyo to rejoin the Fourteenth Army. I ordered it to fly one brigade into Mandalay in its maintenance aircraft at once, and to concentrate the rest of the division as quickly as possible to relieve the 19th Division, in such clearing-up operations as were still going on in the area Mandalay–Maymyo–Myittha–Ava. Unfortunately the 36th Division's American transport aircraft were to be withdrawn on May 1, and therefore the division would before that date have to be flown out to India. My use of this division could only be very temporary. Actually, I managed to keep one brigade in action until May 10.

On March 7, the Chinese First Army, under my old friend Sun, captured Lashio, the Japanese falling back in good order in front of it. A few days later the first regiment of the Mars Brigade was ordered to China, to be followed later by the rest of the brigade. The loss of the Mars Brigade, its only American formation, would greatly weaken N.C.A.C., but its maintenance by air in mobile operations required a greater effort than that needed for a much larger Chinese force, and Sultan therefore wisely let it go first. On March 16, Hsipaw, on the railway thirty-five miles southwest of Lashio and about a hundred from Mandalay, was occupied. The Chinese then sat down on the line they had reached, while the Japanese, who had withdrawn intact before them, now broke all contact and, leaving only a few scattered detachments to watch them, transferred their forces south directly to oppose the Fourteenth Army or into the Shan Hills to threaten its flank. When the Chinese halted, some twenty-five hundred local tribesmen under American officers took over responsibility for the safety of the Stilwell road against possible marauders.

From now on the Chinese, for all practical purposes, ceased to take any part in the Burma war. To me, of course, this was most disappointing, as I had hoped that a Chinese push towards Loilem would have engaged at least some enemy and helped to protect my very vulnerable left flank. However, there seemed to be nothing that I, or apparently anyone else, could do about it, except to remember our motto, 'God helps those who help themselves,' and to get on with the war without the Chinese. So with little hope of help on either of my flanks, I continued the main battle.

When in the last days of February 1945 IV Corps gripped Meiktila in a stranglehold, the divisions of XXXIII Corps were poised in their bridgeheads along the Irrawaddy to the north and west of Mandalay ready to strike. The 19th Division forty miles north of the city, after its struggle, first to hold and then to extend its bridgeheads, was straining at the leash for a dash down the east bank on Mandalay. The 20th Division, fighting without pause, had a deep, firmly-held eight-mile stretch of the southern shore of the river, forty miles west of Mandalay, in which it was collecting to break out. The 2d British Division had been left almost unmolested in the last gained bridgehead, some twenty-five miles west of Mandalay, and was now drawing up its tail across the river.

The crisis of the great battle was at hand. Kimura's gaze was fixed on Mandalay and its neighbourhood, his troops faced north and were marching hard to meet us there, yet he could not fail within a few days, perhaps hours, to awake to the danger behind him at Meiktila. When he did, I must prevent him, as far as I could, from reinforcing that area until Messervy had firmly established IV Corps across the Japanese rear—the anvil to meet the hammer from the north. To do this, Kimura, just as he began to realize what the loss of Meiktila meant to him, must be struck about Mandalay till he reeled, so that he could detach forces from there only at great peril to his Irrawaddy line. Then as disruption spread outward from Meiktila, XXXIII Corps must be loosed in an all-out offensive to the south—the hammer to the anvil. It was not Mandalay or Meiktila that we were after but the Japanese Army, and that thought had to be firmly emplanted in the mind of every man of the Fourteenth Army.

On February 27 an A.L.F.S.E.A. Operation Instruction was issued directing Fourteenth Army to:

(i) Destroy the Japanese forces in the Mandalay area.
(ii) Seize Rangoon before the monsoon.

As orders, based on the Fourteenth Army Operation Instruction of December 19, 1944, to achieve these objects had already been given to corps two months previously, no changes in our plans or dispositions were necessary. Operations continued at an increasing tempo.

Rees's 19th Division was the first to be slipped. On February 26 one of its brigades (64) broke out from the Kyaukmyaung bridgehead and bit into the foothills to the east, gaining elbow room for the second brigade (62), which next day thrust through the Japanese lines on the riverbank. The two brigades then drove south, like a rush of waters over a broken dam. The enemy were swept away, leaving a few crumbling islets of resistance, to be engulfed later, as the third brigade (98) raced from the northern Thabeikyin bridgehead to catch up with the rest of the division. By March 3 the 19th Division was in tankable country; on the 4th, Rees was able to report that the wretched 15th Japanese Division, that had been first shattered at Imphal, then bled white again in the attacks on his bridgeheads, had now disintegrated and was incapable of further organized resistance. Leapfrogging his brigades, next day he crossed the Chaungmagyi River, eighteen miles north of Mandalay and the last natural obstacle before the city. The Japanese had prepared strong positions about Madaya, just south of the Chaungmagyi, where the railway from Mandalay ended, but a motorized column of Rees's men swept into their trenches with or before the enemy trying to occupy them, and went on to clear the town in street fighting. As Mandalay was approached, opposition stiffened but was still uncoordinated, and, by dawn on March 8 one brigade (64) was fighting two miles east of Mandalay Cantonment, while another (98) with its motorized column had reached the northern outskirts of the city. Japanese resistance outside Mandalay was now reduced to small parties roaming the countryside with little knowledge of what was happening around them, but in two places the defence was still strong and well organized—on Mandalay Hill and in the city itself at Fort Dufferin.

Mandalay Hill is a great rock rising abruptly from the plain to nearly eight hundred feet and dominating the whole northeastern quarter of the city. Its steep sides are covered with temples and pagodas, now honeycombed for machine guns, well supplied, and heavily garrisoned. Throughout the day and night of March 9, the fiercest hand-to-hand fighting went on, as a Gurkha battalion stormed up the slopes and bombed and tommy-gunned its way into the concrete buildings. Next day two companies of a British battalion joined them, and the bitter fighting went on. The Japanese stood to the end, until the last defenders, holding out in cellars, were destroyed by petrol rolled down in drums and ignited by tracer bullets. It was not until March 11 that the hill was completely in our hands. When, shortly afterwards, I visited it, the blackened marks of fire and the sights and stench of carnage were only too obvious, while distant bumps and bangs and the nearer rattle of machine guns showed that the clearing of the city was still going on. Through all this noise and the clatter of men clearing a battlefield came a strange sound—singing. I followed it. There was General Rees, his uniform sweat-soaked and dirty, his distinguishing red scarf rumpled around his neck, his bush hat at a jaunty angle, his arm beating time, surrounded by a group of Assamese soldiers whom he was vigorously leading in the singing of Welsh missionary hymns. The fact that he sang in Welsh and they in Khasi only added to the harmony. I looked on admiringly. My generals had character. Their men knew them and they knew their men.

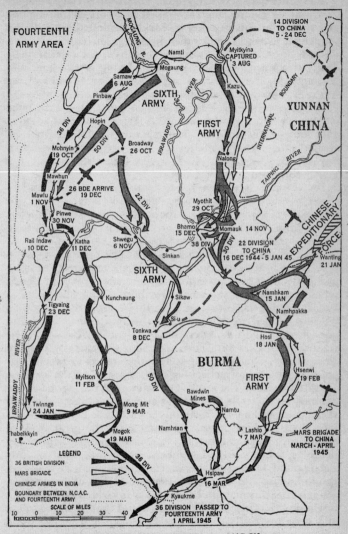

NORTHERN FRONT, AUGUST 1944—MARCH 1945

The other Japanese stronghold, Fort Dufferin in Mandalay City, was a great, rectangular, walled enclosure containing one and a quarter square miles of parkland, dotted with official residences, barracks, and other buildings including the fantastic teak-built Royal Palace of Theebaw, the last Burmese king, its upturned eaves rich with carving, vermillion, and gilding. The crenellated, twenty-foot-high outer walls of the fort were faced with thick brickwork and backed by earth embankments seventy feet wide at their base. All round lay the moat, over two hundred feet wide, water filled and studded with lotus—a picturesque but hampering weed. Fort Dufferin, an immense edition of the toy fortress I used to play with as a boy, manned by Japanese, was a very formidable object to a lightly equipped army in a hurry.

For the next few days Rees's battalions fought their way street by street through the city, suffering heavily, especially in officers, from snipers, until on the 15th the fort was completely surrounded. The attack on Fort Dufferin might well have been a scene from the Siege of Delhi in the Indian Mutiny. Medium guns were brought up within five hundred yards to breach the walls, rafts and scaling ladders prepared, storming parties detailed, and attempts to enter made through the great pipes that ran into the moat. On the night of March 16, in attacks on the northwest and northeast corners of the fort, 'Forlorn Hopes' were repulsed by heavy automatic fire, and our men withdrew, after most gallantly rescuing their wounded. On the 18th and 19th, four separate attempts to cross the moat failed. Such attacks threatened to become expensive, so a more modern aspect was given to the siege by aircraft attacks on the walls. The interior of the fort had been bombed on the 13th, and serious attempts to breach the walls with 500-pound bombs began on the 16th. The bombs, like 5.5-inch shells, only damaged the outer face; the great bank of earth behind was unbreached. Recourse was then had to skip bombing, when Mitchell bombers, flying low, tried to drop 2,000-pound bombs on the waters of the moat so that they would bounce into the walls. After several days of these attacks a small breach some fifteen feet wide up which troops might scramble was made, but the assault would have been hazardous and certainly costly. I was therefore against it, as we could now by-pass the fort, and its eventual capture was inevitable, more, indeed, a matter of news value than military advantage.

I was prepared to wait.

However, during the night of March 19–20 there was extra activity in and around the fort, and after the morning air strike a group of Anglo-Burmese waving white flags and Union Jacks appeared at one of the gates. The garrison, they reported, during darkness had crept through drains from the moat into the southern part of the town. Many were intercepted by our troops, others who hid in deserted houses were hunted down during the next few days, only a handful escaped into open country. Our men entering the fort found large dumps of Japanese stores and ammunition, a number of European and Anglo-Burmese civilian prisoners, and a fair sprinkling of booby traps. Rees himself, as was proper, hoisted the Union Jack again over Fort Dufferin and revisited Government House, now sadly battered, where years before, in more peaceful days, he had served as military secretary. To our great regret, Theebaw's palace had been burned down, whether fired by our shelling and bombing, although we had tried to avoid it, or by the Japanese to destroy the stores they had in it, I do not know. A day or two later I staged a more formal ceremony at which both corps and all divisional commanders were present, when I hoisted the Union Jack over Mandalay. The capture of Mandalay had been as much the result of operations at Meiktila and elsewhere as of those around the city itself. Every one of my divisions had played its part; it was an army victory. I thought it would be good for everyone to have that fact demonstrated.

While these dramatic events had been taking place in Mandalay, the 19th Division had achieved another triumph of daring and mobility. As early as March 6, one of its brigades (62) had been pulled out of the race for Mandalay when still twenty miles north of the city, and next day struck off southeast for Maymyo, the summer capital of Burma in the hills twenty-five miles east of Mandalay. Marching for four days by smugglers' tracks, across two mountain ranges, and through a deep valley, the brigade suddenly burst into the quiet of that lovely hill station to the utter surprise of its Japanese garrison and the numerous administrative troops located there. Some fled north in a train that, luckily for them, happened to be standing with steam up in the station, but the majority were wiped out among the pleasant bungalows and along the flower-bordered roads. An enemy convoy, trying to slip away in the night was ambushed and yielded a gun and forty or fifty lorries which proved a valuable supplement to the pack transport of the brigade. The capture of Maymyo cut the road and railway, which were the only direct and effective lines of communication from the Japanese supply depots of Central Burma to their troops till opposing Sultan's forces. It also did much to secure my left, which, now far ahead of his Chinese, had been something of an anxiety to me. Leaving a battalion to block any hostile move from the northeast and to collect the Japanese stragglers and vehicles that still hopefully made for Maymyo, the remainder of the brigade marched to Mandalay and rejoined their division. Since reaching the Irrawaddy, in ten weeks of hard fighting and rapid movement, the 19th Division had not only cleared the enemy out of Mandalay, Maymyo, and a large area, but had counted six thousand Japanese killed on its battlefields.

The other Indian division of XXXIII Corps, Gracey's 20th, pushed rapidly east, clearing village after village, expanding its bridgehead towards that of the 2d Division. The Japanese losses in the prolonged fighting along the river had sapped their powers of resistance and, on March 2 our two divisions joined up. Three days later the two bridgeheads of the 20th Division also linked up, and from then onward expansion was rapid. The enemy had lost heavily in guns and much of their armour had been destroyed; they were obviously breaking.

As far as we could deduce in this fluid battle, Kimura meant to halt us on a line running southwest from Kyaukse, with its bastions at Kyaukse itself, Myingyan, Taungtha, Mount Popa, Kyaukpadaung, and Chauk. He would have his three armies, sadly depleted, all in the line, from right to left, the Fifteenth, the Thirty-third and the Twenty-eighth. Whether he hoped to hold us off while he made another attempt to regain Meiktila or to cover a general withdrawal to the south we did not know. I hoped the former; the longer he stayed in Central Burma the better chance I had to destroy him. For us the moment had come to strike boldly, to complete the Japanese confusion, to cut lanes through them, to break up their communication systems so that their commanders' already weakening grip should be completely broken. No one was more fitted to do this than Gracey and his men. Never have I seen troops who carried their tails more vertically.

On March 8 20th Division broke out into rocky, undulating

country, interspersed with villages, mango groves, and small banana plantations. Spearheaded by armoured and motorized columns, meeting increasingly disorganized but at times stubborn resistance, one of his brigades fought through Myotha and, by March 12, was clearing the country south of it. Another brigade (100) struck southeast for forty miles and took Pindale, and by March 19, breaking through stiff opposition, and inflicting heavy casualties, had surprised and seized the adminstrative centre of the Japanese 18th Division at Wundwin. From there an armoured column moved rapidly north for thirty miles, spreading consternation and death among the Japanese installations along the railway line. On March 29 the brigade made touch with other troops of the division attacking Kyaukse. Among its captures was a small hospital—seized before the staff had time to kill the patients—which yielded fifty-three sick and wounded prisoners—the largest single bag yet obtained.

While 100 Brigade thus played havoc around Wundwin the other two brigades of the division (80 and 32) struck east and southeast on Kyaukse and Myittha. They were opposed by small but tough parties of isolated Japanese in every village, but on the 16th some of our columns reached the Mandalay–Rangoon railway, twenty miles south of Mandalay. Next day 32 Brigade closed in on Kyaukse, ten miles farther south. This town was of the greatest importance to the Japanese, for not only was it their chief supply centre for a large part of their army, but it was the bastion behind which Kimura hoped to restore some order in his shattered units. It was easily defensible, and already considerable numbers of Japanese, fleeing from the north and west, had rallied there, so that it took several days of stubborn fighting to drive the enemy out of their positions. To the last they clung to the town itself, in the effort to have at least some of the great quantities of stores it contained, and it was not until March 30 that it fell. When our troops reached the railway station, they found a wrecked train fully loaded with the last stores the Japanese had hoped to get away, medical equipment, photographic supplies, sewing machines, and, strangely enough, books and magazines.

This breakout of the 20th Division was a spectacular achievement which only a magnificent division, magnificently led, could have staged after weeks of the heaviest defensive fighting. In three weeks the division had swept clear of the enemy an area forty-five miles by forty and was across the Rangoon–Mandalay railway on a fifty-mile stretch. The Japanese had left two thousand dead and fifty guns behind them. Their 15th and 31st Divisions were now little more than groups of fugitives seeking refuge in the Shan Hills to the east. It is interesting to note that the 20th Indian Division was the only formation of Fourteenth Army to have been trained since its inception for war in Burma. It had been well trained. Nor did it rest on its laurels, but in every direction continued with mobile columns to strike at any Japanese groups located, and to surprise and slaughter them.

In all these operations, and particularly in those aimed at the disruption of the enemy command, the Allied air forces played a notable part. As soon as a Japanese divisional or army headquarters opened up, our wireless location unit, recognizing their call signs and even the mannerisms of their individual operators, quickly pinpointed their positions. Then American and British light bombers and ground-support aircraft were on them like terriers on to rats, while a motorized and armoured column often followed before the dust had settled. The life of a Japanese general and his staff in these days was not a happy one.

The 2d British Division, which on February 25 had been the last to cross the Irrawaddy, at once began to extend its bridgehead. Although it did not meet the strong opposition that had faced the 19th and 20th Divisions and indeed was never seriously counterattacked, the resistance of small Japanese parties in villages, supported by artillery, made the advance somewhat slow. By March 6 troops of the division were five miles south of the Irrawaddy and the bridgehead was expanding to both the east and the west along the riverbank. On the 11th the small town of Kyauktalon was taken by the eastern advance and two days later Myinthi, twelve miles to the southeast, was occupied. The advance east along the riverbank continued and, after a stiff fight on March 17, Ava Fort was cleared of the enemy; next day a Japanese detachment holding the southern end of the Ava bridge was driven out. The great bridge which we had destroyed in the 1942 retreat was of course still down, but its northern end had already been occupied by our 268 Independent Brigade.

On the same day, the 18th, troops of the 2d Division met patrols of the 20th sweeping far around their southern flank.

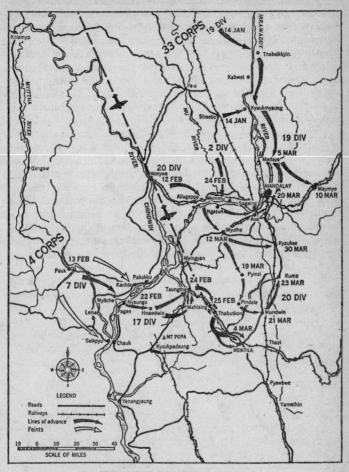

THE BATTLE OF CENTRAL BURMA

On March 20 Nicholson's men occupied Amarapura, the great railway workshops seven miles south of Mandalay, now largely destroyed by our bombing and by Japanese demolition, and on the 21st made contact with patrols of the 19th Division pushing south. The casualties inflicted on the enemy in the 2d Division's breakout had not been severe, but a great deal of booty fell into our hands including much needed engineer stores and, most valuable of all, some serviceable rolling stock.

Although all offensive action, either by N.C.A.C. on our left or by XV Corps on our right, had ceased and the Fourteenth Army alone faced practically the whole of the Japanese forces in Burma, our position was now, I thought, very favourable. Both banks of the Irrawaddy from Mandalay to Chauk and the main road and railway to Rangoon as far south as Wundwin were in our hands. Meiktila was firmly and finally held, the road to it from Myingyan was open, and we were steadily expanding our grasp over the surrounding country. The enemy formations, although still fighting stubbornly, had lost almost all their armour, a large proportion of their guns, and much of their transport. Everywhere they were in great and growing confusion. Kimura's only hope, now, was to extricate himself, fall back to the south, and collect what troops he could to hold us off from Rangoon. *Our* best hope was to rush him off his feet before he could regain balance—and to pray for a late monsoon.

BOOK VI: VICTORY

CHAPTER XXI

THE RACE TO RANGOON

In mid-March 1945 the Battle of Central Burma was drawing to its close, yet Kimura still obstinately refused to admit defeat—an admirable trait in a commander, but one which he was in danger of carrying to excess. His divisions, especially those of Katamura's Fifteenth Army, were in a bad way; they had lost not only guns, transport, and equipment but were now losing their cohesion. If he wished to avoid destruction, Kimura could not fight much longer anywhere north of a line from Yenangyaung to Pyawbwe, and I did not intend he should fight long on that line. The time had come to take our next step—Rangoon.

Our own divisions, although they had been operating strenuously and continuously for several months without rest, were still in great heart. Our casualties, despite the amount of close fighting, had not been unduly heavy, and, as far as Indian units were concerned, had been largely replaced. British reinforcements, as so often in this theatre, lagged behind casualties, and owing to the consequent wastage I had again to replace British battalions by Indian. The state of our road transport, too, caused anxiety. We had lost neither guns nor vehicles to the enemy, but much of our motor transport was on its last legs, and replacements were short. There could be no pause either in operations or in the movement of supplies by road, so that time for overhaul was scant. In spite of heroic efforts to make all possible vehicles serviceable for the next phase, we could only hope that, with forward formations largely on air supply and with an increasing use of river and railway, we should just manage to keep enough lorries running. In the event, we saved the situation only by taking all serviceable vehicles from formations going out of Burma and issuing them to those remaining.

The state of our armour worried me even more. Our striking power, and with it our speed, would depend, beyond anything, on the armoured spearheads of our advance. Yet our Shermans, Lee-Grants, Stuarts, and armoured cars were all obsolete and mostly long overdue for replacement. They had been used hard, and it was only the skill and determination of their crews, British and Indian, backed by the devoted I.E.M.E. and I.A.O.C. men, that had kept them on the road up to now. With daily demands on our armour, opportunities for the extra maintenance so badly needed were not easy to find. I visited the tank and armoured car units to thank them for their magnificent efforts in the past battle and to impress on them how much I should rely on them for the next. I told them that, when I gave the word for the dash on Rangoon, every tank they had must be a starter, and that every tank that crossed the starting line must pass the post in Rangoon. After that they could push them into the sea if they wanted! But they had to get to Rangoon!

It would be a race, and a stern one, against two tough competitors, the enemy and the monsoon. The Japanese, in spite of the hammering we had given them, were still numerous and formidable; the shadow of the monsoon loomed over us, only seven or eight weeks away. If we did not take Rangoon before it broke, we should, with landing grounds out, even dropping hazardous, roads dissolving and health deteriorating, find ourselves in a desperate situation with the prospect of a disastrous withdrawal. It was now the middle of March; a normal monsoon would break somewhere about May 15. Before we could begin to drive south, we had to finish the present battle, clear the large areas to the north of Meiktila and Yenangyaung, rearrange our forces, and break the crust of any new line of Japanese resistance. We could not expect to do all that before the first week of April. Then, with luck, we should have some forty days to reach—and take—Rangoon. From Meiktila, by the railway route, Rangoon is three hundred and twenty miles; from Chauk, via the Irrawaddy Valley, three hundred and seventy. We should have to move at an average of eight or ten miles a day. That, against opposition and demolitions, was fast. There would be no time to stage elaborate attacks; positions that could not be taken by quick assault would have to be by-passed. Even when they were taken, there could be no pause for thorough mopping up, nor could we wait to deal with the very large bodies of Japanese already driven into the hills on the flanks of both routes. Inevitably large enemy masses would be left behind us. As soon as we had got Rangoon, the troops would have to turn in their tracks, come north again, and hunt them. Thinking of that, I hoped that my armoured units would not take too literally my permission to push their tanks into the sea at Rangoon.

The possibility that alarmed me most, however, was that the Japanese would, as they had in other towns, put a suicide garrison into Rangoon that would keep us out for the monsoon. I could not contemplate with anything but dismay a repetition of the Meiktila battle, around Rangoon at the end of a most precarious supply line, in the midst of the rains. I therefore urged that when the Fourteenth Army approached within striking distance of Rangoon from the north, an amphibious and airborne assault—our old friend 'Dracula'—should be put in from the sea. I had always opposed 'Dracula' if it were to be done at the expense of the Fourteenth Army, but now, when divisions were being released from both Arakan and from my army, I believed we had enough troops to stage it without seriously affecting my offensive. Air support for the actual assault would, I realized, have to be at my expense, but our air superiority was so marked that I was prepared to accept that. The naval position had improved and we now had the landing craft necessary for a limited operation. The original 'Dracula' had been planned to take Rangoon while the Fourteenth Army was still far to the north; the new one would be, I hoped, a hammering on the back door while I burst in at the front. It could, therefore, be on a reduced scale and within our means. All the same, General Leese, more confident in the Fourteenth Army's powers than I was, still condemned 'Dracula.' It was discarded and a new corps, numbered 34, was formed in India from the 23d Indian and 81st West African Divisions to capture Phuket Island off the Kra Isthmus as a preliminary to the reconquest of Singapore. Roberts of the 23d Division, whom I had seen go in four years from colonel to lieutenant-general, was given this corps, and I felt rather complacent about the Staff College report I had written on him ten years before.

The last edition of Operation 'Sob,' our Fourteenth Army private plan to reach the sea, envisaged a double advance, by the railway and by the Irrawaddy, with a full corps and a tank brigade on each. The Japanese would not, I calculated, be able to produce enough troops to stop us on both; if they held one corps, the other would break through. However, the state of our transport and shortage of supply aircraft soon ruled out that plan. We had, at the moment, seven divisions operating in Central Burma, but of these the 36th must leave the theatre almost at once as its American air transport was about to be removed. If we were to advance at all south of Meiktila and Yenangyaung, another division would have to go back to India—probably the 2d British, as its strength was falling and it was more difficult to supply than an Indian. This would leave five divisions, and of these, only three, with the two tank brigades, could be maintained by air in a rapid advance far to the south. Against these comparatively small striking forces the Japanese might still bring superior strength, and it was clear that we should have to concentrate our main effort on one axis. The question was, which?

The nearness of the monsoon made me decide that the essential characteristic of our advance must be speed, and that presupposed a wholly mechanized force on the main axis. The strength of this should be at least a corps of two divisions and a tank brigade, and it was necessary, therefore, to choose the better route for a completely mechanized corps. We were leaving behind the open motorable country of Central Burma; whichever route we took there would be a single road, off which, even in dry weather, it would be difficult to deploy. When the rain set in, the movement of both wheeled and tracked vehicles off the metalled road would be impossible. There was little to choose between the northern half of either axis, but the farther one went south on the Irrawaddy line, the more numerous became the water channels that had to be crossed. All bridges would be blown, and, even if we carried an inordinate quantity of Bailey bridging, there would be serious delays—delays which we could not afford. In distance, too, the railway route had an advantage of some fifty miles. Most important of all, the farther east we drove through the Japanese, the more of them would be cut off in the roadless jungles of the Yomas, to struggle out as best they could during the monsoon—a second retreat with, I hope, even more disastrous consequences to them than that from Imphal. There were, of course, disadvantages to the railway route. On it we should meet the stronger enemy group, and we should be liable to counterattack in flank from the Shan and Karen

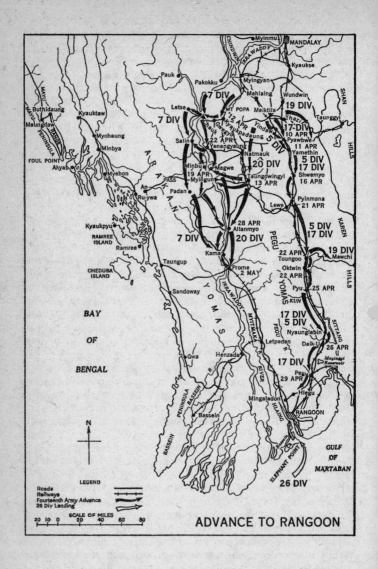

ADVANCE TO RANGOON

Hills, where increasing hostile concentrations were being daily reported. In spite of these disadvantages, I chose the railway axis for my main advance. At the same time, to engage the enemy on as wide a front as possible, to split his forces and distract his command, I would push down the Irrawaddy Valley the maximum mobile force I could maintain. If we were held on the railway, I would at least have a second string to my bow.

The choice of formations for the two lines of advance was not difficult. The 5th and 17th Division of IV Corps were both on the new mechanized and airborne basis, and, in addition, the bulk of that corps was collected in the Meiktila area, some fifty miles south of the general location of XXXIII Corps. It was obvious, therefore, that IV Corps should follow the railway axis and be the main striking force. This did not mean that XXXIII Corps on the Irrawaddy route would be idle. Stopford could be relied on to push his divisions hard. Indeed, with less Japanese opposition, it was not beyond the bounds of possibility that he might reach Rangoon first. On the railway axis, all troops south of Toungoo would have to be completely on air supply; those north of it, as far as possible, on road and perhaps rail. For XXXIII Corps, on the river, there would be air supply for one division and part of the tank brigade only; the rest would have to manage on road and water transport.

At this stage a development took place which promised some embarrassment to the enemy. Even in 1943 we had heard that Aung San, the Burman whom the Japanese had placed in command of their puppet Burma National Army, was disappointed with his masters. Through agents we kept in touch with the various Burmese Nationalist parties and knew that at this time the B.N.A. was being sent to the front. Our contacts reported that Aung San was ready to defect to us but, in spite of our parachuting in a British officer of Force 136, we had no clear indication that he would. However, on March 26 the B.N.A. mutinied and killed some Japanese officers.

Immediately a dispute arose between Force 136, who wished to support Aung San and our Civil Affairs Organization who claimed, with a good deal of reason, that the B.N.A., especially after the liberation of Burma, would be more trouble than use. However, I thought the B.N.A. prowling on their lines of communication, cutting an occasional throat, ambushing small parties, would give the Japanese an uncomfortable feeling on

dark nights. Besides, if these Burmese were not with us as well
as against the Japanese, we should end up by having to fight
them, too; there were also political advantages in having the
only nationalist army force actually with us. I therefore re-
commended that we should supply Aung San with arms and
supplies in return for some tactical control of his forces.
Admiral Mountbatten had come to the same conclusion and I
was given permission to act on these lines. I did not expect the
B.N.A. to exert serious influence on the campaign and I made
no changes in my plans in the expectation of their help.

It was very plain to me—and if it had not been, plenty of
people were willing to enlighten me—that this dash for Rangoon by a mechanized force, confined to one road, thrusting
against time through superior numbers, was a most hazardous
and possibly rather un-British operation. I knew the risks and
the penalties of failure but, as I checked over the final plans, I
was ready to accept them. Whatever the risks, we were winning. We had kicked over the anthill; the ants were running
about in confusion. Now was the time to stamp on them. My
soldiers were out for Rangoon, and anyone who was with them
and had seen them fight could not doubt that they would get
there. Once more the exhilaration running through the army
was a tangible thing that could be seen and felt. I shared it.

On March 18 I ordered 'the capture of Rangoon at all costs
and as soon as possible before the monsoon.' Phase 1 of the
operation was the completion of the present battle. In Phase 2,
Messervy's IV Corps would strike at Pyawbwe while XXXIII
Corps cleared the whole area behind, freeing roads and railways for our use; both corps would then position themselves
for the advance south. Phase 3 would be the twin pushes for
Rangoon, IV Corps down the railway, XXXIII Corps down
the Irrawaddy Valley.

Towards the end of March 1945 Kimura at last accepted
defeat in the great battle of Central Burma, but before doing so
he had used up every reserve available to him. He had run
true to Japanese form : he had left it until too late. Nonetheless, in spite of his plans and his armies crumbling about him,
he prepared resolutely and energetically to deny us the two
routes to the south.

The line from Kyaukse to Chauk, on which he had hoped to
halt our onrush, was gone. Katamura's Fifteenth Army, with
its 15th, 31st and 33d Divisions, had disintegrated, and with

the fall of Kyaukse now imminent, any chance of reorganizing and re-equipping it in the forward area had vanished. Fugitive and scattered it was now scrambling into the foothills to the east, but in those very Shan Hills the Japanese 56th Division in reasonably good order was arriving from the moribund Chinese front. Kimura ordered the shattered Fifteenth Army to collect on this division, and then to make for Toungoo, where, given time, he hoped to re-form it, and thus provide himself with a much needed reserve. His other armies, the Twenty-eighth and Thirty-third, though battered and short of artillery, transport, and much else, were still capable of fighting, especially defensively, with all the savage tenacity of the Japanese soldier. Kimura's thoughts, like mine, must have turned to the advent of the monsoon; his with hope, mine with dread. If he could hold somewhere well north of Rangoon until the rains, he would at least gain the respite he so desperately needed. To this end he placed an army to bar each of our routes.

On the railway axis Honda's Thirty-third Army, with the 18th, 49th, and 53d Divisions, was ordered to hold us about Pyawbwe, astride the road and railway to Toungoo. In addition, Kimura planned to use the 56th Division, now in the Shan Hills, not only to cover the collection of what was left of the Fifteenth Army, but to threaten and perhaps counter-attack in flank any advance of ours to the south along the railway.

Sakurai's task with the Twenty-eighth Army was to prevent our advance down the Irrawaddy at or north of Yenangyaung, while blocking any attempts by our forces to break eastward through the passes from Arakan. Under him were seven infantry and three artillery battalions in Yamamoto's Force, the 54th and 55th Divisions and the 2d Indian National Army Division. Like most plans drawn up by generals, Kimura's was near enough on paper. What it would look like on the ground was another matter.

As March drew on with Kyaukse still uncaptured, Phase 1 of my operations was behind schedule. Time was running out and the spectre of a Japanese stand in Rangoon began again to haunt me, so I renewed my pressure for an attack from the sea. Unknowingly the British Chiefs of Staff came to my help; the seizure of Phuket Island, they declared, should not be attempted until we were about to take Rangoon. Admiral

Mountbatten, therefore, reversed the earlier decision and ordered an amphibious assault on Rangoon by one division and a parachute battalion. I was glad of this though the loss of two Dakota squadrons to the paratroops threw a still heavier burden on the hard-pressed Fourteenth Army supply system.

I took advantage of the regrouping necessary for the advance on Rangoon to sweep the large block of Central Burma between Myingyan–Mandalay–Wundwin–Chauk where scattered but sometimes strong Japanese groups were either holding out with dull ferocity or trying to escape to the south or east. In what I called the 'Union Jack' method, strong columns of the 5th Division moved across the area diagonally from northwest to southeast, while the 2d Division similarly passed from northeast to southwest. It was the quickest way to comb the country and, as my divisions were well trained in rapid movement, I had little fear that this rather complicated pattern of moves across one another's communications would cause confusion.

Eager to recover time, I started Stopford off on his Union Jack manoeuvre even before Phase 1 at Kyaukse had ended; by March 26 most of the area was cleared and the 2d British Division was withdrawn to India. It was then discovered that the most serious resistance remained on Mount Popa, an extinct volcano, which towers abruptly and majestically five thousand feet above the plain. Several hundred Japanese with artillery clung tenaciously to the steep slopes, but eventually that useful maid-of-all-work, 268 Indian Brigade, after brisk fighting in rugged country, turned them out.

The rest of Phase 2 on XXXIII Corps' Irrawaddy front had gone more smoothly but with a good deal of fighting. The 7th Division, taking Kyaukpadaung, the road centre where three years before I had argued with the Chinese commander, pushed down both banks of the Irrawaddy and, on April 18 took Chauk with considerable loss to the enemy.

While these events were taking place east of the Irrawaddy, on the west bank the rather battered Yamamoto Force about Letse was stubbornly covering the withdrawal of the Japanese 54th Division from Arakan. Our advance on the west bank, owing to the necessity to relieve the 28th East African Brigade by troops of the 7th Division from the east was necessarily slower in starting. Points on the east bank were reached several days ahead of corresponding locations on the west, and thus large bodies of the enemy were being constantly cut off from escape to the east and driven back across the river until, with the 54th Division, they built up to some nine or ten thousand. Our troops on the west bank thus met increasing opposition, but the 7th Division pushed on to take the chief centre of resistance at Padan. The whole Japanese situation on the west of the Irrawaddy had by now become perilous, not only from the 7th Division's pressure on that bank but because of the rapid advance of the 20th Division on the other, which compelled the enemy to seek farther and farther south for a crossing to the east.

While the rest of XXXIII Corps had been moving in the 'Union Jack' manoeuvre over to the Irrawaddy, the 20th Division had been left behind to deal with the last stubborn resistance of the Japanese at Kyaukse. Then, having taken Kyaukse on March 30 and harried the last of Katamura's unhappy divisions into the hills, it handed over to the 19th Division and collected south of Meiktila. There, with characteristic energy, Gracey flung himself into preparations for Phase 3. With serviceable vehicles from the 2d Division, which was about to fly out to India, he was able rapidly to reorganize two of his brigades on a motorized establishment. On April 11, the conversion complete, he set out with all speed to take part in the XXXIII Corps advance south. His task was to strike at the Japanese rear at Magwe and Allanmyo.

Sakurai, commander of the Japanese Twenty-eighth Army, entrusted with the defence of the Irrawaddy Valley, was facing north and east. His main communications, road and river, ran south, but his link with the Thirty-third Army, eighty miles away on the railway axis, bent east at Magwe and went through Taungdwingyi. The latter town could be either a bastion to defend his right rear or a threat to it. Everything depended on who occupied it. Sakurai was short of troops, no British were nearer to Taungdwingyi than Meiktila, the country between was waterless, and the road unfit for motor transport; there would be time enough for warning. Sakurai, therefore, concentrated his Japanese troops at places nearer to our forces and on our direct lines of approach; he left Taungdwingyi mainly to Indian National Army units and to his administrative troops. In this he made a fatal mistake—he miscalculated the speed at which we could move. On April 11 no British forces were within sixty miles of Taungdwingyi; on the 14th, one of Gracey's mechanized brigades had seized it. The blow was so sudden that for some days the Japanese command did not realize what had happened, and continued to send convoys via Taungdwingyi to the great profit and entertainment of the 20th Division. Small parties of Japanese and larger ones of Jiffs were encountered by our patrols in the neighbourhood, but the only serious hostile action was an attempt to collect a force to hold a position about ten miles south on the road to Allanmyo. On April 18 a small armoured column from Taungdwingyi reached the Irrawaddy, eleven miles south of Magwe, and sank three boatloads of Japanese trying to escape across the river. The other mechanized brigade, which had halted at Natmauk, thirty miles north of Taungdwingyi, advanced from there and occupied Magwe, against light opposition, on April 19.

The 7th Division continued to push down both banks of the Irrawaddy and on the 22d it occupied the town and oil field of Yenangyaung. The Japanese, bewildered by the speed, strength, and direction of the 20th Division's thrust were, in their efforts to escape, forced either to abandon all vehicles and take to side tracks or to cross the river again to the west. The 20th Division columns, brushing aside hurriedly assembled enemy parties, entered Allanmyo on April 28. High morale was no longer universal among Japanese troops, but their savagery remained; we found Burmese villagers tied to trees and bayoneted. By May 1, XXXIII Corps Headquarters was established in Magwe with the 7th Division, 268 Brigade was at Allanmyo, and 20 Division just starting its advance on Prome and Rangoon.

By the end of March IV Corps with its headquarters at Meiktila, was gathering for the main drive south. Grouped around the town were the 17th Division, the 5th Division, with one brigade still to arrive, and 255 Tank Brigade. In addition, the headquarters and one brigade of the 19th Division were there, ready to take over as soon as the corps left, while the remaining brigades of this division were along the Mandalay road to the north. I found a rather noticeable jam of headquarters in Meiktila, and I decided I should have to wait for some of them to move before I brought mine there. I felt, too, that perhaps the Japanese were a little close as yet for an army headquarters in Meiktila to be really comfortable.

In fact, the Japanese were still a good deal in evidence, and it became daily plainer that Honda would try to regroup his divisions on the good defensive position astride the main road at Pyawbwe. His 49th Division, detailed to hold the centre, was already in place digging hard, his 18th, about Thazi, was to occupy the right, and the 53d, coming in from the northwest, to take up the line on the left. Given a little time, the Japanese position could become most formidable and, if we were seriously delayed by it, our chances of getting to Rangoon would be slight. On the other hand, if we really smashed Honda's army, it was unlikely that Kimura could produce another force capable of holding us farther south. Honda's stand so far north should be all to our advantage, but we must crush him, and quickly.

On March 30 Messervy's IV Corps with the 17th Division and 255 Tank Brigade set about doing so. Cowan, the divisional commander, was in tactical control of the battle and his plan was for a converging attack. His 99 Brigade was to move first east to take Thazi then, turning south, to seize the high ground southeast of Pyawbwe. The 48 Brigade was to strike straight down the main road from Meiktila, while 63 Brigade was to swing around Pyawbwe on the west and occupy the rising ground southwest of the town. A fourth tentacle of envelopment would be an armoured and motorized infantry column, which, driving still wider on the west, would cut the Rangoon road south of Pyawbwe. Having gained these positions, the whole force would close in on the main defences and assault them from all sides.

No sooner had the various advances gained contact than it became clear that the Japanese, while surprised by the speed with which we had mounted our attack, were determined at all costs to halt us. Scattered over the country around Pyawbwe were many villages, some large, some small, and almost all of these had been made into strong points, mutually supporting and self-supplied from dumps within them. The enemy thus held a wide defensive zone which had to be fought through before his main positions could be reached. It would have been difficult to devise a scheme of defence more suited to the Japanese soldier or more calculated to delay us.

The first hitch in our proceedings occurred when 99 Brigade found a strong garrison firmly embedded in Thazi to which the enemy clung as cover for the escape route into the Shan Hills. Direct assault would, at the best, be costly; any other form of attack would necessarily be slow. Similarly, on the Meiktila road, 48 Brigade was soon fighting its way forward from village to village—a dogged process. Whether these Japanese had been caught by our advance before they could fall back on to positions nearer Pyawbwe, or whether it was the policy of their higher command to hold in such depth, I did not know, but they fought like cornered wildcats. When you knew the way—and our men did—they were not difficult to kill, but it took time. And we had not got much time. With this in mind, on April 2 I flew to Meiktila.

I found Messervy and Cowan quite as well aware as I was of the need for speed. Cowan intended to recover the momentum of his advance by leaving a small detachment to contain Thazi, while 99 Brigade, ignoring it, pushed on again. We improved on that by calling in the brigade of the 19th Division from Meiktila to deal with Thazi. This they did a few days later, after some hard fighting. Cowan was confident that, as the result of other steps he was taking, the push astride the road would gather speed. Having seen for myself everywhere the obvious urge to get on and close with the enemy, I left, feeling much happier than when I had arrived—as so often happened after contact with the forward troops.

For some days the 17th Division, forcing its way south from Thazi, fought through villages held by the enemy until, at Yindaw, ten miles from Pyawbwe, it found the toughest nut its teeth had yet met in this battle. Yindaw, part of the Japanese permanent defences, with a strong garrison ordered to hold to the last had great natural strength and was a mass of anti-tank guns, obstacles, and mines. On the 8th, to save time and lives, the 17th Division was told to bypass it and leave it to be dealt with by the 5th Division, following hard on the 17th's heels. This the 5th Division faithfully did. Cowan, pushing on, gained the high ground just north of Pyawbwe and closed in on the town from two sides, while his armoured column fought its way to the Rangoon road to the south and completed the encirclement. The Japanese after dark counter-attacked with their armour but were heavily repulsed—the only night tank versus tank encounter of the campaign.

Then, on April 10, the 17th Division tackled the heart of the Japanese line, Pyawbwe itself. The enemy 49th Division, thoroughly dug in, fought grimly, beating back in hand-to-hand fighting assault after assault, but our troops gradually ate into the defences, and when our armoured column drove north on a broad front, this attack from the rear finally cracked the Japanese resistance. Two thousand enemy dead were counted in the town and many more were caught and killed outside. Great dumps of supplies and ammunition with vehicles, guns, and tanks fell to us. The Japanese 49th Division, clinging to its defences, had been destroyed in them; their 18th Division in Thazi had been unmercifully hammered and their 53d Division, caught as it tried to take up its positions, had been thumped and banged right out of the ring. This battle of Pyawbwe did more than shatter Honda's army, it settled the fate of Rangoon.

Now the straight, all-out drive on Rangoon could be loosed. Early on the morning of April 11, as the 17th Division cleared the battlefield and hunted down enemy stragglers, the 5th Division went through. They were off! I stood beside the road outside Pyawbwe and saw them go. Three hundred miles and, with luck, some thirty days before the monsoon to do it in. It would be a close thing, but after yesterday's battle I was sure IV Corps would pull it off. They certainly meant to, and they looked like it; there was an air of purpose about every truck that rolled dustily by. Mansergh, commanding the 5th Division, drew his to one side, stopped, and got out to greet me. Fresh, alert, and eager, he somehow, for a flash, made me think of the start of a dawn duck shoot in India, but we spoke of more serious business, before he, too, moved on. I watched vehicle after vehicle pass, loaded with Indian soldiers grasping their weapons, and on their faces was the same look as on their commander's, alert and eager. I had begun the war as a brigadier in this division in 1939, and I was proud of them. We should get there all right! A dull roar above made me look up. That noise, three years ago, would have sent us all diving for cover. Now, I was the only one to raise my head and see our fighters streaking south across the sky. We took them for granted, yet it was they who made possible this swift move of soft vehicles, almost nose to tail, down one road. I went back to Cowan's headquarters and found him grimly cheerful, as a commander who had won such a battle might well be. With Messervy we discussed on the map the way the advance would go.

We had often talked of this before; now we were to see if the methods we had devised would be the right ones. The leading division, at the moment the 5th, would move with an armoured and motorized infantry group ahead. There would be a bound forward, as rapid as possible, to seize an air strip or a site for one, the fly-in to it of airfield engineers, and the quick follow-up of the air-transported brigade. Then, while that brigade held the air base, cleared the surrounding country, kept open the road, or, if necessary, reinforced an attack, the rest of the division would make its next bound. Each division would lead in turn, reach its objective, halt, and let the other through. There must be no pause. Air strips would be required at least every fifty miles, but preferably, to save road transport, at more frequent intervals. The rate of our advance would be in direct ratio to the speed with which they could be brought into operation. In fact, after the first day or two we put airfield engineers with the tanks at the head of the column, so as to start work on air strips at the earliest possible moment.

The armoured group ahead of the 5th Division quickly covered the twelve miles to Yamethin, drove through the town, and pushed on. When darkness fell, however, a Japanese suicide party some three or four hundred strong with anti-tank guns infiltrated into the town from the east and dug in among the houses. At dawn next day they commanded the only road and the soft vehicles, which had halted for the night north of Yamethin, were held up. The intruders proved extremely difficult to dislodge, and it was not until the 14th that the last of them was exterminated and vehicles could pass freely. Angry at the delay, the 5th Division pushed rapidly on for thirty miles to Shwemyo, which it occupied on the 16th. Just beyond the village the road runs through a deep valley with the Shwemyo Bluff, a ridge some seven hundred feet high, completely dominating it for several miles, and forcing it to pass through narrow defiles. There is no other way for wheels past the Bluff, and we had always feared that we might be held up there. For a time it looked as if we should.

The Japanese had rushed up from South Burma a fresh regiment of their 55th Division, which was now hurriedly digging in on the Bluff. Pressing in front with his leading brigade, Mansergh debussed his second and sent it by a forced, out-flanking march, deep through hills and jungle, to take the enemy in the rear. On the 18th our men suddenly fell upon them, still digging, and flushed them from their half-completed entrenchments at the bayonet point. Meanwhile, to save air transport which was urgently needed to bring in supplies, especially petrol, several lorry loads of which had been destroyed by Japanese fighters in an attack on our armoured group, the air transported brigade was brought by road to the landing ground at Shwemyo. That night our leading troops harboured two hunded and forty miles from Rangoon.

On the 19th the armoured group, still in the lead, rumbled twenty miles down the road, to find Pyinmana strongly held. While the main column was catching up, the tanks bulldozed a by-pass road around the town, went ten miles farther, and seized the airfield at Lewe—a more valuable prize than the town. In a matter of hours the air strip was repaired and troops and stores were being steadily flown in.

Lieutenant-General Honda, commanding the Japanese Thirty-third Army, with several of his staff, was visiting Pyinmana when our troops were suddenly reported on its outskirts. Luckily for him, his staff car was faster than our tanks. Leaving one mechanized brigade to clear Pyinmana, the other, with its armoured group from 255 Tank Brigade, swept on. The situation at this stage had in it an element of comedy. IV Corps was charging south down the road and railway, while, driven off these, in the hills on each flank, faint but pursuing, enemy parties of all sizes were marching hard in the attempt to reach Toungoo before us. If Radio Tokyo had announced, 'Our forces are pursuing the enemy rapidly in the direction of Rangoon,' it would have been nearer the truth than usual.

All eyes were now on Toungoo. Japanese and British alike were converging on it in desperate endeavours to forestall one another. We must occupy it before the enemy could concentrate there if we were to avoid the long delay of clearing the town house by house. There was another reason. Its group of airfields, some of the best in Burma were the most northerly within good fighter range of Rangoon and, if the amphibious landing there were to be practicable, we must have them as bases for its air cover. The landing was now scheduled for May 2; on naval advice it could not be later owing to weather. This date provided us with our last and, I was beginning to think, the most formidable competitor in the race. We were beating the Japanese, there was as yet no sign of the monsoon, but, if we were to beat 'Dracula,' too, we should have to step up our timetable. We had eleven days to be in Rangoon, and over two hundred miles to go—twenty miles a day. That put us on our mettle!

Kimura was driving his men as hard as Messervy and I were driving ours. He had ordered all troops in the Shan Hills to get to Toungoo with sleepless speed. Their roads were the fair-weather hill tracks that ran roughly parallel to our route, sixty or seventy miles to the east. Opposite Toungoo and about seventy miles from it this track turned abruptly west and joined the Rangoon road in the town. Led by the partly re-organized 15th Division, the Japanese, ferrying fast in any kind of vehicle left to them, made for Toungoo, and it looked as if they might beat us to it. But I still had a shot in my locker for them. As they drew south, their way led them through the country of the Karens, a race which had remained staunchly loyal to us even in the blackest days of Japanese occupation, and had suffered accordingly. Over a long period, in prepara-tion for this day, we had organized a secret force, the Karen Guerrillas, based on former soldiers of the Burma Army, for whom British officers and arms had been parachuted into the hills. It was not at all difficult to get the Karens to rise against the hated Japanese; the problem was to restrain them from rising too soon. But now the time had come, and I gave the word, 'Up the Karens!' Japanese, driving hard through the night down jungle roads for Toungoo, ran into ambush after ambush; bridges were blown ahead of them, their foraging parties massacred, their sentries stalked, their staff cars shot up. Air strikes, directed by British officers, watching from the ground the fall of each stick of bombs, inflicted great damage. The galled Japanese fought their way slowly forward, losing men and vehicles, until about Mawchi, fifty miles east of Toungoo, they were held up for several days by road blocks, demolitions, and ambuscades. They lost the race for Toungoo.

Still leading IV Corps' advance, the 5th Division, brushing aside disjointed opposition, in three days covered fifty miles and, on April 22, with a final spurt, our armour crashed into Toungoo. Although we had heavily bombed the town the day before, the arrival of our ground forces was a complete sur-prise. The signals of a protesting Japanese military policeman on point duty were disregarded, and the first tank went over him. Panic reigned as our tanks roamed the streets, the enemy flying in all directions, intent only on escape. They left behind them only fifty dead, so fast did the living make for the jungle to swell the numbers trudging south. Honda had established his army headquarters in Toungoo and had issued the usual optimistic orders that it was to be defended to the last. He staged another hurried flight, but this time he abandoned most of his headquarters equipment and it was several weeks before he recovered any control over the remains of his army. We had not expected so swift a victory at Toungoo. Now it was one hundred and sixty miles to go and eight days left. The race between IV Corps and XV Corps, which was to make the Rangoon landing, promised a close finish. Betting at this stage was three to one on IV Corps, but even the most optimistic of its supporters would have liked a 31st April in the calendar.

Without a pause the 5th Division, sweeping aside Japanese fugitives, next day reached Pyu, over thirty miles south of Toungoo. Here, although the important bridge had been demolished, the site was undefended and the construction of a new bridge was quickly in hand. On the way the 1st Division of the Indian National Army was encountered. It surrendered en masse, with its commander, one hundred and fifty officers, and more than three thousand men. They were just in time to begin work on the captured airfields. On April 24 the 17th Division, close up and ready, was due to pass through and take the lead, but the 5th, its blood thoroughly up, went on another twenty miles to Penwegon. Here, when our first armoured car crept up, the Japanese demolition party was already in position at the bridge—but asleep. They never woke. In the 17th Division indignation battled with consternation when the 5th thus overran their mark. We were now one hundred and fourteen miles from Rangoon with seven days to May 2.

I knew that with the loss of Toungoo Kimura must realize that the situation in South Burma was critical. He was probably out of touch with his army commander, now a fugitive, and he could not have much left in the way of reserves. We learned, on the 24th, that he was moving his headquarters to Moulmein, but whether this meant that Rangoon would be abandoned or whether, as I had always feared, he would leave a garrison there, I could not tell.

I did not think he would risk running the gauntlet of our Navy and Air Force in an evacuation by sea. Whatever he did, he would have to hold Pegu, as it covered his last withdrawal route to the east, and all our intelligence confirmed that the enemy were concentrating for its defence. Although, of course, we did not know it at the time, Terauchi, the Japanese Supreme Commander, had ordered Kimura to hold South Burma at all costs and, if possible, Rangoon, too. Kimura decided that to hold Rangoon was not possible. He again showed energy in crisis, and called every man and unit to the defence of Pegu. Disregarding the possibility of a sea landing, which in any case he believed we should not attempt so near the monsoon, he brought 24 Independent Mixed Brigade from Moulmein, and hastily formed two new brigades, each under a major-general, from the miscellaneous units of the Rangoon garrison and the lines of communication. One of these brigades contained several anti-aircraft batteries and they brought with them their guns to be used in an anti-tank role. Into these improvised brigades Kimura swept shore-based naval units, fishermen, and civilians. By April 28 this force of three brigades, with numbers of fugitives from the north, was collected at Pegu, and, apart from a handful left to carry out demolitions, no Japanese were in or south of Rangoon. I calculated that Kimura would try to hold Pegu throughout the monsoon if it were only to allow his troops in the Irrawaddy Valley to escape over the Salween River. We could expect bitter resistance.

On April 25 the 17th Division took the lead. After some twenty miles, its armoured spearhead ran into a Japanese rear guard, many of whom were horsed cavalry, and ploughed through them, killing some and scattering the rest. On the 26th Daiku was reached—eighty miles from Rangoon with five days to go and Pegu in between. Next day, where fifteen miles farther south the road passed through a defile between the six-mile-wide Moyingyi Reservoir on the east and swampy ground on the west, more serious resistance was met. Here the enemy had laid a considerable mine field, which took toll of our tanks and was defended by suicide parties of Japanese engineers and infantry. By evening a way had been forced through the mine field, in which the defenders left three hundred dead. All night skirmishing went on and, next morning, the 28th, our advance again met stiff opposition ten miles north of Pegu. After heavy air bombardment, at the approach of our troops the Japanese pulled out, but it was not until evening that our armour reached the outskirts of Pegu to find the town strongly held.

That morning another of our armoured infantry columns had hooked round the Moyingyi Reservoir and cut the Japanese escape road to the east of it, compelling their retreating vehicles to be abandoned or to take the cross-country tracks farther south. A Jiff officer who surrendered reported that more than four hundred British and American prisoners of war were in a village some distance away. They were being escorted from Rangoon towards Moulmein, when their Japanese guards, hearing the road ahead was cut by our rapid advance, abandoned them and fled. Patrols were at once sent out to locate the party and did so, unfortunately not before some of our aircraft, seeing a column of men in khaki, as distinct from the green all our troops wore, had dived and strafed them, killing and wounding several. Some of the officers and men rescued were from the 17th Division, captured in the 1942 fighting, and now found themselves back with their old formation.

The troops of IV Corps were already on reduced rations, having given up food for petrol and ammunition, but the knowledge that they were only forty-seven miles from Rangoon and that the Japanese at Pegu were the only obstacle between them and the capital, spurred them on. The town of Pegu stands on both banks of the winding Pegu River. The road to Rangoon crosses the river by the main bridge in the town itself; the railway crosses twice, by two bridges to the north. The Japanese were cunningly entrenched in the town and covered both railway bridges which they had demolished. Cowan's plan was first to clear the part of the town on the east bank by a double assault, delivered by a brigade from the north and his armoured column from the east and southeast. On the morning of April 29 both these attacks were launched. The northern attack broke into the town but was held short of the road bridge. The armoured column, hampered by mine fields and canals, was unable to use its tanks to the full, and although the infantry pushed on alone they were not, unsupported, able to penetrate far among the houses where Japanese resistance was desperate.

Undismayed, Cowan now extended his operations to the west bank. In a series of small dogfights the approaches to the railway bridges on the east were cleared and attempts to cross made. These were held back by heavy fire, until a platoon of Indian infantry, crawling over the wrecked girders of the southern bridge, succeeded most gallantly in gaining the west bank. With the bayonet they cleared the nearest Japanese trench and held out until more of their battalion, swimming, rafting, and scrambling over the wrecked bridge, joined them. We now had a footing, even if a somewhat precarious one, on the west bank. While this was going on, our troops on the east bank, against bitter opposition, overran almost the whole of the northern residential area of Pegu, but at nightfall on the 30th the enemy still covered the intact road bridge.

I had spent April 29 at my headquarters, now established in Meiktila, where I had received rather alarming reports of a Japanese counterattack directed down the Mawchi road against our line of communication at Toungoo. I was told the main Rangoon road was already under Japanese artillery fire. We had only one brigade of the 19th Division to hold this attack and it might prove very embarrassing if the enemy made any further headway, so on the 30th I flew to Toungoo. As I drove down the main road towards Rees's headquarters, I had convincing evidence of the accuracy of at least one item of my intelligence report—the Japanese were quite noticeably shelling the road. I found Rees cheerful and unalarmed as usual, although at that moment superior enemy forces were pressing on his brigade not very far to the east of us. His troops had dug in among the hills astride the road and he was confident they would hold. I visited some of his units, and stayed to watch a battery firing at Japanese reported to be collecting for an attack. One of the gunners, stripped to the waist, his bronzed body glistening with sweat, was slamming shells into the breach of a twenty-five-pounder. In a lull in the firing I stepped into the gun pit beside him. 'I'm sorry,' I said, 'you've got to do all this on half rations.' He looked up at me from under his battered hat. 'Don't you worry about that, sir.' He grinned. 'Put us on quarter rations, but give us the ammo and we'll get you into Rangoon!' I did not doubt it; with men like that who could?

The Japanese on the Mawchi road tried hard to carry out their orders and cut our communications, but my gunner and his comrades were too good for them. Helped by the Karens, who clung to the Japanese coat-tails, Rees was able in the days that followed, not only to hold them, but to push them back farther into the hills, until the Rangoon road, at any rate, was no longer under their fire. An unspectacular task, out of the limelight of the race for Rangoon, but essential and carried out, as were all 19th Division's tasks, cheerfully, promptly, and with no little grief to the enemy.

During the night at Toungoo reports of the Pegu fighting had come in which made me eager to see what was happening there. Accordingly, on the morning of May 1, taking with me Messervy and two or three others, including Major Robert Fullerton, one of my American staff officers, I set off by air. As we approached Pegu I committed a very foolish and culpable act. I told my pilot to fly on south as I wished to see for myself what the country over which the 17th Division would have to operate was like. Sitting beside the pilot, I had just seen, far away in the direction of Rangoon, tall columns of smoke—which might be bombing or perhaps evidence of evacuation—when we came under considerable anti-aircraft fire. We received several hits, one of which exploded against Fullerton's leg. My pilot with great skill and coolness took evasive action in clouds and landed us on a newly-made advanced strip just north of Pegu. There was a dressing station alongside the airfield and by the greatest good fortune John Bruce, the consulting surgeon of the Fourteenth Army, happened at that very time to be visiting a forward surgical team. Bruce, one of the foremost British surgeons, saved Fullerton's life, but nothing could have saved his leg. I felt—and still feel—very guilty about this. I had no business as army commander to go where I did, and, if I was so stupid as to go, I had no excuse for taking Messervy or the others with me.

After this unhappy introduction to Pegu I found that during the night the situation had improved. We had kept our hold on the west bank and, on the east, patrols probing forward in the dark had reported the enemy thinning out and the sound of motor transport driving away. At dawn our troops had advanced to the attack, but found the whole of Pegu on the east bank clear, except for mines and booby traps. Leaving his air-transported brigade to deal with the west bank and the small parties of Japanese roaming the countryside, Cowan prepared for the final stage of the advance on Rangoon. If the only delay was to come from the Japanese, he could have pushed through the remaining forty miles in the next two days and reached Rangoon some hours ahead of the landing party. Unfortunately, it was not.

On the afternoon of May 1 a great misfortune befell IV Corps. Pegu was in our hands and the advance resumed, when a torrential storm burst over the whole area, followed throughout the night by continuous heavy rain. The monsoon was on us—a fortnight before its time! By morning much of the country was waterlogged, air strips going out of action, and the Pegu River rising ominously. As a precautionary measure, all IV Corps was immediately placed on half rations.

The troops slipped, splashed, and skidded forward, but all streams were in spate and all bridges down. On the evening of the 2d, when news of the successful landing south of Rangoon and of the Japanese evacuation had been received, the 17th Division was halted in drenching rain forty-one miles by road from its goal. More heavy rain during the night swept away approaches to bridges already built, and a whole brigade found itself marooned on what had suddenly become an island. The leading infantry, soaked, hungry, but still full of ardour, wading and often swimming, tried to push on. They were delayed by two miles of heavily-mined road, while the side tracks were often submerged and, like the road, mined. They were still struggling to reach Hlegu, when, late on May 3, they heard XV Corps had occupied Rangoon.

In spite of their disappointment at losing the race, the 17th Division, having lifted the mines, pushed on with determination. On the 4th, a battalion, have long ago left all transport behind, swam and rafted itself across a wide and rapidly flowing *chaung* to reach Hlegu, twenty-eight miles from Rangoon. It was here, on May 6, that a small column of the 26th Division from Rangoon linked up with IV Corps, meeting the 1/7th Gurkha Rifles who, in January 1942, had fired the first shots of the Burma War.

The landing south of Rangoon on May 2 had gone smoothly. I had always wanted it to be a little later, but naval advice was unanimous—and as it proved right—that the 2d was the latest date the weather would allow. It had been a great achievement by Rear-Admiral Martin, Lieutenant-General Christison, and Air Vice-Marshal the Earl of Bandon, the responsible commanders, to have had all ready for D Day. The assault force, mounted at Akyab and Ramree Islands, sailed in six convoys, slowest first, between April 27 and 30. It was covered on passage by 224 Group fighters and a naval carrier force of four escort carriers. Twelve bomber squadrons, British and American, from Strategic Air Force, were allotted to the operation. The naval covering force of one British and one French battleship, two escort carriers, two British and one

Dutch cruiser, and six destroyers put to sea from Trincomalee in Ceylon on April 30. Its duty was to prevent any interference by Japanese naval forces, and it cruised south of Rangoon and east of the Andamans, filling in time by bombarding those islands and Car Nicobar. A destroyer force was also in position south of Rangoon and on April 30 it intercepted eleven enemy craft, escaping with about a thousand troops from Rangoon to Moulmein and sank nine of them.

The overture to the landing was on D-1 Day, May 1, when a heavy bombing attack was delivered on all located defences on both sides of the Rangoon River. Some hours later a battalion of the 50th Indian Parachute Brigade dropped at Elephant Point. A party of about thirty Japanese, either left for observation or just forgotten, offered resistance to the Gurkha paratroops. One wounded Japanese survived. Early on the same morning a pilot, flying over Rangoon, saw written in large letters on the gaol roof the words, '*Japs gone, Exdigitate*.' The R.A.F. slang was not only evidence of the genuineness of the message, but a gentle hint to speed up operations. However, it was determined, wisely, I think, to continue according to plan. Early on the 2d the weather became worse and there was some doubt whether the small landing craft could face the sea. However, it was decided to risk it, and by skilful seamanship all reached and entered Rangoon River. A brigade of the 26th Division, under Major-General Chambers, was landed on each bank and the advance began. Within a few hours a deluge of rain descended, making all movement arduous. Nevertheless, the troops advanced several miles, and by nightfall the eastern brigade was within twelve miles of Rangoon.

While the 26th Division was thus plodding forward, the pilot of a Mosquito aircraft of 221 Group, flying low over Rangoon and seeing no signs of enemy, decided to land on Mingaladon airfield at the cantonment, about eight miles north of the city. The strip was in bad repair and he crashed his aircraft in landing, but, undismayed, he walked into Rangoon, visited our prisoners at the gaol, and assured himself that the Japanese had really gone. In the evening, commandeering a *sampan*, he sailed down the river and met the advancing 26th Division. We were rather pleased about this in Fourteenth Army. If we could not get to Rangoon first ourselves, the next best thing was for someone from 221 Group, which we regarded in all comradeship as part of the Fourteenth Army, to do it. On this confirmation of the Japanese flight, further bombing was called off and the build-up by sea, that was to follow the landing of the 26th Division, was cancelled.

It was not until the evening of May 3 that the brigade on the east bank, struggling through waterlogged country, appeared on the Hlaing River, immediately south of Rangoon. It was ferried over and entered the town. The population in thousands welcomed our men with a relief and a joy they made no attempt to restrain. We were back!

CHAPTER XXII

THE LAST BATTLE

A Burman once told me that the name Rangoon means 'The End of the War.' Whether that is so or not, it certainly was not its end for us. We now had two major tasks: one, the expulsion of all remaining Japanese from Burma, and two, planning, re-equipping, and regrouping for the imminent invasion of Malaya and the capture of Singapore. We pursued both projects simultaneously, often finding one antagonistic to the other, but always giving preference to the new campaign.

The tactical situation in Burma was unusual. Our double dash for Rangoon had left two long gashes across the Japanese body. The easterly of these, made by IV Corps, was more than three hundred miles long with an average width of less than a couple of miles, often indeed not more than a few hundred yards each side of the road—the longest and narrowest salient in history. In the Irrawaddy Valley XXXIII Corps had driven a similar though much broader salient for more than two hundred miles. The 26th Division, newly landed at Rangoon, had gained touch with both corps, thus completing the incisions which severed the Japanese from north to south. In addition, the 19th Division was driving two west-to-east corridors, from Meiktila to Tuanggyi and from Toungoo to Mawchi. We estimated—underestimated as Japanese figures later showed—that there were still between sixty and seventy thousand Japanese west of the Salween, scattered in groups of various sizes, all lacking transport, supplies, equipment; exhausted, diseased, near starving in the terrible monsoon conditions, but enough, even so, to become formidable if they could unite. There was also the threat of large hostile forces in Siam and Indo-China.

As far as we could judge, the Japanese in Burma were trying to collect in four main groups:

(i) *In the Irrawaddy Valley,* where the Twenty-eighth Army had some fifteen thousand men from several formations, all slowly trekking eastward through the Pegu Yomas, hoping to cross the Meiktila–Rangoon road and reach the Sittang.

(ii) *In the Shan Hills east of Meiktila,* the 56th Division and remnants of three others, about six thousand in all, making their way south.

(iii) *East of the Sittang River,* opposite our cordon from Toungoo to Nyaunglebin, the shattered Thirty-third Army, a hotch-potch of units from six or seven different divisions, about twenty-five thousand men.

(iv) *In the south,* about Mokpalin–Moulmein, Kimura had collected from 24 Independent Brigade, the Rangoon garrison, the Pegu battle survivors and lines of communication troops about another twenty-four thousand men.

Already several of the Fourteenth Army divisions were being withdrawn for the invasion of Malaya, but in spite of this, of the appalling climatic conditions, and of the fatigue of our remaining troops I could allow no respite. I ordered IV Corps to destroy all enemy attempting to emerge from the Pegu Yomas, to take Mokpalin, and to secure our line of communication. The XXXIII Corps I told to clear the Irrawaddy Valley and capture Bassein; the 26th Division to secure the Rangoon area.

In the Irrawaddy Valley Sakurai with his Twenty-eighth Army had the bulk of his force still on the west bank and his aim was to get them, especially his 54th Division, intact over the river into the Pegu Yomas. Our 7th Division destroyed his rear guard, but the Japanese had formed a bridgehead at Kamu about twenty miles above Prome and were hurriedly beginning to cross. Our troops closed in on Kama on both banks; on the west they accounted for the Japanese who were not yet over the river and on the east, reinforced by part of the 20th Division, encircled the bridgehead. While parties of the enemy delivered fanatical night attacks on our containing positions, others strove to infiltrate through the inevitable gaps. At the end of ten days of this, fourteen hundred Japanese dead were counted before our lines; more lay in the jungle. The enemy had lost all his transport and almost all his guns while many even of the small fugitive parties making for the Pegu Yomas had been intercepted. The remnants of the Japanese Twenty-eighth Army which reached the shelter of the sodden hills were capable only of concentrating on escape to the east.

As the monsoon grew in intensity so did the difficulties of our maintenance. We were rapidly losing our American air-transport squadrons and our own R.A.F. ones were terribly in need of rest before they could be used over Malaya. Our rail-head was still Dimapur, now nine hundred miles away; our roads, for hundreds of miles unmetalled, were crumbling away under rain of projectile force and ceaselessly battering wheels. The short isolated lengths of railway we tried to use and the river craft we had built or salvaged were ramshackle in the extreme. Our convoys were always liable to run into desperate gangs of Japanese making east across the road or lurking beside it, and no tribute to the determination, skill, and courage of the men who brought the supplies through could be too high. The fact that they *did* bring them through was possible only because among them reigned the same high spirit as in the combat units of the Fourteenth Army. But even these men could not continue indefinitely; it was imperative to reopen the port of Rangoon, smashed and sabotaged as it was. All possible engineer resources and labour were at once turned to this task. They succeeded beyond my hopes. In six weeks we had three thousand tons a day coming over the patched-up wharves; the maintenance crisis was passed.

With startling suddenness the army found itself responsible, too, for the care, administration, and, to a considerable extent, for the supply of four-fifths of Burma with some thirteen million inhabitants. Government had completely disappeared, insecurity and dacoity were rife, trade had ceased, the ruined towns were deserted, and the almost complete absence of consumer goods had spun the Japanese paper currency into wild inflation. We were welcomed, somewhat embarrassingly, as saviours who would in no time restore the carefree conditions of happy Burma before the war. But it was not so easy.

The first necessity was to restore the framework of government throughout the country, but we were hampered by an acute shortage of qualified officials who could be installed in the civil districts which we rapidly, one after the other, liberated. Of the original British civil servants, some had in the past years vanished into other services or joined the armed forces. Too many, it seemed to me, were held in India under the exiled Burmese government. Our own Civil Affairs staff were all allotted to the parts of Burma already in our hands before the last advance. As they retreated, the Japanese had taken with them many of the Burmese officials, who, mostly unwillingly, had served under them, while those who supported Ba Maw's puppet government had fled, to avoid their own countrymen as much as to escape us. Gradually Burmese civil officials of all ranks began to come out of hiding and report for duty; others were located and persuaded to return; but all had to have their records checked before they could be reinstalled. However, in a surprisingly short time, considering all the difficulties, a civil administration, somewhat skeleton in form, was set up and, with increasing efficiency, functioning.

It was an even more difficult matter to get the economic life of the country running again. Not only were we lacking many requirements for the army, but outside Burma there was a world shortage of the articles most needed to supply the desperate necessities of the civil population—notably cotton goods. Even were imports from abroad obtainable, they would not relieve the situation until communications within Burma were restored, and the ports, especially Rangoon, operating again. Nevertheless, even before we got the army back to full rations, we diverted some of its supplies and part of our precious air lift to succour the most distressed areas.

Parallel with this problem of the civil administration was a smaller Burmese politico-military one. How to treat the Burmese National Army, originally Japanese sponsored, but now in arms against them? I had all along believed they could be a nuisance to the enemy but, unless their activities were closely tied in with ours, they promised to be almost as big a nuisance to us. It seemed to me that the only way satisfactorily to control them was to get hold of their commander in chief, Aung San, and to make him accept my orders. This, from what I knew of him and of the extreme Burmese nationalists, I thought might be difficult but worth trying.

Aung San had had a chequered career. In 1930 as an undergraduate at Rangoon University, like most Asian students, he took an active, and at times a rather violent, interest in politics. By 1939 he was the secretary of the extremist Nationalist Minority Group and served a seventeen-day prison sentence for his activities. About this time he was contacted by Japanese agents, who saw in the energetic and able young nationalist a promising tool for their own ripening designs. It thus happened that when in 1940 Aung San's organization was proscribed, he and some thirty others of its members were able to evade the police and reach Japan. Here they were given military training in a Japanese officers' school and were indoctrinated with the belief that Japan would shortly drive the British out of Burma and bring freedom to its people. When the invasion did occur, Aung San and his companions came with it. The Japanese used them as a nucleus around which to collect irregular Burmese forces and to organize a Fifth Column throughout the area of operations. They were undoubtedly a help to their masters in many ways and, on one or two occasions during the retreat, fought bravely against us, although their chief combat duties were the ambushing and murdering of stragglers.

Aung San, whose intelligence and courage had brought him to the fore, showed anxiety to set up a Burmese government, but the Japanese, although they wanted a puppet government, were not prepared to accept him as its head. Perhaps they had already sensed he would not be the pliable and submissive dupe they required, and in any case they had Ba Maw, who was much more what they wanted. Instead, they appointed Aung San commander in chief of the Burma Defence Army, later the Burma National Army, that was set up under the closest Japanese control.

It was not long before Aung San found that what he meant by independence had little relation to what the Japanese were prepared to give—that he had exchanged an old master for an infinitely more tyrannical new one. As one of his leading followers once said to me, 'If the British sucked our blood, the Japanese ground our bones!' He became more and more disillusioned with the Japanese, and early in 1943 we got news from Seagrim, a most gallant officer who had remained in the Karen Hills at the ultimate cost of his life, that Aung San's feelings were changing. On August 15, 1944, he was bold enough to speak publicly with contempt of the Japanese brand of independence, and it was clear that, if they did not soon liquidate him, he might prove useful to us. Force 136 through its agents already had channels of communication and, when the revolt of the Burma National Army occurred and it was clear Aung San had burned his boats, it was time to deal directly with him. With the full approval of Admiral Mountbatten, the agents of Force 136 offered Aung San on April 21 a safe conduct to my headquarters and my promise that, whether we came to an understanding or not, I would return him unharmed to his own people. He hesitated until May 15, but on that day it was reported to me that he and a staff officer had crossed the Irrawaddy at Allanmyo, and were asking to meet me. I sent an aircraft, which flew them to my headquarters at Meiktila the next day.

The arrival of Aung San, dressed in the near-Japanese uniform of a major-general, complete with sword, startled one or two of my staff who had not been warned of his coming. However, he behaved with the utmost courtesy, and so, I hope, did we. He was a short, well-built, active man in early middle age, neat and soldierly in appearance, with regular Burmese features in a face that could be an impassive mask or light up with intelligence and humour. I found he spoke good English, learned in his school and university days, and he was accompanied by a staff officer who spoke it perfectly, as well he might, if it were true, as I was told, that his father had been a senior British official who had married a Burmese lady.

At our first interview Aung San began to take rather a high hand. He was, he said, the representative of the Provincial Government of Burma, which had been set up by the people of Burma through the Anti-Fascist People's Freedom League. It was under this provisional government that he and his National Army served and from whom they took their orders. He was an Allied commander, who was prepared to cooperate with me, and he demanded the status of an Allied and not subordinate commander. I told him that I had no idea what his Anti-Fascist People's Freedom League was or represented. As far as I and the rest of the world were concerned, there was only one government of Burma and that was His Majesty's, now acting through the Supreme Commander, Southeast Asia. I pointed out that he was in no position to take the line he had. I did not need his forces; I was destroying the Japanese quite nicely without their help, and could continue to do so. I would accept his cooperation and that of his army only on the clear understanding that it implied no recognition of any provisional government. He would be a subordinate commander, who would accept my orders and see that his officers and men also obeyed them and those of any British commander under whom I placed them. He showed disappointment at this, and repeated his demand to be treated as an Allied commander.

I admired his boldness and told him so. 'But,' I said, 'apart from the fact that you, a British subject, have fought against the British government, I have here in this headquarters people who tell me there is a well-substantiated case of civil murder, complete with witnesses, against you. I have been urged to place you on trial for that. You have nothing in writing, only a verbal promise at second hand, that I would return you to your friends. Don't you think you are taking considerable risks in coming here and adopting this attitude?'

'No,' he replied shortly.

'Why not?'

'Because you are a *British* officer,' he answered. I had to confess that he scored heavily—and what was more I believe he meant it. At any rate, he had come out on my word alone. I laughed and asked him if he felt like that about the British, why had he been so keen to get rid of us? He said it was not that he disliked the British, but he did not want British or Japanese or any other foreigners to rule his country. I told him I could well understand that attitude, but it was not for us soldiers to discuss the future government of Burma. The British government had announced its intention to grant self-government to Burma within the British Commonwealth, and we had better limit our discussion to the best method of throwing the Japanese out of the country as the next step towards self-government.

We resumed in good temper, and I asked him to give me the strengths and present disposition of his forces. This he was either unwilling or unable to do—I thought a bit of both. I pressed him in this but could get nothing definite. I had the impression that he was not too sure what his forces were, where they were, or what exactly some of them were doing. I said I had had reports that there were many bands of armed Burmans roaming about, claiming to belong to his army, who were no better than dacoits preying on their own countrymen. Rather to my surprise, he agreed and said he hoped we would both of us deal severely with these men, who were no troops of his. He went on to say that, at first, he had hoped the Japanese would give real independence to Burma. When he found they would not, but were tightening the bonds on his people, he had, relying on our promises, turned to us as a better hope. 'Go on, Aung San,' I said. 'You only come to us because you see we are winning!'

'It wouldn't be much good coming to you if you weren't, would it?' he replied simply.

I could not question the truth of this. I felt he had scored again, and I liked his honesty. In fact, I was beginning to like Aung San.

I told him that after the war we should revive the old regular Burma Army, under British officers, on the basis of the Burma Rifles battalions which still existed, and that there would then be no place for any other army—his would have to go. He at once pressed that his forces should be incorporated in the new army as units. This was obviously not altogether the solicitude of a general for his men, but the desire of a politician to retain personal power in postwar Burma. I answered that I thought it most unlikely that the Burmese government would accept them as units, but that I saw no reason why they should not, subject to a check of their records, be enlisted as individuals on the same terms as other recruits. He persisted in pressing for incorporation as units, but I held out no hopes of this. He then asked me if I would now supply and pay his units in the field? He was obviously finding this beyond his powers, and I knew that, if we did not accept the responsibility, his men would be reduced, as many were already, to living by exactions from the people—as dacoits, in fact. I said I would not consider paying or supplying his troops unless he and they were completely under my orders. In our final talk he had begun to take a more realistic view of his position, but he still would not definitely commit himself. Before he accepted the role of a subordinate commander, he said, he must consult with his 'government,' and he asked to be returned, suggesting that he should meet me again in about a week's time. I agreed, warned him of the consequences of refusing terms which, in view of his past, were most generous, shook hands, and sent him off by air again.

I was impressed by Aung San. He was not the ambitious, unscrupulous guerrilla leader I had expected. He was certainly ambitious and meant to secure for himslf a dominant position in postwar Burma, but I judged him to be a genuine patriot and a well-balanced realist—characters which are not always combined. His experience with the Japanese had put his views on the British into a truer perspective. He was ready himself to cooperate with us in the liberation and restoration of

436

Burma and, I thought, probably to go on cooperating after that had been accomplished. The greatest impression he made on me was one of honesty. He was not free with glib assurances and he hesitated to commit himself, but I had the idea that if he agreed to do something he would keep his word. I could do business with Aung San.

Operations against the Japanese were continuing over wide areas, and I wanted to get the role of Aung San's forces clear before clashes occurred between them and our troops. Having reported to my superiors the results of our interview and my views on his reliability, I therefore, instead of waiting for him to come in again, sent him, a few days later, definite proposals.

I would employ and ration all units of the Burma National Army then in action, provided they reported to and placed themselves unreservedly under the orders of the nearest British commander. I would recommend that suitable individual members of the B.N.A. should be allowed to volunteer for recruitment in the future Burma defence forces. Aung San accepted these terms without haggling, asking only that he should be consulted on major decisions on the employment of the B.N.A. and on the enlistment of its members into the regular forces. On May 30 my deputy chief civil affairs officer told Aung San that I had informed the Supreme Commander of our arrangement and that it was in force. Accordingly, somewhat to their surprise, our troops began to meet parties of Burmese in Japanese uniforms, who marched in, and whose officers stated they were reporting for duty with the British. They were regarded with considerable suspicion at first but, almost without exception, obeyed orders well. They proved definitely useful in gaining information and dealing drastically with small parties of Japanese. Aung San had kept his word. I have always felt that, with proper treatment, Aung San would have proved a Burmese Smuts.

In our preparations for the invasion of Malaya, which were pushed on simultaneously with all these activities in Burma, a factor which had already caused us anxiety rapidly assumed serious proportions and threatened to cripple all our plans. This was the repatriation of British troops. Many of my British soldiers and officers had served continuously for four or five years in the East, most of them in the often heartbreaking conditions of the Burma front, without in all that time a sight of their homes. In danger and discomfort, keyed up under strain, they suffered the soldiers' dumb pain of separation. Letters were late and sometimes irregular; time and distance seemed to make strangers of those they loved. In their months' old newspapers from home they read of the unfaithfulness of soldiers' wives, and saw pictures of English girls gambolling in the harvest fields with Italian prisoners. They heard that men on other fronts got home leave. Their own newspaper, *Seac*, was full of articles and letters urging the return home of men with long service in Southeast Asia. They heard of protests and read of promises by distant politicians that their experience and their common sense made them doubt. There was a danger that 'Repat' would become an obsession. When I asked a man in his fox hole or sitting beside the track what he was, he would often, instead of answering, 'I am a Lancashire Fusillier,' 'an F.O.O.'s signaller,' or 'the Bren gunner of this section,' say 'I am four and two,' or 'Three and ten.' He meant that was the number of years and months he had served in the East, and the unspoken question in his eyes, was, 'How many more?' I could not answer him. The British officers, N.C.O.s, and privates who had served longest were our key men. If we sent them home without replacement, neither our British nor our Indian formations could continue to fight efficiently.

It was not for want of representations by their commanders, from the Supreme Commander downward, that these men remained; their replacement was out of our hands. That being so, it would have been wiser and kinder if we had confined ourselves to doing all we could to speed up repatriation—as indeed we did—and everything possible to discourage so much talk about it. Yet, when all was said and done, we still had men with four and even five years in the East without leave home, and that is trying a man higher than he should be tried. The British soldier is accustomed to longer periods of overseas service than any other, yet it is not surprising that, under this growing spate of repatriation talk, among some of them the *élan* which they had shown for so long began to fade. To their honour, my British soldiers, officers and men, endured to the end; never did they shirk duty or hesitate to enter battle, but the strain was telling on them.

The War Office had decided, some time before, that the period of unbroken service in the East for officers and men of the British Army should be four years. In Burma we had many who had served longer than that but whose repatriation had been delayed for one cause or another. In 1945 the period was reduced from four years to three years eight months and, although we did our best to get men home, for reasons of transportation and partly because replacements were not forthcoming for key men, the backlog of those overdue for repatriation began to pile up. This reduction to three years eight months removed the framework of units and made considerable alterations necessary. There was much reorganization and retraining, and almost all British and many Indian and African units lost battle worthiness. This forced the postponement of the planned date of the landing in Malaya to September 9. Then without warning on June 7 the Supreme Commander was told by the Secretary of State for War that next day he was announcing in Parliament that the period of service in the East was reduced to three years four months, and that the men affected would be sent home as soon as possible without waiting for their replacement.

This news was a bombshell that shattered all the plans we had been making. The number of men affected was very large; one-third of the British officers and men in S.E.A.C., and those the most experienced with a high proportion of N.C.O.s, would have to be returned to the United Kingdom before October. Admiral Mountbatten and Generals Auchinleck and Leese at once cabled protests, pointing out that, unless they were authorized to carry out this crippling reduction gradually and in accordance with operational necessity, all Malayan operations would have to be postponed indefinitely. Nevertheless, the Secretary of State duly made his statement without any of the suggested qualifications, and it was broadcast throughout Southeast Asia. Every man in the army now knew when he was due for repatriation, and thousands were already overdue. The Secretary of State considered that in his statement there was provision for retaining men on the grounds of 'operational necessity,' but certainly no soldier so detained would think other than that a clear promise had been broken. It would have been not only unfair to land such men on the Malayan beaches, but unwise. Supported by all his senior commanders, Admiral Mountbatten refused to do this. The only alternatives then were to postpone indefinitely, that is until reinforcements were received from Europe, the Malayan invasion, or to take the grave risk of carrying it out with much-reduced and less-experienced forces. There were many advantages in holding to the September date for the landing; delay would certainly mean increased Japanese preparation and resistance. Both General Leese and I were in favour of taking the risk and Admiral Mountbatten agreed. So the re-sorting of units began all over again as the long-service men were sent to India to await passage home. Some key men, mostly officers, had to be retained under the operational-necessity clause, and they took their fate philosophically. Others, with more thought for their regiments and their men than for themselves, volunteered to stay. We pressed on, both in India and in Burma, in greater urgency than ever with our preparations.

Meanwhile, a considerable reorganization of the higher army command in Southeast Asia was being carried out. I had been chosen to succeed General Leese as Allied Land Forces commander. Fourteenth Army Headquarters moved from Rangoon, where I had established it, to India, there to continue planning the Malayan invasion and to await the arrival of my replacement Lieutenant-General Sir Miles Dempsey who had brilliantly led the Second Army in Europe. To control further operations in Burma, Stopford's XXXIII Corps was transformed into a new army, the Twelfth, to include IV Corps Headquarters, the 7th, 17th, and 19th Divisions, 268 Brigade and 255 Tank Brigade with, temporarily, also the 82d West African Division and 22 East African Brigade. The 5th Division was to return almost at once to India; the 20th and later the 7th also were to be mounted from Rangoon for the Malayan invasion.

I had not seen England for seven years, and I asked for and obtained leave for a short visit home before undertaking what I expected to be an arduous and possibly long new campaign. This leave was granted perhaps the more readily as I had never met Mr. Churchill, the Prime Minister, and I suspect he may have wanted to see what I was like before confirming me in so important an appointment. My wife and I had a hectic but happy month touring Great Britain.

While I was on leave, the last battle of the Burma Campaign, the Battle of the Breakout, was fought. It was obvious that, unless they were reconciled to dying of exposure, disease, and starvation in the Pegu Yomas, Sakurai's Twenty-eighth Army must sooner or later break out from the hills, cross the Mandalay–Rangoon road, and make a desperate attempt to rejoin the rest of Kimura's forces east of the Sittang River.

Sakurai's men were in a bad way. They had been very roughly handled by XXXIII Corps, for transport they were reduced to a few pack animals and such bullock carts as they could seize from the villagers. Their remaining supplies were meagre in the extreme, and they subsisted mainly by foraging from the wretched Burmese. Of artillery they had only a few light guns and of armour none. The monsoon was in full blast, every *chaung* was in spate, the rain was ceaseless, and they had little shelter. The sick received scant medical attention; they could only be left to die. Few armies in their situation would have thought of anything but surrender. Yet, when our aircraft showered the areas in which they were with leaflets inviting surrender and promising good treatment, there was no response. Instead, Sakurai collected his men and prepared to break out.

The IV Corps, under Lieutenant-General F. I. S. Tuker who was temporarily relieving Messervy on leave, had its two divisions, the 19th and 17th, strung out along the road from Pyinmana to Pegu. Our reconnaissance was handicapped, not only by the monsoon conditions for flying but by shortage of aircraft, as all American squadrons were withdrawn by June 1 and several of the R.A.F. had left Burma to prepare for Malaya. However, our patrols pushing westward across water-logged country into the hills began to make contact with the enemy and even took some prisoners. Gradually we traced out the pattern of enemy concentrations as Sakurai, deep in the Yomas, collected his men in five groups from north to south and prepared for his desperate bid to reach the Sittang. Luck was with us, and a long-distance patrol captured an order of the Japanese 55th Division giving full details of the enemy plan. Sakurai proposed in several columns to break out across the Rangoon road on a front of one hundred and fifty miles between Toungoo and Nyaunglebin by escape routes which led mainly through the 17th Division sector. Stopford therefore strongly reinforced that division from the 19th and 20th Divisions and even from the 7th, at the same time calling up Aung San's army, now called the Patriot Burmese Forces. Patrols were pushed into the hills along the tracks the Japanese were expected to use and these routes blocked by strong points where they debouched from the hills. Farther east, mobile columns were ready to intercept as the enemy attempted to cross the road or to engage them on to the plain between the

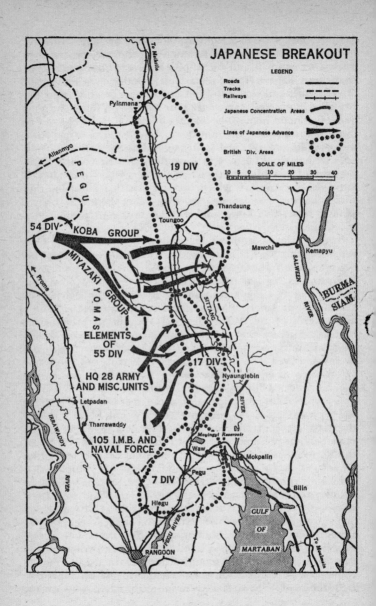

JAPANESE BREAKOUT

LEGEND

Roads
Tracks
Railways

Japanese Concentration Areas

Lines of Japanese Advance

British Div. Areas

SCALE OF MILES
10 5 0   10   20   30   40

To Mahtila

Pyinmana

Allanmyo

P E G U

19 DIV

Thandaung

Toungoo

54 DIV   KOBA   GROUP

Mawchi   Kemapyu

MIYAZAKI GROUP

Prome

YOMAS

SITTANG

BURMA
SIAM

SALWEEN RIVER

ELEMENTS
OF
55 DIV

HQ 28 ARMY
AND MISC. UNITS

17 DIV

Nyaunglebin

RIVER

Letpadan

105 I.M.B. AND
NAVAL FORCE

Tharrawaddy

Moyingyi Reservoir

Waw   Mokpalin

IRRAWADDY RIVER

7 DIV   Pegu

Bilin

Hlegu

PEGU RIVER

GULF

OF

MARTABAN

RANGOON

To Moulmein

road and the Sittang. On the west bank of the river were the P.B.F., stiffened by some Indian battalions, and even beyond this on the east bank lurked patrols of Force 136 and Burmans to ambush any survivors who did contrive to cross. It was a severe gauntlet Sakurai would run.

The first main moves in the Battle of the Breakout came from the Japanese Thirty-third Army which, with about ten thousand men, was east of the Sittang. Strong columns, crossing through three bridgeheads on the west bank of the river, advanced towards Waw, with the aim of distracting and drawing off our troops facing the Twenty-eighth Army, now about to stage its breakout. To meet the formidable Thirty-third Army counterstroke we had only one under-strength brigade of the 7th Division facing east on a twelve-mile front. On July 3 heavy Japanese attacks were delivered on its positions, all of which held, and continued for several days, alternating with bombardments. It was a fantastic battle, which could, in more senses than usual, be described as 'fluid.' The whole battlefield was a swamp; the only bits of comparatively solid ground were the railway embankments and the villages which rose like islands from a waste of water, two or three feet deep, and in places, as the 7th Division ruefully reported, 'too deep for Gurkhas to operate.' We were thin, even on what ground there was, and our casualties mounted steadily. Wisely, Tucker refused to weaken his forces waiting for Sakurai's breakout and preferred to order the forward brigade of the 7th Division to fall back. This it did by night, wading in hollow square through the water. Our men took with them many wounded, and through the long hours of the night the bearers, in the centre of the square, stumbling through mud and water, could never put down a stretcher to rest themselves. Had they done so, the man on it would have drowned. Oddly enough, the Japanese, too, had had enough, and they withdrew at the same time, although later they tried to follow up, and were repulsed decisively. There was one more inconclusive fight, when both sides simultaneously advanced into the 'island' in the loop of the Sittang Old Channel. Then, the Japanese having abandoned all hope of taking Waw, fighting died down, and interest moved farther north, where the long-expected breakout of the Twenty-eighth Army had begun.

Very wisely, Tuker had not allowed the Japanese counter-attack by their Thirty-third Army to distract him from preparations to receive the Twenty-eighth when it broke east. The captured order enabled every escape track to have its standing piquet, and 'V' Force patrols pushed farther west into the hills. There would thus be ample warning of the breakout, which was expected on July 20. Actually it began the day before with an attack by about one hundred Japanese on a platoon post of the 17th Division. This was followed almost daily by enemy parties, of from two to five or six hundred strong, emerging from the Yomas and trying to force their way across the road. Luckily, they did not arrive simultaneously, and they could be dealt with piecemeal. With typical Japanese tenacity—and stupidity—they followed one another by the same routes, and the numerous encounters that took place followed a uniform pattern. First, the Japanese party would strike our detachment blocking their exit to the road. After suffering heavily in the attempt to destroy it, the enemy would split into several smaller bodies and get past on each side. Pursued by our columns and harried by the planes of 221 Group, the Japanese would take refuge in villages to await darkness. Our men would cut the few tracks, still above water, that led east. Then artillery concentrations would shell the villages, inflicting heavy loss at the water made it impossible to dig trenches. After a day or two's siege the wretched Japanese in small groups would try to escape under cover of darkness, only to meet our troops on the west bank of the Sittang, and to be stalked and ambushed by the Burmese Patriot Forces and the armed resistance parties we had by now organized in many of the villages. Crossing the Sittang itself was the worst of the enemy's ordeals, and few succeeded. They were surprised as they launched their rafts, shot as they swam and drifted across on logs, or swept away by the rapid current to drown. In a few days a post of our troops on the riverbank counted more than six hundred bodies floating down from the slaughter at one of the main Japanese crossing places upstream.

The last Japanese to attempt the breakout were 12 and 13 Naval Guard Forces, formed from the Port and Shore Establishments of the Imperial Navy in Burma. They amounted to about twelve hundred men in all and, strangely enough, chose to make their attempt last and alone, on July 31. As they struggled across the road, losing heavily in the process, all our forces within reach were turned on them. Rapidly growing fewer, as our troops and artillery took toll, they approached the Sittang, only to find their way blocked by one of our battalions and to be caught between it and another pursuing one. The country was flooded and numerous *chaungs* near the river were in spate. It took nearly a week for an Indian and a Gurkha battalion to close in on the sailors, but of the four hundred to which they were now reduced, as the Japanese themselves afterwards told us, only three escaped. By August 4 such Japanese fugitives, as had run the gauntlet were over the Sittang, and the last battle in Burma had ended.

Sakurai, lacking transport and communications, and with his troops in the state they were, had indeed done well to stage any sort of organized breakout at all, but his losses were devastating. At the time it was difficult to estimate accurately the Japanese casualties, but more than six thousand bodies were recovered by our troops, hundreds were claimed by the Burmese irregulars, and many more lay undiscovered in water and long grass. Of the seventeen or eighteen thousand men of the Twenty-eighth Army who debouched from the Pegu Yomas, the Japanese themselves later stated that less than six thousand, and these starved, exhausted, and diseased, reached the east bank of the Sittang. In addition, between one and two thousand sick, too weak to march, had been abandoned to die in the Yomas.

Throughout this battle there were two startlingly noticeable features. First, the scale of Japanese surrenders. For the six thousand bodies they had picked up, IV Corps had taken seven hundred and forty prisoners—an unheard-of ratio, at least ten times as high as ever before. Then there was the astonishing smallness of our own casualties. Against the admitted Japanese twelve thousand killed and missing, we had suffered only ninety-five killed and three hundred and twenty-two wounded. We were killing Japanese at a rate of more than a hundred to one. The fact was that this final disaster had not only destroyed the Twenty-eighth Army, but had struck a mortal blow at the fighting spirit of the whole Japanese Army in Burma.

While I was on leave in England I had been told of atomic bombs, of their devastating power, and of the intention to drop them on Japan. Opinions differed widely as to whether, even after this, Japanese fanaticism would hold in desperate resistance to the brink of mass national suicide in Japan itself and elsewhere. On August 6 the first atomic bomb destroyed

Hiroshima and on the 9th the second fell at Nagasaki, so that I was not altogether surprised when my wife and I, flying back to my command, heard in Rome on the 14th that Japan had surrendered unconditionally.

Two days later I arrived at Headquarters Allied Land Forces, Southeast Asia, which were comfortably installed near Supreme Headquarters in Kandy, Ceylon, and there I took over my new and extended command. The staff with the exception of Walsh, who had been General Leese's chief of staff and who had left with him and been replaced by Major-General Pyman, was unchanged. Unchanged, but, remembering how they had displaced General Giffard's officers, a little apprehensive that the new broom would in turn brush them away to make room for its own favourites from Fourteenth Army, and a number of sweepstakes were being run on which officers would be dismissed first. However, as I brought with me only my military secretary, my aides-de-camp, and my Gurkha orderly, Bajbir, who would displace no one, anxiety soon subsided and, although I did make some reductions without replacement, we all got on very well together.

It would have been my fault if we had not, for I found a first-class staff, in excellent running order under Pyman and Bastyan, the principal administrative officer. We soon had our hands full. The area of Southeast Asia Land Forces had suddenly expanded to include Malaya, Singapore, Siam, Indo-China, the Dutch East Indies, Hong Kong, Borneo, and the Andaman Islands. Each confronted us with special and urgent problems. In two of them, Indo-China and the Dutch East Indies, nationalist movements, armed from Japanese sources, had already seized power in the vacuum left by the surrender and were resisting the restoration of French or Dutch sovereignty—fighting had already begun or seemed inevitable. In all areas were intact Japanese forces amounting to about half a million men, whose acceptance of the surrender was not certain, and many thousands of British, Australians, Indians, Americans, Dutch, and French, starving and dying of disease in the brutal and barbaric Japanese prison camps. It was obviously vital that we should occupy all Japanese-held territory at the earliest possible moment not only to enforce the surrender, but to succour these unfortunates.

Appeals from our French and Dutch Allies, cries for help, demands for troops, threats of continued Japanese resistance, apprehensions of wholesale massacre, forebodings of economic collapse, warnings of the starvation of whole populations, poured into our headquarters from every quarter. There were excellent reasons why we should rush to respond to each one. We should have liked to do so, but our shortage of air transport —we had lost more than half our former allotment—and the fact that almost all available shipping had already been loaded for the Malayan invasion, hampered and delayed our attempts to move forces rapidly to so many different points. Our first decision, in this welter of conflicting claims, was immediately to carry out the Malayan landing as planned—that is as if the war were continuing. It would have meant immense confusion had we unloaded and redistributed the troops and stores; besides, at this time Itagaki, the Japanese commander in Malaya, was breathing defiance, and it was quite possible that resistance would be encountered. In any case, to treat the landing as an operation of war was the quickest way to disembark the force, and, should that go peaceably, we could then direct its later echelons elsewhere.

At the same time, using all available air resources, we prepared to fly the 7th Division from Burma into Siam and, using the Bangkok airfield as a staging station, to lift part of the 20th Division into Indo-China to control Terauchi's Supreme Headquarters in Saigon. The 5th Division, if not required in Malaya, was to sail to Singapore and 3 Commando Brigade to Hong Kong. As soon after the occupation of Singapore as possible, the 26th Division was to be landed in Java and Sumatra. All these operations were about to begin, indeed the first ships of the Malayan force were already at sea and all headquarters buzzing with activity, when, on August 19, a very considerable spanner was thrown into their busy works.

The British and American Combined Chiefs of Staff had, ignoring Admiral Mountbatten, their Supreme Commander in Southeast Asia, entrusted the over-all control of the Japanese surrender to General MacArthur, the Supreme Commander in the Pacific. He decreed that the formal surrender in Southeast Asia could take place only after it had been ceremonially completed in his own theatre. This, though inconvenient, might not have mattered so much had he not ordered also that no landings in or re-entry into Japanese-held territory would be made until he had personally received the formal surrender of the Japanese Empire. This ceremony was fixed for August

31, and thus for twelve days—actually fourteen, as it was postponed until September 2—the forces of Southeast Asia had to mark time.

This delay in the formal surrender of the enemy in Southeast Asia did not prevent preliminary meetings, on our ground, between our plenipotentiaries and theirs, at which, after an initial tendency to argue, promptly and firmly suppressed, the Japanese showed a proper submissiveness and readiness to obey orders. But the delay could have had most serious consequences for our prisoners in Japanese hands. Admiral Mountbatten, now assured there would be no resistance, decided, in spite of the ban on landing, to fly in help to the prisoners. Our men and those of our Allies were daily dying in their foul camps; thousands were at the limit of weakness and exhaustion. Had he delayed for even a few days in sending supplies and relief personnel, many more would have died pathetically at the moment of rescue. The relief teams parachuted into the camps with magnificent courage, for they were by no means sure of the Japanese reaction to their arrival, but they could not, of course, bring with them great quantities of stores, medicine, or clothing. All that, and the evacuation of the prisoners to Burma, had to await the arrival of our troops. This was held up for a couple of weeks by the delays imposed in the surrender arrangements, and condemned our prisoners to a correspondingly longer stay in their camps.

The state of these camps and of their wretched inmates can only be realized by those who saw them as they were at this time. Except for derelict huts and *bashas*, the camps were little more than barbed-wire enclosures in which wild beasts might have been herded together. The Japanese and Korean gaolers, almost without exception, were at the best callously indifferent to suffering, or, at the worst, bestially sadistic. The food was of a quality and a quantity barely enough to keep men alive, let alone fit them for the hard labour that most were driven to perform. It was horrifying to see them moving slowly about these sordid camps, all emaciated, many walking skeletons, numbers covered with suppurating sores, and most naked but for the ragged shorts they had worn for years or loincloths of sacking. The most heartmoving of all were those who lay on wretched pallets, their strength ebbing faster than relief could be brought to them. There can be no excuse for a nation which as a matter of policy treats its prisoners of war in this way, and no honour for an army, however brave, which willingly makes itself the instrument of such inhumanity to the helpless.

Once the ceremonial surrender to General MacArthur had been staged on September 2, we were free to occupy the Japanese-held territories. On the 3d our first detachments, mainly medical units to aid the prisoners, were landed by air near Bangkok, followed by headquarters and a brigade of the 7th Division. On September 11 Gracey and a small detachment of his 20th Division were staged through to Saigon and took control of Field Marshal Terauchi's headquarters. The situation in Siam was well in hand, as the Regent and his government had for some time during the Japanese occupation been secretly working with us, organizing a resistance movement, and concerting measures for the day of liberation. In Indo-China fighting between local nationalist movements and the French, now released from internment, was already going on, and Gracey was faced with a most difficult politico-military situation in Allied territory, which he handled in a firm, cool, and altogether admirable manner.

The landing of Robert's XXXIV Corps over the beaches in the Port Swetenham–Port Dixon area, on the west coast of Malay, went in on September 9 as a tactical operation. There was no resistance, and even if there had been I think the operation would have been a success, for the Japanese plans, as we afterwards discovered, were based on our landing elsewhere. The local inhabitants, Malays and Chinese, gave our men a great welcome. When, a little later, I landed myself to see how things were going, the first British soldier I met was a linesman of the Royal Signals, with his rifle slung, holding by one hand a little Chinese boy and by the other a little Chinese girl. Linked with these two grinning youngsters were half-a-dozen others, all laughing and shouting. The soldier was a little embarrassed to be found patrolling a telephone line with this unofficial escort, but the children enjoyed it immensely. Anyway, soldiers and children always go very well together.

On September 3 Royal Marines from the fleet had taken over Penang Island from its Japanese garrison and, steaming on, the 5th Division had reached Singapore amid great local rejoicing on the 5th. Later the 26th Division, staging from Singapore, landed at Batavia in Java to deal with a very complicated and unhappy situation that had developed in the Dutch East Indies. Hong Kong was reoccupied by 3 Commando Brigade on September 10. We were then ready to begin the disarmament and collection in prisoner-of-war camps of the five hundred thousand Japanese troops in our area.

I had already, before the receipt of General MacArthur's orders, issued instructions to all my commanders as to how the Japanese surrender was to be conducted in our area. In these I had laid down that all senior Japanese officers were to surrender their swords to appropriate British commanders in front of parades of their own troops. There had been some protests at this from our Japanese experts who averred that:

(i) The Japanese officer's honour was so bound up with his Samurai sword that, rather than surrender it, he would go on fighting.

(ii) Alternatively, as the lawyers say, if he did surrender it before his men, he would never again be able to exercise command over them.

(iii) He would in fact, rather than be so publicly shamed, commit suicide.

My answers to these forebodings had been:

(i) If the Japanese liked to go on fighting, I was ready for them.

(ii) If the officers lost their soldiers' respect, I could not care less, as I intended to separate them from their men in any case.

(iii) If the officers committed suicide, I had already prepared for this by broadcasting that any Japanese officer wishing to commit suicide would be given every facility.

I was convinced that an effective way really to impress on the Japanese that they had been beaten in the field was to insist on this ceremonial surrender of swords. No Japanese soldier, who had seen his general march up and hand over his sword, would ever doubt that the Invincible Army was invincible no longer. We did not want a repetition of the German First War legend of an unconquered army. With this in mind, I was dismayed to be told that General MacArthur in his over-all instruction for the surrender had decided that the 'archaic' ceremony of the surrender of swords was not to be enforced. I am afraid I disregarded his wishes. In Southeast Asia all Japanese officers surrendered their swords to British officers of similar or higher rank; the enemy divisional and army commanders handed theirs in before large parades of their already-disarmed troops. Field Marshal Terauchi's sword is in Admiral Mountbatten's hands; General Kimura's is now on my mantelpiece, where I always intended that one day it should be.

In Singapore on September 12, 1945, I sat on the left of the Supreme Commander, Admiral Mountbatten, in the line of his commanders in chief and principal staff officers, while the formal unconditional surrender of all Japanese forces, land, sea, and air, in Southeast Asia was made to him. I looked at the dull impassive masks that were the faces of the Japanese generals and admirals seated opposite. Their plight moved me not at all. For them I had none of the sympathy of soldier for soldier that I had felt for Germans, Turks, Italians, or Frenchmen that by the fortune of war I had seen surrender. I knew too well what these men and those under their orders had done to *their* prisoners. They sat there apart from the rest of humanity. If I had no feeling for them, they, it seemed, had no feeling of any sort, until Itagaki, who had replaced Field Marshal Terauchi, laid low by a stroke, leaned forward to affix his seal to the surrender document. As he pressed heavily on the paper, a spasm of rage and despair twisted his face. Then it was gone, and his mask was as expressionless as the rest. Outside, the same Union Jack that had been hauled down in surrender in 1942 flew again at the masthead.

The war was over.

CHAPTER XXIII

AFTERTHOUGHTS

Generals have often been reproached with preparing for the last war instead of for the next—an easy gibe when their fellow countrymen and their political leaders, too frequently, have prepared for no war at all. Preparation for war is an expensive, burdensome business, yet there is one important part of it that costs little—study. However changed and strange the new conditions of war may be, not only generals, but politicians and ordinary citizens, may find there is much to be learned from the past that can be applied to the future and, in their search for it, that some campaigns have more than others foreshadowed the coming of modern war. I believe that ours in Burma was one of these.

This may seem a curious claim to make for the struggles of comparatively ill-equipped men groping through jungles. Yet a painter's effect and style do not depend on how many tubes of colour he has, the number of his brushes, or the size of his canvas, but on how he blends his colours and handles his brushes against the canvas. Looking back on the Burma campaign, which presented, at least to me, a strange unity and completeness, I have many afterthoughts. Of these I have here chosen a few, not because they are, perhaps, the most unusual or dramatic, but because they seem—again to me—to have some interest for the future.

Higher Direction

For the poor showing we made during the first phase of the war in Burma, the Retreat, there may have been a few excuses, but there were many causes, most of them beyond the control of local commanders. Of these causes, one affected all our efforts and contributed much to turning our defeat into disaster—the failure, after the fall of Rangoon, to give the forces in the field a clear strategic object for the campaign. As a result, our plans had to be based on a rather nebulous, short-term idea of holding ground—we were not even sure what ground or for what purpose.

When the loss of Rangoon made it impossible to reinforce, or even adequately to maintain, the army in Burma, still more when the Chinese divisions began to give way, it was only too plain that the Allies had no immediate hope of driving back the Japanese and very little even of holding them. At this time those concerned in London and Washington with the conduct of global war, hard pressed as they were on more vital fronts, tended to overlook Burma. Yet a realistic assessment of possibilities there and a firm, clear directive would have made a great deal of difference to us and to the way we fought. Burma was not the first, nor was it to be the last campaign that had been launched on no very clear realization of its political or military objects. A study of such campaigns points emphatically to the almost inevitable disaster that must follow. Commanders in the field, in fairness to them and their troops, must be clearly and definitely told what is the object they are locally to attain.

The organization of the command in a theatre is, of itself, of the utmost importance. The first step towards ultimate victory in Southeast Asia was the setting up of a supreme command, controlling all Allied forces, land, sea, and air, in the area. There will always be difficulties, national and personal, in the creation and working of such a headquarters. In Southeast Asia these were greater than in similar commands in Africa, Europe, or the Pacific, because of the underlying difference between the British and American attitudes towards the Burma campaign. The clash of personalities, too, was fierce and often, as with Stilwell and Chiang Kai-shek, aggravated by distance. There will always be these frictions to a greater or lesser degree but where Allied forces are operating together there is no effective solution other than a Supreme Headquarters.

The Japanese Army

This was the first time since the Crusades, with the possible exception of some of our Indian wars of the eighteenth and early nineteenth centuries, that the British had fought an Asian or African enemy whose armament and military organization had been comparable to their own. Like our predecessors, the Russians in their war against Japan, we found a war against such a foe, at any rate to begin with, an extremely unpleasant and startling experience. Yet, because we possessed certain basic qualities which the Russians of that day did not, we eventually succeeded where they failed.

The Japanese, in the earlier stages of the campaign, gained the moral ascendancy over us that they did because we never seriously challenged their seizure of the initiative. They bought that initiative, fairly and inevitably, by paying for it with preparation. Our lack of preparation in Burma, military, administrative, and political, made it difficult for our commanders even to bid for the initiative. But we should have tried harder than we did and taken more risks to gain it. Even when weaker, as we were in the earlier stages, to adopt a static defence, to try merely to hold ground, unless relief and reinforcement are at hand, is fatal. The only hope is to take the offensive at least locally whatever the risk and by daring and surprise throw out the enemy's plans. The Japanese were ruthless and bold as ants while their designs went well, but if those plans were disturbed or thrown out—antlike again—they fell into confusion, were slow to readjust themselves, and invariably clung too long to their original schemes. This, to commanders with their unquenchable military optimism, which rarely allowed in their narrow administrative margins for any setback or delay, was particularly dangerous. The fundamental fault of their generalship was a lack of moral, as distinct from physical, courage. They were not prepared to admit that they had made a mistake, that their plans had misfired and needed recasting. That would have meant personal failure in the service of the Emperor and loss of face. Rather than confess that, they passed on to their subordinates, unchanged, the orders they had themselves received, well knowing that with the resources available the tasks demanded were impossible. Time and again this blind passing of responsibility ran down a chain of disaster from the commander in chief to the lowest levels of leadership. It is true that in war determination by itself may achieve results, while flexibility, without determination in reserve, cannot, but it is only the blending of the two that brings final success. The hardest test of generalship is to hold this balance between determination and flexibility. In this the Japanese failed. They scored highly by determination; they paid heavily for lack of flexibility.

The strength of the Japanese army lay, not in its higher leadership which once its career of success had been checked became confused, nor in its special aptitude for jungle warfare, but in the spirit of the individual Japanese soldier. He fought and marched till he died. If five hundred Japanese were ordered to hold a position, we had to kill four hundred and ninety-five before it was ours—and then the last five killed themselves. It was this combination of obedience and ferocity that made the Japanese army, whatever its condition, so formidable, and which would make any army formidable. It would make a European army invincible.

Our Forces

In Burma we not only fought against an Asian enemy, but we fought him with an army that was mainly Asian. In both respects not a few among us with little experience of Asians had to readjust many ideas, including that of the inherent superiority of the white man as a soldier. The Asian fighting man is at least equally brave, usually more careless of death, less encumbered by mental doubts, little troubled by humanitarian sentiment, and not so moved by slaughter and mutilation about him. He is, by background and living standards, better fitted to endure hardship uncomplainingly, to demand less in the way of subsistence or comfort, and to look after himself when thrown on his own resources. He has a keen practiced eye for country and the ability to move across it on his own feet. He has not the inherent disinclination to climb hills that the city-bred, motor-riding white man has. Much—I had almost written most—of our fighting in Burma took place at night. Night fighting is, in effect, a form of dispersed fighting because, although men may be close together, they see little and suffer the fears and anxieties of isolation. The more civilized we become, the more we draw our soldiers from well-lighted towns, the more clumsy and frightened shall we be in the dark, and the greater the odds in favour of a more primitive foe.

While field craft comes naturally to the Asian, he can learn as well as the white man how to handle new weapons, even complicated ones. The European, on the other hand, can at present more readily design and produce such equipment and find the vitally important skilled men to maintain it. He is superior, not so much in natural intelligence, as in education, and thus is able to find a higher proportion of potential officers. He should be able to understand better what he is fighting for, be capable of higher training, and, if it is properly developed, of more sustained morale. Yet with all these advantages, it is foolish to put white men against Asians and expect them to win just because they are white; to win they must be better trained, better disciplined, and better led. If they are not, even superior armament will not overcome the numerical and natural advantages of the Asian. We began by despising our Japanese enemy; the pendulum then swung wildly to the other extreme. We built up our enemy into something terrifying, as soldiers always will to excuse their defeats, and frightened ourselves with the bogey of the superman of the jungle. Both attitudes were calamitous to us. It was not until we taught ourselves to take a balanced view of our enemy as a formidable fighting man, who nevertheless had certain weaknesses, and of ourselves as being able with training to beat him at his own, or any other game, that we won.

In an army such as ours, drawn from many nationalities, administration and supply were complicated. In Indian army formations we began with a proportion of British units among the Indian—about one-third to two-thirds. For a variety of reasons, I came to the conclusion that it was preferable, certainly in infantry brigades, to have either all British or all Indian. Then each race fought better, supply was greatly simplified, and we could more easily suit divisions to their tasks. My Indian divisions after 1943 were among the best in the world. They would go anywhere, do anything, go on doing it, and do it on very little.

Matériel

At the beginning of the war there was the greatest contrast between the Japanese and the British logistical outlook, between what they required to operate and what we *thought* we required. They launched their troops into the boldest offensives on the slenderest administrative margins; our training was all against this. The British army, ever since the terrible lesson of the Crimea, had tended to stress supply at the expense of mobility. The static conditions of World War I, followed by fast-rising standards of living, inevitably increased this bias. In many theatres of World War II, the complexity of equipment, the growth of specialized organizations, the expansion of staffs, and the elaboration of communications still further increased the ratio of administrative to fighting strengths and swelled the amount of transport required. In Africa and Europe the decline of the enemy's air power from 1941 onward and the relative abundance of motorable routes concealed what, in other circumstances, would have been the tactical impossibility of manoeuvre with such tail-heavy formations. With us in Burma, from its complete dominance in 1942, the Japanese air force became, from 1944, less and less of a danger to movement until it practically disappeared even as a threat. Yet the difficulty of the country with its lack of roads remained and still forced us to limit transport on the ground, while shortage of aircraft compelled the same economy in the air. We discovered that, instead of the four hundred tons a day not considered excessive to keep a division fighting in more generous theatres we could maintain our Indian divisions in action for long periods, without loss of battle efficiency or morale, on one hundred and twenty. As we removed vehicles from units and formations which joined us on European establishments, they found to their surprise that they could move farther and faster without them. The fewer vehicles on the roads or tracks, the quicker they travelled, and an enforced ingenuity in combining ferrying by lorry with marching covered long distances in remarkably short time. This relation between tactical mobility and numbers of vehicles, between the size of staff and effective control, will increase in importance in any future war. Unless they are constantly watched and ruthlessly cut down, vehicles and staffs will multiply until they bog down movement.

With us, necessity was truly the mother of invention. We lacked so much in equipment and supplies that, if we were not to give up offensive operations altogether, we had either to manage without or improvise for ourselves. We learned that if the spirit could be made willing the flesh would do without many things and that quick brains and willing hands could, from meagre resources, produce astonishing results. Our mass-production river shipyards, our methods of building roads and airfields, our 'parajutes,' our huge market gardens almost in the battle line, our duck farms, our fish saltings, and a hundred other things were gallant and successful efforts by the Army in the field to live up to its motto, 'God helps those who help themselves.' My soldiers forced the opposed crossing of great rivers using ludicrously inadequate equipment, stretched brittle communication links to fantastic lengths, marched over the most heartbreaking country on reduced rations, fought disease with discipline and beat it. The Japanese first demonstrated painfully on us that it is not so much numbers and elaborate equipment that count in the tough places, but training and morale. We had to learn this lesson in a hard school before we could turn the tables on them.

New Techniques

In Burma we fought on a lower scale of transport, supplies, equipment, supporting arms, and amenities than was accepted in any other British theatre. Yet, largely because of this lack of material resources, we learned to use those we had in fresh ways to achieve more than would have been possible had we clung to conventional methods. We had not only to devise new tactics but to delve deeply into the motive forces of human conduct and to change our traditional outlook on many things. The result was, I think it true to say, a kind of warfare more modern in essence than that fought by other British forces. Indeed, by any Allied force, with the exception of the Americans in the Pacific. There, their problem, the opposite of ours, was to use the immense resources that became increasingly available to them most effectively in the peculiar circumstances of an ocean war. They solved it brilliantly and evolved a new material technique. We also in strange conditions evolved our technique of war, not so much material, as human.

Compared with those in Europe, the combat forces used in Burma were not large. Including Stilwell's Chinese, the greatest number of divisions I ever had under my command in action at one time was eighteen. They fought on a front of seven hundred miles, in four groups, separated by great distances, with no lateral communications between them and beyond tactical support of one another. My corps and divisions were called upon to act with at least as much freedom as armies and corps in other theatres. Commanders at all levels had to act more on their own; they were give greater latitude to work out their own plans to achieve what they knew was the army commander's intention. In time they developed to a marked degree a flexibility of mind and a firmness of decision that enabled them to act swiftly to take advantage of sudden information or changing circumstances without reference to their superiors. They were encouraged, as Stopford put it when congratulating Rees's 19th Division which had seized a chance to slip across the Irrawaddy and at the same time make a dart at Shwebo, to 'shoot a goal when the referee wasn't looking.' This acting without orders, in anticipation of orders, or without waiting for approval, yet always within the over-all intention, must become second nature in any form of warfare where formations do not fight closely *en cadre*, and must go down to the smallest units. It requires in the higher command a corresponding flexibility of mind, confidence in its subordinates, and the power to make its intentions clear right through the force.

Companies, even platoons, under junior leaders became the basic units of the jungle. Out of sight of one another, often out of touch, their wireless blanketed by hills, they marched and fought on their own, often for days at a time. They frequently approached the battle in scattered columns, as they did for the crossing of the Irrawaddy, and concentrated on the battlefield. The methods by which they did this and, above all, the qualities they needed to make these tactics possible and successful repay study. They may be needed again.

Discipline

The more modern war becomes, the more essential appear the basic qualities that from the beginning of history have distinguished armies from mobs. The first of these is discipline. We very soon learned in Burma that strict discipline in battle and in bivouac was vital, not only for success, but for survival. Nothing is easier in jungle or dispersed fighting than for a man to shirk. If he has no stomach for advancing, all he has to do is to flop into the undergrowth; in retreat, he can slink out of the rear guard, join up later, and swear he was the last to leave. A patrol leader can take his men a mile into the jungle, hide there, and return with any report he fancies. Only discipline—not punishment—can stop that sort of thing; the real discipline that a man holds to because it is a refusal to betray his comrades. The discipline that makes a sentry, whose whole body is tortured for sleep, rest his chin on the point of his bayonet because he knows, if he nods, he risks the lives of the men sleeping behind him. It is only discipline, too, that can enforce the precautions against disease, irksome as they are, without which an army would shrivel away. At some stage in all wars armies have let their discipline sag, but they have never won victory until they made it taut again; nor will they. We found it a great mistake to belittle the importance of smartness in turnout, alertness of carriage, cleanliness of person, saluting, or precision of movement, and to dismiss them as naïve, unintelligent parade-ground stuff. I do not believe that troops can have unshakable battle discipline without showing those outward and formal signs, which mark the pride men take in themselves and their units and the mutual confidence and respect that exist between them and their officers. It was our experience in a tough school that the best fighting units, in the long run, were not necessarily those with the most advertised reputations, but those who when they came out of battle at once resumed a more formal discipline and appearance.

Air Power

The fabric of our campaign was woven by the close intermeshing of land and air operations, yet we began in Southeast Asia with exaggerated ideas of what air power by itself could accomplish. We discovered, both when it was overwhelmingly against us and equally when it was overwhelmingly with us, that it could not *stop* movement on the ground; it could only impede and delay it. Neither the Japanese air forces nor our own prevented divisions being moved or troops being supplied. They made these things more difficult.

One of the characteristics of air power is its ever-increasing flexibility, but even this has certain limitations. As long as our squadrons, fighter or bomber, could operate from bases within reasonable range of their objectives, this flexibility was obvious and marked. When, however, as sometimes happened on a front as wide as ours with distances as great, we had to find another airfield, the flexibility of air power temporarily, at least, vanished. We built earth landing strips even with little machinery in a matter of hours, but the all-weather airfield capable of acting as a base, of which at least a certain number were required, was a much slower business. During our rapid advances we solved the problem only by making Japanese airfields the primary objectives of our foremost troops. Even then we should have been gravely embarrassed if the enemy had concentrated more thoroughly than they did on destroying runways, road rollers, equipment, and repair materials.

As we were, compared with most Allied armies, short of artillery (and even if it had been available the country would have hampered its use) we came to rely for close support more and more on the air. We developed our own and adapted other people's methods of calling up air support, of indicating targets, and of coordinating movement on the ground with fire from the air. We as confidently dovetailed our fire plans with the airmen as with the gunners. Talked in by Air Force officers with the forward troops, our fighters would place their cannon shells and rockets within a hundred yards of our men, and by dummy runs keep down the enemy's heads for the last infantry rush. Quick and accurate cooperation of this sort did not come in a day; it grew with the airmen's and soldiers' mutual confidence, understanding, and pride in one another's achievements. In peace the function of tactical air support of land operations is apt to fade, but in war its urgency will increase.

A most distinctive aspect of our Burma war was the great use we made of air transport. It was one of our contributions towards a new kind of warfare, and I think it fair to say that, to a large extent, we discovered by trial and error the methods of air supply that later passed into general use. We were the first to maintain large formations in action by air supply and to move standard divisions long distances about the fighting front by air. The second Chindit expedition in March 1944, when we landed some thirty thousand men and five thousand animals far behind the enemy's lines and maintained them for months, was the largest airborne operation of the war. The decisive stroke at Meiktila and the advance on Rangoon were examples of a new technique that combined mechanized and air-transported brigades in the same divisions. To us, all this was as normal as moving or maintaining troops by railway or road, and that attitude of mind was, I suppose, one of our main reformations. We had come a long way since 1928 when, as a junior staff officer, I had been concerned with other Indian army officers in a struggle, not entirely without success, to introduce operational air transport and supply on the North-west Frontier.

Although we moved great tonnages and many thousands of troops by air, the largest number of transport aircraft we ever had was much less than would elsewhere have been considered the minimum required. It was quite easy theoretically to demonstrate that what we were doing was impossible to continue over any length of time. Yet the skill, courage, and devotion of the airmen, British and American, both in the air and on the ground, combined with the hard work and organizing ability of the soldiers, not only did it, but kept on doing it month after month. As in so many other things, we learned to revise accepted theories and, when worth it, to risk cutting our margins.

A feature of our airborne operations and movements was that the troops employed were not of some special kind. No soldiers of the Fourteenth Army were taught to believe there was anything mystic, strange, or unusual about air movements or maintenance; to them, of whatever race, these were normal administrative methods. The only exception was parachute jumping. I would, if I had had the aircraft available for practice, have made it an ordinary part of, at least, every infantryman's training. The incidence of serious injury is, I should think, no higher among soldier parachutists than among soldier motorcyclists. Unfortunately, the lack of training aircraft prevented our using parachutists on a large scale, but even so we were undoubtedly the most air-minded army that ever existed. We had to be.

More publicity was given to air transport than to any other feature of the Burma war and, perhaps as a result, certain fallacies about it gained currency. The first was to overlook the fact that our pattern of operations depended, almost entirely, on a very large measure of air supremacy. Until a degree of air superiority, amounting at least locally to dominance, had been secured, neither air supply, movement, nor tactical support could be carried on with the certainty and regularity our operations demanded. The fighter and the bomber between them had to sweep the skies and push back the enemy landing grounds; the air battle had to be won first—and from now on it will always have to be won first. A second fallacy was that air supply is entirely a matter to be arranged by air forces; that the only things required are the aircraft and the men to fly and maintain them. The organization of air supply is as much a job for the army as for the air force. It is as important as flying the aircraft that the immensely varied stores, properly packed, should arrive at the right air strips for loading at the right time; that they should be sent to the right units, and that on arrival unloading, distribution, and delivery should be swift and unerring. All these and a dozen other things are the province of the army and entail the most difficult—at least we found it so—of all requirements, a complicated mass of signal communications. Among the most strategically dangerous ideas that half-baked thinking on air supply provoked, was that, even if surrounded, positions could be held for months provided they might be maintained from the air. In fact, troops thus cut off even if fed and maintained eventually lost heart, and air supply is so easily interrupted; the weather or a few well-sited anti-aircraft weapons can easily put a stop to it. Air supply is only half the answer. The other half is an adequate relieving force which, however good the prospect of air supply, must appear in a reasonable time and which the beleaguered garrison must know will appear.

There is one other thing about combined land and air operations—and all operations on land are that. The land and air commanders responsible at each level must not only be in close touch, they should live together as we did. Ours was a joint land and air war; its result, as much a victory for the air forces as for the army.

Special Forces

The British army in the last war spawned a surprising number of special units and formations, that is forces of varying sizes, each trained, equipped, and prepared for some particular type of operation. We had commandos, assault brigades, amphibious divisions, mountain divisions, long-range penetration forces, airborne formations, desert groups, and an extraordinary variety of cloak-and-dagger parties. The equipment of these special units was more generous than that of normal formations, and many of them went so far as to have their own bases and administrative organizations. We employed most of them in Burma, and some, notably the Chindits, gave splendid examples of courage and hardihood. Yet I came firmly to the conclusion that such formations, trained, equipped, and mentally adjusted for one kind of operation, were wasteful. They did not give, militarily, a worth-while return for the resources in men, matériel, and time that they absorbed.

To begin with, they were usually formed by attracting the best men from normal units by better conditions, promises of excitement, and not a little propaganda. Even on the rare occasions when normal units were converted into special ones without the option of volunteering, the same process went on in reverse. Men thought to be below the standards set or over an arbitrary age limit were weeded out to less-favoured corps. The result of these methods was undoubtedly to lower the quality of the rest of the army, especially of the infantry, not only by skimming the cream off it, but by encouraging the idea that certain of the normal operations of war were so difficult that only specially equipped *corps d'élite* could be expected to undertake them. Armies do not win wars by means of a few bodies of super-soldiers but by the average quality of their standard units. Anything, whatever short cuts to victory it may promise, which thus weakens the army spirit, is dangerous. Commanders who have used these special forces have found, as we did in Burma, that they have another grave disadvantage—they can be employed actively for only restricted periods. Then they demand to be taken out of the battle to recuperate, while normal formations are expected to have no such limits to their employment. In Burma, the time spent in action with the enemy by special forces was only a fraction of that endured by the normal divisions, and it must be remembered that risk is danger multiplied by time.

The rush to form special forces arose from confused thinking on what were, or were not, normal operations of war. In one sense every operation of war is a special one, whether it is attack, defence, withdrawal, penetration, raids behind the enemy's lines, destruction of his detachments, assault over a beach, river crossings, jungle, or mountain warfare, or any of the rest; each has its peculiar requirements. Yet all are and have always been familiar operations of war; any standard unit should expect that, at some time or other, it may be called upon to engage in any of them. The level of initiative, individual training, and weapon skill required in, say, a commando, is admirable; what is not admirable is that it should be confined to a few small units. Any well-trained infantry battalion should be able to do what a commando can do; in the Fourteenth Army they could and did. This cult of special forces is as sensible as to form a Royal Corps of Tree Climbers and say that no soldier, who does not wear its green hat with a bunch of oak leaves stuck in it, should be expected to climb a tree.

I would lay it down that any single operation in which more

than a handful of men are to be engaged should be regarded as normal, and should be carried out by standard formations. The only exception I would allow to this is a parachute landing, which, until facilities for training much larger numbers in the drill of jumping are available, must require something of a special force. The absence of such forces does not, of course, mean that ordinary units would not, as they have always done, practice and train for particular operations, but it would avoid having large numbers of picked troops, either waiting long periods to be used for short periods, or of eventually being employed for something quite different from that for which they have so long and laboriously prepared. Private armies—and for that matter private air forces—are expensive, wasteful, and unnecessary.

There is, however, one kind of special unit which should be retained—that designed to be employed in small parties, usually behind the enemy, on tasks beyond the normal scope of warfare in the field. There will be an increasing need for highly qualified and individually trained men—and women— to sabotage vital installations, to spread rumours, to misdirect the enemy, to transmit intelligence, to kill or kidnap individuals, and to inspire resistance movements. They will be troops, though they will require many qualities and skills not to be expected of the ordinary soldier and they will use many methods beyond his capacity. Each small party would study and train intensively for a particular exploit and should operate under the direct control of the Higher Command. They should rarely work within our own lines. Not costly in man power, they may, if handled with imaginative ruthlessness, achieve strategic results. Such units, based on the army, but drawing on all services and all races of the Commonwealth for specially qualified men and women, should be an essential component of our modern Armed Forces.

The question of control of these clandestine bodies is not without its pitfalls. In the last war among the Allies, cloak-and-dagger organizations multiplied until to commanders in the field—at least in my theatre—they became an embarrassment. The trouble was that each was controlled from some distant headquarters of its own, and such was the secrecy and mutual suspicion in which they operated that they sometimes acted in close proximity to our troops without the knowledge of any commander in the field, with a complete lack of coordination among themselves, and in dangerous ignorance of local tactical developments. It was not until the activities of all clandestine bodies operating in or near our troops were coordinated, and where necessary controlled, through a senior officer on the staff of the commander of the area, that confusion, ineffectiveness, and lost opportunities were avoided.

The Future

In Burma we thus developed a form of warfare, based more on human factors than on lavish equipment, which had certain characteristics. The chief of these were:

(i) The acceptance as normal of the regular movement and maintenance of standard formations by air.

(ii) Great tactical freedom for subordinate commanders.

(iii) The operation, over wide distances in most difficult country, of comparatively small forces in tactical independence but strategic combination.

(iv) Reduced scales of transport and equipment, supplemented by ingenuity and improvisation from local resources.

(v) The high quality of the individual soldier, his morale, toughness, and discipline, his acceptance of hardship, and his ability to move on his own feet and to look after himself.

War in the future may vary in scope from unlimited nuclear war aimed at the complete annihilation of a whole people, to a restricted tactical employment of nuclear weapons, or even to the small war of traditional pattern. Whatever form its takes, especially when nuclear weapons are employed as they will be in any war between great powers, one thing is reasonably certain. Modern war, with its destruction of bases, disruption of communications, and disorganization of control, will, if they are to operate at all, compel armies to disperse.

Dispersed fighting, whether the dispersal is caused by the terrain, the lack of supplies, or by the weapons of the enemy, will have two main requirements—skilled and determined junior leaders and self-reliant, physically hard, well-disciplined troops. Success in future land operations will depend on the immediate availability of such leaders and such soldiers, ready to operate in small, independent formations. They will have to be prepared to do without regular lines of communication, to guide themselves, and to subsist largely on what the country offers. Unseen, unheard, and unsuspected, they will converge on the enemy and, when they do reveal themselves in strength, they will be so close to him that he will be unable to atomize them without destroying himself. Such land operations, less rigidly controlled and more individualistic than in the past, will not be unlike ours as we approached the Chindwin and the Irrawaddy, and stalking terrorists in a Malayan jungle is today, strange as it may seem, the best training for nuclear warfare. The use of new weapons and technical devices can quickly be taught; to develop hardihood, initiative, mutual confidence, and stark leadership takes longer.

The air attacks we sustained and delivered were, compared with what they might be now, feeble things. Yet determined troops, especially in close or broken country, who are prepared to jettison all but fighting essentials and move in small, self-contained formations, will, I believe, make their own way even through the chaos of atomic bombing. In unlimited war, after the first shock of mutual devastation had been survived, victory would go, as it did in our other jungle, to the tougher, more resourceful infantryman. The easier and more gadget-filled our daily life becomes, the harder will it be to produce him. It took us some time to do so in Burma. It can be done in peace; in war, there will no longer be so much time.

Until the very horror of modern mass destruction forces men to find some more sensible way of settling national disputes, war will remain, and while it remains it will continually change. Yet, because it is fought between men rather than between weapons, victory will still go, when armaments are even relatively equal, to the side which is better trained and of higher morale—advantages which are obtained neither easily, quickly, nor without the sacrifice of more than money in peace. War remains an art and, like all arts, whatever its variation, will have its enduring principles. Many men, skilled either with sword or pen, and sometimes with both, have tried to expound those principles. I heard them once from a soldier of experience for whom I had a deep and well-founded respect. Many years ago, as a cadet hoping someday to be an officer, I was poring over the 'Principles of War,' listed in the old Field Service Regulations, when the sergeant-major came upon me. He surveyed me with kindly amusement. 'Don't bother your head about all them things, me lad,' he said. 'There's only one principle of war, and that's this. Hit the other fellow as quick as you can and as hard as you can, where it hurts him most, when he ain't lookin'!' As a recruit, I earned that great man's reproof often enough; now, as an old soldier, I would hope to receive his commendation. I think I might, for we of the Fourteenth Army held to his 'Principle of War.'

In these pages I have written much of generals and of staff officers; of their problems, difficulties, and expedients, their successes and their failures. Yet there is one thought that I should like to be the over-all and final impression of this book—that the war in Burma was a *soldier's* war. There comes a moment in every battle against a stubborn enemy when the result hangs in the balance. Then the general, however skilful and farsighted he may have been, must hand over to his soldiers, to the men in the ranks and to their regimental officers and leave them to complete what he has begun. The issue then rests with them, on their courage, their hardihood, their refusal to be beaten either by the cruel hazards of nature or by the fierce strength of their human enemy. That moment came early and often in the fighting in Burma; sometimes it came when tired, sick men felt alone, when it would have been so easy for them to give up, when only will, discipline, and faith could steel them to carry on. To the soldiers of many races who, in the comradeship of the Fourteenth Army, *did* go on, and to the airmen who flew with them and fought over them, belongs the true glory of achievement. It was they who turned Defeat into Victory.

INDEX

469

475

476

A SELECTION OF FINE READING
AVAILABLE IN CORGI BOOKS

War

☐ 552 08738 6	THE BARREN BEACHES OF HELL	Boyd Cochrell	35p
☐ 552 08603 7	LIQUIDATE PARIS	Sven Hassel	30p
☐ 552 08779 3	GESTAPO	Sven Hassel	35p
☐ 552 08799 8	WHITE COOLIE	Ronald Hastain	30p
☐ 552 98558 9	FOURTEEN EIGHTEEN (illustrated)	John Masters	105p
☐ 552 08756 4	THE OTHER SIDE	John Murdoch	35p
☐ 552 08621 5	MEDICAL BLOCK: BUCHENWALD	Walter Poller	35p
☐ 552 08536 7	THE SCOURGE OF THE SWASTIKA	Lord Russell	30p
☐ 552 08537 5	THE KNIGHTS OF BUSHIDO	Lord Russell	30p
☐ 552 08757 2	DEFEAT INTO VICTORY	Field-Marshal Sir William Slim	40p

General

☐ 552 08786 6	COFFEE TEA OR ME?	Trudy Baker & Rachel Jones	35p
☐ 552 98789 1	INVESTING IN MAPS (illustrated)	Roger Baynton-Williams	125p
☐ 552 08747 5	JOGGING (illustrated)		
		William J. Bowerman & W. E. Harris, M.D.	30p
☐ 552 08768 8	SEX MANNERS FOR OLDER TEENAGERS (illustrated)		
		Robert Chartham	30p
☐ 552 07593 0	UNMARRIED LOVE	Dr. Eustace Chesser	25p
☐ 552 07950 2	SEXUAL BEHAVIOUR	Dr. Eustace Chesser	25p
☐ 552 08805 6	WHO DO YOU THINK YOU ARE?	Dr. Eustace Chesser	25p
☐ 552 98572 4	NEE DE LA VAGUE (illustrated)	Lucien Clergue	105p
☐ 552 98711 5	INVESTING IN CLOCKS AND WATCHES	P. W. Cumhaill	125p
☐ 552 08800 5	CHARIOTS OF THE GODS? (illustrated)	Erich von Daniken	35p
☐ 552 08745 9	MAGIC AND MYSTERY IN TIBET	Alexandra David-Neel	35p
☐ 552 08677 0	ON THE EDGE OF THE ETHERIC	Arthur Findlay	30p

Western

☐ 552 08532 4	BLOOD BROTHER	Elliott Arnold	40p
☐ 552 08813 7	SUDDEN AT BAY	Frederick H. Christian	25p
☐ 552 08660 6	RUN FOR THE BORDER	J. T. Edson	25p
☐ 552 08706 8	SLIP GUN NO. 65	J. T. Edson	25p
☐ 552 08783 1	HELL IN THE PALO DURO No. 66	J. T. Edson	25p
☐ 552 08673 8	NORTH TO THE RAILS	Louis L'Amour	25p
☐ 552 08742 4	THE MONSTER FROM YUMA No. 8	Louis Masterson	20p
☐ 552 08802 1	THE DEVIL'S MARSHAL No. 9	Louis Masterson	20p
☐ 552 08803 X	GUNMAN'S INHERITANCE No. 10	Louis Masterson	20p

Crime

☐ 552 08761 0	THE TOFF IS BACK	John Creasey	25p
☐ 552 08739 4	TRAITOR'S EXIT	John Gardner	25p
☐ 552 08809 9	MADRIGAL	John Gardner	25p
☐ 552 08782 3	THE LITTLE WAX DOLL	Norah Lofts	30p
☐ 552 08640 1	RED FILE FOR CALLAN	James Mitchell	25p
☐ 552 08758 0	SURVIVAL . . . ZERO	Mickey Spillane	25p
☐ 552 08801 3	THE SILENT LIARS	Michael Underwood	25p

All these books are available at your bookshop or newsagent; or can be ordered direct from the publisher. Just tick the titles you want and fill in the form below.

CORGI BOOKS, Cash Sales Department, P.O. Box 11, Falmouth, Cornwall.
Please send cheque or postal order. No currency, and allow 5p per book to cover the cost of postage and packing in U.K., and overseas.

NAME...

ADDRESS ....

(Oct. '71) ....